ISBN 978-0-282-35393-3
PIBN 10848624

English
Français
Deutsche
Italiano
Español
Português

www.forgottenbooks.com

Mythology Photography **Fiction**
Fishing Christianity **Art** Cooking
Essays Buddhism Freemasonry
Medicine **Biology** Music **Ancient
Egypt** Evolution Carpentry Physics
Dance Geology **Mathematics** Fitness
Shakespeare **Folklore** Yoga Marketing
Confidence Immortality Biographies
Poetry **Psychology** Witchcraft
Electronics Chemistry History **Law**
Accounting **Philosophy** Anthropology
Alchemy Drama Quantum Mechanics
Atheism Sexual Health **Ancient History**
Entrepreneurship Languages Sport
Paleontology Needlework Islam
Metaphysics Investment Archaeology
Parenting Statistics Criminology
Motivational

Mr Wm Bradford

THE

CREDIBILITY

OF THE

Gospel History :

OR, THE

FACTS

Occasionally mention'd in the

NEW TESTAMENT;

Confirmed by PASSAGES of

ANCIENT AUTHORS

Who were contemporary with our
SAVIOUR or his APOSTLES,
or lived near their Time.

With an APPENDIX concerning the Time of
HEROD's Death.

Part I

VOL. II.

By NATHANIEL LARDNER.

LONDON:

Printed for JOHN CHANDLER at the CROSS-KEYS in the
POULTRY. 1727.

THE

CONTENTS·

BOOK II.

CHAP. VI.

The CONTENTS.

ERRATA.

PAGE 110. l. 3. from the bottom of the page, for *Quirinius* read *Quirinus.* 126. l. 14. for προ ঠ r. προτ𝑔. 129. l. 10. after *Saint* r. *Luke.* 144. in the margin for *Deut.* r. *Numb.* 145. l. 1. for *this case,* r. *this rule in this case.* 255. l. 6. for *Antoninies.* r. *Antonines.* 285. l. 10. for *Pso* r. *Piso.* p. 376. l. 15. for *would* read *it would.* In the Notes p. 26. l. 1. for χηρυττόμεν℧ r. κηρυττόμενος. 71. l. ult. for χὺν r. ἰχὺν 55. l. ult. for 142. r. 1242.

THE
CREDIBILITY

OF THE

GOSPEL HISTORY.

BOOK II.

CHAP. I.

Three Objections againſt *Luke,* ch. ii. *v.* 1, 2.

§. I. *The firſt Obj. That there is no mention made by any ancient Author of a Decree in the reign of* Auguſtus *for taxing all the world, Stated and anſwered.* §. II. *The ſecond Obj. That there could be no taxing made in* Judea, *during the reign of* Herod, *by a Decree*

B   *of*

of Auguſtus, *ſtated and anſwered.*
§. III. *The third Obj. That* Cyrénius
was not Governour of Syria *till ſe-*
veral years after the birth of Jeſus,
Stated, together with a general an-
ſwer. §. IV. *Divers particular Solu-*
tions of this Obj. §. V. *The laſt So-*
lution confirmed and improved. §. VI.
Divers particular difficulties attending
the Suppoſition, that this taxing was
made by Cyrenius, *conſidered.*

H E Hiſtory of the *New Teſta-*
ment is attended with many
difficulties. *Jewiſh* and *Hea-*
then authors concur with the
ſacred Hiſtorians in many things. But it is
pretended, that there are other particulars in
which they are contradicted by authors of
very good note.

A M O N G theſe, the difficulties which
may be very properly conſidered in the firſt
place, are thoſe which relate to the account
St. *Luke* has given of the *Taxing* in *Judea,*
which brought *Joſeph* and the Virgin to
Bethlehem a little before the birth of Jeſus.

A N D it came to paſſe in thoſe days,
ſays St. *Luke, that there went out a decree*
from

from Cefar Auguftus *that all the world fhould be taxed.* (*And this taxing was firft made when* Cyrenius *was governour of* Syria) *And all went to be taxed, every one in his own city. And* Jofeph *alfo went up from* Galilee, *out of the city of* Nazareth, *into* Judea, *unto the city of* David, *which is called* Bethlehem (*becaufe he was of the houfe and linage of* David) *to be taxed with* Mary *his efpoufed wife, being great with childe.*

Luke ii. 1. —5.

AGAINST this account feveral objections have been raifed (*a*). They may be all reduced to thefe three.

I. IT is objected, That there is no mention made, in any ancient *Roman* or *Greek* Hiftorian, of any general taxing of people all over the world, or the whole *Roman Empire*, in the time of *Auguftus*, nor of any Decree of the Emperour for that purpofe: Whereas, if there had been then any fuch thing, it is highly improbable, that it fhould have been omitted by them.

II. ST. *Matthew* fays, that Jefus was born *in the days of* Herod *the king*. *Jude a* there-

Matth. ii. 1.

(*a*) Vid. Spanhem. Dubia Evangelica Part ii. Dub. iv. v. &c. Huet. Demonft. Evangel. Prop. ix. cap. x. & Commentatores.

fore

fore was not at that time a Roman province, and there could not be any *taxing* made there by a Decree of *Augustus.*

III. *CYRENIUS* was not Governour of *Syria* till nine or ten, perhaps twelve years after the birth of Jesus. St. *Luke* therefore was mistaken, in saying, that this Taxing was made in his time. This objection will be stated more fully hereafter.

§. I. By way of answer to the first objection,

1. I allow that there is not any mention made by ancient writers of any general taxing all over the world, or of all the subjects of the *Roman Empire,* in the reign of *Augustus.*

Many learned men having been of a different opinion, I am obliged to consider their proofs.

TILLEMONT (*a*) puts the question (for he does not assert it) whether *Plinie* has not referred to such a thing. But it is plain from *Plinie*'s words, that he speaks of a partition of *Italie* only into several districts (*b*).   There

(*a*) Tillemont Memoires Eccles. Tom. i. Not. ii. Sur *Jesus Christ.*   (*b*) Nunc ambitum ejus, urbesque enumerabimus. Qua in re praefari necessarium est, auctorem nos Divum Augustum

THERE is a paſſage alſo of *Dio,* which has been referred to upon this occaſion : But it has evidently no relation to the matter before us.   The *Romans* had a Tax called the *twentieth.*   This tax was grievous to many people.   *Auguſtus* therefore deſired the Senate to conſider of ſome other.   ‘ But ‘ the Senate not finding any proper expedient, ‘ he intimated that he would raiſe mony upon ‘ lands and houſes, without telling ’em what, ‘ or in what manner, it ſhould be ; and hereup- ‘ on ſent officers abroad, ſome one way and ‘ ſome another, to make a ſurvey of the e- ‘ ſtates both of particular perſons and cities. ‘ But upon this the Senate complied imme- ‘ diately, and the old tax of the twentieth was ‘ confirmed, leſt a worſe ſhould come in its ‘ room.   This was all *Auguſtus* aimed at, ‘ and the Survey was laid aſide (*a*)’.   Beſides, this affair happened, A. U. 766. A. D. 13. long after the taxing which St. *Luke* ſpeaks of.

Auguſtum ſecuturos, deſcriptionemque ab eo factam Italiae totius in regiones xi. *Plin.* lib. iii. cap. v.

(*a*) Καὶ παραχρῆμα μηδὲν εἰπὼν, μήθ’ ὅσον, μήθ’ ὅπως αὐτὸ δώσουσιν, ἔπεμψεν ἅμας ἄλλη τά τε τ̃ ἰδιωτῶν κỹ τὰ τ̃ πόλεων κτήματα ἀπογραψομένυς· ἵνα ὡς κỹ μειζόνας ζημιωθησόμενοι δείσωσι, κỹ τὴν εἰκοσὴν τελεῖ ἀντέλωνται· ὁ κỹ ἐγένετο· Dio. lib. 56. p. 588. E.

THE paſſage, which *Baronius* (*a*) has quoted from *Aethicus*, he does himſelf allow to relate only to a geometrical deſcription of the Empire, begun by order of *Julius Ceſar*, and finiſhed in thirty two years, and therefore over long before the *taxing* mentioned by St. *Luke.*

I am afraid to mention his argument from *Plinie*, leſt it ſhould be thought, that I intend to divert the reader, when we ought to be ſerious. *Plinie* ſays : ' And as for ' *Auguſtus* himſelf, whom all mankind ' rank in this claſſe [*of fortunate perſons*] if the whole courſe of his life be ' carefully conſidered, there will be obſerved ' in it many inſtances of the fickleneſſe and ' inconſtance of human affairs (*b*).' But *Baronius* ſuppoſes, that *Plinie* ſays, that *in every cenſus mention is made of* Auguſtus, *and that there was ſo particularly in that made by* Veſpaſian *and* Titus, *becauſe he firſt made* (*c*) *a ſurvey of the whole Roman*

man

<hr>

(*a*) Apparat. N. 97.   (*b*) In Divo quoque Auguſto, quem univerſa mortalitas in HAC CENSURA nuncupat, ſi diligenter aeſtimentur cuncta, magna ſortis humanae reperiantur volumina Lib. 7. cap. 45.   (*c*) Idemque dum haec alibi ait: [lib. 7. cap. 45.] *In Divo quoque Auguſto, quem univerſa mortalitas in haç cenſura nuncupat,* nempe eam, quam Veſpaſianus & Titus recens egerunt, de qua idem inferius [ibid. cap. 49.]

man Empire : Thus making *Plinie* to refer, in the paſſage he quotes from him, not to what went before, but to a paſſage which follows *four* chapters lower.

SOME have alleged, as a proof of this general taxing, ſome words of *Suidas*, who in his Lexicon (*a*) ſays, ' That *Auguſtus* ' ſent out twenty men of great probity into ' all parts of his Empire, by whom he made ' an aſſeſſement of perſons and eſtates, order- ' ing a certain quota to be paid into the ' treaſury. This was the firſt Cenſus, they ' who were before him having at pleaſure ex- ' acted tribute of thoſe who had any thing ; ' ſo that it was a public crime to be rich'.

BUT it is very difficult to take this upon *Suidas's* authority alone, ſince he ſays not in what part of *Auguſtus's* reign it was done, quotes no author for it, and it is not to be

---

49.] Meminit, ſignificare videtur, in quolibet repetito in orbe Romano luſtris ſingulis cenſu, mentionem Auguſti fieri ; quod primus omnium univerſum orbem Romanum ſubjectum imperio cenſuiſſet. At de cenſibus ſatis. *Baron.* ubi ſupra.

(*a*) In Voc. Ἀπογραφὴ· Ἀπογραφὴ ἡ ἀπαρίθμησις· Ὁ δ Καῖσαρ Αὔγυς⊙, ὁ μοναρχήσας, εἴκοσιν ἄνδρας τὰς ἀρίςυς τὸν βίον κ᾽ τὸν τρόπον ἐπιλεξάμεν⊙, ἐπὶ πᾶσαν τὴν γῆν τ̃ ὑπηκόων ἐξέπεμψε· δι᾽ ὧν ἀπογραφὰς ἐποιήσατο τ̃ τε ἀνθρώπων & ὐσιῶν, αὐτάρκην τινὰ προςάξας τῷ δημοσίῳ μοῖραν ἐκ τέτων εἰσφέρεαξ· Αὕτη ἡ ἀπογραφὴ πρώτη ἐγένετο, τ̃ πρὸ αὐτῆ τὰς κεκτημένυς τὶ μὴ ἀφαιρημένων, ὡς εἶναι τοῖς εὐπόροις δημόσιον ἔγκλημα τὸν πλῦτον.

B 4   found

found in any ancient writer now extant. Tho',
poſſibly, he refers to the ſtory juſt now told
from *Dio*; who aſſures us, that project, he
mentions, was never executed. Beſides,
Suidas ſays, this was the *firſt Cenſus*; which
is a very great miſtake. There had been before *Auguſtus* many aſſeſſements of Roman
citizens, and likewiſe of divers provinces of
the *Roman Empire*.

IN another place *Suidas* ſays, ' *Auguſtus*
' had a deſire to know the number of all the
' inhabitants of the *Roman Empire* (*a*).
And he mentions the number, which, he
ſays, was found upon the enquiry. But
Suidas muſt have been miſtaken. Archbiſhop *Uſher's* remark upon this paſſage is
worth placing here. ' In their Conſulſhip
' [*Caius Marcius Cenſorinus*, and *C. Aſinius*
' *Gallus*] there was a ſecond muſter made
' at *Rome*, in which were numbered 4233000
' Roman Citizens, as is gathered out of the
' fragments of the *Ancyran* marble. In
' *Suidas*, in Ἀύγυϛος the number is far leſſe
' of thoſe that were muſtered, 4101017.
' which yet he very ridiculouſly obtrudeth

(*a*) V. Ἀύγυϛ⊙· Ἀύγυϛ⊙· Καῖσαρ δόξαν αυτῷ πάντας τὺς
οἰκήτορας Ῥωμαίων κατὰ πρόσωπον ἀριθμεῖ, βυλόμεν⊙· γνῶναι
πόσον ἐϛ1 πλῆθ⊙·· ϗ ἑυρίσκονται ὁι τὰ Ῥωμαίων οἰκῦντες ὑί μυυ-
ριάδὲς ϗ χίλιοι ιζ', ἄνδρες.

' upon

' upon us not for the mufter of the city only
' but of the world (*a*)'.

T H E late learned Editor (*b*) of *Suidas*
does alfo highly approve of this cenfure paffed upon his Author by our moft learned
and excellent Arch-bifhop.   It is obfervable
that they both ufe here the word *City* [*urbis
cenfu*].   I hope however they mean not the
City of *Rome* only and the country round
about it, but the Roman Citizens all over
the *Roman Empire*, or at left all *Italie* :
for otherwife, with fubmiffion, I fhould
think them, in this particular, almoft as unreafonable as *Suidas*.   It is incredible, that
there fhould have been at *Rome* and in the
country round about it, befide ftrangers and
flaves, which were very numerous, fo many
Roman Citizens as are mentioned on the
Ancyran Marble ; even though all, who
were entered in a Cenfus, be fet down there ;

(*a*) *Annals* :   year of the world, 3996. p. 786. *Engl. Edit.*
Lond. 1658. In the *Latin* the laft words are : Qui tamen non
pro Urbis tantùm fed pro Orbis etiam Romani cenfu ridiculè
nobis ibi obtruditur.

(*b*) De hoc loco vide omnino Cafaubonum contra Baron.
Exerc. 1. Num. 93.   Et Uffer.—qui recte obfervarunt, Suidam
hic cenfum urbis pro cenfu orbis Romani lectori obtrudere:
cum ridiculum fit credere, non plures fuiffe totius imperii Romani incolas, quam quot Suidas hic exprimit.

which

which however is denied by fome. I fup-pofe then, that by the Mufter of the City, thefe learned men mean the mufter or cen-fus of Roman Citizens in any part of the *Roman Empire*; as oppofed to all the peo-ple in general living in the fame Empire. And in this fenfe only (*a*) I adopt their cenfure of *Suidas*: and cannot but think it very juft. The number of the inhabitants of the *Ro-man Empire* muft needs have exceeded the numbers mentioned by *Suidas*, or on the marble; though it fhould be fuppofed, that none are included in thefe numbers but thofe who were arrived at military age. This might be fufficient to fhew, that the number on the Ancyran marble is not the number of all the people of the *Roman Em-pire*: but other reafons may appear prefent-ly.

I muft in the next place take the liberty of confidering what Dr. *Prideaux* has faid upon this fubject, who, with *Huet* (*b*), and others, thinks, that this defcription or furvey in *Judea* belonged to one of the furveys made by *Auguftus*; and that in particular,

(*a*) I think this evidently *Kufter's* fenfe. His *Orbis Romani* is explained afterwards by *totius imperii Romani Incolas*. There fore his *urbis cenfus* imports Roman Citizens living any where.

(*b*) Demon. Evang. ubi fupra §. iii.

it was a part of his *second* Cenfus. ' The
' firft was in the year when he himfelf was
' the fixth time, and *M. Agrippa* the fecond
' time Confuls, that is, in the year before the
' Chriftian Aera 28. The fecond time in the
' Confulfhip of *C. Marcius Cenforinus* and
' *C. Afinius Gallus*, that is, in the year be-
' fore the Chriftian Aera 8. And the laft
' time in the Confulfhip of *Sextus Pom-*
' *peius Nepos*, that is, in the year of the
' Chriftian Aera 14. In the firft and laft
' time he executed this with the affiftance of
' a Collegue. But the fecond time he did it
' by himfelf alone, and this is the defcription
' which St. *Luke* refers to. The Decree con-
' cerning it iffued out the year I have menti-
' oned, that is, in the 8th year before the
' Chriftian Aera, which was three years be-
' fore that in which Chrift was born.------
' That we allow three years for the execu-
' tion of this decree can give no juft reafon
' for exception------The account taken by
' the decree of *Auguftus* at the time of our
' Saviour's birth extended to all manner of
' perfons, and alfo to their poffeffions, eftates,
' qualities, and other circumftances. And
' when a defcription and furvey like this was
' ordered by *William* the Conqueror, to be
' taken

' taken for *England* only, I mean that of
' the Domefday Book, it was fix years in
' making; and the Roman province of *Syria*
' was much more than twice as big as all
' *England* (a).'

To all this I fhall only fay (1.) that the
furveys made by *Auguflus* were of ROMAN
CITIZENS only. So he fays himfelf in the infcription on the Ancyran marble (b). And
the Roman Hiftorians fay the fame thing (c).
But the Cenfus or Defcription made in
Judea, according to St. *Luke's* account, was
of all the *inhabitants* of that country, which
certainly were not, all of them, Roman
Citizens.

(a) Prideaux Conn. Part. ii. pag. 650. 652. 8*vo.* Edit. 1718.

(b) Et. In Confulatu. Sexto. Cenfum. POPULI. Collega,
M. Agrippa. Egi—Quo. Luftro. CIVIUM. ROMANORUM. Cenfita
funt. Capita. Quadragiens. Centum. Millia. Et. Sexaginta. Tria.
——Cum——Nuper. Luftrum. Solus. F.ci. Legi. Cenforum.
SINIO. Cof. Quo. Luftro. Cenfa. funt. CIVIUM. ROMANORUM.
Quadragens. Centum. Millia. Et. Ducenta. Triginta. Tria.——
In confulatu. FI.——Cum. nuperrime——Luftrum. Cum.
Lega. Tiberio. Sext. Pompeio. Et. Sext. Apuleio. Cof. Quo.
Luftro. ROM. CAPITUM. Quadragens. Centum. Mil.—IGINTA.
Et. Septem. Mil. Legi.

(c) Recepit & morum legumque regimen aeque perpetuum:
quo jure, quamquam fine cenfurae honore, cenfum tamen
POPULI ter egit. *Suet.* in *Aug.* cap. 27.

(2.) THE

(2.) THE years which the Doctor mentions were not the years, in which the de-
crees were iſſued out, but in which the ſurveys
were finiſhed. This appears to me the
moſt natural meaning of the words of the
Inſcription.

PERHAPS it will be objected, that the
conſulſhips here ſet down do not denote the
years, in which a cenſus was finiſhed, but in
which it was reſolved upon and entered in
the *Faſti*, or Public Acts ; and that the ſenſe
of the Inſcription may be thus : In ſuch, and
ſuch a Conſulſhip I made a cenſus, by which
cenſus, when finiſhed, the number of Citizens was found to be ſo and ſo. It may be
likewiſe ſaid, that the phraſe *Luſtrum feci*
does not neceſſarily import the making the
Luſtrum, which was done when the Cenſus
was over, but that *Luſtrum* is *here* Synony-
mous with Cenſus. And it may be urged,
that when *Luſtrum* denotes the ſolemn ſa-
crifice at the concluſion of the cenſus, the
verb *condo* is uſed, and not *facio*, which we
have here.

TO this I anſwer, that by the account here
given of the *third* cenſus we are obliged to
ſuppoſe, that the Conſulſhips here named
denote the times, when each Cenſus was
finiſhed

finished. *Sextus Pompeius* and *Sextus Apuleius*, in whose Consulship the last census is placed, were Consuls A. U. 767, A. D. 14. And *Augustus* died the 19th of *August* that very same year. If the census had been only begun, and not finished, he could not have set down on the Table, as he has done, the number of Citizens which was found in that Census. Moreover, it is plain from (*a*) *Suetonius*, that *Tiberius* was nominated for Collegue of *Augustus* in this Census, the year before, if not sooner. It is likely the Census might be *then* entered in the public Acts. But however that be, it is plain, that the date on the Ancyran Marble signifies the compleating of the Census. And I think, that the passage I have just quoted from *Suetonius* may remove the scruple relating to the phrase ; since he has used the verb *condo*, by which we are fully assured, that the census was finished, and the solemn sacrifice performed at the conclusion of it, in the year set down on the Ancyran Marble.

(*a*) A Germania in urbem post biennium regressus, triumphum, quem distulerat, egit.—Dedicavit & concordiae aedem.—Ac non multo post lege per Coss. lata, ut provincias cum Augusto communiter administraret, simulque censum ageret, condito lustro in Illyricum profectus est. *vit.* *Tiber.* cap. 20, 21.

FARTHER, *Auguſtus* in the Ancyran marble places his firſt cenſus in his own ſixth Conſulſhip, *Agrippa* being his collegue. And *Dio* ſays expreſly that *Auguſtus* made, or *finiſhed* (a) the cenſus in that year. This being the caſe as to the *firſt* and *third* cenſus of *Auguſtus,* we may conclude the ſame thing alſo with reference to the *ſecond*, and that it was finiſhed the *eighth* year before the Chriſtian Aera: conſequently, it is impoſſible, that St. *Luke's* deſcription ſhould have been a part of it.

AFTER *Auguſtus's* death there were three books found among his papers: and one of theſe is alleged as a proof that there had been made ſome general ſurvey of the *Roman Empire,* and that about this time. Doctor *Prideaux's* words are theſe : ' Of the ' book, which *Auguſtus* made out of the ' ſurveys and deſcriptions which were at ' this time returned to him out of every Pro- ' vince and depending Kingdome of the *Ro-* ' man *Empire, Tacitus* (b)*, Suetonius* (c)*, and

(a) Καὶ τὰς ἀπογραφὰς ἐξετέλεσε· l. 53. p. 496. c.

(b) Cum proferri libellum recitarique juſſit. Opes publicae continebantur. Quantum civium, ſociorumque in armis : quot claſſes, regna, provinciae, tributa aut vectigalia, & neceſſitates & largitiones, quae cuncta ſuâ manu perſcripſerat Auguſtus. *Tacit. Ann.* lib. i. cap. xi.

(c) De tribus voluminibus, uno, mandata de funere ſuo com-

' and *Dion Caſſius (a)*, make mention, and
' repreſent it to be very near of the ſame
' nature with our Domeſday Book above-
' mentioned'.

BUT I do not ſee how *Auguſtus's* having had by him a *little book* (*libellum, Breviarium imperii*) written with his own
hand, containing a ſmall abridgement of
the public taxes, impoſts, and revenues,
can be any proof that this ſtate of the empire was formed upon a ſurvey made at this
time, or indeed upon any general ſurvey
made at any other time, by virtue of any one
ſingle decree (that is St. *Luke's* phraſe) for
the whole empire. This ſtate which *Auguſtus* had by him of the public ſtrength
and riches might have been formed upon
ſurveys made at different times. Nay, he
might have in this *Book* the ſtate of dependent Kingdomes, in ſome of which a Cenſus had never been made. And it is likely

complexus eſt: altero, indicem rerum a ſe geſtarum, quem vel-
let incidi in aeneis tabulis, quae ante Mauſoleum ſtatuerentur:
tertiò, breviarium totius imperii, quantum militum ubique ſub
ſignis eſſet, quantum pecuniae in aerario & fiſcis, & vectiga-
lium reſiduis. *Suet.* in Aug. cap. 101.

(*a*) Τὸ τρίτον τά τε τ̃ ϛρατιωτῶν ϗ τὰ τ̃ προσόδων, τῶντε
ἀναλωμάτων τ̃ δημοσίων, τό, τε πλῆθ⊙ τ̃ ἐν τοῖς θησαυροῖς
χρημάτων· *Dio.* lib. 56. p. 591. B.

it may appear in the progreſſe of this argument, that there were ſeveral countries,
branches of the *Roman Empire*, which had
never been obliged to ſubmit to a Cenſus.

BESIDE that there is not found in any
ancient Roman hiſtorian any account of a
general Cenſus of all the countries and people of the *Roman Empire*; there are conſi-
derations taken from the nature of the thing,
which render it very improbable, that a general Cenſus ſhould ever have been appointed at one time. The Roman Aſſeſſments
were always diſagreeable things in the provinces, and often cauſed diſturbances. An
univerſal Cenſus at the ſame time ſeems to
have been impracticable. And there does
not appear in any Roman hiſtorian ſo much
as a hint, that ſuch a thing was ever thought
of by any of their Emperours.

WHAT is juſt now ſaid of the difficulty of making a general ſurvey at one and
the ſame time, affects chiefly the Doctor's
Sentiment, who ſeems to think that the taxing St. *Luke* ſpeaks of was a proper Roman
Cenſus. They who ſuppoſe that it was only
a numbring of the people, are not particularly concerned with it.

2. I am of opinion, that St. *Luke* fpeaks only of a *taxing* in *Judea:* and that the firft verfe of his fecond chapter ought to be rendered after this manner: *And it came to pafs in thofe days, that there went forth a decree from* Cefar Auguftus *that all the* land *fhould be taxed.* So Monfieur *Lenfant* has tranflated it (*a*). *Bynaeus* likewife is of the fame Sentiment, and has fupported it, in my judgment, very well (*b*).

I have fhewn in another (*c*) place that the word we have here does fometimes denote a particular country only, and that St. *Luke* has ufed it for the land of *Judea.* And he muft be fo underftood in this place. The Decree relates to the land of *Judea* only, becaufe (*d*) the account that follows is

of

(*a*) En ce temps là, il fût publié un Edit de la part de Céfar Augufte, pour faire un dénombrement de tout le païs. *Nouveau. Teft.* voyez les notes.　　(*b*) Antonius Bynaeus de natali J. Chrifti. lib. i. cap. iii. §. v. vi.

(*c*) See V. 1. p. 521. n. a.　　Some time after this whole chapter was in a manner quite finifhed, I met with *Keuchenii* Annotata in *N. T.* He has upon this text alleged fome other examples of this ufe of οἰκυμένη I rely upon thofe I have produced in the place referred to, and fhall not trouble the reader with more.

(*d*) What is above was writ feveral months before I had feen *Keuchenius.* But my Sentiments are fo much confirmed by what he has fa'd upon the fame fubject, that I am perfwaded the reader will allow me to take the advantage of

fub-

of that country only. And muſt not every one perceive ſome deficience if οἰκεμένη be here rendered the whole world or the *Roman Empire.* Let us ſee what St. *Luke* ſays, omitting at preſent the parentheſis. *And it came to paſſe in thoſe days that there went out a decree from* Ceſar Auguſtus *that all the world ſhould be taxed. And all went to be taxed, every one in his own city. And* Joſeph *alſo went up from* Galilee *out of the city of* Nazareth. If the account of the Decree had been worded by St. *Luke* ſo generally as to comprehend the whole world, would be not have taken ſome notice of the land of *Judea* before he came to relate particularly what was done in it?

I F it be enquired: If the land of *Judea* only be meant, what does the term *all* ſignifie? I anſwer, it was very neceſſary to be added. At the time when St. *Luke* wrote, and indeed from the death of *Herod,* which happened ſoon after the nativity of Jeſus,

ſubjoining here from him what follows: Praeterea, an veri ſpeciem habet, Auguſtum uno eodemque tempore deſcriptionem per totum orbem Romanum inſtituere voluiſſe? accedit quod *omnes* v. 3. ad civitatem patriam protecti leguntur, ut deſcriberentur, nimirum illud πάντες reſpicit ad πᾶσαν τὴν ἰκεμένην, cujus deſcriptio injuncta fuiſſe verſ. 1. legitur, & iſtius mandati authoritate *omnes* impulſi, & ad propriam civitatem profecti eſſe memorantur.

the

the land of *Judea* or of *Ifrael* had fuffered a difmembring. *Archelaus* had to his fhare *Judea* properly fo called, together with *Sa-maria* and *Idumea*. And the province of *Judea*, which was afterwards governed by Roman Procurators, was pretty much of the fame extent. But *Galilee, Iturea,* and other parts of the land of *Ifrael,* had been given to other defcendents of *Herod* the Great.

St. *Luke's* words therefore are extremely proper and expreffive, That ALL THE LAND *fhould be taxed* ; to fhew, that this decree of *Auguftus* comprehended *Galilee,* the country in which *Jofeph* lived. That this was the intention in adding this term of uni-verfality, is evident from St. *Luke's* fpecifying immediately afterward the name of the City, from which *Jofeph* came to *Bethlehem ;* which City was not in the country that originally belonged to the tribe of *Judah,* was not fituated in the bounds of the pro-vince of *Judea* at the time in which Saint *Luke* is fuppofed to write, but was of the kingdome of *Judea* in the reign of *Herod.*

I T feems needleffe to obferve that it was very common to add the term *all* or *whole* to *Judea* or *Land,* when perfons intended the

the Land of the *Ifraelites*. There are divers inftances in the *Old* and *New Teftament*. And *Jofephus*, fpeaking of *Agrippa* the Elder, who had been poffeffed of all the territories fubject to his grandfather *Herod* the Great, fays: ' He had now reigned ' three years over the WHOLE land of ' *Judea* (a)'.

THOUGH I am very well fatisfied from the context, that St. *Luke* comprehends nothing in *Auguftus*'s decree befide the land of *Judea*; yet it is no fmall confirmation of this interpretation, that the moft early chriftian writers feem to have underftood St. *Luke* in the fame manner. For when they fpeak of this circumftance of our Saviour's nativity, they never fay any thing of a general Cenfus all over the world, or the *Roman Empire*.

JUSTIN MARTYR in his firft a- pology informs the Emperour and the Senate, of the time and place of Chrift's nativity. ' *Bethlehem, fays he,* in which Jefus Chrift ' was born, is a village in the country of ' the *Jews*, at the diftance of five and thir- ' ty ftadia from *Jerufalem*. You may af-

(a) Τρίτον ὁ ἔτῷ αὐτῶ βασιλεύοντι τῆς ὅλης Ἰεδαίας πεπλή- ρωτο· Jofeph. pag. 871. v 34.

C 3   ' fure

' fure your felves of this from the Cenfus
' made in the time of *Cyrenius* your firft
' procurator in *Judea* (a)'.   He mentions
this Cenfus alfo in feveral other places,
and always in the fame manner (b).   I do
not recollect above one paffage of *Irenaeus*,
in which there is any notice taken of this
Cenfus (c), and that is not very material.

St. *Clement* of *Alexandria* fays : 'Our
' Lord was born in the eight and twen-
' tieth year, when they firft ordered a cenfus to
' be made in the time of *Auguftus* (d)'

O R I G E N confounds this cenfus with
that afterward made in *Judea* by (e) *Cyre-*
nius.   But fays nothing of its being univerfal.

(a) Κώμη δέ τις ἐςὶν ἐν τῇ χώρᾳ Ἰυδαίων, ἀπέχουσα ϛαδίυς
τριάκοντα πέντε Ἱεροσολύμων, ἐν ᾗ ἐγεννήθη Ἰησῦς Χριϛὸς, ὡς κỳ
μαθεῖν δύνασθε ἐκ τῶν ἀπογραφῶν τ̄ γενομένων ἐπὶ Κυρηνίυ τῦ
ὑμετέρυ ἐν Ἰυδαίᾳ πρώτυ γενομένυ ἐπιτρόπυ· Juſt. Mart. Apol.
1. p. 75. E.   (b) Πρὸ ἐτῶν ἑκατὸν πεντήκοντα
γεγεννῆσθαῖ τὸν Χριϛὸν λέγειν ὑμᾶς ἐπὶ Κυρηνίυ· ibid. pag. 83. B.
Ἀπογραφῆς ὄσης ἐν τῇ Ἰυδαίᾳ τότε πρώτης ἐπὶ Κυρηνίυ κ. τ. λ.
Dial. ii. p. 303. D.   (c) Sed proxima aetatis dicebant,
[*Judaei Joh.* viii. 56. 57.] five verè ſcientes ex conſcriptione
cenſus, five conjicientes ſecundum aetatem, quam videbant
habere eum ſuper quadraginta. Iren. lib. ii. cap. xxii. § 6.
(d) Ἐγεννήθη ⁊ ὁ Κύριϛ⊙ ἡμῶν τῷ ὀγδόῳ κỳ εἰκοϛῷ ἔτει, ὅτε
πρῶτον ἐκέλευσαν ἀπογράφας γενεάς̄ Clem. Strom. lib. 1. pag.
339. D.   (e) Καὶ μετ' ἐκεῖνον [Θευδᾶν] ἐν ταῖς τῆς
ἀπογραφῆς ἡμέραις, ὅτ' ἔοικε γεγεννῆσθαῖ ὁ Ἰησῦς, Ἰυδας τις Γαλι-
λαῖ⊙ πολλὺς ἑαυτῷ συναπέϛησεν ἀπὸ τῦ λαῦ τ̄ Ἰυδαίων· Orig.
cont. Celſ. lib. i. p. 44.

And

And indeed the paſſage amounts almoſt to a poſitive proof, that he thought the cenſus related to *Judea* only.

TERTULLIAN has often made mention of the time of the riſe of Chriſtianity in his apology addreſſed to the Roman Magiſtrates (*a*), in his books inſcribed to the *Gentiles* (*b*): of this and the cenſus, in his treatiſes, wrote againſt the *Jews* (*c*), and againſt *Heretics* (*d*): but yet there is no notice taken of any Cenſus beſide that in *Judea.*

I F any think that we are to expect no mention of a general Cenſus from the Chriſtian writers, becauſe the Cenſus in *Judea* was all that was to their purpoſe: I ſay, that a general Cenſus of all the people and countries of the *Roman Empire* was very much to their purpoſe, the more to illuſtrate the

(*a*) Apol. cap. v. vii. xxi.   (*b*) Ad Nat. lib. i. cap. vii.   (*c*) Fuit enim de patria Bethlehem, & de domo David, ſicut apud Romanos in cenſu deſcripta eſt Maria, ex quâ naſcitur Chriſtus. *adv. Judaeos* cap. 9.   (*d*) Aufer hinc, inquit, moleſtos ſemper Caeſaris cenſus. *De carne Chriſti* cap. 2. Sed & cenſus conſtat actos ſub Auguſto nunc in Judaea per Sentium Saturninum, apud quos genus ejus inquirere potuiſſent. *adv. Marc:* lib. iv. cap. 19. Tam diſtincta fuit a primordio judaea Gens per tribus & populos, & familias, & domos, ut nemo facile ignorari de genere potuiſſet, vel de recentibus Auguſtinianis cenſibus, adhuc tunc fortaſſe pendentibus. *ibid.* cap. 36.

epocha

epocha of our Saviour's nativity. A general
Cenfus muft have been better known than
one that was particular. Would *Juſtin Mar-*
tyr, Origen, and *Tertullian* have omitted
this circumſtance, if St. *Luke* had mentioned
it? Or if they themſelves were aware of it?
And yet in their time certainly an univerſal Cenſus, made in the reign of *Auguſtus,*
could not have been forgotten.

Nay, though the univerſality of the
Cenſus had been a circumſtance of no importance at all in their argument; yet it is
almoſt impoſſible, but it muſt have dropped
from them in ſome one of thoſe many occaſions, in which they have mentioned our
Saviour's nativity, and the cenſus which accompanied it.

I shall proceed but one ſtep farther
to obſerve, that *Euſebius* has made no mention of any more than the cenſus performed
in *Judæa,* neither in his Hiſtory (a) nor in
his Chronicle (b).

I cannot ſay, that this interpretation
is ſupported by any ancient verſion. But

(a) Vid. Hiſt. Ecc. lib. i. cap. v.   (b) Ἐν τῷ λγ
Ἡρώδꙋ Κυρήνιꙍ ὑπὸ τῆς συγκλήτꙋ βꙋλῆς ἀπιϛάλμενꙍ εἰς τὴν
Ἰꙋδαίαν ἀπογραφὰς ἐποιήσατο τ᾽ ꙋϛιῶν κⱝ τ᾽ οἰκητόρων. p. 76.
vid. & p. 200.

Bynaeus

Bynaeus (*a*) obferves, that in an ancient glofs there is this explanation of it : *That all the world fhould be taxed*] *or furveyed: not the orb of all the earth, but the orb of* Judea *and* Syria.

IF then the Cenfus or Defcription ordered by the Decree of *Auguftus* at the time of our Saviour's nativity was of the land of *Judea* only, the filence of ancient hiftorians is no objection at all againft St. *Luke*'s account.   There muft have been many furveys of provinces of the *Roman Empire* in the reign of *Auguftus*, of which there is no notice taken by any of the *Roman* or *Greek* authors now in our hands.

THE only writer, in whom we could expect any mention of it, is *Jofephus.* Whether he has fpoke of it or not, will be confidered hereafter.   But fuppofing at prefent, that there is no notice at all taken of it by him, this is no objection againft St. *Luke.*   It is not to be expected, we fhould find in one fingle

---

(*a*) Hoc a nemine interpretum, quod quidem ego fciam, animadverfum effe nifi in fpecimine Gloffae Ordinariae, quod Robertus Stephanus edidit, legimus.   *Octavius* xlii. *imperii fui anno, publico decreto edixit, ut univerfus orbis Judaeorum & Syriae defcriberetur, & paulo poft* [*ut cenferetur totus orbis*] *five defcriberetur: non quidem orbis terrarum, fed orbis Judaeorum & Syriae.* Bynaeus. De natali Jefu Chrifti p. 306.

Hifto-

Hiftorian all the affairs that were tranfacted in
his country.   We have undoubted evidence
of this enrollement in the early teftimonies
of the chriftian writers.   I have already ex-
hibited more than enough of them. *Juftin*
Martyr fpeaks of it in his *apology* to the
Emperour and the Senate before the midle
of the fecond century.   *Tertullian* mentions it in feveral of his pieces.   There is
fcarce any one occafional fact or circumftance relating to the hiftory of Jefus, which
was more frequently and more publicly mentioned by the chriftian writers.   And yet it
was never contefted, that I know of, in all
antiquity, not even by the adverfaries of the
Chriftian Religion.   *Julian* fpeaks of it as
a thing univerfally known.   I fubjoin his
words. ' The Jefus, *fays he,* whom you
' extol, was one of *Cefar's* fubjects. If you
' deny it, I'll prove it by and by.   Though
' it may be as well done now.   For you fay
' your felves that he was enrolled with his
' father and mother in the time of *Cy-*
' *renius* (a)'

(a) Ὁ παρ' ὑμῖν χηρυττόμενΘ- Ἰησᾶςι ἕις ἦν τ Καίσαρ Θ-
ὑταχόων ἒι ἢ ἀπιςεῖτε, μικρὸν ὕςερον ἀποδείξω· μᾶλλον ἢ ἤδη
λεγέσθω· Φατὲ μέν τοι αὐτὸν ἀπογράψας μετὰ τᾶ πατρὸς κ̣
τῆς μητρὸς ἐπὶ Κυρηνίᾳ· Apud *Cyrill.* lib. vi. pag. 213. ed. *Spanh.*

I PRE-

I PRESUME, I have anſwered this objection : but it is upon the ſuppoſition that
St. *Luke* ſpeaks of a Cenſus or enrollment
in *Judea* only. I have not taken up this
interpretation to avoid a difficulty, but becauſe I really think it to be St. *Luke*'s meaning. However, if St *Luke* be ſuppoſed to
ſpeak of a general Cenſus of the *Roman
Empire,* I own it, that the ſilence of antiquity would be a very great objection. Nor
is the difficulty much leſſened by ſuppoſing
this enrollment was of Perſons only, and
not of lands or goods.   The numbring the
people was far from being the principal deſign
of a Cenſus of Roman Citizens.   But yet,
oftentimes, when an hiſtorian mentions a
Cenſus, he gives very little account of any
thing relating to it, beſide the number of Citizens that was found.   If ever the number
of all the people of the *Roman Empire*
had been taken in the reign of *Auguſtus,*
it would have been a very great curioſity ;
and hiſtorians would have been very fond of
gratifying their readers with it.   Though
we have but few writers of thoſe times, yet
it is with me unqueſtionable, that in ſome
of thoſe we have, there would have been a
particular account of ſo remarkable an event,

or

or at left many references to it: whereas there are none at all.

§. II. S т. *Matthew* says, that Jesus was born in the days of *Herod*. *Judea* therefore was not at that time a Roman Province: and there could be no taxing made there by virtue of a Decree of *Augustus*.

T н i s objection has been answered already. For it is evident from what has been alleged from the Christian writers in the reply to the former objection, that there was some Census, Description, or Survey made in *Judea* at the time of our Saviour's nativity, by a Decree of *Augustus*. However, that no scruples may remain in the minds of any from a false notion of the state of *Judea* under *Herod*, I shall particularly consider the matter of this second objection.

B e f o r e I distinctly consider this objection, I would observe in general; that though we have the word *Taxing* in our version, *that all the world should be taxed*; *This taxing was first made*; yet the words used by St. *Luke* do not import a Tax, or laying a Tax or Duty upon a people. In the margin of our Bibles we have the word *enrolled*. And in most other translations (*a*) a word of like fignification is ufed.

I MUST alfo premife, that fome have thought, that this Enrolment was to be only of names and perfons; and that all *Auguftus* aimed at by this decree was to know the number of people inhabiting the *Roman Empire,* with their employments and conditions of life. Doctor *Whitby* paraphrafes thefe words thus: *that all the world fhould be taxed: i. e.* ' fhould have their ' names and conditions of life, fet down ' in court rolls, according to their families'.

OTHERS have thought, that this Decree obliged to a Regiftry not only of the names of perfons and their conditions of life, but alfo of their goods and poffeffions; and that in fhort, it was a Roman Cenfus which was now made, in order to the peoples paying taxes for the future, according to the value of their eftates. I own it, I am inclined to this latter opinion; and that Saint *Luke* fpeaks only of a Cenfus in *Judea,* as I have already declar'd.

(*a*) Ut defcriberetur univerfus orbis. Haec defcriptio prima facta eft: *Verf. vulg.* pour faire un denombrement—ce denombrement fe fit. *Mons.* verf. & *Mr. Le Clerc, Lenfant,* &c.

HAVING

HAVING premised these things, that we may find out what kind of *enrolment*, or regiſtring was now ordered by *Auguſtus*, whether a decree of *Auguſtus*, could be obligatory at this time upon the people of *Judea* ; and whether, it is likely there was a Roman Cenſus made there at this time, I ſhall conſider theſe following particulars.

1. I SHALL explain the nature of a Roman Cenſus.

2. I SHALL conſider the force of Saint *Luke*'s words.

3. I SHALL deſcribe in general the ſtate of *Judea* under *Herod*.

4. I SHALL enquire what grounds there are to believe, that a Roman Cenſus was made in *Judea* at this time.

1. I SHALL explain the nature of a Roman Cenſus. A Cenſus (as I take it) conſiſted of theſe two parts: *firſt*, the account, which the people gave in of themſelves and their eſtates ; and *ſecondly*, the value ſet upon their eſtates by the Cenſors, who took the account from them. The people did undoubtedly repreſent in ſome meaſure the value of the things they entered ; but the Cenſors ſeem to have had the power of determining and ſetling the value.

THERE

THERE was indeed another thing which belonged to the office of the Cenfors at *Rome*, fc. the Cenfure or Correction of manners : but, as I fuppofe this belonged only to a Cenfus of Roman Citizens, and that it was no part of a Cenfus of all the inhabitants of a Province, or of a Country fubject to a dependent Prince, I take no notice of it here.

THE Roman Cenfus was an inftitution of *Servius Tullius*, the fixth King of *Rome*. *Dionyfius* of *Halicarnaffus* gives us this account of it ; that ' He ordered all the ' Citizens of *Rome* to regifter their eftates ' according to their value in money, taking ' an oath, in a form he prefcribed, to deli- ' ver a faithful account according to the beft ' of their knowledge, fpecifying withal the ' name of their parents, their own age, and ' the names of their wives and children, ad- ' ding alfo what quarter of the City, or ' what town in the country, they lived in (*a*).

(*a*) Ἐκέλευσεν ἅπαντας Ῥωμαίους ἀπογράφεσθαί τε κỳ τιμᾶσῇ τὰς ὀσίας πρὸς ἀργύριον, ὀμόσαντας τὸν νόμιμον ὅρκον, ἢ μὴν τ'ἀληθῆ κỳ ἀπὸ παντὸς τῶ βελτίςυ τετιμῆσῇ, πατέρων τε ὧν εἰσι γράφοντας, κỳ ἡλικίαν ἣν ἔχυσι δηλῦντας, γυναῖκάς τε κỳ παῖδας ὀνομάζοντας, κỳ ἐν τίνι κατοικῦσιν ἕκαςοι τῆς πολέιας τόπῳ, ἢ πάγῳ τῆς χώρας προςιθέντας· Dionyf Hal. Ant. Rom. L. iv. c. 15. p. 212. init. *Hudf. Edit.*

AND

A N D after much the fame manner do we find a Roman Cenfus defcribed in the (*a*) Fragments of the Twelve Tables, and in the Roman (*b*) Orators, (*c*) Hiftorians, and (*d*) Lawyers. From all whom it appears, the people were required to give in an account of their names, their quality, employments, wives, children, fervants, and eftates.

B E S I D E what the people did, there feems to have been fomething done by the Cenfors more than the bare taking the account the people gave in : That is, they were to determine the value of each particular of their eftates, and the amount (*e*) of the whole: and from this feems to have been taken the name or title of this office both

(*a*) *Cenfores populi aevitates, foboles, familias, pecuniafque cenfento. Cic. de Leg.* Lib. iii. cap. 3.   (*b*) *Jam (ut cenforiae tabulae loquuntur) fabrum & procüm, audeo dicere, non fabrorum & procorum. Cic. Orator. Num.* 156.   (*c*) *Ab hoc (Servio Tullio) populus Romanus relatus in cehfum.*——— *Summâque regis folertiâ ita eft ordinata refpublica, ut omnia patrimonii, dignitatis, aetatis, artium, officiorumque difcrimina in tabulas referrentur, ac fi maxima civitas minimae domus diligentiâ contineretur. Florus Lib.* i. cap. vi. vid. Liv. L. 1. cap. 42. & feq.   (*d*) Vid. Digefta. Tit. *de Cenfibus.* (*e*) *In cenfu habendo poteftas omnis aeftimationis habendae, fummaeque faciundae cenfori permittitur. Cic. in Verr.* Lib. ii. *Num.* 131.

in

in the (*a*) *Latin,* and in the (*b*) *Greek* language.   For not only was the compaſs of ground which any one poſſeſſed to be conſidered, but the nature of it, and the profits, it might yield : Nor the number only of ſlaves or ſervants which any one had ; but alſo the work (*c*) they were employed in, according to which their Service was to be valued.   And therefore, every one reckoned himſelf worth ſo (*d*) much as the Cenſors valued his eſtate at.

THIS power which the Cenſors had of rating or valuing the eſtates of all perſons, gave them an opportunity of committing inʲuſtice, in favouring ſome and oppreſſing others. For tho' there were (*e*) rules by which they ought to regulate their eſtimation of

---

(*a*) Cenſio aeſtimatio, unde Cenſores. *Feſtus.* de verb. Sign. Cenſores ab re appellati ſunt. *Liv.* Lib. iv. cap. 8. fin. (*b*) Τιμητής.   (*c*) In ſervis deferendis obſervandum eſt, ut & nationes eorum, & officia, & artificia ſpecialiter deferantur. l. 4. §. 5. fi. de *cenſibus.*   (*d*) Cenſores dicti, quod rem ſuam quiſque tanti aeſtimare ſolitus ſit, quantum illi cenſuerint. *Feſtus. V. Cenſores.*   (*e*) Formâ cenſuali cavetur, ut agri ſic in cenſum referantur,——arvum quod in decem annos proximos ſatum erit, quot jugerum ſit,——illam aequitatem debet admittere cenſitor, ut officio ejus congruat, relevari eum, qui in publicis tabulis delato modo frui certis ex cauſis non poſſit. l. 4. pr. eod.

D   every

every particular, and the fupreme Cenfors (a)
were wont to iffue out Precepts to their
under officers, injoining Juftice and equity
in their pofts; yet if the fupreme Cenfors
were men of ill principles, very great enor-
mities often went unpunifhed (b).

Th a t the reader may have a compleat
idea of the defign of thefe enrolments among
the *Romans*, at leſt fo far as is neceffary to
our purpofe ; I fhall add here the account
which *Dionyfius* has given of the Cenfus
made by *T. Lartius* the Dictator, A. U.
258. before Chriſt, 496. Being chofen
Dictator, ' He immediately ordered, that all,
' according to the excellent inftitution of
' *Servius Tullius*, fhould in their feveral
' tribes give in an account of their eftates,
' fetting down the names of their wives and
' children, and their own age and that of
' their children. All having in a fhort time
' offered themfelves to be affeffed (for the
' penalty of neglect was no lefs than for-
' feiture of eftate and citizenfhip) there were
' found to be one hundred fifty thoufand and

(a) Edicis enim, te in decumanum, fi plura fuftulerit, quam
debitum fit, in octuplum judicium daturum effe. *Cic. in Verr·*
Lib. iii. Num 26.   (b) Sic cenfus habitus eft, te
Praetore, ut eo cenfu nullius civitatis refpublica poffet admini-
ftrari. ·Nam locupletiffimi cujufq; cenfus extenuãant, tenuif-
fimi auxrant. ibid. L. 2. n. 138,

' feven

' feven hundred *Romans* at Man's eftate.
' After this, he feparated thofe who were of
' military age from the elder; and difpofing
' thofe into centuries he formed four bodies
' of horfe (*a*) and foot.' From this paffage
it appears, that the knowledge of the military ftrength of the ftate was intended in
this inftitution, as well as the regulating the
public revenue. It was neceflary to obferve
this here, that the reader may the better judge
of fome arguments that follow.

2. W E fhall now confider the force and
import of the words St. *Luke* makes ufe of
in his account of the matter before us.

No w it muft be allowed, that the Verb
made ufe of by St. *Luke* in the firft verfe,
that all fhould be taxed or enrolled (*b*), is
ufed by *Greek* Authors, for the making of
any kind of entry or enrolment. Thus
Servius Tullius obferving many Roman Ci-

(*a*) Τὸ κράτιϛον ᾓ ὑπὸ Σερϐίϗ Τυλλίϗ ᾓ δημοτικωτάτϗ βασιλέως καταϛαϑέντων νομίμων, πρῶτ⊙ ἐπέταξε Ῥωμαίοις ἅπασι
ποιῆσαι, τιμήσεις κατὰ φυλὰς ᾓ βίων ἐνεγκεῖ, προϛγράφοντας
γυναικῶν κὴ παίδων ὀνόματα, κὴ ἡλικίας ἑαυτῶν τε κὴ τέκνων· ἐν
ὀλίγῳ δὲ χρόνῳ πάντων τιμησαμίνων, διὰ τὸ μέγεϑ⊙ τῆς τιμωρίας·
τήν τε ᾓϛ ϗσίαν ἀπολίσαι τὰς ἀπειϑήσαντας ᾔει, κὴ τὴν πολιτέιαν
ἑπτακοσίοις πλέϗς εὑρέϑησαν οἱ ἐν ᾗβῃ Ῥωμάιων πεντεκάιδεκα
μυριάδων· μετὰ τϗτο διακρίνας τὰς ἔχοντας τὴν ϛρατέυσιμο-
ἡλικίαν ἀπὸ ᾓ πρεσβυτέρων κ. λ. lib 5 c. 75. p. 324.

(*b*) Ἀπογάφεϛαᾗ πᾶσαν τὴν ὁκϗμένην (Ἀύτη ἡ ἀπγραφὴ κ τ.λ.)

tizcns

tizens to be in debt, ordered all of them who had not where-withal to fatisfie their Creditors to enter (*a*) their names and the fum they owed in public rolls, that it might be known what the whole amounted to, and provifion might be made for payment.

This word is likewife ufed concerning the enrolments which were made, when the Roman Citizens gave in their names and inlifted themfelves in the Service of a General (*b*).

So that perhaps there may be fome reafon to queftion, whether St. *Luke* intended not a bare entry or enrolment made by the people of *Judea*, of their names and condition of life, as many learned men have fuppofed.

But yet on the other hand, it is certain, that the whole of a Cenfus is oftentimes expreffed by the *Greek* authors, by the words which St. *Luke* has ufed. Thus *Dio Caffius* fpeaking of *Auguftus*'s firft cenfus, fays, ‘ in the fame year he finifhed (*c*) the en- ‘ rolments'.

(*a*) Ἀπογράφεαϑ κελεύσας τὰς ἀποχρέυς, ὅσοι τὴν πίςιν ἀδύνατοι ἦσαν φυλάττειν τοῖς ὀφείλυσι, κ̀ πόσον ἕκαςος. Dionyf. *Hal.* L. iv. c. 10. p. 207.   (*b*) Συνέρρεον ἀπογραφόμενοί τε πρὸς τὰς ἡγεμόνας τὰ ὀνόματα, κ̀ τὸν ςρατιωτικὸν ὀμνύντες ὅρκον· *Dion. Hal.* Lib. x. cap. 16. init.   (*c*) Ἐν δ' ἐν τῷ τότε παρόντι τάτε ἄλλα ὥσπερ εἴθιςο ἔπραξε, κ̀ τὰς ἀπογραφὰς ἐξετέλεσε.

' rolments :' Hereby meaning, the whole of a Cenfus, including alfo the cenfure of manners, which belonged to a Cenfus of Roman Citizens.   And in another place, when he particularly defcribes the office of a Cenfor, he fays : ' As Cenfors, They [The Empe' rours] enquire (*a*) into our lives and man' ners and make enrolments.'   He intends therefore in this place the whole of a Cenfus, except the correction of manners, by the noun, which St. *Luke* makes ufe of in the fecond verfe : only it is in the plural number.

FARTHER St. *Luke's* narration contains in it fo many circumftances of a Roman Cenfus, that I cannot but think, there was at this time a proper Cenfus. The fubftance of the Decree was, that all the land fhould be enrolled.   Again, *All went to be taxed,* or enrolled.   And he intimates very plainly, that *Mary* alfo was enrolled with *Jofeph.*   All thefe are particulars extremely agreeable to the nature of a Roman Cenfus.

ἐξετέλεσε· *Dio.* L. 53. p 496. c. ad A U. C. 726.—vid. etiam pag. 512. B κỳ αὐτῶν (ſc Galiorum) κỳ ἀπογραφὰς ἐποιήσατο, &c.

(*a*) Ἐκ ỳ τῦ τιμητεύειν, τάς τε βίας κỳ τὰς τρόπας ἡμῶν ἐξετάζεσι, κỳ ἀπογραφὰς ποιῦνται· id. L. 53. p. 508. B. C.

THOUGH

T H O U G H therefore the words in Saint *Luke*, and especially the Verb in the first verse, is used for the making of any kind of entry, yet the whole relation obliges us to understand it concerning this particular kind of enrolment.

A N D St. *Luke's* words appear to be extremely proper. The Edicts for a Census seem to have generally run in this form, expressing the duty of the people. There is in *Cicero* the title of such an Edict, published by *Verres* Praetor of *Sicilie*; when a Census was to be made in that Province. It is called An EDICT concerning the EN-ROLMENT (*a*).

I N a Census of the Citizens of *Rome,* the number of the people was always taken and observed, but there was a census made of goods and lands, as well as of persons. This appears from passages already quoted from *Dionysius* of *Halicarnassus* and others. And *Livie* says expresly, that the very design of the institution was, that people might contribute to the expences of the

(*a*) EDICTUM DE PROFESSIONE. *Cic. in Ver.* Lib. iii. Num. 26.

state

ftate not by the Head, but in proportion to their eftàtes (*a*).

AND for ought that appears, the fame views were purfued in the affeffements made in the provinces. *Tacitus* indeed fays that the *Batavi* paid no tribute to the *Romans*, and furnifhed the ftate with arms and (*b*) men only upon occafion. And fome may be difpofed to infer from hence that there might be enrolmentsmade, in fuch a province, of the names of the people, and their con-ditions of life; in order to know what number of troops it might furnifh the ftate with.

THIS is very poffible, and I think, not unlikely. Though I have not yet feen any particular inftance of it referred to by learn-ed men upon this occafion. Some how-

(*a*) Ut quemadmodum Numa divini auctor juris fuiffet, ita Servium conditorem omnis in civitate difcriminis, ordinum-que, quibus inter gradus dignitatis FORTUNAEQUE aliquid inter-lucet, pofteri fama ferrent: Cenfum enim inftituit, rem falu-berrimam tanto futuro imperio: ex quo belli pacifque munia NON VIRITIM, UT ANTEA, SED PRO HABITU PECUNIARUM, FIERENT. *Liv.* lib. 1. cap. 42.

(*b*) Nec opibus Romanis, focietate validiorum attriti, viros tantum armaque imperio miniftrant. *Tacit. Hift.* lib. iv. cap. 12. Nam nec tributis contemnuntur, nec publicanus atterit, exempti oneribus & collationibus, & tantum in ufum proelio-rum fepofiti, velut tela atque arma bellis refervantur. Id. de *Morib. Germ.* cap. 29.

ever

ever do suppose that the survey of *Judea*
at this time was made by *Augustus* with
this very view (*a*). But I believe *Judea* was
the last place in which the *Romans* would
look for Soldiers. The *Jews* had formerly
served the Kings of *Syria* and *Egypt* in
their wars : They had likewise been in the
Roman armies. But now they had scruples
about serving *Heathens* in this way. And
all of them who were in the service of the
Romans had been discharged in form (*b*).
Their own Kings kept foreign troops in
Judea. After the conquest of *Egypt*, *Augustus* made *Herod* a present of four hundred
Gauls that had been the Life Guard of
Cleopatra Queen of *Egypt* (*c*). And in
the description of *Herod's* funeral solemni-
ty, *Josephus* reckons up three distinct corps
of foreign soldiers, *Thracians*, *Germans*,
and *Gauls* (*d*). Indeed the *Jews* were at
this time so self-willed and tumultuous, that
(as it seems) no Prince was very forward to
put weapons into their hands.

(*a*) Breviario igitur quod meditabatur Augustus, quantum
militum Judaea suppeditare posset, includi debuit. Basnage. Ann.
Polit. Ecc. ante D. 5. n. xi.

(*b*) Joseph. Ant. lib. 14. cap. x. §. 12.

(*c*) Id. de B. J. Lib. 1. p. 1006. 15.   (*d*) Ibid. cap. ult.
sub. fin.

I RECOLLECT

I RECOLLECT but one inftance that looks like a defign of any of the Roman Emperours to take *Jews* into their Service. This was in the reign of *Tiberius,* who, as *Suetonius* fays, fent the *jewifh* youth (who were at *Rome*) under a fort of a military oath into the more unhealthful provinces *(a).* But this feems to me to have been more like fending them to the mines than taking them into military fervice. We are certain the *Jews* did afterward pay tribute to the *Romans.* And perhaps I may hereafter make it appear they were now, and had been, before this, tributary to the *Romans.* It is therefore much more likely, that furveys fhould be made in *Judea* with a view to tribute than to military fervice.

NOR do I perceive, what learned men gain by this. They think it difhonourable to *Herod* to have the goods of his fubjects enrolled and rated by a Roman officer for the payment of tribute. But where lies the difference between this, and the numbring and entering his people in order to demand for Soldiers as many men as his country could afford? If indeed this enrolment of

(a) Judaeorum juventutem, per fpeciem facramenti, in pro- vincias gravioris coeli diftribuit. *vit. Tiber.* cap. 56. vid. & *Tacit. Ann.* 2. cap. 85.

his

his people had been made by *Herod*, by his
own authority, and at his own difcretion,
in order to furnifh the Emperour with a certain quota of men upon occafion, *Herod*'s
honour had been faved.   But this is not
St. *Luke*'s account. *There went out a decree
from* Cefar Auguftus *that all the land fhould
be taxed.*   And by virtue of this decree of
Auguftus all *Herod*'s fubjects, men and women, in every part of his dominions, were
enrolled, with great exactneffe, and as it
feems with great expedition.   And the order
of enrolment muft have been very preffing.
I do not fuppofe indeed, that the Virgin was
obliged at all by the decree to go to *Bethlehem :* But I think, that *Jofeph* would not
have gone thither when fhe was fo near the
time of her delivery, if the enrolment would
have admitted of a delay, or could have been
done at another time.

A N D that this enrolment was performed
by fome Roman officer, as well as ordered
by an Imperial decree, may be very fairly
concluded from the parenthefis, *v.* 2.   Since
the main intention of it is to diftinguifh it
from another, which was certainly made by
a Roman Officer.

M R

Mr. *Whiston* indeed says, *It is very pro-bable that the enrolment of the* Jews *was made by* Herod, *at the request of* (a) Auguſtus. It would have been to Mr. *Whiston's* purpoſe to give a few ſpecimens of this ſtile of *Auguſtus* or of the Republic toward'ſome of their dependent nominal Kings. But it would not have ſignified much in this caſe, becauſe St. *Luke* does not ſay, *there went out a requeſt from Ceſar Auguſtus,* but a *Decree*. And therefore we ſhould'have been ſtill obliged to call it a *Decree*. And I believe, we may do ſo very ſafely. We ſhall' find 'by and by, from the hiſtory of *Herod,* that it is very unlikely, that *Auguſtus* ſhould have ſent *Herod* any *requeſts* about this' time.

AGAIN: Mr. *Whiſton* ſuppoſes *that* Herod *the King of the* Jews *was requeſted or required to get him* (Auguſtus) *a like exact account of the jewiſh nation, as he had already attained of the reſt of the Ro-man Empire.* But if this had been all that *Auguſtus* did, namely, *requiring* or *requeſt-ing* this of *Herod,* then *Herod* muſt have iſſued a command or order to all his people to enrolle themſelves. But how came Saint *Luke* to mention *Auguſtus's* requirement or

(a) Short view of the Harm; of the four Evang. p. 149.

requeſt

requeſt to *Herod*, and call it a decree too, and yet ſay nothing of *Herod's* order? I think St. *Luke* does plainly repreſent the peo- of *Judea* in motion for enrolling themſelves in their ſeveral cities in obedience to *Au-guſtus's* decree; and he ſays nothing of *Herod*.

S o m e have thought that this enrolment was the effect of *Auguſtus's* curioſity. And ſome expreſſions of *Claudius* (a) in his ſpeech to the Senate about giving the free-dom of the City to the *Gauls* have been al-leged by learned men as a proof, that aſſeſſe-ments were ſometimes made in the provinces purely out of curioſity. For he ſays, that he had found a Cenſus to be a very difficult work, even when nothing more was intend-ed by it, than to know, what his Eſtate (or riches) was. But even from theſe words it appears, that an account was taken of the Eſtates of the people, as well as their names and conditions of life. And the Cenſors muſt have made an eſtimation: Otherwiſe the value could never have been known with

(a) Et quidem cum ad cenſus novo tum opere & inadſueto Galliis, ad bellum avocatus eſſet. Quod opus, quam arduum· nobis ſit, nunc cum maxime, quamvis nihil ultra quam ut pub. lice notae ſint facultates noſtrae exquiratur, nimis magno experi. mento cognoſcimus. vid. *Lipſ. excurſ.* ad Tacit. Ann. xi. A.

any

any certainty. Befides, I think, that all the Emperour intends here, is, that he could eafily conceive with what difficulty a Cenfus was at firft introduced into a Province, when even now a frefh Cenfus was feldom made without fome difturbance. And as a proof of this, he inftances in the rebellion, which the firft cenfus of *Gaul* produced in that country (a). And though he calls this renewing a Cenfus, only an inquiry that his eftate or revenue might be publickly known: yet certainly the tribute to be paid according to the Cenfus is not to be excluded. Princes do not, nor is it reafonable they fhould reckon their people only, all their riches. The revenue arifing from the tribute or taxes which they pay is certainly a part of the Prince's riches. The Emperours meaning therefore is, that the making of a Cenfus now is not the impofing any new hardfhip: the great ufe of them is to preferve exactneffe and order in the ftate of his revenues; and yet they give people uneafineffe: How much more muft they have done fo formerly?

(a) *Livie* fpeaks likewife of this difturbance. Tumultus, qui ob Cenfum exortus in Gallia erat, compofitus. *Epitome libri* 137. *Liviani.*

MORE-

MOREOVER, the taxing afterwards made in *Judea* was certainly a Census of Goods as well as Persons. And yet when St. *Luke* makes mention of it in *Gamaliel's* (a) speech, he uses the same word he does here.

ALL the first Christians thought this was a census of goods. It is apparent that *Justin Martyr* thought so, in that he tells the Emperour and the Senate, it was made by their first Procurator in *Judea*. *Tertullian* makes no scruple to call it very plainly a Census. And *Eusebius* in his chronicle says expresly, that enrolments were then made of goods as well as of persons. All these considerations, if I mistake not, render it highly probable, that according to St. *Luke*, there was now a proper census made in *Judea* throughout the territories of *Herod*.

BUT though it be supposed, that here was now a Census made, yet a Census is not a Tax. Assessments were certainly made, that tribute might be paid according to them: and where a Census was made, a tribute might be required. But yet it might be forbore or remitted. And whether any Tri-

(a) Μετὰ τῦτον ἀνέςη Ἰῦδας ὁ Γαλιλαῖ$\odot$ ἐν ταῖς ἡμέραις τῆς ἀπογραφῆς, *Act.* v. 37.

bute

bute was raifed upon this Cenfus or not, I leave at prefent undetermined.

SUPPOSING the affair St. *Luke* gives us an account of to have been a Roman Cenfus, it is poffible two or three enquiries may be here made. (1.) What occafion was there for *Jofeph* to enrolle himfelf, fince he was a poor man; as may be concluded from the leffer offering, which the Virgin made at the Temple, for her purification?

I anfwer, that it was the Cuftom in a Roman Cenfus, for perfons of all employments and characters to enter themfelves; as appears from the defcriptions given of it, in the authors which I have before quoted. And though *Jofeph* was not a rich man, it does not follow he had nothing. However, whatever his condition was, the Edict obliged him to give in an account of himfelf to the officers unlefs there was a particular exception made, and only fuch perfons were required to appear who were poffeffed of eftates to fuch a value. *Auguftus* feems once to have made fuch a Cenfus of the Roman Citizens (*a*). But that this was not

the

(*a*) Ἀυτὸς ἢ ἀπογραφὰς, τ̃ ἐν τῇ Ἰταλίᾳ κατοικέντων, ἢ μὴ ἐλάττω πέντε μυριάδων ὕσιαι κεκτημένων, ἐποιήσατο· Τὰς ⅋ ἀσθενεστέρυς

the ufual method, is evident, becaufe this particular circumftance of that cenfus is mentioned as fomewhat extraordinary.

(2.) S I N C E *Jofeph* lived in *Galilee*, how came he to go up from thence, to be regiftered at *Bethlehem ?*

T o this I anfwer, that poffibly he might be obliged to it by virtue of fome claufe in the Edict. *Ulpian* fays (*a*), that perfons ought to enrolle themfelves in the place where their eftate lies. Though *Jofeph* was not rich, yet he might have fome fmall inheritance in or near *Bethlehem,* and might be obliged to go thither upon that account. But this I do not infift upon here.

S t. *Luke* gives us this reafon of his going to *Bethlehem : becaufe he was of the houfe and linage of David, v.4.* It is probable, that this journey was owing to the Cuftom of the *Jews,* who, whenever they were numbred, entered themfelves according to their tribes and families. If againft this, it be

ἀσθενεςέρας, τάς τε ἔξω τῆς Ἰταλίας οἰκῦντας ἐκ ἠνάγκασεν ἀπογράψαϑ, δείσας μὴ νεωτερίσωσί τι ταραχθέντες· Dio.L. 55. p. 557. B.

(*a*) Is verò qui agrum in aliâ civitate habet, in eâ civitate profiteri debet, in quâ ager eft. Agri enim tributum in eam civitatem debet levare, in cujus territorio poffidetur. l. 4. §. 2. ff. *de cenfibus*

ob.

objected, That the *Jews* had loft the regifters of their families before this time: I
anfwer, that this does not appear. They
were reckoned by them to be of great importance. And it is not unlikely, that many,
if not moft of them, had the regifters of
their families till the final ruine of their
ftate and conftitution, and perhaps for fome
time after it. *Anna* is faid to be the *daugh-*
ter of Phanuel, *of the* TRIBE OF ASSER *. * Luke ii.
36.
Barnabas was a LEVITE †, *Paul* affirms, † Acts iv.
that he was of the TRIBE OF BENJAMIN ||. || Rom. xi.
And thefe two were born in foreign coun- Phil iii. 5.
tries, the one in *Cyprus*, the other at *Tarfus.*

   JOSEPHUS, the *jewifh* Hiftorian
having mentioned the time of his birth,
and the names of feveral of his anceftors,
fays: ' Thus have I given an account of my
' family, as I found it in the publick re-
' cords' *(a)*. It is true, *Jofephus* was of
the race of the priefts, and their regifters
might be kept with greater care and exactneffe than others: But it is evident from
what he fays of the marriages of the priefts,
that the regifters of other families were in

  (a) Τὴν μ̄ ἒν τῦ γένυς ἡμῶν διαδοχὴν ὡς ἐν ταῖς δημοσίαις
Δέλτοις ἀναγεγραμμένην εὗρον, ὅτως παρατίθεμαι· *Jofeph.* in vit.
init.

           E   being

being likewise. ' Every prieſt, ſays he, a-
' mong us is obliged to marry a woman of
' his own nation, and not ſo much to re-
' gard money or any other advantages, but
' to make an exaçt enquiry into her deſcent,
' and to accept of no account but what is
' well atteſted. This is done not in *Judea*
' only; but in all places, wherever there is
' any part of our nation, this law relating to
' the marriages of the prieſts is moſt careful-
' ly obſerved ; I mean in *Egypt* and *Ba-*
' *bylon*, and every other part of the world,
' in which any of our prieſts live (*a*).

(3.) WHAT neceſſity was there, for the
Virgin Mary to go to *Bethlehem?* Surely,
every maſter of a family was not obliged by
a Roman Cenſus, to appear before the officer, with his wife, children and ſervants,
if he had any.

I ANSWER, that I know not of any obligation ſhe was under by virtue of *Auguſtus's*
Ediçt to go to *Bethlehem* at this time : But
yet, *Joſeph* and *Mary* might chooſe it. And

(*a*) Δεῖ γὸ μετέχοντα τῆς ἱεροσύνης ἐξ ὁμοεθνῆς γυναικὸς παιδο-
ποιεῖσϑ, κ μὴ πρὸς χρήματα μηδὲ τὰς ἄλλας ἀποβλέπειν τιμὰς,
ἀλλὰ τὸ γένῳ ἐξετάζειν ἐν τ ἀρχαίων λαμβάνοντα τὴν διαδοχὴν,
κ πολλὺς παραχόμενον μάρτυρας· κ ταῦτα πράττομεν ᵘ μόνον ἐπ'
αὐτῆς Ἰυδαίας ἀλλ' ὅπυ ποτὲ σύσημα τῦ γένυς ἐςὶν ἡμῶν, κὰκε͂ι
τὸ ἀκριβὲς ἀποσώζεται τοῖς ἱερεῦσι περὶ τὺς γάμυς. κ. τ. λ. *Cont.*
Apion. lib. i. §. 7.

they

they might have very good reasons for it that
we are unacquainted with.   St. *Luke* says
ch. ii. 41, 42.   *Now his parents went to*
Jerusalem *every year, at the feast of the*
Passover.   And when he was twelve years
old, they went up to Jerusalem, *after the*
custom of the feast.   And yet by the Law
of *Moses*,   the males only were obliged to
appear before God at the great Feasts.   And
many learned men are of opinion, that our
Saviour did not go up to *Jerusalem* till this
passover (which St. *Luke* here speaks of)
when he was *twelve years* of age : though
his Parents, *Mary*, as it seems, as well as
Joseph, had gone up to *Jerusalem* every
year ; *i. e.* from their last settlement in *Ga-*
lilee, after their return from *Egypt*.

3. I SHALL now give a general description of the state and condition of *Judea*
under *Herod*, that we may be able to judge
whether a Roman Census could be made in
it by virtue of a decree of *Augustus*.

THE *Roman Empire* extended at this
time to all the most considerable countries of
the known world, whether situated in *Eu-*
rope, *Asia*, or *Africa*.   Beside those countries which were properly called Provinces,
and were governed by Officers sent from

E 2   *Rome,*

Rome, with the title of Prefidents, Praetors, or Proconfuls; there were other countries governed by Kings, Tetrarchs or Dynafts dependent upon the Roman State.

In the ftate and condition of thefe dependent Princes, there was a confiderable difference. Some few received their crown from the Emperour, and acknowledged a dependence, but paid no tribute (*a*); among the reft, who were in a more proper fubjection fome were called Friends of the Emperour or the Roman State. This was undoubtedly a very great honour, efpecially when conferred in form (*b*). Thefe Friends of the *Romans* furnifhed them with a part of their troops, or with fums of money upon particular occafions; or made prefents to the Emperour and his minifters, when needful. That is, they paid tribute in the genteeleft way. Others were more properly tributary, and were obliged to the payment of certain fums of money: but it is generally fuppofed

(*a*) Ἧς ['Αρμενίας] 'Ρωμαῖοι ἐκ ἄρχωσι μ̅ ἐς φόρε κομιδὴν, αὐτοὶ ᾖ αὐτοῖς ἀποδεικνύωσι τὰς βασιλέας· *Appian. in Praef. init.*

(*b*) Cognitis dehinc Ptolemaei per id bellum ftudiis, repetitus ex vetufto mos, miffufque è fenatoribus qui fcipionem eburnum, togam pictam, antiqua munera patrum daret, *regemque & Socium, atque amicum* appellaret. *Tacit. Ann.* lib. iv. cap. 26. vid. & aliud exemplum apud *Dionyf. Hal.* lib. v. cap. 35. pag. 291.

that they raifed it themfelves among their people by their own officers. But I fufpect that many of thofe princes called Friends were properly tributary, and that the Emperour had an officer in the territories of moft of them who took care of his revenue. Befide thefe, there were (if I miftake not) fome countries under the government of dependent Kings, in which a tribute was raifed in the way of a Roman Cenfus.

THAT *Herod* was a dependent Prince, I think, was never denied. He obtained the kingdome of *Judea* at firft by virtue of a decree of the Roman (*a*) Senate; and was affifted in taking poffeffion of it by Roman troops commanded by their own (*b*) officers. *Auguftus* gave him leave to nominate for his Succeffor which of his fons he pleafed. But yet in his laft will there was a claufe, by which the final determination of all was fubmitted to the will and pleafure of the Emperour. And after his death his fons were obliged to go to *Rome* (*c*) to obtain the grant and confirmation of *Auguftus*, before they dared to take poffeffion of the territories affigned them by their father.

(*a*) Jofeph de Bell. lib. 1. cap. 14. fin.
(*b*) Ibid. cap. 13.
(*c*) De Bell. lib. 2. cap. 2.

E 3   THAT

T H A T *Herod* was tributary to *Augustus* immediately before his death, feems evident from the Sentence pronounced by the Emperour after he had confidered *Herod*'s will. ' To *Archelaus* were given, *fays Jofephus,* ' *Idumea,* and *Judea,* and the country of ' the *Samaritans.* Thefe were eafed of a ' fourth part of their tribute, *Cefar* decree- ' ing them this relief, becaufe they had not ' joined with the other people in the late ' difturbances (*a*)'. I think it moft reafonable to underftand this of a tribute paid, or to be paid, not to *Herod* or *Archelaus* but to the Emperour. If the *Samaritans* were tributary to *Cefar,* the *Jews* were fo likewife. It is plain thefe were not more favoured than the former. And they were both equally fubject to *Herod* and *Arche-laus.*

T H A T *Herod* had been always tributary to the *Roman Empire,* may be inferred from what *Agrippa* the younger fays to the *Jews* in his Speech to diffuade them from the war. ' At this time, *fays he,* the defire of

(*a*) Τὰ ᵹ Ἀρχελάῳ συντελῦντα Ἰδυμαῖά τε κֿ Ἰυδαία, τό, τε Σαμαρειτικὸν τετάρτֿ μέρֿֿ ֿֿτοι ᵗ φόρων παρελέλυντο, Καίσαρֿֿ ἀֿτοῖς κֿφισιν ψֿφισαμένֿ, διὰ τὸ μὴ συναποֿֿῆσαι τῇ λοιֿֿ πλֿθύֿ *Jofeph. Ant.* lib. 17. cap. xiii. §. 4. vid. & *de Bell.* lib. ii. cap. vi.

liberty

' liberty is unseasonable.   It had been much
' better to have maintained it with vigour
' formerly.---Then all ought to have been
done that was possible, to have kept out
' the *Romans*, when *Pompey* first entered
' into this land.   But our ancestors, and
' their kings, superior to you in wealth, in
' strength and conduct, yielded to a small
' part of the Roman power.   And you
' now the hereditary subjects of the *Romans*
' attempt to resist their whole Empire (*a*).'
And *Josephus* in his speech to the *Jews*
besieged in *Jerusalem*, to persuade them to
surrender to *Titus*, plainly dates the beginning of the *jewish servitude* to the *Romans* from *Pompey's* conquest of *Judea* (*b*).
It may be concluded from hence, that from
that time the *Jews* were tributary to the

(*a*) Ἀλλὰ μὴν τόγε νῦν ἐλευθερίας ἐπιθυμεῖν ἄωρον, δέον ὑπὲρ
τῆ μηδὲ ἀποβαλεῖν αὐτὴν ἀγωνίζεσθαι πρότερον ——τότε ἦ ἐν
ἐχρῆν πάντα ὑπὲρ τῆ μὴ δέξασθαι Ῥωμαίυς ποιεῖν, ὅτε τὴν ἀρχὴν
ἐπέβαινε τῆς χώρας ὁ Πομπήϊ(Θ)· ἀλλ' οἱ μ̄ ἡμέτεροι πρόγονοι, κ̄
οἱ βασιλεῖς αὐτῶν, κ̄ χρήμασι κ̄ σώμασι κ̄ ψυχαῖς ἄμεινοι ὑμῶν
πολλῶ διακείμενοι, πρὸς μοῖραν ὀλίγην τῆς Ῥωμαίων δυνάμεως ἐκ
ἀντέχον ὑμεῖς ἠ, οἱ τὸ μ̄ ἰσχακύειν ἐκ διαδοχῆς παρειληφότες——
πρὸς ὅλην ἀνθίσασθε τὴ Ῥωμαίων ἡγεμονίαν *Joseph. de Bell*. lib.
ji. cap. 16 pag. 1085. 1086.   (*b*) Πόθεν δ' ἠρξάμεθα
δυλείας, ἀρ ὀχὶ ἐκ στάσεως τ̄ προγόνων, ὅτι ἡ Ἀριστοβύλε, κ̄
Ὑρκανῆ μανία, κ̄ ἡ πρὸς ἀλλήλες ἔρις Πομπήϊον ἐπήγαγε τῆ πόλει,
κ̄ Ῥωμαίοις ὑπέταξεν ὁ Θεὸς τὸς ἐκ ἀξίες ἐλευθερίας· id. ibid. lib.
v. cap. ix. p. 142. fin.

E 4   *Romans*

Romans. Subjection and Servitude muſt needs imply the paying of Tribute.

A P P I A N mentions *Herod* King of the *Idumeans* and *Samaritans* among the other Kings, who, according to *Mark Antony*'s direction, were to bring in a certain preſcribed tribute (*a*). *Antony* and *Herod* were always very good friends, and it cannot be ſuppoſed that *Herod* was better uſed by *Auguſtus* than he had been by *Antony*.

I N the ſtory of the difference between *Herod* and *Syllaeus* the *Arabian,* which difference ſeems to have aroſe about three years before *Herod*'s death, and to have continued a year or two at leſt, if not as long as *Herod* lived, there is a paſſage that deſerves to be obſerved in this place. ' *Syllaeus* more-
' over bribed *Fabatus, Caeſar*'s Procurator,
' and employed him againſt *Herod*. But *Herod*
' by a larger ſum of money drew off *Fabatus*
' from *Syllaeus,* and by him required the
' performance of thoſe things which *Ceſar*
• had ordered (to be done by *Syllaeus*).
' However *Syllaeus* went on in his old way,
' performed none of thoſe things ; and more-
' over accuſed *Fabatus* to *Ceſar,* ſaying, that

(*a*). Ἴση δέ ποι ϰỳ βασιλέας ὓς δοκιμάσειν, ἐπὶ φόροις ἄρα τεταγμένοις.——᾿Ιδυμαίων ᷉ ϰỳ Σαμαρέων, Ἡρώδην· *Appian. de Bell. Civ.* lib. v. pag. 1135.

' he

' he was a Procurator more in *Herod's* interefts than the Emperours (*a*)'.   By *Procurator* can be meant no other than an
officer that took care of the Emperour's
revenue. And the nature of the charge feems
to imply, that *Fabatus* had a truft under the
Emperour in *Herod's* dominions.   This
indeed may be queftioned, becaufe that afterwards, *Syllaeus* having killed *Fabatus*, *Aretas* the King of *Arabia* profecuted *Syllaeus*
at *Rome* for the murder of *Fabatus*, as well
as for other crimes committed by him (*b*).
And from hence it may be inferred by fome,
that *Fabatus* was rather an officer in *Arabia*.
Let it be fo.   However, here is a proof, that
the Emperour had a Procurator to take care of
his tribute or revenue in the country of a
dependent Prince : for fuch was the King of
Arabia.   And it is not impoffible, that
Fabatus might be concerned in both thofe
Kingdoms, of *Judea* and *Arabia*.

(*a*) Πείσας ⅗ [Συλλαῖ۞] πολλοῖς χρήμασι Φαβάτον τὸν Καίσα-
ρ۞ διοικητὴν, ἐχεῖτο βοηθῷ ϗ καθ᾽ Ἡρώδου πλέιονα ⅗ ὃὖς Ἡρώδης,
ἀφίςησί τε ἀπὸ Συλαίŏ Φαβάτον, ϗ δι᾽ αὐτῷ τὰ κελευσθέντα ὑπὸ
Καίσαρ۞ εἰσέπραττεν· ὁ ⅝ μηδὲν ἀποδὒς, ἔτι ϛ κατηγόρει Φαβάτŏ
πρὸς Καίσαρα, διοικητὴν ἔιναι λέγων, ὖ Ϯ ἐκείνŏ, Ϯ ⅝ Ἡρώδŏ συμ-
φερόντων· *Joſeph. de Bell* lib. 1. cap. 29. pag. 1030. v. 21.——
   (*b*) Vid. *Joſeph. Ant.* lib. 17. cap. 3.

UPON

UPON the whole then, *Herod* was always a dependent tributary Prince. Whether he was at laſt obliged to ſubmit to a Cenſus, will be the ſubjeᵉᵗ of enquiry under the next head.

ALL that I would ſhew farther here is, that a Cenſus was not inconſiſtent with the rights allowed to theſe dependent Princes, according ro the Roman conſtitution. This is generally denied, and therefore ſome proof muſt be given of it. But it cannot be ex-expecᵗed, that I ſhould produce many examples of a Cenſus made in dependent kingdoms: partly, becauſe the Roman Hiſtorians never take any notice of theſe things, un leſs they are attended with ſome accidents that render them remarkable : and partly, becauſe the *Romans* had ſeveral ways of raiſing tribute ; and a Cenſus, which was the moſt diſagreeable way of all, was not uſed in all thoſe countries that were properly provinces.

AFTER the battle of *Philippi*, in which *Brutus* and *Caſſius* were defeated, *Mark Antony* went over into *Aſia*, and coming to *Epheſus*, ſummoned the ſtates of the nations thereabout to give him a meeting. In a ſpeech he made to theſe States, among other

other things, he tells them : ' Your King *Attalus* bequeathed his kingdome to us by
' teſtament. Our government has been mil-
' der than his was. For we remitted the
' taxes you had been wont to pay to him,
' till men of turbulent ſpirits aroſe amongſt
' us, and laid us under a neceſſity of demand-
' ing tribute of you. And even then we did
' not impoſe it upon you in the way of a
' Cenſus, that we might collect it with the
' leſs hazard and trouble to ourſelves, and
' required only the annual payment of a ſum
' of money out of the produce of your
' country (*a*).' In the concluſion they a-
greed to pay a whole nine years tribute in
two years time. The battle of *Philippi*
was fought (*b*) A. U. 712. *Attalus* died
(*c*) A. U. 621. So that *Aſia* (*Propria*) had
been then a Province 90 years, and yet they
had not had any Cenſus among them. It is
not likely therefore, that we ſhould meet with
many inſtances of a Cenſus made in dependent kingdoms.

(*a*) Ἐπεὶ ὃ ἐδέησεν, ὃ πρὸς τὰ τιμήματα ὑμῖν ἐπιθήκαμεν, ὡς
ἂν ἡμεῖς ἀκίνδυνον φόρον ἐκλέγοιμεν, ἀλλὰ μέρη φέρειν ᾧ ἑκάϛοτε
καρπῶν ἐπιτάξομεν· *Appian. De Bell. Civ.* lib. V. pag. 1074.
 (*b*) Vid. Petavii Rationarium Temporum Part. i. lib. iv. cap. 20.
 (*c*) Vid. ibid. cap. 14.

TACITUS

TACITUS however has given us one inftance. About this time, *fays he,* ' the
' *Cilicians* fubject to *Archelaus* the *Cappa-*
' *docian* (*a*), being required to enrolle them-
' felves in our way, and to pay tribute ac-
' cordingly, withdrew into the faftneffes of
' mount *Taurus* : and by the advantage of
' the fituation, maintained themfelves againft
' the weak forces of the King ; till *Marcus*
' *Trebellius* came into his affiftance from
' *Vitellius* Prefident of *Syria* with four
' thoufand Roman Soldiers, and a body of
' Auxiliaries, *&c.* (*b*).

By *Cilicia* I here underftand not *Cilicia the Plain* [*Cilicia Campeftris*], which had been a Roman Province long before this, but *Cilicia the Rugged* [*Afpera*], which had been annexed by *Auguftus* to the Kingdome of *Cappadocia* (*c*). It is true, that upon the death of old *Archelaus,* A. U. 770,

(*a*) Or, that had been fubject to *Archelaus* the *Cappadocian.*

(*b*) Per idem tempus Clitarum natio Cappadoci Archelao fubjecta, quia noftrum in modum deferre cenfus, pati tributa adigebantur, in juga Tauri Montis abfceffit: locorumque in-genio fefe contra regis imbelles copias tutabantur ; donec M. Trebellius Legatus a Vitellio praefide Syriae cum quatuor millibus legionariorum, & delectis auxiliis miffus, duos colles operibus circumdedit : & erumpere aufos, ferro, ceteros, fiti ad deditionem coegit. *Tacit. Annal.* lib. vi. cap. 41.

(*c*) Vid. *Strabonem* lib. xiv. p. 987. D.

A. D. 17.

A.D. 17. (*a*), the Kingdome of *Cappadocia* was reduced to the ftate of a Province (*b*); and this difturbance, which *Tacitus* here fpeaks of, is placed by him in A. U. 789. A. D. 36. (*c*). But *Tacitus* has no where faid, that this *Cilicia* was made a province. If it had, he muft have known it; and could not have fpoke of it, as he does here. He fays, that the people maintained themfelves in their faftneffes againft the *King's weak forces*, till a General arrived from *Vitellius* with a reinforcement of Roman Soldiers. If it had been a Province, he would have faid, that the people had been too hard for the troops which the Prefect had with him. And this account is in the main confirmed by feveral other Hiftorians, who fay, that this *Cilicia* was governed by Kings till the time of *Vefpafian* (*d*).

Nor is it very hard to trace the fortune of this people from the beginning of the reign of *Caligula* to *Vefpafian*. For *Dio*

(*a*) C. Coelio L. Pomponio *Coff*. (*b*) Regnum in provinciam redactum eft. *Tacit Ann*. lib. ii. cap. 42. (*c*) Q Plautio & Sext. Papinio *Coff*. (*d*) Item Thraciam, Ciliciam, & Comagenem ditionis regiae ufque ad id tempus, in provinciae formam redegit. *Sueton. in Vefpaf*. cap. 8. Item Thraciam, Ciliciam Tracheam, & Comagenem, quae fub regibus amicis fuerant, in provinciarum formam redegit [*Vefpafianus*]. *Eutrop*. lib. vii. cap. xix.

fays,

fays, that *Caligula* gave the Maritime *Cili-cia*, (which was another name of this coun-try) to *Antiochus*, as an acceffion to his kingdome of *Comagene* (a).   Before *Cali-gula* died he took it away from him.   And by *Claudius* it was again reftored to the fame *Antiochus* (b). And from an account, which *Tacitus* has given of another tumult of this people, A. U. 805. A. D. 52. [*Faufto Sulla & Salvio Othone Coff.*] they appear to have been then fubject to *Antiochus* (c). And it is likely they continued under him till it was made a province by *Vefpafian,* becaufe *Comagene* alfo was at that time reduced to a province, as appears from *Sueto-nius* and *Eutropius* already quoted; and from *Jofephus*, who fays, that this *Antiochus* was difpoffeffed of all his dominions in the fourth year of *Vefpafian* (d).

(a) Ὁ γὰρ Ἀντιόχῳ τε τῷ Ἀτιόχε τὴν Κομμαγηνὴν, ἣν ὁ πατὴρ αὐτε ἶχε, κỳ προσέτι κỳ τὰ παραθαλάσσια τῆς Κιλικίας δὺς· Dio. lib. 59. p. 645. D.   (b) Καὶ μετὰ τῶτο τῷ τε Ἀντιόχῳ τὴν Κομμαγηνὴν ἀπέδωκεν (ὁ γὰρ Γάϊθ, ὃ περ αὐτὸς οἱ δὺς αὐτὴν, ἀφήρητο·) id. lib. 60. pag. 670. A·   (c) Nec multo poft agreftium Cilicum nationes, quibus *Clitarum* cog-nomentum, faepe & alias commotae, tunc Trofobore duce, montes afperos caftris cepere.—— Dein rex ejus orae Antiochus, blandimentis adverfus plebem. fraude in ducem, cum barbaro-rum copias diflocaffet, Trofobore paucifque primoribus inter-fectis, ceteros clementia compofuit. *Tacit. Ann.* lib. xii. cap. 55.   (d) Vid. Jofeph. de Bell. Jud. lib. vii. cap. 7.

I   THE

THE only difficulty is, who they were subject to, when this census was ordered to be made among them in the later end of *Tiberius*'s reign. For by the manner, in which the first words of this passage of *Tacitus* are quoted by Cardinal *Noris* (*a*), and by *Pagi* (*b*) from him, they must have understood by *Archelao subjecta*, the people *that had been subject to Archelaus*, that is, to *Archelaus* the King of *Cappadocia.* However, *Lipsius* and *Muretus* (*c*) understand *Tacitus* to say, that they were then *subject to Archelaus*, a son of the former *Archelaus* who died at *Rome*, A. U. 770.

I AM under no obligation to determine this matter, because it is the same thing to my purpose, whether they were now subject to the King of *Comagene* or some other dependent prince; or whether they were subject to a son of the old *Archelaus* King of *Cappadocia:* The *imbelles regis copiae*, the *King's weak forces* proving they were under a King.   But it seems to me most natural to interpret *Tacitus*, as *Lipsius* does. The *imbelles regis copiae* imply, that a King had been mentioned before; and therefore

---

(*a*) Noris Cenotaph. Pif. Diff. ii. pag. 308.   (*b*) Appar. ad Annal. num. 127.   (*c*) In loc.

Archelao

Archelao subjecta cannot be very fairly understood to mean no more than a description of these *Cilicians,* to distinguish them
from others of that name.

TIBERIUS had been indeed very
angry with old *Archelaus.*   But neverthelesse, he might be willing, when he had made
his kingdome of *Cappadocia* a province, to
give one of his sons this small appendage of
it.   This *Cilicia* was far from being any
strong temptation.   The country was moun-
tainous, and the people were apt to turn to
robbery or piracy, and for these reasons
they had been given before by *Augustus* to
the ; above-mentioned *Archelaus* (*a*).   *Cappadocia* had been a very rich booty to *Tiberius.*   Upon its being made a province,
by the ready mony and effects of *Archelaus*
and the revenues of the country, such sums
came into the public treasury of the *Romans,* that their tax called the hundreth
fell immediately to a two hundreth (*b*).   We
may therefore suppose, that by *Archelaus*
here is meant a son of the former King of

(*a*) Vid. *Strabo* lib. xiv. p. 987. D.

(*b*) Regnum ejus in provinciam redactum est; *fructibusque
ejus levari posse centesimae vectigal,* professus Caesar, ducen-
tesim-m in posterum statuit. *Tacit. Ann.* lib. ii. cap. 42.

Capa-

Cappadocia, tho' he be an obfcure perfon. And the weakneffe of the king's forces is an argument, that he was no confiderable prince, and that thefe people were his only fubjects.

THOUGH here be but one example, it is fufficient for my defign.   I believe it was dif-graceful to a Prince, to have a Cenfus made in his dominions.   However, *Tacitus* does not infinuate, that there was any injuftice in it, or that it was abfolutely inconfiftent with the rights indulged to dependent Princes: and the King, to whom this people were fubject, fupported this cenfus, as far as 'he was able.

4. I AM now to enquire, whether we have any reafons to believe, that there was a Cenfus made in *Judea* at this time.

WE can hope for no light in this matter from any author but *Jofephus,* except the notice which the Chriftian writers have taken of it.   If we will rely upon them, I think the point is decided already : but at prefent we will lay afide their teftimonies, and con‧fine our enquiries to *Jofephus.*

THAT *Herod* was always tributary has been proved.   I apprehend, that toward the later end of his reign there was fome alte-ration made in his circumftances for the worfe.

F   In

In order to judge of the evidence there is for
it, we muſt trace the hiſtory of *Herod's* affairs about this time.

OBODAS was now King of *Arabia,*
and *Syllaeus* his chief Officer under him,
who indeed adminiſtred all affairs of that
country with almoſt kingly authority. *Herod* had lent *Obodas* a conſiderable ſum of
mony: When the time of payment came,
Herod demanded the mony, but in vain.
Moreover a band of robbers had infeſted
Herod's dominions and carried off ſeveral of
his Subjects, and were afterwards ſheltered
by *Obodas* and *Syllaeus* in *Arabia.* Theſe
differences between the two courts of *Judea*
and *Arabia* were brought before *Saturninus*
and *Volumnius* the Emperour's chief officers
in *Syria,* the neighbouring province. Here
it was ſtipulated, that *Herod* ſhould ſurrender
to *Obodas* all the *Arabians* he had in his
cuſtody, and that *Obodas* ſhould releaſe all
jewiſh priſoners, and pay the mony he owed
in thirty days time (*a*). But, when this
time was expired, none of theſe conditions
were performed on the part of the *Arabians.*
And *Syllaeus* full of reſentment againſt *Herod* ſails for *Rome.* The terms agreed upon

(*a*) Joſeph. Ant. lib. 16. cap ix. p. 7:4.

not

not having been performed by *Obodas*,
Herod, with the confent of *Saturninus* and
Volumnius, marches into *Arabia*, and routs
the forces that oppofed him. Advice of
this is immediately fent to *Syllaeus* then in
Italie. He procures an audience of *Auguftus*, tells him, That *Herod* had made an
incurfion into *Arabia*, laid waft the country,
and killed five and twenty hundred *Arabians*
with their General. *Auguftus* having heard
this, enquires of *Herod*'s friends at *Rome*,
and of perfons who arrived from *Syria*,
whether this was matter of fact. Being affured it was, without ever asking the occafion, ' He writes a letter to *Herod* in very
' angry terms. The fubftance of this letter
' was, That whereas he had hithertotreated
' him as a FRIEND, he fhould for the future
' treat him as a SUBJECT (*a*)'.

HEROD then fent Ambafladors to
Rome : But they were forced to return without fo much as obtaining an audience. A
fecond Ambaffy likewife went to *Rome*
without any effect (*b*).

(*a*) Ὀργή τε μείζων ἐγίνετο τῷ Καίσαρι, κỳ γράφει πρὸς τὸν
Ἡρώδην, τάτε ἄλλα χαλεπῶς, κỳ τῦτο τῆς ἐπιϛολῆς τὸ κεφάλαιον,
ὅτι πάλαι χρώμεν۞ αὐτῷ φίλῳ, νῦν ὑπηκόῳ χρήσιται· id. ibid.
p.735.   (*b*) P. 736 init.

IN the mean time *Obodas* dies, and *Aretas* takes upon him the crown of *Arabia:* and then sends away Ambassadours to *Rome*, with large presents; withal accusing *Syllaeus*, his predecessor's chief minister, of many great crimes. But *Syllaeus* was still in great favour at *Rome*, and *Augustus* was offended, that *Aretas* had taken upon him the government of *Arabia* without first obtaining his leave. And sent back the Ambassadours without receiving the presents, or admitting them to an audience. ' The affairs of these ' two kingdoms of *Judea* and *Arabia* were ' then in a very bad posture. In one there ' was a King not confirmed in his govern- ' ment. And *Herod* having lost the Em- ' perour's favour was forced to submit to ' many disgraces and affronts. Seeing no ' end of these evils, he resolved to send ' once more an Ambassy to *Rome*, and to ' try whether he could gain friends there, ' and by them recover the Emperour's good ' will. The person sent upon this occasion ' was *Nicolas* of *Damascus* (a)'.

THIS

(a) Τὰ ϽΚ περὶ τὴν Ἰȣδαίαν κͿ Ἀραβίαν, ἀεὶ κͿ μᾶλλον ἐπεδίδȣ, —ῢ ΚΚ βασιλέων, ὁ ΚΚ ὔπω τὴν ἀρχὴν βεβαίαν ἔχων.—Ἡρώδης Ͻ, ἐφ' οἷς ἠμύνετο τάχιον, ὀργισθέντ’ αὐτῷ Καίσαρ’, ἁπάσας τὰς εἰς αὐτὸν παρανομίας φέρειν ἠναγκάζετο· πέρας δ' ȣδὲν ὁρᾶν προεςῶτα·

This *Nicolas*, who was ever firm to *Herod*'s intereſt, was a man of great abilities and of admirable addreſſe. When he came to *Rome*, *Syllaeus*'s power was declining: New informations againſt him had been brought from *Arabia*, and *Nicolas* artfully joining in with the *Arabians* procures an audience of *Auguſtus*; and having fiſt ſupported the charges brought by them againſt *Syllaeus*, he proceeded to the defenſe of *Herod*. Here the Emperour ſtopped him ſhort, ' and bid him anſwer, whether *Herod* had not ' marched his forces into *Arabia*, and ſlain ' five and twenty hundred men? To which *Nicolas* replied: That the things the Emperour had heard concerning *Herod* were in part true and in part falſe, and that the occaſion of all had been conceaied from him. He informed the Emperour of the differences between *Obodas* and *Herod*: That certain ſtipulations had been entered into in the preſence of *Saturninus* and *Volumnius*: That *Syllaeus* had ſworn by the Emperour's Fortune, that the terms agreed upon ſhould be punctually executed, but that nothing had

προεςώτων κακῶν, ἔγνω πάλιν ἐις Ῥώμην ἀποςέλλειν, ἔι τι δύναιτο μετριώτερον ευρεῖν διά τε τ̃ φίλων, ἢ πρὸς ἀυτὸν Καίσαρα την ἐντυχίαν ποιησάμενΘ∙ κ. τ. λ. p. 736.

　　　　　　been

been done : That *Herod* had not moved his
forces, till he had firſt obtained the conſent
of the Emperour's chief officers in *Syria,*
and that the numbers of the ſlain had been
very much magnified. *Auguſtus,* perceiving
that his diſpleaſure againſt *Herod* had been
built upon miſrepreſentations, was appeaſed ;
and at length pronounced a Sentence, that
Syllaeus ſhould return home, give *Herod*
ſatisfaction, and then be puniſhed for his
crimes (*a*).

SOME time after this we have an account
of ſome diſturbances in *Herod's* family. A
very ſtrict friendſhip had commenced between *Antipater Herod's* eldeſt ſon, *Pheroras
Herod's* brother, and *Pheroras's* wife, who
was particularly diſagreeable to *Herod.* *Salome, Herod's* ſiſter, who knew every thing,
ſuſpected that theſe three were carrying on
deſigns againſt her brother. She came and
told him what ſhe knew, and *Herod* had had
ſome intelligence before, and was full of
ſuſpicions, but what he had heard was not
fully confirmed. There follows immediately upon this, a paſſage of ſo extraordinary a
nature, that it muſt be tranſcribed without
any abridgement. ' There was moreover,

(*a*) Id. ibid. cap. x pag. 740, 741.

ſays,

' *says (a) Josephus*, a certain Sect of *Jews*,
' who valued themselves highly for their
' exact knowledge of the law, and talking
' much of their interest with God, were
' greatly in favour with the women. They
' are called *Pharisees*, men who had it in
' their power to controle Kings, extremely
' subtle, and ready to attempt any thing a-
' gainst those whom they did not like.
' When therefore the whole *jewish* nation
' took an oath to be faithful to *Cesar* and
' the interests of the King, these Men to the

(a) Καὶ ἦν ζν μόριόν τι Ἰεδαικῶν ἀνθρώπων ἐπ᾽ ἀκριβώσει μέγα
φρονεν τῷ πατρίῳ νόμῳ, οἷς χαίρειν τὸ θεῖον προσποιεμένων ὑπῆκτο
ἡ γυναικωνῖτις· Φαρισαῖοι καλεῦνται, βασιλεῦσι δυνάμενοι μάλιϛα
ἀντιπράσσειν, προμηθεῖς, κἀκ τῷ προπετῶς εἰς τὸ πολεμεῖν τε κ᾽
βλάπτειν ἐπηρμένοι· παντὸς γεν τῷ Ἰεδαικῷ βεβαιώσαντ Ⓢ δι᾽
ὅρκων ἦ μὴν εὐνοῆσαι Καίσαρι, κ᾽ τοῖς βασιλέως πράγμασι, οἱ δε,
οἱ ἄνδρες ἐκ ὤμοσαν, ὄντες ὑπὲρ ἑξακισχίλιοι· κ᾽ αὐτὲς βασιλέας
ζημιώσαντ Ⓢ χρήμασιν, ἡ Φερώρα γυνὴ τὴν ζημίαν ὑπὲρ αὐτῶν.
ἐισφέρει· οἱ ᾖ ἀμειβόμενοι τὴν εὐνοιαν αὐτῆι, πρόγνωσιν ᾖ ἐπεπιϛεύοντο
ἐπιφοιτήσει τῷ Θεῷ, προέλεγον ὡς Ἡρώδῃ μ κατάπαυσεως ἀρχῆς
ὑπὸ Θεῷ ἐψηφισμένης αὐτῷ τε κ᾽ γένει τῷ ἀπ᾽ αὐτῶ, τῆς τε
βασιλείας εἴς τε ἐκείνην περιελθέσης κ᾽ Φερόραν, παῖδάς τε οἱ εἶεν
αὐτοῖς. Καὶ τάδε, ἀ ᾖ ἐλάνθανεν τι Σαλώμην, ἐξαγγελτὰ βασιλεῖ
ἦν, κ᾽ ὅτι τ περὶ τὴν αὐλὴν διαφθείροιεν τινας· Ⓔ ὁ βασιλεὺς τ
τε Φαρισαίων τὰς ἀιτιωτάτες ἀναιρεῖ, κ᾽ Βαγώαν τὸν εὐνῆχον,
Καρόν τε τινα τ τότε πρεύχοντα ἀρετῇ τῷ εὐπρεπῆς, κ᾽ παιδικὰ
ὄντα αὐτ· κτίνει ᾖ Ⓔ πᾶν ὁ, τι τῷ οἰκείῳ συνεισῆκει εἰς ὁ Φαρισαῖ Ⓢ ἔλεγεν· Ἦρτο ᾖ ὁ Βαγώας ὑπ᾽ αὐτῶν ὡς πατήρ τε Ⓔ εὐεργέτης
ὀνομασθησόμεν Ⓢ, τῷ ἐπικαταϛαθησομένῳ προρρήσει βασιλέως,
κατὰ χεῖρα ᾖ ἐκείνῳ πάντα ἵναι, παρέξοντ Ⓢ αὐτῷ γάμυ τε
χῦν, Ⓔ παιδώσεως τίκνων γνησίων. *Antiq.* 17. cap. 2. § 6.

　number

' number of above fix thoufand refufed to
' fwear. The King having laid a fine upon
' them, *Pheroras*'s wife paid the money for
' them. They, in requital for this her kind-
' neffe, (for they were fuppofed by their
' great intimacy with God to have attained
' to the gift of foreknowledge) foretold, that
' God having decreed to put an end to the
' government of *Herod* and his race, the
' kingdome would be transferred to her and
' *Pheroras* and their children. *Salome*,
' who was ignorant of none of thefe things,
' came and told the King of them, and af-
' fured him likewife, that many of the court
' were corrupted by them. Then the King
' put to death the moft guilty of the *Phari-*
' *fees*, and *Bagoas* the eunuch, and one
' *Carus*, the moft beautiful young man a-
' bout the Court, and the great inftrument
' in the King's unlawful pleafures. He like-
' wife flew every one of his own family
' which adhered to thofe things which were
' faid by the *Pharifees*. But *Bagoas* had
' been elevated by them [*above all the reft*],
' for he was to be called father and bene-
' factor, the King who was to be appointed
' according to their prediction (for all things
' would be in his power) being to give him
a capacity

‘ a capacity of marriage, and of having
‘ children of his own.’

IN the margin (*a*) I juſtify my verſion
of this paſſage, as to one particular, in which
it is ſingular. But beſide that, poſſibly,

(*a*) THIS paſſage of *Joſephus* has been already quoted very
often by learned men, who have treated of this *Cenſus*, or
of the true time of our Saviour's nativity. But all, whom I
have ſeen, have followed *Gelenius*'s verſion of theſe laſt words,
which is thus: Nam Bagoas in eam ſpem ſublatus erat, quaſi
parens & benefactor appellandus regis, quem deſtinarent vaticinia ;
proſpere enim ceſſura novo regi omnia, conſtabiliendo ſucceſ-
ſionem prolis legitimae. They certainly did not look upon the
original. If they had, they would have eaſily perceived his
miſtake. By this means they have loſt one ſtrong argument, that
this affair has a reference to our Cenſus, as will appear by and
by. Doctor *Hudſon* has very much corrected *Gelenius*'s verſion,
and tranſlates the concluding words thus: Fuit autem per eos
elatus Bagoas, quod dicerent eum patrem beneficumque appel-
latum iri ejus, qui ex eorum praedictione creandus rex eſſet :
habiturum enim eum regem omnium rerum poteſtatem, &
Bagoae vires conciliaturum cum muliere congrediendi, propriof-
que liberos gignendi. But, methinks, the ſenſe of this is not
very extraordinary, *Bagoas* is to receive a great benefit from the
King, and beſtowes none upon him, that I ſee ; and yet he *is to
be called his Father and Benefactor.* I think, that *Joſephus*
ſays, that the *Phariſees* gave out, that *Bagoas* was to become,
or *to be called, a Father*; and hereby, that is, by his having
children would alſo be a benefactor to his country. I have
made no alteration in the original words of *Joſephus*. I have
only inſerted a comma after ὀνομασθησόμεν⊙-, and changed the
colon after βασιλέως to a comma. This interpretation is not
my own. I had it from a learned and ingenious friend, to
whom I am very much indebted for this, and divers other
critical obſervations which I highly value.

ſome

fome may have a fcruple about this Sentence:
*He likewife flew every one of his own
family, who adhered to thofe things which
were faid by the Pharifees.* The original
word is in the fingular number, *which were
faid by the Pharifee,* or which *the Pharifee
faid.* If any fhould be apt to think from
hence, that this has reference to fome thing
faid by fome particular *Pharifee,* I muft defire them to confider the context. It is evident from what goes before and follows that
period, that the *Pharifees* in general are
concerned in this affair, though fome only
were punifhed, the *moft guilty,* as *Jofephus*
calls them. The fame phrafe is in another
place ufed by *Jofephus,* where the *Pharifees* in general are intended. Thus he
fays: ' The *Sadducees,* when in office,
' ufually go into the meafures (*a*) of the
' *Pharifees*': in the original it is, *of the
Pharifee.*

I TAKE this oath, which *Jofephus* here
fpeaks of, to be the fame thing with Saint
Luke's taxing, for thefe reafons.

(1.) As far as I can perceive, this oath muft
have been taken much about the fame time

(*a*) Ὁπότε ⲅⲁⲣ ἐπ' ἀρχὰς παρέλθοιεν,——προχωρῦσι δ' ἔν οἷς ὁ Φαρισαῖ ⲗⲉⲅⲉⲓ Antiq. 18. c. 1. §.4.

with

with the taxing or Cenſus mentioned by St. *Luke,* according to all thoſe who place the nativity of Jeſus ſome time between twelve, or fifteen months and two years before the death of *Herod.*

(2) T H E R E is a great variety of circumſtances attending this oath in *Joſephus,* that accord with the hiſtory the Evangeliſts have given us of the birth of Jeſus.   I imagine I am very much prevented by the reader, but I ſhall ſpecifie ſome of them.

S T. *Luke* ſays : *There went out a decree from* CESAR AUGUSTUS, *that all the land ſhould be taxed.*   The ſubſtance of the oath in *Joſephus* was, to *be faithful to* CESAR, as well as to *Herod.*   An oath is a formal acknowledgement of ſubjection, as well as an engagement to fidelity.   No greater acknowledgement of ſubjection could be made than an enrolment in a Roman Cenſus.   St. *Luke* ſays, the decree was, that *all the land* ſhould be taxed, and that *all went to be taxed.* *Joſephus* agrees with him ſurpriſingly, when he ſays, that *All the jewiſh nation* took the oath, except ſix thouſand *Phariſees.*

S T. *Luke's Taxing* and *Joſephus's Oath* are followed with parallel events.   When the wiſe men came, ſaying : *Where is he,*

that

that is born King of the Jews? Herod *was troubled and all* Jerusalem *with him.* Jo-sephus's account is a perfect comment upon this text of St. *Matthew.* St. *Matthew* says: *When he* [Herod] *had gathered the* CHIEF PRIESTS AND SCRIBES *of the people together ,* he demanded of them where CHRIST *should be born. And they said unto him, in* Bethlehem *of* Judea : *for thus it is written by the* PROPHET ; *and thou* Bethlehem----*art not the least among the princes of* Juda : *for out of thee shall come a* Go-VERNOUR THAT SHALL RULE MY PEOPLE ISRAEL. So that all the disturbance at *Jerusalem,* which St. *Matthew* speaks of, was on account of the birth of a King of the *Jews.* And it is the same thing in *Josephus.* And the *chief priests* and *Scribes* of Saint *Matthew* were undoubtedly of the *Pharisees,* which are the persons so much spoken of by *Josephus.* The *King* in *Josephus* has a cha-racter of the Christ or Messias : *for All things would be in his power.* Whether the jest upon *Bagoas,* or rather upon the *Pha-risees,* be of *Josephus's* own invention ; o whether it was an old piece of wit in use a-mong profane people to banter those who ex-pected great things from the Messias ; or

whether

Mat.ii.4,5.

whether it be matter of fact, that some of the *Pharisees* did at this time give any such assurances to some person of influence in *Judea*, the better to carry on selfish designs, I do not determine.   But it is an evidence, that the King, who was then the subject of discourse, was supposed to be an extraordinary person.

I N *Josephus* the *Pharisees* give out a prediction, that *God had decreed to put an end to* Herod's *government*, &c.   This I take to be the very same thing with *the chief priests and scribes (a): Thus it is written by the prophet*, in St. *Matthew :* That is, what *Josephus* calls a *prediction* or *prophecy* of the *Pharisees* is no more than an interpretation or application of an ancient prophecy.   Thus *Josephus* took upon himself the aire and character of a prophet, when he applied the ancient *jewish* prophecies of

(a) Unde putas factum, ut eo ipso tempore, proxime post descriptionem Judaicam Pharisaei vaticinia ista tractarent, & pro lubitu suo interpretarentur? Numquid res ipsa testimonium perhibet Matthaei narrationi? Nonne audis magos ab oriente quaerentes, ubi natus sit Rex Judaeorum? Nonne Herodem sciscitantem a Pharisaeis, ubi Christus nasceretur? His enim occasionibus, his Herodis mandatis, Pharisaei ad Prophetarum libros remissi, vaticinia de quibus quaerebatur prolata, ad placitum uxoris Pherorae, secretis colloquiis detorserunt. *Kepler.* de Anno Natal. Christ. cap. 12.

the

the Meffias to *Vefpafian.*   He was taken prifoner by *Vefpafian* then General in *Judea*
under *Nero.*   *Jofephus,* hearing that *Vefpafian* had a defign to fend him to the Emperour, defired he might fpeak with the General in private.   Being brought before *Vefpafian,* and all the company being difmiffed,
except *Titus* and two friends, *Jofephus* begins : ' You think *Vefpafian,* that you have
' in *Jofephus* a meer prifoner.   But I am
' come to you as a meffenger of great things.
' Had I not been fent to you by God, I
' knew what the law of the *Jews* is, and
' how it becomes a General to die.   Do
' you fend me to *Nero ?* What! are they
' who are to fucceed *Nero* before you to
' continue? You *Vefpafian* will be *Cefar :*
' You, and this your fon will be Emperour.
' Bind me therefore ftill fafter, and referve
' me for your felf.   For you fhall be Lord
' not of me only, but of the earth and the
' fea and all mankind.   And for punifhment
' I deferve a clofer confinement, if I now
' fpeak falfhood to you in the name of
' God (*a*).'

. (*a*) Ἐγὼ ϳ ἐπὶ τιμωρίαν δέομαι φρικᾶς μείζον⊙-, ἢ κατε-
χεδιάζω ϗ Θεῦ· Jof. de B. lib. iii. cap. vii. §. 9.

HOWEVER,

HOWEVER, befide the anfwer given by the *Scribes* to *Herod's* enquiry, we are to remember the fpeech made by old *Simeon*, an eminent *Pharifee*, at the prefentation of Jefus at the temple; and that *Anna* a PROPHETESSE *gave thanks unto the Lord, and fpake of him to all them that looked for redemption in Ifrael.* And there might be many other fuch like things faid there by others, to all which *Jofephus*, a Prieft, and well informed of what was faid and done at the temple, may be juftly fuppofed to have a reference.

ST. *Matthew* fays, that *when* Herod *faw, that he was* MOCKED *of the wife men, he was* EXCEEDING WROTH, *and fent forth, and flew all the children that were in* Bethlehem, *and in all the coafts thereof.* And *Jofephus* has given us the tokens of an uncommon rage in *Herod*. And though Saint *Matthew* has related, upon this occafion, no other inftance of *Herod's* cruelty, befide the orders for deftroying the *children* in and near *Bethlehem*; yet nothing is more likely, than that *Herod*, the moft jealous of mortals fhould, upon the retreat of the wifemen, be filled with fufpicions, that the *Scribes* and *Pharifees*, whom he had lately confulted about the birth-place of the King of the

Jews,

Jews, had been acceffory to the difappoint-
ment he had met with from the faid wifemen: and that being heated by the infinua-
tions of his fifter *Salome* (provided *Jofephus* has not brought her in here for the fake
of a jeft) and by the barbarous counfels of
his fon *Antipater,* now in *Judea* and in
high favour, he fhould then make alfo that
cruel ravage in his court and at *Jerufalem,*
of which our *jewifh* hiftorian has given us a
fummary account.

(3.) As I think, that *Jofephus* was a very
firm *Jew* ; fo his indecent way of fpeaking
of this affair is a ftrong proof it relates to
the tranfactions at *Jerufalem* after the birth
of Jefus. Is it not ftrange, that *Jofephus*
fhould banter the *Pharifees* for pretending
to the gift of foreknowledge, when he himfelf, a *Pharifee,* has been moft notorioufly
guilty of it ? I intend not only his fpeech to
Vefpafian, juft now tranfcribed. There are
other, rather more flagrant inftances, and
that in the hiftory of (*a*) the *jewifh War,*
writ long before his Antiquities, in which is
the paffage we are upon. His ridicule of the

(*a*) Vid. de Bell. lib. iii. cap. 7. §. 3. vid. & quae fequuntur
Jofephi ad Vefpafianum alloquium, ibid. §. 9.

Pharifees.

Pharifees appears to me very unfeafonable
in an account of fuch a fcene of cruelty,
and when they were under very heavy fuf-
ferings : And for what ? For refufing the
oath of fidelity ? No. They had efcaped
with a *fine* for *not fwearing to* Cefar, *&c.*
if there had not followed fome offenfes more
particularly againft *Herod,* as is pretended.
And what are thefe? Why predictions and
expectations, that the kingdome was by the
decree or appointment of God to be tranf-
ferred to fome perfon not of *Herod's* race :
another inftance of agreement with the
time that fucceeded the birth of Jefus, which,
according to the Evangelifts, was a time of
great expectation of a King predicted and
prophecied of. But here is not one riotous
or feditious action mentioned or hinted, the
utmoft is feditious words. And yet *Jofephus* juftifies, triumphs in thefe terrible executions. In a word, he, who ufes to con-
demn *Herod* as a man of an inhumane difpofition, here treats the *Pharifees* of this
time with *Herodian* cruelty.

ALL this is abfolutely unaccountable to
me, but upon the fuppofition, that this affair relates to the birth of Jefus. Nor do I
think, that I wrong *Jofephus* in the leaft. It

G   is

is to me more than probable, that every *Jew*, who did not believe Jesus to be the Chrift, as *Josephus* did not, had a great deal of ill-will againft him and all his followers. That any *Jew* of thofe times fhould have been long in a ftate of indifference upon this point, was impoffible.

IF it be faid, that the predictions mentioned by *Josephus* relate not to Jesus, but to *Pheroras's Wife, and her Children:* I do not deny, but that fhe might pay a regard to what the *Pharisees* faid at this time, as well as others did: but that fhe, or *Pheroras*, or any one iffuing from them was the perfon then difcourfed of, and the chief fubject of the *Pharisees* predictions, I do not believe, becaufe it is inconfiftent with the reft of *Josephus's* ftory. If *Pheroras's* wife had been the perfon chiefly concerned in this affair, as *Josephus* pretends here, would fhe have efcaped with her life in fo wide a fcene of cruelty, in which even the former favourites of *Herod* were involved? If the difpofitions of people ran now all toward *Pheroras* and his wife, would *Antipater* have been ftill great with them ? Would *Antipater*, fo defirous of the Crown, have gone away to *Rome*, as he did foon after this execution, and

and leave things in this posture? Would he,
when he went away, leave securely in the
hands of *Pheroras* and his wife the work
of poysoning his father, and securing the
succession for himself? Would not *Antipater*, who had lately, with exquisite artifice
and cruelty, accomplished the death of his
two brothers, sons of *Herod* by *Mariamne*,
have been able to have effected the ruine of
Pheroras's wife? It is true, after this execution was over, she was called to account by
Herod.

THAT it may not be insinuàted, that I
conceal any difficulty, I will here give the
reader *Josephus*'s words which follow next
after the long passage we are concerned with.
' *Herod* having punished the *Pharisees*, who
' had been convicted of concerning them-
' selves in this affair, calls a council of
' his friends, and there accuses *Pheroras*'s
' wife : ascribing to her the affront that
' had been offered to the virgins (A), and
' therein to him : adding, that she did all
' she could to create a difference between
' him and his brother, that the fine imposed

(A) *The virgins*] The meaning is: *Pheroras*'s wife had been
his servant. *Herod* had offered *Pheroras* one of his daughters,
and after that, another. But *Pheroras* refused them both out
of his affection for this woman.

' upon

' upon the *Pharisees* had been evaded by her
' means, and that in the present affair no-
' thing had been done without her :----and
' that if *Pheroras* had any regard for him,
' he would of his own accord put away his
' wife.   You will then, says he to *Pheroras*,
' be my brother indeed, and we shall live
' (*a*) together in friendship.'

I F the meaning of the last words of the *charge* against this woman be not, that in the *present affair nothing had been done without her*, as I have rendered them, but that *Now a days nothing was done without her*, as Doctor *Hudson* translates them (*b*), then her conduct in the late affair is not so much as made a particular crime, but is only

(*a*) Ἡρώδης ᵹ, κολάσας τ̃ Φαρισαίων τὰς ἐπὶ τοῖςδε ἐληλεγμένας, συνέδριόν τε ποιεῖται τ̃ φίλων, ᴋ, κατηγορίαν τῆς Φερώρε γυναικὸς, τήν τε ὕβριν τ̃ παρθένων τῆ τολμῆ τῆς γυναικὸς ἀνατιθεὶς, ᴋ, ἔγκλημα ταύτην ἀτιμίαν αὐτῶ ποιύμεν☉, ὥςε ἀγωνοθετεῖν ςάσιν αὐτῶ πρὸς τὸν ἀδελφὸν ᴋ, πόλεμον ἐκ φύσεως αὐτοῖς ⱕ λόγω ᴋ, δι' ἔργων ὅσα δύναιτο, τήν τε διάλυσιν τῆς ζημίας τῆς ὑπ' αὐτῶ ἐπιβληθείσης τέλεσι διαφευχθῆναι τοῖς ἐκείνης, τ̃ τε νῦν πεπραγμένων ἐδὲν ὅ, τι ἐ μετ' αὐτῆς· ἀνθ' ὦν Φερώρα καλῶς ἔχειν, ἐ δεήσει ἐδὲ γνωμῶν ἐισηγήσεως τ̃ ἐμῶν, αὐτοκέλευσον ἀποπέμπεαϑ γυναῖκα ταύτην, ὡς πολέμε τε πρός μοι σοὶ ἀιτίαι ἐσομένην ᴋ, νῦν, ἔιπερ ἀντιποιῆ συγγενείας τῆς ἐμῆς, ἀπείπαϑ τήνδε τὴν γαμετήν· μενεῖς ᵹ ἔτας ἐμὸς ἀδελφός τε ᴋ, σέργειν ἐκ ἀπηλαγμέν☉· Antiq. 17. c. 3. §. 1.

(*b*) Suisque impendiis evitata esset solutio mulctae ab ipso impositae, nihilque jam sine illa ageretur.

comprehended

comprehended in a general charge of an over busy intriguing temper.

B u t let it be granted that *Josephus* says, her conduct in this affair was an express charge in *Herod's* accusation; yet the punishment proposed confutes the supposition, that she was the main agent in this concern. *Herod* assures *Pheroras*, they two should be very good friends, if this woman were but *put away*. Would this disgrace have satisfied *Herod*, if beside many other provocations, she had now been the Principal in a crime, for which many accessories, and those in all other respects very acceptable persons, had been punished with death? I hope we may be allowed not to credit *Josephus* in a circumstance so inconsistent with the rest of his account. And, I think, it is not hard to guesse, why *Josephus* gave some false turns in this story.

I h a v e one thing more to desire of the reader, that is, that he will be pleased to consider, whether *Josephus* does not contradict himself in the main passage, in which he is so merry. He tells us at first, that the *Pharisees*, in requital for the kindnesse shewed to them, foretold, that God had decreed to transfer the kingdome to *Pheroras's*

G 3   *wife,*

wife, and Pheroras, *and their children:* But at the end, it is *the King, who was to be appointed according to their prediction.* How comes *Pheroras's wife,* and Pheroras, *and their children* to be all a *King ?* Or how came the *King* to be all them? If the reader can reconcile thefe things together, it will be very well. But if he cannot, I hope he will come over to me, and allow, that here are fome things faid of *Pheroras's* wife and the *Pharifees* without foundation. I ever take it, that inconfiftences are a certain fign, that an author has not confined himfelf barely to matter of fact, but has indulged his fanfy and gone into fiction.

FOR thefe reafons then I think, that the Oath in *Jofephus,* taken by all the *jewifh* nation, is the fame thing with the taxing or enrolement mentioned by St. *Luke.* And I think, that this oath refers to a cenfus made in *Judea,* for the following reafons. In a cenfus the people gave in an account of themfelves and their eftates upon *oath.* It feems to me very probable that a cenfus was made, or at left ordered by *Auguftus,* during the time that *Herod* lay under his difpleafure. Under the former particular I fhewed that *Herod* had been, before this, a tributary prince.

prince. His great fubjection appears likewife in the difference between him and *Obodas*. He was obliged to refer the matter in difpute to the Emperour's officers in *Syria*. After *Obodas* had broke the ftipulations, *Herod* did not dare to move his forces without the confent of the before-mentioned officers. And *Auguftus* fuppofing that he had done fo, was very angry, and threatens, that whereas he had *hitherto ufed him as a friend, he fhould for the future treat him as a fubject.* Thefe words are undoubtedly proper and expreffive words. If *Herod*, when a *friend* of *Auguftus*, was in fuch fubjection, what can the treating as a *fubject* mean, but the reducing him to the loweft ftate of dependent princes? Which feems to be that of obliging them to fubmit to a cenfus, and then raifing tribute in their dominions according to it.

JOSEPHUS fays, that after the receit of this letter from *Auguftus*, *Herod* fent in vain two Ambaffies to *Rome*, that the ftate of *Judea* grew worfe and worfe, that *Herod* was obliged to fubmit to many difgraces. The Emperours difpleafure againft *Herod* was manifeft therefore, not at *Rome* only, but in all the countries about *Judea*.

G 4 (1.) But

(1.) B u t it may be objected, that *Jofe-phus* has no where faid, that there was any enrolement made of the *Jews*, much lefs that there was a proper Cenfus made in *Judea*.

T o this I anfwer, that it is apparent, there was an enrolement and numbring of the people. How elfe fhould all the people have taken an oath, except *fix thoufand Pharifees?* Did they not enter the people that took the oath? If they did not, how fhould it have been known who fwore and who did not?

N o r can it be inferred there was no en-rolement or Cenfus, becaufe *Jofephus* has not exprefly faid there was. *Jofephus*'s account of this matter is very flight and de-fective. If it had not been for fome things which followed after the oath, and had fome connexion with it, it feems that he would have taken no notice of it at all. An oath had been taken by all the *jewifh* na-tion to *Cefar* and *Herod*, and great ex-actneffe had been obferved in relation to it. The numbers and characters of thofe which had refufed were known. This was an af-fair of importance, and deferved a much more particular account than he has given us. And we are allowed to fuppofe fome

things,

things, not expreffed, which muft neceffari-
ly have been concomitants of it.

I DO not pretend to affign pofitively the
reafons of his flight mention of this affair.
But, I apprehend, I can give fome probable
account of it. *Herod's* fubjects were all enrolled in a Cenfus, but there was no tribute
demanded upon it. *Herod* had great dexte-
rity, or very good fortune in furmounting
the difficulties he met with in the feveral
parts of his life. He was himfelf a man of
a great Genius, and fome of his fervants were
men of great abilities. *Nicolas* of *Damafcus* in particular was eminent for learning and addreffe. And *Herod* knew very
well how to beftow a prefent or a bribe.

I AM moreover the rather inclined to
think, that no tax was raifed upon this Cenfus, becaufe it appears that after thefe troubles, of which *Jofephus* has given us an account, *Auguftus* was in a great meafure reconciled to *Herod*. Perceiving, that his
refentment againft *Herod* had been very
much founded upon afperfions, he might be
difpofed to forbear exacting the tribute upon the Cenfus, and to let things go on in
the old way. Then *Herod* had taken care
that the Decree had been obeyed and executed

cuted in his dominions without difturbance : all had fworn or enrolled themfelves, ex- cept *fix thoufand Pharifees,* and they were fined.

MOREOVER, *Herod* was now an old man, and had many Sons. It was therefore very likely, there would be fome partition made of his dominions at his death. And *Auguftus* might be very willing there fhould be fo. Three or four little princes are bet- ter governed then one that is powerful. Tri- bute could not be paid according to this Cenfus any longer than the feveral parts of the kingdome continued united in one perfon. When it came to be divided or parcelled out, a new cenfus would be neceffary.

IF then no tribute was paid upon this Cenfus, an hiftorian could the more eafily pafs it by without a very particular defcrip- tion, efpecially fince it had been finifhed without any popular tumults.

IT may be inferred from the manner in which St. *Luke* mentions this furvey, that it was not very much taken notice of. If it had been univerfally known, there had been hardly any occafion, upon the mention of a decree of *Auguftus* in the reign of *Herod* to enrole all the land, to fubjoin a parenthefis, the

the chief intent of which seems to be to di-stinguish this from another that happened not till after the removal of *Herod's* successor.

IF this Census was not universally known when *Josephus* wrote, he might be well pleased to touch upon it but slightly. The *jewish* writers were very forward to enume-rate the honours done to their people by the Roman Senate, or the chief men of the com-monwealth, or the Emperours afterwards; the better to gain some regard among other nations, by whom they were generally de-spised and hated. But as for any disgraces they received from the *Romans*, the case was very different.

THUS *Josephus* has mentioned many favours conferred on the *Jews* by *Julius Cesar*, *Augustus*, *Livia*, *Marcus Agrippa*, *Claudius*, and other *Romans:* but yet he says nothing of the Journey which *Caius*, *Augustus's* eldest adopted son, made through *Judea*, in the beginning of the reign of *Archelaus*. This we have from (a) *Sueto-nius* only, an author very little concerned in *jewish* affairs. The reason seems to be,

(a) Sed & Caium Nepotem, quod Judaeam praetervehens apud Hierosolymam non supplicasset, collaudavit [Augustus]. *Suet.* in *Aug.* cap. 93.

that

that *Caius* offered no facrifice at *Jerufalem*, nor made any prefent to the temple, which was deemed a piece of contempt fhewn to their religion.

P O S S I B L Y, *Jofephus* found but a flender account of this tranfaction in the Hiftory of *Nicolas* of *Damafcus*, from which he took his materials for this reign. Though *Nicolas* was no *Jew*, yet he was a great friend and flatterer of *Herod :* and it could not but be an ungrateful task to him, after that he had in the former part of his work drawn his mafter as a great genius, a founder of cities, and friend of *Auguftus*, to defcribe at laft fo difagreeable a fcene as that of one of the Emperour's officers enrolling all the fubjects of his dominions.

N I C O L A S (a) had great intimacies with *Herod*. *Jofephus* has affirmed more than once, that he was a great flatterer (b) of him. And in one place fays particularly, ' That living in his kingdome and together · with him he compofed his hiftory with a ' view to pleafe the King and advance his ' intereft, touching upon thofe things only

(a) Καὶ Νικόλαος ὁ Δαμασκηνὸς φίλος τε ὢν τῷ βασιλέως, κỳ τὰ πάντα συνδιαιτώμενος ἐκείνῳ, κ. λ. Antiq. 17. c. 5. §. 4.

(b) Ibid. l. 14. c. 1. § 3.

' which

' which made for (a) his honour.' This
inrolement, even though it was not a proper
affeffement, but only an entry of the names
of all the people, their age and condition,
accompanied with an oath of ftrict fidelity
to the Emperour, muft have been the greateft mortification of *Herod*'s whole life: and
from the character of *Nicolas*, juft fet down,
it may be concluded almoft with certainty,
that he did not give a particular account of
this affair. Nor had *Jofephus* any inducements to fupply his defects in this place.

(2.) BUT it will be faid, that the filence
of *Jofephus* is not the only difficulty : there
is in him well nigh pofitive proof, that there
had been no cenfus or enrolement made in
Judea before the removal of *Archelaus*.
For upon the occafion of this, he fays :
' Moreover *Cyrenius* came into *Judea*, it
' being annexed to the province of *Syria*, to
' to make an affeffement of their goods and
' feife *Archelaus*'s eftate. The *Jews* were
' at firft very much moved at the (b) men-
' tion of the enrolements, but by degrees

(a) Ζῶντι γ̓ ἐν τῇ βασιλείᾳ ⓒ σὺν αὐτῷ, κεχαρισμένας ἐκείνῳ
κỳ καθ' ὑπηρεσίαν ἀνέγραφεν, μόνον ἀπτόμεν⊙· ᵗ πρὸς εὔκλειαν
αὐτῷ φερόντων· Antiq. 16. c. 7. §. 2.

(b) Ὁι ჳ κάιπερ τὸ κατ' ἀρχὰς ἐν δέινῳ φέροντες τὴν ἐπὶ ταῖς
ἀπογραφαῖς ἀκρόασιν· Antiq. 18. c. 1. §. 1.

' they

' they were brought to acquiefce at the per-
' fwafion of *Joazar* the High Prieft'. He
obferves alfo, ' that at this time *Judas* the
' *Gaulanite* excited them to a rebellion,
' telling them, that a cenfus would intro-
' duce downright (a) flavery.' It will be
faid: It may be hence inferred, that there
had been no enrolments made before: if
there had, they could not have been fo fright-
ful now.

I ANSWER, that there muft have been an
enrolment made, when the oath mentioned
by *Jofephus* was taken : And that oath was
likewife an exprefs and folemn acknowledge·
ment of fubjection to the *Romans*.

BESIDES, though this *oath* had been
quite omitted by *Jofephus*, it would not
have followed, that there had been no enrolment made before this time in *Judea*.
People are not always of the fame temper.
Judas of *Galilee* now broached or revived
the principle, that they ought to obey none
but God : and for fome reafons it was received with great applaufe, fpread and gained
ground. But the *Jews* muft have been
more fubmiffive, when they all took the
oath to *Cefar*, except fix thoufand. And af-

(a) Ibid.

tèr *Herod* was dead, there was a very nume.
rous Embaffy fent to *Rome* in the name of
the whole *jewiſh* nation, entreating, that
inſtead of being governed by any of *Herod's*
defcendents, ' they might be annexed to the
' Province of *Syria*, and be fubject to Prac-
' tots fent from thence, promiſing likewiſe
' a moſt quiet and peaceable behaviour under
' fuch a government (*a*).

IN another place *Joſephus* reprefents
Judas's arguments in thefe terms : ' And
' at this time a certain man called *Judas* the
' *Galilean* excited the people to rebellion,
' telling them they had a mean fpirit if they
' could endure to pay tribute to the *Ro-*
' *mans*, and acknowledge mortal men for
' their Lords......after God had been their
' King (*b*)·   It might be as well inferred
from what *Judas* fays here, that the *Jews*
had never before paid tribute to the *Romans*,
or been fubject to mortal Lords, as from
what he fays in the other place, that they
had never before been enrolled.   I prefume

(*a*) Ἧν ὃ κεφάλαιον αὐτοῖς τ ἀξιώσεως, βασιλείας μ κ τοιῶν
δὲ ἀρχῶν ἀπηλλάχθαι, προσθήκην ᐤ Συρίας γεγονότας ὑποτάστεᐧ
τοῖς ἐκεῖσι πεμπομένοις σρατηγοῖς· κ. τ. λ. *Joſ. Ant.* 17. p. 784·
v. 35.   (*b*) Κακίζων, εἰ φόρον τε Ῥωμαίοις τελεῖ ὑπομέ-
ινσι, κ μετὰ τὸν Θεὸν ὄψουσι θνητὸς δεσπότας· *De Bell.* lib. ii.
cap. 8. §. 1.

it need not be proved, that they had been subject, before this, to *mortal Lords.* I think too, that I have shewn, they had been tributary to the *Romans* in the reign of *Herod.* They had likewise paid Tribute to the *Romans* before *Herod's* reign : For *Josephus* says, that *Cassius* ' imposed a heavy ' tribute upon the people [*in Syria*]. And in ' particular bore very hard upon *Judea,* ex- ' acting of them seven hundred talents of ' silver (*a*)'. This sum was laid in several portions upon the several parts of *Judea,* and *Herod,* then Governour of *Galilee* under *Hyrcanus,* brought in his quota the first, and thereby very much obliged *Cassius.* *Judas's* speech therefore is no proof, that there had been no enrolment or Census made in *Judea* before the removal of *Archelaus.*

(3.) I can think of but one difficulty more. Perhaps some will say, my argument is defective, and that in order to make it out, that this *oath,* taken by the *Jews,* in *Josephus,* was a census, I ought to produce some passage of an ancient writer, in

(*a*) Καὶ φόρꙋς αὐταῖς μεγάλꙋς ἐπετίθει· μάλιϛα ἡ τὴν Ἰꙋδαίαν ἐκάκωσεν, ἱπτακόσια τάλαντα ἀργυρίꙋ ἐισπραττόμενΘ· *Ant.* lib. 14. cap. xi. §. 2.

which

which a cenfus is called an *Oath*, or the act of the people enrolling themfelves in a cenfus is expreffed by *taking an oath*. I own then, that I have not any fuch example by me. However, I would offer here two or three confiderations.

[1.] IN a Roman Cenfus the people gave in their account of themfelves and their eftates upon oath. And that oath, as reprefented by *Dionyfius*, has a very near refemblance with the words of *Jofephus*. *Dionyfius* fays, the people were commanded to *take an oath to give in a true account according to the beft of their knowledge:* and *Jofephus* fays, that the whole *jewifh* nation engaged by an (*a*) oath to be *faithful to* Cefar *and the interefts of the King*.

[2.] WE have in the ancient writers very few accounts of affeffements made in provinces. The Roman hiftorians fcarce ever take any notice of them, but when they were attended with fome difturbances which

(*a*) THERE is another thing which may deferve notice. *Dionyfius* fays, That the penalty at *Rome* for not enrolling in a cenfus was lofs of eftate and citizenfhip. Perhaps the *fine* impofed on the *Pharifees*, who refufed to fwear, was now ordered in conformity to the Roman Cuftoms upon like occafions. For *Herod* had been wont before to inflict punifhments of another kind for refufing to fwear fidelity to him. *Antiq.* 15. c. 10. § 4.

H made

made them remarkable. As we have but
very few writers of thofe times, efpecially
fuch as lived in the provinces ; it is not to be
wondered that we meet with fome fingular
phrafes in thofe we have, and which we cannot parallel in any other authors now in
our hands. If we had before us the works
of a good number of provincial writers, it is
not unlikely, but we might fee fome of
them reprefent their nation enrolling themfelves in a Cenfus, efpecially in the firft Cenfus made in their country, by the taking an
oath of Allegiance and Fidelity to the
Emperour. I fhall give an inftance from
Jofephus, and which has likewife fome affi-
nity with our fubject. In the *jewifh* war he
calls *Fabatus Cefar's* Procurator (*a*) : In his
Antiquities (*b*) he calls him *Cefar's* fervant.
He alfo calls one *Stephen,* who was in
Judea in the time of *Cumanus, Cefar's* fervant. ' And (*c*) at this time, *fays he,* fome
' who aimed at innovations fet upon *Stephen*
a fervant

(*a*) Πείσας ἢ πολλοῖς χρήμασι Φαβάτον τὸν Καίσαρ۞ διοκη-
τὴν· *De Bell* lib. 1 cap 29. p 1030. v.22. vid. & v. 29.

(*b*) —ἀνηρηκέναι ἢ κỳ Φάβατον Καίσαρ۞ δἔλον· *Antiq.* 17.
cap. 3. p.755. v 6.

(*c*) Τῶν ᾧ ἐφεςώτων ἐπὶ νεωτερισμῷ τινὲς, κατὰ τὴν δημοσίαν,
ὁδὸν ὡς ιαχτὸν ςαδίων ἀπωθεν τῆς πόλεως, Στέφανον Καίσαρ۞
δἔλον

' a servant of *Cesar*, in the High-way about
' a hundred Stadia from the city, and robbed
' him of all he had'. I have shewn above,
that *Fabatus* was *Augustus*'s Procurator in
the Kingdom of *Arabia*, if not also in
Judea. And that *Stephen* also was Procurator in *Judea*, may be concluded, from the
treasure he had with him, and from his being
particularly the object of the spite of the se-
ditious *Jews* who were uneasy under the
Roman government. So that, with *Josephus*, the *Emperour's servant* and the *procurator of the Emperour's revenue* were sy-
nonymous terms. If *Josephus* appears at
present singular in this stile, yet I doubt not,
but it was at that time very common.

[3.] I APPREHEND, that though the
Jews entered themselves and their estates in
the way of a Roman Census, yet there was
no tribute raised upon it. Which might be
the reason of *Josephus*'s representing this
affair simply by taking an oath, rather than
by the name of a Census.

I HAVE now laid before the reader the
evidence I have for this supposition, that
there was a Census made in *Judea* a little

δῆλον ὁδοιποροῦντα λῃσεύσαντες, ἅπασαν αὐτῷ τὴν κτῆσιν διαρπάζεσιν.
Antiq. 10. cap 4. §. 4. vid. & *de Bell.* p. 1072. v. 32.

H 2　　　before

before the death of *Herod*. The particulars mentioned by St. *Luke*, and the expreſſions he uſes, are very ſuitable to a Cenſus. And the poſture of *Herod*'s affairs about this time incline me to think there was an enrolment, after the manner of a Roman Cenſus, made in his dominions by order of *Auguſtus*.

But whether I am in the right or not, St. *Luke* certainly ſays, that there was an enrolment: And *Joſephus* ſays, that the whole *jewiſh* nation had taken an oath to be faithful to *Ceſar* and *Herod*. Some entry therefore muſt have been made. And if St. *Luke* be underſtood to ſpeak only of an enrolment of names and perſons, his account is confirmed by *Joſephus* as fully as one could wiſh.

And though it ſhould be thought, that I have not fully proved, that there was at this time a proper aſſeſſement made in *Judea*; yet I have, I think, ſhewn undeniably, that about this time that country was brought into a very ſtrict ſubjection to *Auguſtus*: And herein alſo St. *Luke* and *Joſephus* agree entirely.

I am ſenſible that they, who have hitherto ſuppoſed, that Jeſus was not born till a few weeks before the death of *Herod*, will

very

very unwillingly allow, that the oath in
Jofephus has any relation to St. *Luke*'s enrolement.   But then, befide the task of eva-
ding all the many concurring circumftances
in St. *Luke* and *Jofephus*, they will labour
under one very great difficulty.   For this
oath appears to have been taken by the
Jews fo very near the end of *Herod*'s reign,
that it will be utterly inconceiveable, that
the *Romans* fhould have ordered another general enrolment and harrafle the people again
before *Herod*'s death.   Nor will they be able
to remove this difficulty by faying, that the
fwearing began about the time it is placed in
by *Jofephus*, but was not finifhed till a few
weeks before *Herod* died : For it was all
over at the time *Jofephus* fpeaks of it.   All
had taken the oath, but fix thoufand *Pharifees*; they had refufed, and were fined.

§. III. T H E third objection, is this. *Cyrenius* was not Governour of *Syria* till nine
or ten, perhaps twelve years after our Saviour
was born: therefore St. *Luke* has made a miftake in faying, that this taxing happened in
the time of *Cyrenius*.

T H I S objection muft now be ftated more
at length.   In our tranflation the words are:
And this taxing was firft made when Cy-

renius *was governour of* Syria.   What is
the fenfe of our tranflation, I do not know :
and it muft be owned likewife, that the words
of the Original (*a*) feem to have in them an
uncommon ambiguity.   Many think, the
moft genuine natural fenfe of the original
words is : *This firft taxing* (or enrolment)
was made when Cyrenius *was governour
of Syria.*   And upon this fenfe of them the
objection is founded.   And it is urged, this
cannot be agreeable to the truth.   For the
Evangelifts have affured us, that Jefus was
born in the later end of *Herod's* reign. But
Jofephus fays, that (*b*) *Quintilius Varus* was
then Prefident of *Syria,* and he muft have
been fo at leaft a year before *Herod* died. And
Saturninus was his predeceffor.   Moreover
Jofephus fays, that *Cyrenius* was fent Governour into *Syria,* when *Archelaus* was removed from his government of *Judea,* who
yet reigned there between nine and ten
years after *Herod.   Jofephus* relates this
matter, in his *Antiquities,* thus.

‘ BUT in the tenth year (*c*) of *Arche-
‘ laus's* government, the chief of the *Jews*

(*a*) Ἀύτη ἡ ἀπογραφη πρώτη ἐγίνετο ἡγεμονεύοντ@ τῆς Συρίας
Κυρηνίʿ   (*b*) *Ant.* L. 17. cap. v. §. 2.   (*c*) Δεκάτῳ
Ͻ ἔτει τῆς ἀρχῆς Ἀρχελάʿ

and

' and *Samaritans* not being able to bear his
' cruelty and tyranny accufed him to *Cefar*'.
The Emperour fent an officer into *Judea* to
bring him to *Rome*. ' When he came thither,
' *Cefar*, having heard what he had to fay in
' anfwer to his accufers, banifhed him, ap-
' pointing *Vienna* a City in *Gaul* for the
' place of his abode (*a*).   And the country
' of *Archelaus* being annexed to the pro-
' vince of *Syria, Cyrenius* a Confular perfon
' was fent by *Cefar* to make an affeffement
' in *Syria*, and to feile *Archelaus*'s eftate (*b*)'.

AFTERWARDS he fays: 'In the mean
' time *Cyrenius* a Roman Senator, who had
' ferved all other offices, and through them
' arrived at the Confulfhip, and was diftin-
' guifhed likewife by divers other honours
' and dignities, came into *Syria* with a few
' troops, being fent thither by *Cefar* to ad-
' minifter juftice to that people, and to make
' an affeffement of their goods. And *Copo-*
' *nius* a perfon of the *Equeftrian* rank was
' fent with him to govern in *Judea* with
' fupreme authority. *Cyrenius* alfo came in-
' to *Judea*, now annexed to *Syria*, both

(*a*) Ant. L. 17. C. 15. §. 2.

(*b*) Τῆς δ᾽ Ἀρχελάυ χώρας ὑποτελῦς προσκεμηθείσης τῇ Σύρων,
πέμπεται Κυρήνιος ὑπὸ Καίσαρος, ἀνὴρ ὑπατικὸς, ἀποτιμησόμενος,
τὰ ἐν Συρίᾳ, ℭ ἀποδωσόμενος οἶκον· ibid. §. 5.

' to affeffe their eftates, and to feife *Arche-*
' *laus*'s effects and treafure (*a*)'.

I t is objected therefore, that St. *Luke* has
committed a very groffe miftake, in faying,
that *this taxing was made when* Cyrenius
was governour of Syria : Since it appears
from *Jofephus*, that *Cyrenius* was not prefident of that province till after the banifhment of *Archelaus, Herod*'s fon and fucceffor.

To this I anfwer, that though the fenfe
of the words, as they now ftand in St. *Luke*'s
Gofpel, fhould be fuppofed inconfiftent with
this account taken from *Jofephus* ; yet it
would be unreafonable to conclude, that
St. *Luke* had really made any miftake.
St. *Luke* appears in the reft of his hiftory, and
from many particulars of this account before
us, to be fo fully mafter of the ftate of *Judea*,
and of the nature of this affair he is here
fpeaking of, that it is impoffible he fhould
commit any fuch miftake.

(*a*) Κυρίνι⊙ 5. τ̃ εἰς τὴν βελὴν συναγομένων ἀνήρ, τάς τε
ἄλλας ἀρχὰς ἐπιτετελεκὼς, κỳ διὰ πασῶν ὁδεύσας ὕπατος γενέῶ,
τότε ἄμα ἀξιώματι μέγας, σὺν ὀλίγοις ἐπὶ Συρίας παρῆν, ὑπὸ
Καίσαρος δικαιοδότης τ̃ ἔθνες ἀπεσαλμένος, κỳ τιμητὴς τ̃ ἐσιῶν
γενησόμενος· Κωπώνιός τε αὐτῷ συγκαταπέμπεται, τάγματος τ̃
ἱππέων, ἡγησόμενος Ἰεδάιων τῇ ἐπὶ πᾶσιν ἐξεσίᾳ παρῆν ↄ κỳ
Κυρήνιος εἰς τὴν Ἰεδάιων προσθήκην τῆς Συρίας γενομένην, ἀποτιμη-
σάμενός τε αὐτῶν τὰς ἐσίας, κỳ ἀποδωσόμενος τὰ Ἀρχελάε χρήματα·
Antiq. 18. c. 1. §. 1.

IN

IN the beginning of his third chapter St. *Luke* has moſt exactly ſpecified the State of all *Judea*, or the land of *Iſrael*, as it was in the fifteenth year of *Tiberius*, by ſetting down the ſeveral Tetrarchs and Go-vernours of it, and the true extent of their territories.

ST. *Luke* underſtood the nature of enrol-ments, as made by the *Romans*. The enrol-ment now made, was by virtue of a Decree of *Auguſtus*. And he ſays that *Joſeph went to be taxed with* Mary *his eſpouſed wife.* This was the cuſtom of the *Romans,* as has been ſhewn from undoubted teſtimonies, to enrole *women* as well as men, whereas the *Jews* uſed to number or enrole *Males* only.

MOREOVER, St. *Luke* appears to be well acquainted with the Cenſus which *Jo-ſephus* gives us an account of. *Gamaliel* ſays: *After this man roſe up* Judas *of* Galilee, *in the days of the taxing, and drew away much people after him: he alſo periſhed, and as many as obeyed him, were diſperſed.* I think it may be fairly ſuppoſed, that Saint *Luke* underſtood what he has related from *Gamaliel.* And then, here are particulars enough to ſatisfie us, he wanted no infor-mation

Acts v. 37.

mation concerning the Cenſus which *Joſe-phus* ſpeaks of.

THAT *Gamaliel* here ſpeaks of the Cenſus made in *Judea* after the baniſhment of *Archeláus* is evident, becauſe it was at that time, that *Judas* of *Galilee* raiſed a diſturbance. *Gamaliel* calls them *the days of the taxing*, which implies, that this was a very noted and remarkable Period: as it is certain, it was.

GAMALIEL here calls this *Judas* by his proper name. *Joſephus* does in one place call him *Judas Gaulanites* (*a*), but he often ſtiles him *Judas* the *Galilean*, or of *Galilee* (*b*). *Gamaliel* ſays, that he *drew away much people after him*. *Joſephus* ſays the ſame thing of him in almoſt the ſame words (*c*).

GAMALIEL does exactly ſpecifie the time in which this man *roſe up*, namely in *the time of the taxing*, or of the enrolment; for *Joſephus* ſays, ' he perſuaded, ' not a few not to enrole themſelves, when

---

(*a*) Ant. L. 18. cap. 1. pag. 792. v. 3.

(*b*) Ὁ Γαλιλαῖος Ἰέδας p. 974. 3. τὶς ἀνὴρ Γαλιλαῖος, Ἰέδας ὄνομα· p 1060. 8.

(*c*) Ἐλεάζαρος ἀπόγονος Ἰέδα τῦ πείσαντος Ἰεδαίων ἐκ ὀλίγες μὴ ποιεῖαζ τὰς ἀπογραφὰς, ὅτε Κυρήνιος τιμητὴς εἰς τὴν Ἰεδαίαν ἐπεμφθη de B. Jud. L. vii. pag. 1313. v. 41.

Cyre-

' *Cyrenius* the Cenfor was fent into
' *Judea* (a).

GAMALIEL fays *he alfo perifhed,
and all, even as many as obeyed him, were
fcattered.* Jofephus has no where related
particularly the end of this *Judas*. But that
his enterprize was defeated at that time, we
may be certain : otherwife the Roman Government could not have fubfifted in that
country with any quièt, which yet it did
for near fixty years after the banifhment of
Archelaus. Nor is there after this any mention made, in *Jofephus*'s hiftory, of any
action or attempt of *Judas.*

PERHAPS it will be here objected, that
Gamaliel's words imply, that this defign of
Judas was quite confounded, and his principles funk at once : And yet it feems likely from the uneafineffe which the *Jews* exprefs under the Roman tribute in fome places
of the Evangelifts, that his principles were in
being long afterwards : And from *Jofephus*
it appears, that his notions were very pre-
valent, and were one caufe of their war at
laft with the *Romans.*

BUT if any fo underftand *Gamaliel,* they
appear to me very much to miftake the de-

(a) Ibid. & pag. 792. init.

fign

fign of his Argument. Doubtlefs it was not without fpecial reafon that *Gamaliel* alleged thefe two inftances. And he fpeaks of each in a very different manner. Of *Theudas* he fays: *He was flain, and all, as many as obeyed him, were fcattered and brought to nought* [διελύθησαν, κỳ ἐγένοντο εἰς ἐδὲν·] They were ruined and came to nothing. Of *Judas* he fays: *he alfo perifhed, and all, as many as obeyed him were* difperfed [διεσκορπίσθησαν]. Having mentioned thefe two inftances, which the councel were well acquainted with, and hereby laid a foundation for the advice he propofed to give, he goes on: *And now I fay unto you, refrain from thefe men, and let them alone: for if this counfel or this work be of men,* (as *Theudas's* was), it *will come to* (a) *nought* (as his did.) *But if it be of God, ye cannot overthrow it, left haply ye be found even to fight againft God.*

I T is not to be fuppofed, that *Gamaliel* fhould fay: *Judas's* defign was *of God.* However the chief men of the *jewifh* nation might approve his principles, they were wifer than openly to efpoufe them: they left that to the common people.

(a) Καταλυθήσεται·

T H E force of *Gamaliel's* argument is this:
Theudas and his measures came to nothing.
After him *Judas* rose up: He himself perished, and his people were dispersed; but yet
his principles prevail.   You likewise may
now punish these men, and put an end to
their lives; but if their principles be of
God, they will prevail notwithstanding;
and all the issue will be, that you will contract guilt, fight against God, but in vain.

A N D to this seems to be owing the great
successe of *Gamaliel's* reasoning, and the
service he did the Apostles at this time.   He
insinuates some hopes, that their design
might be of the same nature with *Judas's.*
This may be inferred from his way of expressing himself: *left haply ye be found to fight
against God.*   This was *Judas's* peculiar
principle, that they were to own no mortal
Lords, but God only (*a*).   And it is not unlikely, that *Gamaliel* intended hereby to in-
sinuate, not only that there was danger of
their opposing a design which came from
God, and of opposing it with no other
effect, but that of contracting guilt to themselves; but also of opposing the very King-

(*a*) Joseph pag. 1060. v. 10.

dom

dom and government of God which they wished to be under.

It deserves likewise to be observed, that *Gamaliel* mentions *Theudas* with contempt and indignation. *Before these days rose up* Theudas, *boasting himself to be some body* : but nothing like this follows the mention of *Judas.*

GAMALIEL concludes upon the whole, that they should *let these men alone.* We have no occasion to meddle in this matter. It is not unlikely but the *Romans,* our present Governours, will be jealous of these men. But it seems to me an affair we have no reason to concern our selves in.

St. *Luke* therefore must be supposed to be well acquainted with the Census made after the banishment of *Archelaus.*

I must be permitted to observe farther, that St. *Luke* does here call *Cyrenius* by his true name. It has indeed been a dispute among learned men, whether his Roman name was *Quirinus* or *Quirinius. Onuphrius* in his *Fasti* printed it *Quirinius* : *Grotius* (*a*) and *Lipsius* (*b*) thought *Onuphrius* was mistaken, and that it ought to be correct-

(*a*) In *Luc.* ii 2. *ann.* L. iii. c. 48.

(*b*) In not. ad *Tacit.*

ed

ed *Quirinius*. (*a*) *Perizonius* feems to have proved, that *Quirinus* is the true way of writing it in *Latin*: fince it was not the family name, or the *nomen*, but *cognomen*, the third name of this Gentleman. For his name was *Caius Sulpicius Quirinus*, and in the *Syriac* verfion of St. *Luke* he is written *Kurinus*, and in the *Latin* vulgate *Cyrinus*. But however that be, he allows it to be common for the *Greeks* to make fome alteration in the termination of Roman names, when they turn them into their own language. It is certain his name in all the *Greek* authors has the termination of ιος or *ius*. *Strabo* (*b*) and *Dio* (*c*) call him Κυρίνιος (*Cyrinius*). But in *Jofephus* (*d*) his name is always writ-ten, as in St. *Luke*, *Cyrenius*.

MOREOVER it is certain *Cyrenius* was Governour of *Syria*, and he has here a very proper title, by which he muft have been well known in *Judea*, and in all that part of the world.

LASTLY, if we confider that the words now before us are a parenthefis, and that St. *Luke* calls the Enrolment or Cenfus he

(*a*) Differta. de Auguftea orb. Terr. Defcr. §. 30.
(*b*) Lib. 12. p. 854.
(*c*) Vid. *Dio*. lib. 54. ad A.U. 742.
(*d*) P. 791. v. 5, 12. p. 794. v. 21, 37. & alibi.

was

was fpeaking of, the *firft*, we cannot well doubt, but that the original intention of them was, in fome manner or other, to diftinguifh this enrolment, which was now made in the reign of *Herod*, from that, which was afterwards made when *Archelaus* was banifhed.

H E that will ferioufly confider all thefe particulars, will have no fufpicions, that St. *Luke* has made any miftake.

I F then the fenfe, which is now ordinarily given thefe words, is not confiftent with truth, it is highly reafonable to conclude, that either we do not take the true meaning of them, or elfe that fome fmall alteration or other has happened in the text of St. *Luke*.

§. IV. B u t though what has been here offered, and which has alfo been in the main alleged before by thofe who have confidered this place, be fufficient to take away the force of this objection; yet, I prefume, it will be expected, I fhould give fome account of the particular Solutions that have been offered by learned men.

I s H A L L therefore briefly mention fome which appear to me lefs probable, and then reprefent fome others more diftinctly, and

at

at laſt endeavour to ſupport or emprove that which appears to me the faireſt.

1. ONE Solution propoſed by (*a*) *Calvin*, and much approved by *Salmeron* and *Baronius*, is that *Joſephus* was miſtaken in the account which he has given of *Cyrenius*. The two laſt mentioned writers eſpecially are of opinion, that we need pay little regard to *Joſephus*, whoſe hiſtory, they ſay, abounds with miſtakes and falſhoods (*b*). And *Baronius* (*c*) has taken ſome pains to make out a new ſeries of the ſucceſſion of the Governours of *Syria* about this time. For he thinks, that *Cyrenius* was twice, if not thrice, preſident of *Syria*. But this project can be but little approved by learned men at preſent. No one that reads *Joſephus* without prejudice, and that conſiders he had before him the hiſtory of *Herod*'s reign writ by *Nicolas* of *Damaſcus*, who was a learned man, *Herod*'s favourite, and employed by him in affairs of Government, can make any doubt, but that

(*a*) In loc.

(*b*) Praeſtat ut Joſephi verò fidem & hiſtoriam deſeramus, tanquam incertam, & fluctuantem & veritati in multis diſſen. tientem. *Salmeron in Evang.* T. iii. Tractat. 32.

(*c*) Sicque contra Joſephi deliria certo appareret, ſub Auguſto imperatore, vivente Herode ſeniore, reperiri duplicem, immo triplicem Quirinii in Syria praefecturam. *Baron. Ann.* An. *D.* 3. Vid. & app. ad *Ann.* num. 80—86.

I   *Quin-*

Quintilius Varus was Governour of *Syria* when *Herod* died; that *C. Sentius Saturninus* was his predeceſſor, and was in the province at leſt two or three years; and that *M. Titius* was preſident before him. With all theſe Governours of *Syria Herod* had ſome concerns. What *Joſephus* has ſaid of them may likewiſe be confirmed in a great meaſure from other Authors (*a*). So that there is no room for *Cyrenius* at this time.

N o r can there well be any queſtion made, but that *Joſephus* has given us, in the main, a true account of the enrolment or Cenſus made by *Cyrenius* after *Archelaus*'s baniſhment. It appears from the manner, in which *Gamaliel* ſpeaks of the *Taxing* when *Judas* of *Galilee* roſe up, that this was a remarkable event. And the account *Joſephus* gives of it may aſſure us, this was an affair all men were then well acquainted with. The diſturbance raiſed by *Judas* was ſuppreſſed, but yet the principle ſubſiſted. It was the occaſion of much uneaſineſſe under the Roman Government, and many were at times puniſhed on account of it (*b*).

(*a*) Vid. *Noriſ.* Cenot. Piſ. Diſſ. ii. cap. 16. §. 9. 10.
(*b*) *Joſ. Ant.* L. 18. cap. 1. §. 6.

2. ANOTHER

2. ANOTHER Solution propofed by *Calvin* (*a*), and which *Valefius* (*b*) judges to be the moft commodious of any, is, that the Decree of *Auguftus* was iffued in the later end of *Herod*'s reign ; but that for fome reafon or other the Cenfus could not be made, or at left nor finifhed till the time that *Cyrenius* was Governour of *Syria*, ten or twelve years afterwards.

BUT this is to make St. *Luke* fpeak very improperly and confufedly, in what he fays of *Cyrenius*. And it is directly contrary to what follows. Having related, that there *went out a decree from* Cefar Auguftus, *that all the world fhould be taxed,* he fubjoins: *and all went to be taxed every one in his own City.* And there was fo great a refort at this time at *Bethlehem* upon this account, that *Jofeph* and *Mary* were obliged to take up with very indifferent accommodations : *There was no room for them in the inn.*

3. SOME think that inftead of *Cyrenius,* we ought to read *Saturninus*; becaufe, according to *Jofephus*, he was Prefect of *Syria*, within a year or two before *Herod* died ; and *Tertullian* fays this Cenfus was

(*a*) Ubi fupra. Ec. Lib. 1. cap. v. (*b*) Vid. Notas ad *Eufeb.* Hift.

I 2 made

made by him. This is one of the Solutions propofed by (a) *Valefius*, though he rather approves that laft mentioned. But againft this, it has been obferved by many learned men, that *Cyrenius* is in all our Copies of St. *Luke*, and appears to have been there before *Tertullian*'s time ; fince *Juftin Martyr* fays exprefly, that this Cenfus was made by *Cyrenius*.

4. O T H E R learned (b) men have thought it a very eafy and probable conjecture, that originally the name in St. *Luke* was *Quintilius*. *Quintilius Varus* fucceeded *Saturninus*, and was in the Province of *Syria*, when *Herod* died. The Cenfus afterward made by *Cyrenius* was certainly beft known, and fome ignorant tranfcriber might therefore imagine *Quintilius* a miftake, and pretend to correct the original by inferting *Cyrenius* in his room. Befides, the alteration of *Quintilius* to *Cyrenius*, is a change of only a few (c) letters, and therefore might the more eafily happen.

B u t this Solution is liable to the fame objection with the former, *viz.* that *Cy-*

(a) Ubi fupra.   (b) *Huet.* Dem. Evang. Prop. ix. cap. x, *Parker* Demonft. of the truth of the Chrift. Religion, p. 219. 4to. 1681.   (c) Κυϊντιλίs, Κυρηνίs·

renius

renius is in all the Copies of the *Greek* original, and in all the ancient verfions. And befides, has this difadvantage, that this Cenfus St. *Luke* fpeaks of is not afcribed to *Quintilius Varus* by any ancient Chriftian writer whatever, whereas *Saturninus* has been mentioned by *Tertullian*.

THE reader is to judge for himfelf, but there are fome other (*a*) Solutions which feem to me more probable, and to deferve a more particular confideration.

5. THE next I fhall mention is that offered by (*b*) Mr. *Whifton*, which is this; ' that a Defcription or enrolment of the *Jews* ' was made juft before our Saviour's birth, ' but the Tax it felf was not raifed till the ' banifhment of *Archelaus* when *Cyrenius* ' was Governour of *Syria*: And Dr. *Prideaux* feems to approve of this way of folving this difficulty. For he fays : ' If the ' fecond verfe of the 2d. chapter of Saint ' *Luke*, be fo rendered as to imply that the , levying the Tax according to the Defcrip- ' tion mentioned in the former verfe, was ' firft executed, while *Cyrenius* was Gover-

(*a*) I have paffed by the conjecture of thofe who have fuppofed this whole parenthefis to be an interpolation, as not deferving to be mentioned.   (*b*) A fhort view of the Harm. of the Evangelifts Prop. xi.

I 3

' nour

' nour of *Syria*, this will remove all diffi-
' culties.   And the Text can well bear this
' interpretation (*a*).

IN order to support this interpretation,
Mr. *Whiston* says (*b*).   ' The word used for
' the Description at our Saviour's birth is the
' Verb ἀπογράφομαι ; and that used for the
' taxation under *Cyrenius*, is the noun
' ἀπογραφή·   *He adds*, that by custom a
' noun of the same original with a verb does
' vary in signification from it.   Γεομετρεῖν
' is to measure the earth : Γεομετρία is Geo-
' metry ; or the Science that consists of the
' knowledge of numbers and figures.-------
' Nay in *English*, in the words directly ap-
' posite to this matter, the verb to *tax* is
' oftentimes to lay an imputation, while the
' noun a *Tax* is the levy of money only.'

BUT (1.) Mr. *W-----n*'s Argument from
the use of nouns and verbs is not valid here.
He says, ' by custom a noun of the same
' original with a verb does vary in significa-
' tion from it'.   This may be, and there may
be many instances of it.   But it had been
much more material to give an example or
two of the use of the noun ἀπογραφὴ for

(*a*) *Connex*. Part. ii. lib. ix. Anno ante ch. v.
(*b*) Ubi supra.

a *Tax*

a *Tax*, namely in the fenfe in which he
here underftands it. This he has not done,
and I prefume no fuch example can be alleged from any *Greek* author.

I KNOW of but two or at the moft three
Senfes in which this noun is ufed, which can
have any relation to this matter.

[1.] IT is ufed for the act of the people in prefenting themfelves to be enrolled. As when Soldiers offered themfelves to
be inlifted (*a*) or enrolled under a General.
And in a Cenfus it may be ufed for the act of
the people who come and offer themfelves
to be enrolled and affeffed. So the word
feems to be ufed by *Jofephus*, when he fays
in the place above quoted that *Judas* perfwaded not a few (*b*) of the *Jews* not to
make enrolments or entries; that is, not to
offer themfelves to be entered and affeffed.

[2.] THE word is ufed for a Cenfus.
So it is ufed by *Dio* in many places:
ἀπογραφὰς ποιεῖσθαι is the fame as *cenfum
agere*; that is, to make enrolments, is the
fame as to make a Cenfus (*c*).

[3.] THIS

___

(*a*) See above, p. 36. n. b.   (*b*) Ἐλεάζαρος ἀπόγονος
Ἰούδα τῦ πείσαντος Ἰουδαίων ἐκ ὀλίγες μὴ ποιεῖσθαι τὰς ἀπογραφάς.
de B. Jud. L. vii. p. 1313. 40.   (*c*) Πλὴν ἐν ταῖς ἀπογραφαῖς, p. 509. C. αὐτὸς ὃ ἀπογραφὰς τ̄ ἐν τῇ Ἰταλίᾳ κατοι-
κεῖτον

[3.] T H I S noun is uſed for the public Rolls or Court Books, in which the entries were made : This Senſe of the word is very common. Thus *Caligula* being at play at Dice, and having loſt all his money, he asked for the *Gallic* court Rolls (*a*), and ordered ſeveral of the moſt wealthy of that people to be put to death, and ſeiſed their caſh. And the Citizens of *Rome*, whoſe debts were more than they could diſcharge, having entered the ſums they owed in Books opened for that purpoſe, *Servius Tullius*, took the Books or Rolls, [τὰς ἀπογραφὰς ἔλαβε] brought them into the *Forum*, and paid the Creditors (*b*).

T H U S I have reckoned up all the Senſes I know of this noun, relating to this matter. However it never ſignifies a *Tax.* Taxes were paid according to the Cenſus where any had been made. But they were no part of it. They might be remitted, or demanded. And the tribute is never expreſſed by the noun ἀπογραφὴ, but is ever diſtinguiſhed from what that ſignifies. (2.) THIS

κέντων ἐποιήσατο· 557. B. vid. etiam jam citat. pag. 496. C. 508. B. C. See above p. 119.

(*a*) Κυβίνων ἢ ποτὲ κ᾽ μαθὼν ὅτι ἐκ ἴιη οἱ ἀργύριον, ᾔτησέ τε τὰς τ̄ Γαλατῶν ἀπογραφὰς κ. τ. λ. *Dio.* L. 59. p. 657. B.

(*b*) *Dion. Hal,* L. iv. cap. 10. p. 207. 23.

(*c*) Τόν τε φόρον τὸν ἐκ τ̄ ἀπογραφῶν ἀφῆκε, τέλη τέ τινὰ κατέλυσε *Dio.* L. 49. pag. 401. B.

(2.) THIS interpretation of these words is contrary to matter of fact. There was no Tax levyed after the banishment of *Arche-laus* according to the Enrolment made at the birth of our Saviour. But as soon as *Ar-chelaus* was banished, ' *Cyrenius* came into ' *Judea* to make an assessment of their goods.' *Josephus* is as express in this matter as can be (*a*). Then it was that *Judas* of *Galilee* and his followers ' exclaimed that an assesse- ' ment would bring in among them down- ' right slavery (*b*)'.

THIS interpretation therefore is so far from being of any service to us, that it would introduce a new, and, I think, insuperable difficulty, by putting upon these words a sense directly contrary to what *Josephus* has said.

J O S E P H U S is so express, that there seems no need of reasoning upon the matter to confute this supposition. But I can never conceive, how a Tax could be levyed in *Judea*, after the removal of *Archelaus*, upon the Census or enrolment made at our Saviour's birth, without the utmost confusion or the'

(*a*) Παρῶν ἢ κὴ Κυρήνιος εἰς τὴν Ἰεδαίαν ἀποτιμησόμενός τε αὐτῶν τὰς ἐσίας· *Ant.* L. 18. c. 1·   (*b*) Τήν τε ἀποτίμησιν ἐδὲν ἄλλο ἢ ἄντικρυς δελείαν ἐπιφέρειν λέγοντες· Id. ibid.

utmost

utmoſt injuſtice. When the Enrolment which St. *Luke* ſpeaks of was made, *Galilee, Trachonitis,* and other countries were ſubject to *Herod,* beſide *Judea:* many who lived in *Galilee* enrolled themſelves in *Judea,* particularly *Joſeph,* as St. *Luke* aſſures us. But when *Archelaus* was baniſhed, one half of *Herod's* Dominions was in the poſſeſſion of *Herod* the Tetrarch and *Philip,* and had been ſo ever ſince the death of *Herod* called the Great. And only *Judea, Samaria* and *Idumea,* which had been ſubject to *Archelaus,* were thrown into the form of a Roman Province. The *Jews* having enrolled themſelves according to their families at the time of our Saviour's nativity, and many having come into *Judea* properly ſo called from *Galilee* and other parts of *Herod's* territories, a new enrolment was abſolutely neceſſary in *Judea* at the time of *Archelaus's* removal, if they were to pay tribute there in the way of a Cenſus. *Judea,* otherwiſe, muſt have been very much over-burdened. If there was an aſſeſſement of goods made at the latter end of *Herod's* reign, undoubtedly *Joſeph's* ſtock at *Nazareth* was entered and rated at *Bethlehem.* And as the *Jews* in that part of the world were chiefly

chiefly of the tribes of *Judah* and *Benja-min*, the inhabitants of *Galilee*, and *Tra-chonitis*, &c. muſt have very generally en-rolled themſelves in towns that belonged to the province of *Judea*.   But it would have been very unreaſonable in the *Romans* to de-mand tribute of the people of *Judea*, pro-perly ſo called, for eſtates and goods which were in the territories of the Tetrarchs *Herod* and *Philip*.

A N D we are aſſured, that the *Romans* did uſe to act equitably and with great ex-actneſſe in theſe matters.   Many of the Ro-man Citizens had been for a long time op-preſſed with the weight of their debts. A way having been found out A. U. 402, to give them eaſe, *Livie* ſays, that the next year a Cenſus was ordered, becauſe the property of many things had been altered (*a*).

6. T H E Solution I ſhall conſider in the next place, is that, which was firſt offered by *Herwaert* (*b*).   I give it here in the words

(*a*) Quia Solutio aeris alieni multarum rerum mutaverat do-minos; cenſum agi placuit lib. 7. cap. 22. n. 6. vid & c. 21.

(*b*) Ut hoc loco genitivus ἡγεμονεύοντος vocabulo πρώτη ad-ditus, vim comparationis efficiat, & perinde fit, ac ſi diceretur deſcriptionem illam eſſe *priorem*, priuſque factam, quàm Quiri-nius Syriae praeficeretur, praefecturamque ipſius gereret. *Her-waert* nova & vera Chronologa *Monachii* 1612. p. 189.

of

of (*a*) Doctor *Whitby* by whom it is efpoufed. *And this taxing was firft made* (before that made) *when* Cyrenius *was Governour of Syria.* The leraned *Kepler* (*b*) approved of this interpretation as perfectly agreeable to the genius of the *Greek* language. Notwithftanding this (*c*) *Cafaubon* rejected it, and was fuppofed by moft to have confuted *Herwaert's* arguments for it. *Perizonius* in his differtation upon this Subject of the Taxing has afrefh fupported this interpretation. Monfieur *Le Clerc* in his additions to Dr. *Hammond's* annotations expreffes his approbation of it: and has fince declared (*d*) that he thinks it has been fet in fo clear a light as to be inconteftable. And it is now embraced by many other learned men both Proteftants and Catholics.

I AM very defirous, this Solution fhould appear here to as much advantage as an argument fo full of *Greek* criticifms can do in

(*a*) In loc.   (*b*) Cum igitur omnium Graecè doctorum judicio conftet fic optimè verfum effe hunc locum Lucae, multoque emendatius quam habet antiqua verfio, fpero omnes acquieturos hac Solutione objectionis prius propofitae. *De Natal. J. Chr.* p. 116, 117.   (*c*) *Exerc. in Baron.* i. n. 33.   (*d*) *Ce denombrement fe fit avant que Quirinius fut gouverneur de la Syrie.* Des Savans hommes ont mis, cette explication dece paffage de St. Luc dans un fi grand jour qu'elle paroit defformais inconteftable. *Nouv. Teftam.*

a defign

a defign of this nature in our own language.
Perizonius allows, that a great many of
Herwaert's inftances are not to the purpofe.
And Mr. *Le Clerc* has in his writings more
than once referred to *Perizonius's* treatife
for the proofs of this interpretation.   I
reckon therefore, that it will be fufficient
to reprefent this argument, as it is drawn
up by Dr. *Whitby* and *Perizonius* : efpecially
if I take in by the by an inftance or two,
infifted on by others, though neglected by
them.

DOCTOR *Whitby* fays ' I dare not allow
' of the boldnefs of thofe Criticks who for
' Κυρηνίυ read Κυιντιλίυ------I would rather
' read πρὸ τῆς than πρώτη------But neither
' do we need this criticifm, fince the words
' πρῶτ⊙ and πρότερ⊙ are by the Seventy
' oft ufed according to this fenfe ; of the
' word πρότερον, this is beyond doubt, God
' faying twice ἀποσελῶ σφηκίας προτέρας συ,
I will fend hornets before thee, Exod. xxiii.
' 28. Jof. xxiv. 12.-----That πρῶτ⊙ alfo is
' ufed in the fenfe of priority, we learn
' from thefe inftances πρωτότοκ⊙ ἐγώ ἢ
' σύ, I am before thee, I am elder than thou;
' κ ἵνα τι ὒκ ἐλογίσθη ὁ λόγ⊙ μυ πρῶτ⊙ ;
' *Chal.* לי מרםיותא, *Why then was not*
                                        the

‘ the word first spoken to me? *Cur mihi non*
‘ *annunciatum est priori?* 2 Sam. xix. 43.
‘ Isa. lxv. 16. *The former troubles are for-*
‘ *gotten*, Gr. ἐπιλήσονται τὴν θλίψιν αὐτῶν
‘ τὴν πρώτην, and *ver.* 17. ὃ μὴ μνησθῶσι
‘ τῶν προτέρων, *they shall not remember*
‘ *the former*. So *John* i. 15. 30. ὅτι πρῶτός
‘ μυ ἦν, *for he was before me*, and chap. 15.
‘ 18. *know that they hated* ἐμὲ πρῶτον,
‘ *me before you*, 1 Cor. xiv. 30. ὁ πρῶτ⊙
‘ *Let the former hold his peace*; and 1 *Joh.*
‘ 4. 19. *We love him*, ὅτι πρῶτ⊙, be-
‘ cause he loved us before; and in *Aristo-*
‘ *phanes*, ἀλλ᾽ ὐκ ἂν προ τῦ is interpreted,
‘ ἀλλ᾽ ὐκ ἂν πρότερον, *Neph.* p. 122. And
‘ so *Theophylact* interprets the word here.
‘ τυτέςι προτέρα ἡγεμονεύοντ⊙, ἤγυν πρότερον
‘ ἢ ἡγεμόνευε τῆς Συρίας Κυρήνι⊙.

PERIZONIUS understands these
words in the same sense (*a*) with the Doctor, only he differs from him and *Her-*
waert, in that they suppose πρώτη. to
be the same as προτέρα, whereas he says

(*a*) Verus itaque meâ sententiâ verborum sensus est: *Haec*
descriptio prius, vel, *ante, facta est, quam praesideret Syriae*
Quirinus. Dissertatio de Augustea orbis terrarum Descrip-
tione, §. xxi.

thefe

thefe numeral adjectives have the force of adverbs (*a*).

HE alleges divers of the fame examples which the Doctor does, particularly *John* i. 15, and xv. 18. Of the later, ὅτι ἐμὲ πρῶτον ὑμῶν μεμίσηκε, he fays, it muft by all means be underftood (*b*) of priority of time: *It hated me before it hated you.*

HE fuppofes alfo (*c*) that we have a parrellel inftance in a word of an oppofite meaning, 2 *Macc.* vii. 41. ἐσχάτη τῶν υἱῶν ἡ μήτηρ ἐτελεύτησε· *Laft of all after the fons the mother died.* In the fame manner is πρῶτον

(*a*) Voluit autem Herwartus πρώτη poni ἀντὶ ☞ προτέρα, atque hujus locutionis vi, genitivum, qui fequitur, a τῷ πρώτη, tanquam a comparativo, regi. Durum hoc plerifque vifum. Ego rem aliter expediendam omnino cenfeam. Πρώτη fimpliciter, ut adjectivum numerale jungitur verbo, quemadmodum folent adjectiva habitum vel modum rei geftae fignificantia, tanquam fi fint adverbia——Sic plane πρῶτ☺, verbis adjunctum, faepe fignificat folam ordinis & numeri rationem, fine difcrimine, plurefne fint, an unus, qui fequantur; atque adeo tunc non tam fuperlativi, quam pofitivi naturam induit, eandemque fubit conftructionem, quam δεύτερος & feqq. Pati hoc naturam rei fignificatae evidens ex lingua Hebraica, ubi, ut conftat, eodem vocabulo ראישון prior & primus, אחד primus & unus, promifcue fignificantur. Pofitivi autem naturam vere quafi induere aliquando τὸ πρῶτος apud Graecos, vel inde colligas, quod ex eo formatum fuerit aliud plane fuperlativum πρώτιςος id quod non fuiffet opus, fi femper iftius gradus vim retineret πρῶτος· ibid. §. xxii. (*b*) Vertendum omnino cum fignificatu temporis, me primum ante vos ibid. & §. xxiii.

(*c*) Ibid.

the

the adverb uſed in *Ariſtophanes in avibus*
p. m. 564. *de Gallo* ; ἦρχέ τε πρῶτον Δαρεῖ𝛖
χὶ Μεγαϐύζ𝛖, i. e. *imperabatque Perſis priuſ-
quam Darius & Megabyzus.*

PERIZONIUS ſays, that the ge-
nitives that follow πρῶτος are governed by
an Ellipſis (*b*), and that πρῶτός μ𝛖, is the
ſame as πρῶτος πρό μου, πρῶ𝜄ος ὑμῶν the ſame
as πρῶτος πρὸ ὑμῶν· Thus in *Luke* xi. 38.

(*a*) Ibid.

(*b*) Πρὸ enim eſſe particulam, quae in iſta locutione deſide-
ratur, & a qua regitur genitivus, certiſſimum ex eo, quod ubi
ellipſis nulla, & ſententia plene ac integre exponitur, illa potiſ-
ſimum occurrit expreſſa. Apud *Anton.* Liberalem fab. 29.
Καὶ πρὸ Ἡρακλέ𝛖ς ἑορτῇ θύ𝛖σι Γαλινθιάδι πρώτῃ· Galinthias ibi
optime dicitur merita fuiſſe de Hercule, & idcirco Thebanos in
feſto Herculis *ſacrificare Galinthiadi prius*, ſeu primae, *ante
Herculem* ⸻Sed & ipſe *Lucas* Evang. xi. 38. expreſſit ſimi-
liter τὸ πρὸ poſt πρῶτος· ὁ ꝼ Φαρισαῖ☾, inquit, ἰδῶν ἐθαύμασεν,
ὅτι 𝛖 πρῶτον ἐβαπτίσθη πρὸ ἀρίσ𝛖· *quod non primum ſe laverit,
antequam cibum ſumeret.* Vides utrobique poſt πρώτη &
πρῶτον ante genitivum expreſſam hanc praepoſitionem; quod
certo eſt indicio, ab ea etiam regi, quando nulla comparet,
omiſſa per ἔλλειψιν, ſed tamen intelligenda: atque adeo expli-
candum etiam πρῶτον Δαρεῖ𝛖, quaſi dictum eſſet πρῶτον πρὸ
Δαρεῖ𝛖· ἡ ἀπογραφὴ πρώτη Κυρηνί𝛖, quaſi πρώτη πρὸ Κυρηνί𝛖·
§. xxv.⸻mihique idem eſt, ac ſi dixiſſet Lucas, non quidem
προτέρα ἡγομονέυοντος, verum πρώτη πρὸ ἡγεμονέυοντος⸻
Sed nihil ſimilius, quod ad conſtructionis & linguae rationem,
Lucae verbis ſecundum noſtram eorum interpretationem, quam
locus Lxx. Interpretum *Jerem.* xxix. 2. 𝛖τοι οἱ λόγοι, 𝛖ς ἀπέσ-
ειλεʋ Ἱερεμίας εἰς Βαϐυλῶνα ὑςερον ἐξελθόντος Ἱεχονί𝛖 ἐξ Ἱερ𝛖σαλήμ·
Haec ſunt verba, quae miſit, vel ſcripſit Jeremias Babylonem,
poſtquam exiit Jechonias ex Hieroſolymis §. xxviii.

He

He wondered, [ὅτι ἔ πρῶτον ἐβαπτίσθη πρὸ ἀρίϛε] *that he had not washed before dinner.* From th.s and another such instance he concludes, that the genitive is governed by πρὸ understood, when it is wanting.

THIS is the substance of the argument in favour of this meaning of this passage of St. *Luke*.

IT has been thought by some to be an objection against this solution, that then Saint has omitted to name the person by whom this enrolment was made. But methinks, this is a defect which may be dispensed with. This interpretation answers very well what seems to be the main intention of this parenthesis, namely, to distinguish the enrolment now made from that which was made afterward. And if the words will bear this sense, I should think that most persons would acquiesce in it. For my own part, I dare not absolutely reject it : but yet I am not fully satisfied, that this sense can be fairly put upon the words. I think my self obliged to review the arguments here offered by these learned men, and hope it may be done without offense.

K I SHALL

I shall therefore make some remarks upon Doctor *Whitby* and *Perizonius*, and consider likewise some other examples, omitted by them, upon which some others have laid a great stresse.

Doctor *Whitby*'s instances of the use of πρότερος and πρότερον from the *Seventy* are not to the point, because the word in St. *Luke* is πρώτη. There is no doubt, but πρότερΘ, the comparative, is very often followed by a genitive case, and denotes such or such a thing to be *before* another. We want some plain examples of this use of πρῶτΘ· Nor is πρωτότοκΘ· ἐγώ ἢ σύ to the point, because the ἢ is wanting in Saint *Luke*, and the construction is different. The example from *Isa.* lxv. 16. only proves that πρῶτΘ· signifies the *former* : and tho' πρώτη in St. *Luke* should be so rendered, the difficulty will remain in its full force. For, then the sense will be : *This former taxing was made, when* Cyrenius *was governour of Syria.* Nor can the πρῶτΘ· in 1 *Cor.* xiv. 30. or 1 *John* iv. 19. do us any service, for want of a regimen equivalent to what we have in our text. Nor do I see what use can be made of the phrase borrowed from *Aristophanes.* The passage from 2 *Sam.* 19. 43,

as

as it is quoted by *Keuchenius* (*a*), feems
to me more ftrongly to fupport this interpretation, than as it is quoted by the Doctor.
Though, I fuppofe, the Doctor had his reafons for quoting it in that way.   Nor has
Perizonius quoted this text, though he had
Keuchenius before him.   It is obfervable,
that Ἰέδα is wanting in (*b*) *Grabe*'s edition
of the *Septuagint*, as there is nothing an-
fwerable to it in the *Hebrew*.   The inftances
from St. *John*'s Gofpel will be diftinctly confidered by and by.

PERIZONIUS [§. 22.] is concerned to fhew that πρῶτΘ is not always
fuperlative, but fome times only pofitive.
But I cannot perceive the force of his arguments.   Becaufe the *Hebrews* have ufed
fome of their Numerals in this manner, does
it follow that the *Greeks* did?   Is it any
proof that the *Englifh* fay *Henry Seven*, be-

(*a*) Silentio tandem praeterire nequeo quod 2 *Sam.* cap. 19.
43. legitur, *Et vir Ifraelis refpondit viro Judae, & dixit, mihi
funt decem partes in rege,* ubi Lxx. de fuo addere videntur, κ̀
πρωτότοκΘ ἐγὼ ἢ σύ, & etiam in Davide ego prae te: cur
igitur me vilipendifti, & non fuit verbum meum primum feu prius
(inter duos enim fermo eft) mihi ad reducendum regem meum;
quod Lxx. vertunt, κ̀ ἐκ ἐλογίσθη λόγος μϐ πρῶτός μοι ϐ
Ἰέδα ἐπιστρέψαι τὸν βασιλέα ἐμοί; ubi πρῶτός ϐ Ἰέδα manifefte
ponitur pro πρότερος· *Petri Keuchen: annot.* in loc.   (*b*) Καὶ
ἐκ ἐλογίσθη ὁ λόγος μϐ πρῶτός μοι ϐ ἐπιστρέψαι ϐ βασιλέα ἐμοί.

K 2   caufe

cauſe the *French* ſay *Louïs Quatorze* ? And then for the other argument, that πρῶτος *is as it were a poſitive*, becauſe πρώτιςος is formed from it : The Caſe, I think is this ; πρὸ has two or three ſuperlatives : and if *Perizonius* would prove πρῶτος to be a poſitive, he muſt produce ſome example in which it is ſo uſed.

T H E firſt quotation in *Perizonius* [§. 23] which I ſhall conſider is *John* xx. 3, 4. *Peter therefore went forth, and that other diſciple, and came to the Sepulchre. So they ran both together, and the other diſciple did outrun Peter* [καὶ ἦλθε πρῶτος εἰς τὸ μνημεῖον] *and came firſt to the Sepulchre.* Which *Perizonius* would render thus : and came firſt, *viz. before Peter;* and ſays that the meaning cannot be *came firſt of all* [πρῶτος πάντων] becauſe *Mary Magdalene* had been there before. No, for certain, it is not, *came firſt of all,* becauſe two only are here ſpoken of ; and *omnium primus* is not properly ſaid of two. But I wonder *Perizonius* did not perceive the proper ellipſis in this place, and which is very obvious, namely, τοῖν δυοῖν, and came the *firſt of the two. Perizonius* does not deny, that πρῶτος is uſed, where two only are ſpoken
of ;

of; nay, he contends for it. But becaufe it is
generally denied (*a*), and becaufe his proofs
appear to me not very clear, or at left not
fo fully to fuit my interpretation of this
text, I fhall give two undoubted examples.
Thus (*b*) *Dionyfius* fays, that *Servius Tullius*'s wife was *daughter of* Tarquin *the
firft*; though there were but two *Tarquins*
Kings of *Rome*. *Plutarch* thus defcribes
a reftlefs uneafy mind. ' If he is a native of
' a province, of *Galatia* for inftance, or *Bi-
' thynia*; He thinks he is not well ufed, if
' he has not fome eminent poft among his
' Citizens. If he has that, he laments that
' he has not a right of wearing the *Patri-
' cian* habit : If he has that, he grieves that
' he is not a Roman Praetor : If he is
' Praetor, that he is not Conful ; and if
' Conful, that he was not declared firft, but
' (*c*) only the latter (of the two)'.

(*a*) Πρῶτος κỳ πρότερος διαφέρει· πρῶτος γ̓ ἐπὶ πολλῶν, πρότερος
ἢ, ἐπὶ δύο· *Ammon. de Sim. & Diff.* (*b*) Ταρκυνίε
θυγάτηρ ἔσα ϖ πρώτε βασιλέως· *Dionyf. Hal. Antiq.* p.234,
v.13. confer. p.250. v.42. ὅτι Ταρκυνίε ϖ πρότερον βασιλεύσαν-
τος Ῥωμαίων ἀδελφῆ παῖς ἦν· & p.253.10. ϖ πρότερον βασιλέως·
Ταρκυνίε θυγάτηρ· (*c*) Ἐὰν ᵹ κỳ ϛρατηγῶν, ὅτι μὴ
ὑπατεύει κỳ ὑπατεύων ὅτι μὴ πρῶτος, ἀλλ᾽ ὕϛερος ἀναγορεύθη.
Plutarch. de *Anim. Tranq.* p.470. c.

K 5 THIS

THIS text then will not help *Perizo-nius*. All that can be proved from it is, that πρῶτος is uſed very properly where two only are ſpoken of. If πρώτη in St. *Luke* be allowed to ſignify the *firſt* or *former* of *two* taxings, all that will reſult from hence is, that St. *Luke* thought there was another taxing beſide this; and that this now made by *Cyrenius* was the former of the two. No inſtance of this ſort will prove, that the meaning of this paſſage is, This taxing was *before*, or *prior* to, that made when *Cy-renius* was Governour of *Syria*.

THE examples from *John* i. 15, 30. xv. 18. are ſome of the moſt proper exam-ples in the whole number : and if they are rightly underſtood, they are very much to the purpoſe. But, with ſubmiſſion to theſe learned men, I think, they are taken by 'em in a wrong ſenſe. They are both much of the ſame kind; but I chooſe to conſider firſt of all that alleged from *John* xv. 18. εἰ ὁ κόσμος ὑμᾶς μισεῖ, γινώσκετε ὅτι ἐμὲ πρῶτον ὑμῶν μεμίσηκεν· *If the world hate you, know that it hated me before it hated you. Herwart* (*a*) is much pleaſed with this example. IF

_____

(*a*) Ille verò S. joannis xv. 18. locus ad hoc inſtitutum mirificè facit,—*Si mundus vos odit, ſcitote quia me priorem vobis odio habuit.*

I F πρῶτον be fuppofed to be an adverb,
then this is not a parallel inftance. But indeed, as I take it, it is neither an adverb,
nor an adjective, but a noun Subftantive;
or at left, an adjective ufed fubftantively:
and the latter part of the verfe ought to be
rendered : *Know that it has hated me*
YOUR CHIEF. The connexion of the words
may fatisfy us, that this was our Saviour's
meaning. His argument is, that men had
hated him who was fuperior to them ; nay,
they had hated even his father, the difciples
therefore ought not to be furprifed if they
hate them alfo. *v.* 20. *Remember the words
that I faid unto you, the fervant is not
greater than his Lord, if they have perfe-
cuted me, they will alfo perfecute you. v.* 24.
*But now they have both feen and hated me
and my father.* The force of the argument
is not, that the world had hated him *before*
it had hated them : But he bids them confider,
that it hated him who was *their mafter,* and
whom they allowed to be fo. This is the
argument made ufe of in other places with
the fame view. *The difciple is not above* Mat.x.24.
his mafter, nor the Servant above his Lord. 25.
----*If they have called the mafter of the*

K 4 *houfe*

houſe Beelzebub, *how much more ſhall they call them of his houſhold ?*

IF it be ſaid, that there was no occaſion to ſubjoin *your chief* after *me*; that *me* is uſed δειχτιχῶς, and that the diſciples could conſider Jeſus no otherwiſe than as their maſter : I anſwer, that it is apparent from the texts already alleged here by me, that this was not our Saviour's Stile ; and that he did not truſt ſo much to his diſciples underſtandings. When he had occaſion to draw any inferences from his ſuperiority, he always expreſſeth it. *Ye call me Maſter, and Lord, and ye ſay well: for ſo I am. If I then your Lord and Maſter have waſhed* John xiii. *your feet, ye ought alſo to waſh one ano-* 14 *thers feet.*

Πρῶτος is uſed ſeveral times in the *New Teſtament*, in the plural number, for ſuperiority of honour and dignity : Καὶ τοῖς πρώτοις τῆς Γαλιλαίας, is not ill rendered in our Mark vi. verſion, *chief eſtates* of Galilee : γυναικῶν 21. τε τῶν πρώτων ὀκ ὀλίγαι, *of the chief wo-* Acts xv. *men not a few :* or, as perhaps the words 4. might be rendered, not a few of the wives of the chief men.

IT is likewiſe uſed in the ſingular number in the ſame ſenſe. Καὶ ὃς ἐὰν θέλῃ ἐν ὑμῖν

ὑμῖν εἶναι πρῶτος, ἔςω ὑμῶν δ᾽ξλος· *And whoſoever will be chief among you, let him be your ſervant.* There is another un- ^{Matth.} exceptionable inſtance of this uſe of the word: ^{xx. 27.}

ἐν δ᾽ τοῖς--- ὑπῆρχε χωρία τῷ πρώτῳ τῆς νήσε· *In the ſame quarters were poſſeſſions of the* CHIEF MAN *of the Iſland.* Grotius, *in* ^{Acts xxvii.} *his annotations* upon this place, has exhibi- ^{7.} ted a *Greek* inſcription, found in this very Iſland of *Melita,* a part of which inſcription is thus: Λ. Κ. ΚΙΟΣ. ΙΠΠΕΥΣ. ΡΩΜ. ΠΡΩΤΟΣ ΜΕΛΙΤΑΙΩΝ. L. C. *Kius, Roman Knight, chief of the* Melitenes.

T H E word is often ſo uſed in the *Septuagint* verſion: πρῶτος τῶν τριάκοντα, chief of the thirty *. Καὶ Ἀσαφ πρῶτος τῶν ^{* I Chron.} ἀδόντων †, and in many other other places. ^{xi. 11.} And in *Joſephus:* Ἰ᾽ςος ὁ Πίςε παῖς, ὁ ^{† Nehem.} ^{xii. 45.} τῆς τρίτης μερίδος πρῶτος, *Juſtus* the ſon of *Piſtus,* chief or leader of the third faction in (*a*) *Tiberias.* I throw an example or two more from other (*b*) authors into the margin.

(*a*) *Joſeph.* in vit. p. 907. v. 12.   (*b*) Τὸν δ᾽ ᾗ παῖδα ἐόντος πρώτε παρ᾽ ἐμοὶ κ. λ. *Herodot.* lib. i. c. 115. ἦν δ᾽ ἀνὴρ ἀςὸς, κ᾽ ὁ πρῶτος αὐτῶν κ. λ. ibid. c. 173. Καὶ Ἐπαμινώνδας βοιωταρχῶν ἐν Λεύκτροις ἐνίκησι Λακεδαιμονίες, κ᾽ ϯ Ῥωμάιων [Θηβάιων legit Perizonius] κ᾽ ϯ Ἑλλήνων πρῶτος ἐγένετο· *Ælian. Var. Hiſt.* vii. 14.

THERE is likewife in the *New Tefta-*
ment a verb derived from πρῶτ@., according to this fenfe of it ; ἵνα γένηται ἐν πᾶσιν
ἀυτὸς πρωΐευων, *that in all things he might*
Col. i. 18. *have the preeminence :* or, that in all things
he might be chief: a word very common
alfo in other writers.

NOR do I fee, why πρῶτ@. fhould not
be allowed to be ufed fubftantively in divers
of the places I have produced. *Princeps* in
Latin is properly an adjective, and is often
fo ufed : at other times it is a fubftantive. 'Αὐτοκράτωρ is fometimes an (*a*) adjective. It
is alfo ufed fubftantively. No one will deny
it. Ὕπατ@. is a word very near parallel
with πρῶτ@., is often an adjective, at other
times is ufed fubftantively, and denotes a Conful.

I COME now to the other inftance, *John.*
i. 15. ὗτ@. ἦν ὃν ἒιπον, ὁ ὀπίσω μυ ἐρχό-
μεν@. ἔμπροσθέν μυ γέγονεν, ὅτι πρῶτός μυ
ἦν· *This was he of whom I fpake, He that*
cometh after me is preferred before me.
The fame words occur again *v.* 30. with little variation. But the laft claufe ought not,

(*a*) Λαβὼν τὴν ἀυτοκράτορα ἀρχὴν· *Dionyf.* *Hal.* lib. 7.
p. 408. v. 1.

in

in my opinion, to be rendered, *for he was before me*, but, *for he is my Prince or Lord*.

WHAT I have already said in favour of this meaning of πρῶτος in the former instance may, I presume, make way for admitting it here.

I APPREHEND *John* to say: He that *follows me*, or comes behind me, was always before me, or *in my view*, for he is my Prince. Ἔμπροσθεν and ὀπίσω (unless I am much mistaken) are never used in the *New Testament* for priority or posteriority of time, nor for superiority or inferiority in respect of dignity (unless they are so used here in the case of *John the Baptist*) but always have a regard to place. *For we must all appear before the judgment seat of Christ* [a]. [Ἔμπροσθεν τῦ βήματος τῦ Χριστῦ] I said unto Peter before them all [b] [Ἔμπροσθεν πάντων]. *Forgetting the things which are behind, and reaching forth unto those things which are before* [c] [Τὰ μὲ ὀπίσω ἐπιλανθανόμενος, τοῖς ͻͻ ἔμπροσθεν ἐπεκτεινόμενος]· ἐνώπιον and ἔμπροσθεν are frequently used the one for the other [d]. It is true, *John* came before Christ, that is, before his face. He went before him as an

a 2 *Cor.* v 10.

b *Gal.* ii 14.

c *Phil.* iii 13.

d *Matth.* x. 33. *Luke* xii. 9.

officer

officer before a great man. But that is expreffed here in ὀπίσω μᾶ ἐρχόμενος·

BUT I will not contend about this. Perhaps ἔμπερσθέν μα γέγονεν is not ill rendered
in our tranflation, *is preferred before me,*
though it appears to me an unufual fenfe of
the word.

HOWEVER, πρῶτός μα muft neverthe-
leffe be underftood, as I render it. And I
learn from *Beza (a),* that others have been
of the fame opinion before me.

THUS then *John* fays, toward the conclufion of his miniftry : *Ye your felves bear
witnefs that I* [from the beginning] *faid,
I am not the Chrift, but that I came before
him* *.* Referring to what he had declared at
firft : *I am the voice of one crying in the
wildernefse,* MAKE STRAIT THE WAY OF
THE LORD †. That is, I came not on my
own account, but barely as a harbinger that
makes way for his Lord. This is the peculiar charaċter of *John,* under which he was
prophefied of ‖ : And under which he always fpeaks of himfelf. And what in the
15th and 30th verfes of this 1ft. chap. of
John, is ὅτι πρῶτός μα ἦν, *he is my Prince,*

* *John* iii. 20.

† —i. 18.

‖ *Ifa.*xl. 3. *Malach.*iii. 1. iv. 5.

(a) Quamobrem etiam nonnulli πρῶτός μα interpretantur *Princeps meus* : quod mihi penitus infolens videtur. *Bez.* in loc.

is

is in the 27th. *verf.* reprefented by an expreffion that denotes the vaft fuperiority of Chrift
above him : αὐτός ἐςιν ὁ ὀπίσω μȣ ἐρχόμενος,
ὅς ἔμπροσθέν μȣ γέϿονεν· ȣ̃ ἐγὼ ȣ̓κ εἰμὶ ἄξιος
ἵνα λύσω αὐτȣ̃ τὶν ἱμάντα τȣ̃ ὑποδήματος· *He
it is, who coming after me, is preferred before me, whofe fhoes latchet I am not worthy
to unloofe.* That is, I am fo far inferior to
him, and am in fo low a poft under him,
that I am not worthy to perform the meaneft
office about his perfon : or, in other words,
I am a mere harbinger, and he is my Lord.
Athenagoras (*a*) has ufed this word in this
very fenfe of a Prince or chief.

I HOPE it will be no objection againft
this interpretation, that then the words
would not have been πρῶτός μȣ ἦν, but ἐςίν :
for thefe are all one and the fame. I need
go no farther for proof than thefe two verfes:
ȣ̃τος ἦν ὃν ἔιπον in the 15th, in the 30th
is ȣ̃τός ἐςι περὶ ȣ̃ ἐγὼ ἔιπον. So that ἦν
and ἐςὶ fignifie the very fame thing, and are
ufed one for the other.

(*a*) Προσῆκε ϟ τῷ μ̃ τὸ πρωτεύειν κατὰ φύσιν, τῷ δὲ δορυφερȣ̃ν
τὸν ΠΡΩΤΟΝ, ὁδοποιεῖν τε ϟ προανέργειν πᾶν ὁπόσον ἐμποδὼν
ϟ πρόσαντες· Decet enim hoc fecundum naturam principatum
habere, illud autem, fatellitis vice PRINCIPI fuo viam facere,
& praevio curfu, omnia impedimenta & praerupta tollere. *De
Refurr.* p. 50. *D. Parif.* 1636.

I AM

I A M indeed aware, that some Grammarians will except against my notion of πρῶτος
being a Substantive. I will then for the present suppose it to be an Adjective. But yet,
I cannot part with the interpretation I have
given of either of these texts. The context
satisfies me, the sense I affix to the words is
the true meaning : and I can, if I mistake
not, account for it according to the strictest
rules of the Grammarians. Let then πρῶτον
in *John* xv. 18. be inclusive, and be understood partitively, and ὑμῶν will be governed
by the ellipsis ἐξ. This I suppose will not
be contested. But I choose to understand
πρῶτον here exclusively. I think, that is the
best sense. And then the ellipsis may be (*a*)
πρὸ, or περὶ or whatever else the Grammarians like best. Πρῶτος in *John* i. 15,
30. is evidently exclusive, according to my
way of rendring it; and the μ8 following
is governed by an ellipsis of one of the last
mentioned prepositions. This I take to be

(*a*) *Perizonius* says §. 24. Apud Graecos hanc vicem prae-
stant praepositiones πρὸ & περὶ, quarum illa respondet τῷ ante,
haec τῷ prae. Πρὸ is also used to denote preference and preeminence, both simply and in composition. Simply : Καὶ ὅτ@
ποιμὴν ἀποδείκνυται διανοίας, τυφὸν πρὸ ἀληθείας ἀσπαζομένης, ᾧ
πρὸ τ᾽ εἶναι τὸ δοκεῖν ἀποδεχομένης *Philo* p. 193. D. vid. & p. 194.
D. In composition : in προεσ᾽ ὡς, προτιμάω, &c.

perfectly

perfectly agreeable to the rules of the Grammarians. And thus, in one place Jesus tells his disciples, that he was chief *above* them : and in the other *John the Baptist* says, that Jesus was Prince or chief *above* him. And now I have *Beza* on my side, with reference to *John* i. 15. For though he would not allow, that πρῶτός μȣ is *my prince*; yet he says *(a)*, after a very careful examination, he is convinced, it expresses the vast excellence and superiority of Christ above *John*. I am not singular therefore in supposing, that this text does not express directly and simply priority of time, but only virtually and consequentially, as it is implied and comprehended in the superior dignity, of which it is a part.

THERE is another πρώτη in the *New Testament*, which has been understood by some in the same sense, in which these learned men have taken the two former instances, though it is not alleged by them. *Now the first day of the feast of unleavened bread*: Matt. xxvi. 17. Mark xvi. 12.

(a) Caeterum hoc loco diligentius expenso, quam antea,— Declarat igitur praestantiam, sed Christo peculiarem, & ipsi propriam : nempe quasi diceret joannes. Qui me sequitur quasi magistrum praeeuntem discipulus quispiam, mihi ante positus est, idque optimo jure quia infinitis modis est praestantior: quamvis ante docere coeperim quàm ille sese mundo patefecerit. *In loc*

This

This was the fourteenth day of the month: but it is urged here, that the 15th day was the firſt day of the feaſt of unleavened bread; for *Joſephus* ſays, that the 16th day of the month was (*a*) the ſecond day of that feaſt. And the words of the Law agree here with. *And in the fourteenth day of the firſt month is the paſſover of the Lord. And in the fifteenth day of this month is the feaſt.*

Deut.
xxviii.16.
17.
See Exod
xii. 18. *Seven days ſhall unleavened bread be eaten.* The fourteenth day therefore was the day of the Paſſover. The feaſt of unleavened bread was diſtinct from it, and laſted ſeven days from the 14th at night. The fifteenth day of the month was the firſt of unleavened bread. Therefore, when the Evangeliſts, ſpeaking of the 14th day, ſay, it was πρώτη τῶν ἀζύμων, they mean not the *firſt* day of unleavened bread, but the day *before* that Feaſt.

THE *Jews* have a rule, that in the computation of Feaſts, the day (*b*) preceeds the night. What ſtreſſe ought to be laid upon

(*a*) Τῇ ⸰ δευτέρα τ ἀζύμων (ἡμέρα ἕκτη δ᾽ ἐστὶν αὕτη ⸰ δεκάτη) *Antiq.* 3. c. 10. p. 124. v. 20.

(*b*) Quum autem *Matt.* 26. 17. & *Marc.* 14. 12. ipſe dies 14. Niſan appellatur primus dies azymorum, intelligendum id eſt ſecundum canonem Judaeorum, mox traditum, ſcilicet in ſacris comedendis diem praecedere noctem; ſic ut tempus veſpertinum diei 14. & nox ſubſequens hoc modo diei 14. accenſeantur. *Reland. Antiq. Heb.* p. 422.

this

this cafe, I know not. I am fatisfied we do not need it. The *Paffover* was ftrictly fpeaking diftinct from the feaft of *unleavened bread*, and feven days of un-leavened bread followed the day of the paff-over. But their houfes were cleanfed from all leaven on the morning of the day on which the Pafchal Lamb was flain, and there-fore after noon they could eat no leavened bread. For this reafon, perhaps, the day of the paffover was called the firft of unleavened bread. But, whatever was the reafon of it, it is certain, that the paffover and the feaft of unleavened bread are often taken promifcu-oufly the one for the other. And though *Jofephus*, in the particular account of the in-ftitution, diftinguifhes the paffover f.om the feaft of unleavened bread, yet he often calls the one the other. ' At (*a*) that time, *fays* ' *he*, the feaft approaching, in which the ' *Jews* are wont to eat unleavened bread. ' The feaft is called the paffover, it being kept ' in remembrance of their departure out of ' *Egypt*.' And in one place he fays, we keep

(*a*) Ἐνςάσης ᾗ κατὰ τόνδε τὸν καιρὸν ἑορτῆς, ἐν ᾗ Ἰȣδαίοις ἄζυμα προτίθεαᾗ πάτριον. Πάσκα ᾗ ἡ ἑορτὴ καλεῖται, ὑπόμνημα ἔσα τῆς ἐξ Αἰγύπτȣ ἀπάρσεως αὐτῶν γενομένης· *Antiq.* 17. c. 9. §. 3. p.773. v.25. vid. & p. 609. v. 31. 887. v. 10.

L   ' the

(*a*) the feaſt of unleavened bread eight
' days.' According to this method of
computation, the 14th day was the firſt of unleavened bread. So that when theſe two
feaſts were conſidered as one, as they were
very often, and the whole was called by the
feaſt of unleavened bread, the fourteenth
day muſt be the firſt. The Evangeliſts, perhaps, do not write in Syſtem: nor does *Joſephus*, as it ſeems, nor indeed any other
good writers; but according to the uſual
way of ſpeaking.

HERWAERT (*b*) lays great ſtreſſe
upon a paſſage of *Athenaeus*, who quotes

(*a*) Ὅθεν εἰς μνήμην τῆς τότε ἐνδείας ἑορτὴν ἄγομεν ἐφ᾽ ἡμέρας ὀκτὼ, τὴν τ᾽ ἀζύμων λεγομένην· *Antiq.* 2. c. 15. p. 88. *init.*

(*b*) Ille vero locus Ariſtotelis eſt ſingularis. Eum recenſet Athenaeus Lib. xi. p. 505. πρὸ ᷉ αὐτῦ [Πλάτωνⓖ] τῦθ᾽ εὗρε τὸ εἶδⓖ τ᾽ λόγων ὁ Τήⓖ Ἀλεξάμενⓖ, ὡς Νικίας ὁ Νικαεὺς ἱϛορεῖ Ⓖ Σωτηρίαν. Ἀριϛοτέλης ᷉ ἐν τῷ περὶ ποιητῶν ὕτως γράφει· Ουκῦν ἐδὲ ἐμμέτρυς τὰς καλυμένας Σώφρονⓖ μίμυς μὴ φῶμεν εἶναι λόγυς κỳ μιμήσεις, ἢ τὰς Ἀλεξμένυ τῦ Τηίυ τὰς πρώτυς γραφέντας τ᾽ Σωκρατικῶν διαλόγων ἄντικρυς φάσκων ὁ πολυμαθέϛατⓖ Ἀριϛοτέλης πρὸ Πλάτωνος διαλόγυς γεγραφέναι τὸν Ἀλεξάμενον. Haec quidem Athenaeus: Ubi ſane verba í la Ari-
ſtotelis τὰς πρώτυς γραφέντας τ᾽ Σωκρατικῶν διαλόγων. Athenaeus hiſce interpretatur [τὰς πρότερον] πρὸ Πλάτωνⓖ διαλόγυς,κ.τ.λ. Plato enim in ſuis Dialogis introducit Socratem qui hortetur juvenes, ſophiſtas redarguat, viros doceat, unde haud immerito vocantur Socratici——Quemadmodum igitur Ariſtoteles Alex-
ameni Dialogos prius ſcriptos, quam Plato ſuos Socraticos con-
ſcripſiſſet, vocat τὰς πρώτυς γραφέντας τ᾽ Σωκρατικῶν διαλόγων, ſic Divus Lucas, &c. *Herwaert.* ubi ſupra. pag. 197.

Ariſtotle,

Ariſtotle, ſaying (as *Herwaert* underſtands the words) that *Alexamenus*'s dialogues were wrote before the *Socratic* dialogues [that is the dialogues in which *Plato* introduces *Socrates*] expreſly affirming, ſays *Athenaeus*, that *Alexamenus* wrote dialogues before *Plato*.

BUT it is very plain to me, that *Ariſtotle* ſays that *Alexamenus*'s dialogues were the firſt Socratic dialogues; that is, that *Alexamenus* was the inventer of that way of writing. I have tranſcribed the paſſage of *Athenaeus* more at length then *Herwaert* has done. And if the reader will conſider the whole of it, I think he will be convinced : 1ſt, That by *Socratic dialogues* is here meant, not *Plato*'s *dialogues* in which he introduces *Socrates*, but in general that way of writing: and 2dly, That *Ariſtotle* ſays that *Alexamenus*'s dialogues were (*a*) the firſt of the kind. From whence *Athenaeus* infers very juſtly that *Ariſtole* ſays expreſly, that *Alexamenus* wrote dialogues before *Plato*.

I THINK likewiſe, that *Athenaeus* never dreamt of that meaning of *Ariſtotle*'s words which *Herwaert* affixes to them. Interpret

(*a*) So *Athenaeus* ſays expreſly: τῶθ' εὑρε τὸ εἰδῶ- τ λόγων·

L 2   *Ariſtotle*

(*a*) the feaſt of unleavened bread eight
' days.' According to this method of
computation, the 14th day was the firſt of unleavened bread. So that when theſe two
feaſts were conſidered as one, as they were
very often, and the whole was called by the
feaſt of unleavened bread, the fourteenth
day muſt be the firſt. The Evangeliſts, perhaps, do not write in Syſtem: nor does *Joſephus,* as it ſeems, nor indeed any other
good writers; but according to the uſual
way of ſpeaking.

HERWAERT (*b*) lays great ſtreſſe
upon a paſſage of *Athenæus,* who quotes

(*a*) Ὅθεν εἰς μνήμην τῆς τότε ἐνδείας ἑορτὴν ἄγομεν ἐφ᾽ ἡμέρας ὀκτὼ, την ͞τ ἀζύμων λεγομένην· *Antiq.* 2. c. 15. p. 88. *init.*

(*b*) Ille vero locus Ariſtotelis eſt ſingularis. Eum recenſet Athenæus Lib. xi. p. 505. πρὸ ͞γ αὐτῦ [Πλάτων⊙] τῦθ᾽ εὖρε τὸ εἶδ⊙ ͞τ λόγων ὁ Τήϊ⊙ ᾽Αλεξάμεν⊙, ὡς Νικίας ὁ Νικαεὺς ἱϛορεῖ ⊕ Σωτηρίαν. ᾽Αριϛοτέλης ὴ ἐν τῷ περὶ ποιητδν ὕτως γράφει ᾽Ουκῦν ὀδὲ ἐμμέτρες τὰς καλεμένες Σώφρον⊙ μίμες μὴ φῶμεν ἔιναι λόγες κ᷁ μιμήσεις, ἢ τὰς ᾽Αλεξμένε τῦ Τηϊε τὰς πρώτες γραφέντας ͞τ Σωκρατικῶν διαλόγων ἄντικρυς φάσκων ὁ πολυμα-θέϛατ⊙ ᾽Αριϛοτέλης πρὸ Πλάτωνος διαλόγες γεγραφέναι τὸν ᾽Αλεξάμενον. Haec quidem Athenæus: Ubi ſane verba ì la Ari-ſtotelis τὰς πρώτες γραφέντας ͞τ Σωκρατικῶν διαλόγων. Athenæus hiſce interpretatur [τὰς πρότερον] πρὸ Πλάτων⊙ διαλόγες, κ. τ. λ. Plato enim in ſuis Dialogis introducit Socratem qui hortetur juvenes, ſophiſtas redarguat, viros doceat; unde haud immerito vocantur Socratici——Quemadmodum igitur Ariſtoteles Alex-ameni Dialogos prius ſcriptos, quam Plato ſuos Socraticos con-ſcripſiſſet, vocat τὰς πρώτες γραφέντας ͞τ Σωκρατικῶν διαλόγων, ſic Divus Lucas, *&c. Herwaert.* ubi ſupra. pag. 197.

Ariſtotle,

Ariſtotle, ſaying (as *Herwaert* underſtands the words) that *Alexamenus*'s dialogues were wrote before the *Socratic* dialogues [that is the dialogues in which *Plato* introduces *Socrates*] expreſly affirming, ſays *Athenaeus,* that *Alexamenus* wrote dialogues before *Plato*.

BUT it is very plain to me, that *Ariſtotle* ſays that *Alexamenus*'s dialogues were the firſt Socratic dialogues ; that is, that *Alexamenus* was the inventer of that way of writing. I have tranſcribed the paſſage of *Athenaeus* more at length then *Herwaert* has done. And if the reader will conſider the whole of it, I think he will be convinced : 1ſt, That by *Socratic dialogues* is here meant, not *Plato's dialogues* in which he introduces *Socrates*, but in general that way of writing : and 2dly, That *Ariſtotle* ſays that *Alexamenus*'s dialogues were (*a*) the firſt of the kind. From whence *Athenaeus* infers very juſtly that *Ariſtole* ſays expreſly, that *Alexamenus* wrote dialogues before *Plato*.

I THINK likewiſe, that *Athenaeus* never dreamt of that meaning of *Ariſtotle*'s words which *Herwaert* affixes to them. Interpret

(*a*) So *Athenaeus* ſays expreſly: τꝗό' ϵυρε τὸ ειδ☉ ꝗ λόγων·

L 2 *Ariſtotle*

Ariſtotle as *Herwaert* does, and *Athenaeus* is guilty of a ridiculous tautology in his inference.

THAT I underſtand *Ariſtotle* aright, is farther evident from *Diogenes Laertius,* whoſe words upon the ſame ſubject are thus:
' Some ſay that *Zeno* the *Elean* was the firſt
' writer of Dialogues, but *Ariſtotle* in his
' firſt Book of Poets ſays that *Alexamenus*
' the *Teian* was, as does alſo *Phavorinus* in
' his commentaries (*a*).

IT was neceſſary to dwell thus long upon this inſtance, becauſe it is the only inſtance from a profane author which Monſieur (*b*) *Baſnage,* who follows *Herwaert,* has quoted in favour of this interpretation of St. *Luke.*

WE return now to *Perizonius,* and will take next his inſtances [§. 25.] ϗ πρὸ Ἡρακλέυς ἑορτῇ θύυσι Γαλινθιάδι πρώη· and *Luc.* xi. 38. ὁ δὲ φαρισαῖος ἰδὼν ἐθαύμασεν ὅτι ὐ πρῶτον ἐβαπτίσθη πρὸ ἀρίςυ· The leſt that can be ſaid of theſe is, that they avail nothing at all, becauſe they are not parallel with our text. If St. *Luke's* words had

(*a*) Διαλόγυς τόινυν φασὶ πρῶτον γράψαι Ζήνωνα τὸν Ἐλεάτην Ἀρισοτέλης ⸱) ἐν πρώτῳ περὶ ποιητῶν Ἀλιξάμινον Στυρέα ἢ Τήὸν, ὡς ϗ Φαβωρῖνος ἐν ἀπομνημονεύμασι. *Diog. Laert.* Lib. iii. Segm. 48.   (*b*) Ann. Polit. Eccleſ. ant. Dom. 5. num. 14.

been

been, πρώτη or πρῶτον ἐγένετο πρὸ ἤγ, I suppose
we should have been all agreed, and there
would have been no occasion to employ a
good part of a differtation to prove that he
faid, This taxing was *before* Cyrenius's time.
If there had been divers unexceptionable inftances produced, in which πρῶτος followed
by a genitive [without the πρὸ] had been
ufed for priority of time, then thefe here alleged would have been very good proofs
of this way of accounting for the conftruction by way of Ellipfis, and to fuppofe
that πρὸ ought to be underftood where it is
not expreffed. But till that is done, they are
of no ufe.

BUT this is not all : For indeed *Perizo-*
nius could not have fhewn any thing more
againft himfelf than thefe examples. For if
it be the cuftom of the *Greek* authors to fubjoin πρὸ after πρῶτος, when they intend to
fay one thing is *before* another, it is an argument that πρῶτος alone has not this power.
Nay, St. *Luke*, it feems, fubjoins πρὸ to the
adverb πρῶτον. I fuppofe πρὸ is never fubjoined to πρότερος, or πρότερον. But thefe
inftances fhew, it is ufual to fubjoin it to
πρῶτος, when priority before another thing is
intended to be expreffed.

IF I fhould affert that *communicare te* was good *Latin,* and equivalent to *communicare tecum,* would it avail any thing to produce inftances of *communicavit mecum, cum Caio,* and the like ? Would thefe prove that *cum* is needlefs to be added, and that it is included in the Verb? Would not all fuch examples be againft me? This is *Perizonius's* argument.

BUT then it muft be allowed, that *Perizonius's* example from *Ariftophanes,* and another from (a) *Alexander Aphrodifius,* alleged by others in this caufe, prove that πρῶτον the adverb is ufed, without περò following it, to denote the priority they contend for. How far the argument will hold by way of analogy from adverbs to adjectives, I cannot fay. It ought alfo to be allowed, I think, that the paffage [§. 23.] from the *Maccabees,* ἐσχάτη τῶν υἱῶν ἡ μήτηρ ἐτελεύτησε, *laft of all, after the fons, the mother died,* is a parallel inftance. But whether fuch another example can be found in any good *Greek* writer, I very much queftion. And the πρῶτός μοι τῷ Ἰúδα, of 2 *Sam.* xix. 43. but

(a) Ἡ πληγὴ πρῶτον τῆς ἀςραπῆς τὴν βρόντην ἀποτελεῖ, ἢ ἅμα· Ictus prius tonitru perficit quam fulgur, aut fimul. *Alexand. Aphrod. Problem.* Lib. i.

not found in all copies of the Seventy, is likewise an equivalent phrafe to that in St. *Luke*, and to be underftood in the fame fenfe thefe learned men put upon St. *Luke's* words. If I miftake not, the whole ftreffe of the argument for this interpretation relies upon thefe three particulars; provided I un-derftand aright, *John* i. 15. 30. xv. 18, the πρώτη τῶν ἀζύμων, and the paffage from *Athenaeus*: which, whether I do or not, is fubmitted to the judgment of the reader.

A N D it ought to be confidered, whether it be reafonable to affix to πρώτη in Saint *Luke* a meaning fo very unufual, if not unprecedented in any good writer, efpecially confidering the many ways of expreffing the fenfe which thefe learned men contend for, fuch as πρὸ, πρότερα, πρότερον, πρῶτον, πρῶτον πρὸ, πρώτη πρὸ, πρίν, &c.

L A S T L Y, a paffage of *Herodotus* (a) does very ftrongly incline me to think, that it is not very agreeable to the genius of the *Greek* Language to ufe the fuperlative adjective πρῶτος to exprefs the priority of one thing before another either in a pofitive way, or in-ftead of πρότερος. He fays: Οἱ δὲ Ἀιγύπ-

(a) Lib. 2. *init.*

L 4

τιοι,

Ίιοι, πρὶν μὲν ἢ ψαμμήλιχος σφέων βασιλέυσαι,
ἐνόμιζον ἑωϋτὰς πρώτυς γενέσθαι πάντων ἀνθρώ-
πων· ἐπειδὴ δὲ ψαμμήτιχος βασιλεύσας, ἠθέλησε
εἰδέναι ὅι τινες γενοίατο πρῶτοι, ἀπὸ τότε νομί-
ζυσι Φρύγας πρὸτέρυς γενέσθαι ἑωϋτῶν, τῶν δὲ
ἄλλων, ἑωϋτό,· ' The *Egyptians*, before the
' reign of *Pfammetichus*, thought them-
' felves the firft [or moft ancient] of all peo-
' ple. But fince the reign of *Pfammetichus*,
' who made an experiment for finding out
' who were the firft of all people, they have
' thought that the *Phrygians* were before
' them, they, before others'. If πρῶτος
could be ufed in the fenfe contended for,
why did not *Herodotus*, who had here ufed
it twice, ufe it once more? Why did he take
πρὸτερος in the later branch of the Sentence, if πρῶτος would have been as proper?
I do not think he did it for the fake of the
found, but the fenfe.

I HAVE now fet before the reader the
arguments for this interpretation, and have
offered my own remarks upon them. I
muft conclude, as I began, with faying, that
I am in fufpenfe whether this meaning can
be put upon St. *Luke's* words.

7. THERE

7. THERE is another Solution which was firſt propoſed by (*a*) *Beza,* and has been embraced by many learned (*b*) men. The Roman Catholic Authors that approve of this Solution agree to underſtand the words, as they ſtand in the vulgate verſion : *This firſt Deſcription or Enrolment was made by Cyrenius (c).* The Proteſtants generally render them : *This firſt Enrolment was made,* Cyrenius *being Preſident of* Syria *: or, when* Cyrenius *was Preſident of* Syria *(d).*

B Y preſident of *Syria,* they do not underſtand, Preſident in the moſt ſtrict and proper ſenſe of the word ; it being apparent from *Joſephus,* that either *Saturninus,* or *Quintilius Varus* muſt have been Preſident of *Syria* at the time this enrolment was made. And there is no inſtance of two perſons being jointly Preſidents with equal power in the ſame Province, when a Pro-

(*a*) *Bez.* in loc. Vid. & *Huet.* Dem. Ev. Prop. ix. Cap. x. §. 3.

(*b*) *Grot.* & *Hamm.* in loc. *Scaliger.* animad. in Chron. *Euſeb.* ad A. 2016. *Caſaub.* in Bar. Exerc. i. Numb. 31. 32. *Uſſer.* Ann. ant. aer. Chr. v. *Noriſ.* Cenot. Piſ. Diſſert. ii. p.320. —322. *Pagi.* app. ad ann. Bar. Num. 126.—129.

(*c*) Haec deſcriptio prima facta eſt a praeſide Syriae, Cyrino.

(*d*) Haec deſcriptio prima facta eſt praeſidente Syriae Cyrenio. *Bez.* Haec deſcriptio prima facta eſt cum praeeſſet Syriae Cyrenius, *Caſaub.* ubi ſupra. Numb. 31.

vince

vince was in peace, as *Syria* was at this time (a).

THEY suppose, that when *Augustus* had issued his decree that all the world, that is, all the *Roman Empire* should be taxed (for in this wide and extensive sense do these learned men understand these words of St. *Luke*) *Cyrenius* was sent with extraordinary power to make the Census in *Syria* and *Judea*: And *Saturninus* or *Quintilius Varus*, which soever of them was then President, was joined with him: and was subordinate to him, or had equal power with him in this particular work. *Cyrenius* therefore having at this time some power in *Syria*, he is called President of it, though he was not properly President or the ordinary chief Magistrate of that Province.

IN order to justifie this Solution two things are to be considered: 1. Whether *Cyrenius*, though not properly Prefect of *Syria*, may be called so in a loose and general sense: and 2dly, It must be shewn, that it is not unlikely, that *Cyrenius* might be sent upon this affair at this time with extraordinary power.

(a) Vid. *Norif.* Cenotaph. Pif. Diff. ii. cap. 16. §. 10.

As

As to the firft point, it is alleged, that the Title of *Governour* or *Prefident* is often given to others befide thofe who are properly poffeffed of that dignity. *Jofephus* calls *Saturninus* and *Volumnius* Prefidents of *Syria* (a), though *Saturninus* was at that time Prefident, according to his own account, and *Volumnius* Procurator only, *i. e.* the officer that took care of the Emperour's revenue in that Province.

THAT *Cyrenius* might be fent upon this affair with extraordinary power, is not at all unlikely.   For the office of Cenfor in the City was very honourable, and was a diftinct charge from that of the Confuls and Praetors, the ordinary magiftrates.   The Surveys in Provinces alfo were often performed not by the ordinary governours but by perfons fent thither with extraordinary power, and thofe, perfons of the higheft eminence and dignity (b).

SUCH

(a) Ἐκεῖνος ἢ διελέγετο περὶ τέτων τοῖς Καίσαρος ἡγεμόσιν Σατυρνίνωτε κỳ Ουολουμνίῳ-περὶ ὧν ἐπί τε Σατυρνίνε κỳ Ουολομνίε τ Συρίας ἐπιςατέντων· Antiq. L. 16. cap. 9. pag. 734. v. 25. and 37. Πολλάκις μ̃ ἐπὶ Σατυρνῖνον ἐλθόντα κỳ Ουλέμνιον τὲς τῆς Συρίας ἡγεμόνας· ib. cap. 10. p. 741. v. 1.

(b) Regimen fummae rei penes Germanicum agendo Galliarum Cenfui tum intentum. *Tacit. Ann.* Lib. 1. cap. 31. ad A. U. 767. Interea Germanico per Gallias, ut diximus, *cenfus accipienti,*

S u c h an one was this *Cyrenius.* He
was not defcended from a noble, or *Patri-
cian* family : But by his early fervices he had
obtained the honour of the Confulfhip, and
paffed through that and other offices with
great reputation : obtained a memorable victory over the *Homonadenfes,* for which he
received the honour of triumphal ornaments:
Was afterwards Governour to *Caius Caefar,
Auguftus's* eldeft adopted fon : Married
Aemilia Lepida, who had been defigned by
Auguftus for the wife of *Lucius,* his fecond
adopted Son ; and at laft had the honour of
a publick funeral by a Decree of the Senate
in the reign of *Tiberius* (a).

T h i s quick difpatch he made of affairs
of importance rendered him a very fit man

accipienti, *excefiffe Auguftum,* adfertur. Id. cap. 33. vid. &
L. ii. cap. 6.

(a) Sub idem tempus, ut mors Sulpicii Quirinii publicis ex-
fequiis frequentaretur, petivit (*Tiberius*) a Senatu. Nihil ad vete-
rem & patritiam Sulpiciorum familam Quirinius pertinuit, or-
tus apud municipium Lanuvium : Sed impiger militiae, & acri-
bus minifteriis confulatum fub Divo Augufto; mox expugna-
tis per Ciliciam Homonadenfium Caftellis infignia triumphi
adeptus; datufque Rector Caio Caefari Armeniam obtinenti,
Tiberium quoque Rhodi agentem coluerat. *Tacit. An.* L. iii.
c. 48. *Quirinio—deftinata quondam uxor L. Caefari, ac Divo
Augufto nurus, dederetur.* Id. ibid. c 23. De hac re vid. etiam
Sueton. Tib. c. 49. & de victoria in Homonadenfes partâ,
Strabon. Lib. xii. pag, 854.

for

for such an affair as this Census in *Syria* and *Judea*.

MOREOVER there is nothing in the history which we have of *Cyrenius*, which is any way inconsistent with his coming into *Judea* about this time: but divers particulars, which render it very probable he might be employed in this work.

CYRENIUS was Consul of *Rome*, A. U. 742. He might therefore very well be sent upon the expedition against the *Homonadenses* in the year U. C. 747. or, possibly, in 746. It was a piece of prudent advice which *Maecenas* gave (a) *Augustus*, never to bestow a provincial government upon the Senators or other great men, till some time after they had laid down their City Magistracy. Which advice *Augustus* followed, and appointed the space of five years interval between their serving any publick office in the City, and receiving another in the Provinces (b).

As *Cyrenius*'s expedition against the forementioned people was his first action after his Consulship, he might very probably be em-

(a) *Dio.* Lib. 52. pag. 479. fin.   (b) Μηδένα πρὸ πέντε ἐτῶν μετὰ τὸ ἐν τῇ πόλει ἄρξαι κληρῶσθαι· Id. L. 53. p. 505. C. Auctor & aliarum rerum fuit. In queis——ne magistratus deposito statim in provincias mitterentur. *Sueton.* Aug. c 36.

ployed

ployed in it, A. U. 747. Archbifhop *Ufher* (*a*) thinks he was then Proconful of *Cilicia*. Cardinal *Noris* thinks it more likely that he was not then the ordinary Governour of *Cilicia*, but that he was fent upon this expedition with extraordinary (*b*) power. However the learned men that embrace this folution fuppofe, that having finifhed this war, he might be fent into *Syria* and *Judea* to perform the Cenfus there, in the later end of the year of *Rome*, 747, or, as others, in 748, or 749. About which time the Cenfus or Enrolment, which St. *Luke* fpeaks of, muft have been made, for *Herod* died in the year 750, or 751.

CYRENIUS was not appointed Governour to *Caius Cefar* till the Year U. C. 755. Cardinal *Noris* infers this from the words of *Tacitus* above-cited : *datus Rector Caio Caefari Armeniam obtinenti.* It is evidently a miftake of thofe learned men who have thought that *Cyrenius* was Governour to *Caius*, when he firft went into the *Eaft*. It is certain, that M. *Lollius* was then his Governour. And *Cyrenius* was not put into that Poft till after the death of

(*a*) Vid. *Ann.* A. 5. ante aer. Chr, Pi&ff. Diff. ii. pag. 319.

(*b*) Cenotaph.

Lollius

Lollius (*a*), which feems to have happened
fome time in the year of *Rome* 755. Befides, it is certain from *Jofephus*, that *Caius*
was at *Rome* after the death of *Herod*, and
therefore was not yet fet out for the *Eaft*.
For he was one of thofe whom *Auguftus*
called to the Council he held after *Herod's*
death about confirming his laft will (*b*).

CYRENIUS therefore feems to have
been at leifure for this work : And from the
whole of his ftory and character, fo far as it
is come down to us from the *Greek* and
Roman Authors, no man appears more likely to have been employed in it.

THIS folution has one advantage above
moft of thofe above-mentioned, in that it is
here allowed, that this furvey was performed
by *Cyrenius*, in which all the ancient chriftian
write rs agree, except *Tertullian* ; who in
one place (but the only place in which he has
named the chief officer concerned in it) afcribes it to *Saturninus*. And we are much
obliged to thefe learned men for tracing the
hiftory of *Cyrenius*, and thereby removing,
in part at leaft, the objections againft this fup-

(*a*) *Vellerus*, L.ii.c. 102. *Suet* Tib. c. 13. *Norif.* ubi fupra.
p. 317.   (*b*) *Jofeph. Ant.*L. 17. c. 9. p. 775.
v. 14.

pofition

pofition, which has been the current opinion of Chriftians.

THERE is however one difficulty attending this Solution: I mean the fenfe, in which thefe learned men underftand *Cyrenius*'s government or prefidentfhip. I do not at all conteft the validity of their argument, that the title of ἡγεμὼν may be given to one who is not properly Prefident. But fince *Cyrenius* certainly was afterwards the ordinary governour of *Syria*, it is not eafy to underftand this title in St. *Luke* in a loofe and general way. And I can never perfwade my felf, that St. *Luke* intended no more than the power and authority of making a Cenfus in *Syria*. If *Cyrenius* had never been Prefident of *Syria*, perhaps their inftances had been to the point; but now, I think, they are not. Befides, according to the way in which thefe learned men generally interpret St. *Luke*, ἡγεμονέυοντος, *&c.* is here the genitive cafe abfolute, or governed by ἐπὶ underftood: either of which does as fully exprefs *Cyrenius*'s being Prefident of *Syria*, as any form of expreffion can do.

JOSEPH SCALIGER feems to have interpreted thefe words fomewhat differently from other learned men who embrace this

this Solution. He takes them thus. *This Defcription was the firft under Cyrenius prefident of Syria.* I put his words in the margin (*a*), that the reader may judge whether I mifunderftand him. But ftill this interpretation is liable to the objection laft mentioned: for it is implied in it, that *Cyrenius* was Prefident of *Syria*, at the time of both thefe Surveys.

§. V. T H E R E is yet another interpretation, which thefe words are capable of, and which has for fome time appeared to me the genuine meaning of them. *This was the firft affeffement of Cyrenius Governour of Syria.* The natural order of the words is this : Ἀύτη ἐγίνετο ἡ πρώτη ἀπογραφὴ ἡγ΄ Τ. Σ. Κ. There are innumerable inftances of a conftruction parallel with this here of Ἀύτη ἡ ἀπογραφὴ πρώτη. *Matth.* xxii. 38. Ἀυτη ἐςὶ πρώτη ἠ μεγάλη ἐντολή· *This is the firft and great commandment.* Mark xii. 30. Ἀυτη πρώτη ἐντολή· *Numb.* ii. 32. Ἀυτη ἐπίσκεψις τῶν υἱῶν Ἰσραήλ· *Thefe are thofe which were numbred of the children*

dren

(*a*) Ideo S. Lucas non contentus eft dicere Ἀυτη ἀπογραφὴ ἐγίνετο ἡγεμονεύοντ۞ τῆς Συρίας Κυρηνίв. Sed quum duas ἀπογραφὰς fciret fuiffe, addidit, πρώτη : ἀυτη ἡ ἀπογραφη ἐγίνετο πρώτη· Certè, fi eft πρώτη, ergo quaedam fuit δευτέρa ; & fane

τῆς

dren of Ifrael. I put an inftance or two
more into (*a*) the margin. It is eafie for the
reader to obferve, thefe inftances are parallel
with the words before us: the particle ἡ or
αἱ follows Ἀυ7η or Ἀῦται, and preceeds
the Subftantive.

Ἐγένε7ο is not here *facta eft, was made,*
but *fuit, was.* I prefume I need not give
any proofs, that this is a very common meaning of this verb.

THE diftant fituation of ἐγένε7ο in Saint
Luke from ἀυτη need not create any fcruple.
In fome examples the verb fubftantive is quite
wanting, as in *Mark* xii. 30. *Numb.* i. 44.
Sometimes ἐςὶν is expreffed, and follows immediately after ἀυ7η. But it is found in all
kinds of pofitions in paffages parallel with
this of St. *Luke.* I give one inftance which
anfwers the conftruction of this verfe in every
refpect, *Rev.* xix. 9. ὗ7οι ὁι λόγοι ἀληθινόι
ἐισι τῶ Θεῶ. *Thefe are the true fayings of
the word of God.* And another inftance

τῆς δευτέρας meminit idem. *Act.* v. 37. Atque ita diftinguen-
dum effe nemo dubitare poteft. *Scaliger.* animadv. in *Chron.
Eufeb.* ad. A. 2016.

(*a*) Numb. i. 44. Ἀυτη ἡ ἐπίσκεψις ἣν ἐπεσκέψατο Μωῦσῆς.
cap. iii.1. Καὶ ἀυται ἀι γενέσεις Ἀαρών· v. 2. κỳ τάυτα τὰ ὀνόματα
τ̃ ὑιῶν Ἀαρών· vid. cap. iv. 32. 38. *Deut.* vi. 1. & alibi.

from

from *Plato* (a) of ἐγένετο it felf, in a situation exactly parallel with this in St. *Luke*. Ἡ ἢ ἡ τελευτὴ, ὦ Ἐχέκρατες, τῦ ἑταίρου ἡμῖν ἐγένετο ἀνδρὸς, ὡς ἡμεῖς φαῖμεν ἂν, τῶν τότε ὦν ἐπειράθημεν ἀρίσου, κὴ ἄλλως φρονιμωτάτυ κὴ δικαιοτάτυ. ' This, *O Echecrates*,
' was the end of our friend; and as we say,
' the best, wifest and justest man that ever
' we knew'.

I f it be objected, that it must be *this census*; or this *first census* was made, and not this was the first census; because there is no noun substantive preceding αὔτη, by which it can be governed: I answer, that as I interpret the words, αὔτη is governed by the ἀπογραφὴ that follows, or by an ἀπογραφὴ understood. And this is the case of many other (b) passages, which yet must be construed, as I do St. *Luke*.

L e t us proceed. When St. *Luke* calls *Cyrenius Governour of Syria*, I understand the words in the strict and proper sense. Ἡγεμονεύοντος τῆς Κυρίας is not the genitive case absolute, or governed by ἐπὶ understood, and to be construed, *Cyrenius being gover-*

(a) *Phaedo. Fin.*   (b) Ezek. 48. v. 1. Καὶ ταῦτα τὰ ὅρια τῶν φυλῶν. v. 29. 30. Ἅυτη ἡ γῆ, ἣν βαλεῖτε ἐν κλήρῳ ταῖς φυλαῖς τῶ Ἰσραήλ· κὴ ὗτοι οἱ διαμερισμοὶ αὐτῶν----Καὶ ἅυται αἱ διεκβολαὶ τῆς πόλεως.

nour

nour of *Syria*, or *when Cyrenius was governour of Syria*; but it is governed by ἀπογραφή.
They do not exprefs any time at all. But this is
Cyrenius's title, the title, by which he was
well known in that part of the world. As
we fay, *Antony* the *Triumvir*, or *Cato* the
Cenfor, to diftinguifh them from others of
the fame names. Ἡγεμονέ͜οντος, &c. is with
me the fame thing, as if St. *Luke* had faid,
ἡγεμόν@· τῆς Συρίας Κυρηνίυ.

I⊤ is certain, that *Greek* Authors delight
very much in the ufe of participles; and, I
think, more efpecially when they fpeak of
titles and dignities. Thus *Cicero*, in (*a*) *Dio*,
fays: 'We expeẟt that our Praetors and
' Confuls fhould follow the laws of reafon
' and juftice.' Τὲς μὲν ϛρατηγοῦντας τός θ'
ὑπατεύοντας πάντα ἀπ' ὀρθῆς τῆς διανόιας
ποιεῖν ἀξιώσομεν· The fame fame hiftorian
(*b*) fays: ' The three brothers, the *Antonies*,
' had all of them fome office in the City at
' one and the fame time: *Marcus* was Con-
' ful, *Lucius* Tribune, and *Caius* Praetor'.
Τρεῖς γὰρ οἱ ἀδελφοὶ οἱ Ἀντώνιοι ἔτοι ὄντες ἀρχὰς ἅμα πάντες ἔχον· Ὁ μὲν γ͜ὸ Μάρχ@· ὑπα-.
Ίεύων: ὁ δ͜ Λεύκιος δημαρχῶν· ὁ δ͜ Γάιος ϛρατηγῶν.

THESE participles seem to me to be sometimes substantives, or at left, to be (*a*) used
substantively. I believe all are sensible that
ἄρχων is so used. Some of those other titles
of offices or dignities expressed by participles seem to me very near, or altogether parallel with it.

BUT let ἡγεμονεύοντ῀ Θ. be a mere participle; only then it will be said: If it be governed by ἀπογραφὴ, it ought to have been
ἡγεμονεύσαντ῀Θ. To this I answer, that undoubtedly ἡγεμονεύσαντ῀Θ. would have been
very proper, but so is also ἡγεμονεύοντ῀Θ. It
is no uncommon thing for *Greek* authors to
use the Present tense for the first Aorist. I
give an instance or two that fully justify my
interpretation. *Josephus* says: ‘ And it is cer-
‘ tain that *Varus* was of a Royal Family,
‘ since he was a descendent of *Soemus* who
‘ was Tetrarch of a country near mount (*b*)
‘ *Libanus*’. Καὶ ἦν ὁμολογυμένως ὁ Οὐαρ῀Θ.
βασιλικῦ γένυς, ἔγγονος Σοέμυ τῦ περὶ Λίβανον
τετεαρχῦντος. *Dionysius* says, that the *Latins*
were so called from *Latinus* a King of (*c*)

(*a*) Δεκιάνος Κάτ῀Θ. ὁ τῆς ἥσυ ἐπιτροπεύων. DIO. lib. 62.
p. 701. A. Κεσίω Γάλλω τῷ τῆς Συρίας ἡγεμονεύοντι· *Joseph.*
p. 907. v. 12. Αὐτὸς ꝰ ὑπὸ τῦ τῆς χώρας ἡγεμονεύοντος δεθείς.
id. p. 945. v. 35.   (*b*) P. 939. v. 20.   (*c*) Antiq.
R. lib. 2. p. 76 v. 24.

that

that country. Ὄνομα ἢ κοινὸν ὃι σύμπαντες ἔτοι Λατῖνοι ἐκλήθησαν ἐπ᾽ ἀνδρὸς δυναστεύοντος τῶν τόπων Λατίνε. If any should say, it is improper to understand this participle, as I do, because *Cyrenius* was not Governour of *Syria* till after the time in which St. *Luke's* survey was made ; I add one example more, which must fully obviate this exception. *Herodian* says, ' That to *Marcus* the Emperour ' were born several daughters (*a*) and two sons. Τῷ βασιλεύοντι Μάρκῳ θυγατέρες μὲν ἐγένοντο πλείες, ἄῤῥενες ἢ δύο. Yet several of those children were born to him before he was Emperour. This instance shews plainly, that these participles do not always import only the time when men are in office.

I HOPE this is sufficient to shew, that ἡγεμονεύοντος is the same as ἡγεμόνος, at left that it is governed by ἀπογραφή. The supposing ἡγεμονεύοντος Τ. Σ. Κ. to be the Genitive absolute, or governed by ἐπὶ, as it has given occasion for the objection we are now upon, so it seems to have led some learned men into interpretations of this text unsupported by the use of good *Greek* writers.

I APPREHEND I have now justified my interpretation of every part of this verse ;

(*a*) Lib. i. init.

This

This was the firft Affeffement (or furvey)
of Cyrenius the Governour of Syria, or, *of*
Cyrenius who was Governour of Syria.

BUT if any choofe rather to take *Scaliger's*
method, as to the firft part of the verfe, I
fhall not contend about that, provided my
fenfe of the later part be admitted. Then
the Interpretation will ftand thus. This furvey was the firft [furvey] of *Cyrenius* the
Governour of *Syria.*

NOR can I fee any reafon why all thofe
who follow *Beza,* and fuppofe that this
furvey was made by *Cyrenius,* as well as that
made after *Archelaus's* removal, fhould not
receive this interpretation. When they come
to fhew why this is called by St. *Luke* the
firft furvey, though indeed they have not
tranflated the place as I do, (*a*) they una-
voidably run into the fame meaning. *Ba-*

(*a*) Denique dicitur haec defcriptio πρώτη, ut diftinguatur ab
aliâ, de qua *Act.* v. 37. quam Jofephus & Eufebius litteris con-
fignarunt, & fub Cyrenio etiam factam dicunt, licet diverfo
tempore. *Hamm.* in loc. ex verfione *Cleric.*

Hunc igitur cenfum Quirinius habuit A. U. 749 cum ex-
traordinario imperio in Syriam miffus; quae defcriptio *prima*
a S. Luca dicitur, quod idem poftea Quirinius A. U. 760. praefes
ordinarius in Syriam veniens, cenfum iterum in judaea egit,
eâdem tum primum in provinciae formam redactâ. *Norif.*
Cenotaph. Pif. p. 322.

ronius

ronius (*a*) likewife underſtands the words much after the ſame manner, only he falſly ſuppoſed that *Cyrenius* was twice preſident of *Syria*.

So me time after I had been perſwaded this was the ſenſe of this text, I met with theſe words of *Tanaquil Faber* (*b*). *Beatus Lucas*, cap. 2. *ait natum eſſe Chriſtum dominum tempore primi cenſus, ſeu deſcriptionis, quae a Cyrenio ſeu Quirinio faſta eſt.* This paſſage gave me a great deal of pleaſure, though it does not appear how this acute and learned man underſtood ἡγεμονέυοντος.----But I have ſince met with a more explicite authority for my way of tranſlating Ἀυλη ἡ ἀπογραφη. The title of *Origen*'s xi. Homily upon St. *Luke*, in the latin edition of his works, is thus: *De eo quod ſcriptum eſt, Puer autem creſcebat & confortabatur ſpiritu, uſque ad eum locum ubi ait: Haec eſt deſcriptio prima quae faſta eſt ſub praeſide Syriae Cyrino.* And, in the body of the (*c*) Homily are words to the ſame effeſt.

(*a*) Quod igitur ab Evangeliſta ea deſcriptio a Quirino *prima faſta* dicitur: non ſic (ut vidimus) eſt accipiendum, ut tunc primùm judaei fuerint deſcripti atque cenſi: ſed *primam* dixerit reſpeſtu *ſecundae ſub eodem praeſide faſta. App. Num.* 88.

(*b*) Epiſt. lib. i. ep. 43.   (*c*) Haec fuit deſcriptio prima, a praeſide Syriae Cyrino.

THE

THE verfion I here offer does not only appear to me a very natural and obvious meaning of the words, but it is very good fenfe, and extremely fuitable to their pofition in a parenthefis. *In thofe days there went out a decree from Cefar Auguftus that all the world* [Land] *ſhould be taxed. (This was the firſt affeffement of Cyrenius the Governour of Syria).* It is needlefs to obferve, that if this verfion be allowed, the objection we are confidering vanifhes. There is no colour or pretence to fay, that St. *Luke* confounded the cenfus or furvey, made in the time of *Herod*, with that made after the removal of *Archelaus.*

§. VI. I APPREHEND there lies now no objection againſt St. *Luke*, but what may arife from the doubts which fome may have in their minds, concerning *Cyrenius* being the officer employed in making this furvey. I wifh the reader be not quite tired with this long fucceffion of criticifms. But whether he will accompany me any farther or not, I think my felf obliged to take into confidera. tion all the difficulties which attend this particular circumftance.

HERE I adopt at once all that has been already offered by thofe who embrace *Beza's*
Solution,

Solution, to make it appear probable, that *Cyrenius* performed the Cenfus of which St. *Luke* fpeaks. But I now enjoy a peculiar advantage above thofe learned men, in the fuppofition I advanced at firft, that this cenfus of *Cyrenius* was of *Judea* only. They think, that *Auguftus*'s decree extended to the whole Empire; and that *Cyrenius* was fent with extraordinary power to make the cenfus in *Syria* and *Judea.* But they fuppofe, (and indeed they are obliged to allow it) that *Saturninus* was joined with him, if *Saturninus* was then prefident. This has given *Perizonius* (*a*) a fine advantage againft their fuppofition, that *Cyrenius* was concerned in this cenfus. To give *Cyrenius* fuperior or equal power to *Saturninus* in *Syria*, the province of which he was the ordinary governour, would have been an affront, efpecially confidering that *Saturninus* was equal to *Cyrenius,* in every refpect, and fuperior to him in fome : for he was of a better family, and the elder Conful by feven years. And it is no lefs injurious to *Cyrenius* to put him under *Saturninus.*

I AM not at all concerned with this. I think *Cyrenius* performed the Cenfus alone,

(*a*) Differt. de Aug. Defcrip. §. 15, 16, 17.

by

by virtue of the extraordinary power with which he was fent. But if any are inclined to think, that *Saturninus* was joined in the Commiffion with him, this would be no difparagement to *Saturninus*. To give him authority in a neighbouring kingdome where he had none before, would not be to leffen him, but to augment his power. Nor do I fuppofe, it could be any difgrace to *Cyrenius* to have the Governour of *Syria* made his partner.

I PROCEED to confider all the difficulties that can affect the fuppofition that this cenfus was made by *Cyrenius*, as far as I am concerned with them.

1. IT is faid, that it was not cuftomary for the *Romans* to fend any great man twice into the fame country. Since it is certain from *Jofephus*, that *Cyrenius* afterwards made a Cenfus in *Syria* and *Judea*, it may be concluded, he did not perform that Cenfus, which St. *Luke* fays was made in *Judea* at the time of our Saviour's nativity (*a*).

(*a*) Multis de caufis difplicet nobis gemina haec Cyrenii defcriptio. Bis ad eandem rem Quirinium in Syriam fuiffe miffum, fidem vix imperat, nec Romanos ad mores quadrat. *Bafnage. Ann. Pol. Ecc.* ant. Dom. 5. num. 14.

To

T o this I anſwer: I allow, that it was not uſual for the ſame perſon to be more than once made the Preſident of one and the ſame province.---And in this *Baronius,* who thought *Cyrenius* was twice or thrice Governour of *Syria,* is deſerted by all learned men. For none of the defenders of *Beza's* Solution, who maintain the double cenſus of *Cyrenius,* do ſay, that *Cyrenius* was twice the ordinary Preſident of *Syria.*

B u t it was very common for one and the ſame perſon to be ſent twice or oftner into the ſame country in different Poſts or with different degrees of authority. *Caſaubon* (*a*) has produced inſtances enough to ſilence this objection. And *M. Vipſanius Agrippa,* the perſon laſt mentioned by him, was ſent twice into *Syria* by *Auguſtus* with extraordinary power. Firſt of all, A. U. 731. (*b*), and again, A. U. 738. (*c*).   I w i l l

---

(*a*) Neque vero nullum eſt exemplum illorum, qui in eaſdem provincias cum eodem, vel diverſo munere ſunt miſſi. C. Caſſius profectus in Syriam Quaeſtor M. Craſſi, mox ipſo & ejus exercitu deleto, res magnas ibi geſſit, & aliquamdiu provinciam obtinuit: eidemque poſt aliquot annos ſenatus Syriam & bellum contra Dolabellam decrevit. Ventidius Baſſus, quando primum cum Parth's bellum geſſit, Antonii fuit Legatus: poſtea ejuſdem belli gerendi cura illi demandata eſt, ------Agrippa qui per decennium Aſiam adminiſtravit, bis ex Italia eodem, eſt profectus, *Caſaub.* in *Baron.* Exerc. 1. num. 32.

(*b*) *Dio.* l. 53. p. 518. c.   (*c*) Id. l. 54. p. 534. B.

I WILL give an undeniable example of an officer's being twice in the same province with different degrees of power. When *Piso* prefect of *Syria* had been removed by *Germanicus*, and after that *Germanicus* himself died, the officers in the province had a consultation together, who should be made President of *Syria*. *Vibius Marsus* laid claim to it, but at last yielded to *Cn. Sentius Saturninus* (a) the elder officer. Thus *Sentius*, one of the chief officers then in the province, was made president. This alone is a proof, that it was very common for officers to serve different posts in the same Province. But this is not what I aim at. This Consultation (b) was held A. U. 772. A. D. 19. And it appears from *Josephus* (c), and *Tacitus* (d), that long after this, in the (e) reign of *Claudius*, this same *Vibius Marsus* came to be actually president of

(a) Consultatum inde inter legatos, quique alii senatorum aderant, *quisnam Syriae praeficeretur*. Et ceteris modice nisi, inter VIBIUM MARSUM & Cn. Sentium diu quaesitum : dein Marsus seniori, & acrius tendenti Sentio concessit. *Tacit. Ann.* lib. ii. cap. 74.   (b) M. Silano & L. Norbano *Coss.* (c) Καὶ μετ' ὀ πολὺ, Πετρώνιον μὲν Μάρσ©∽ διεδέξατο, ᾗ διεῖπε Συρίαν. *Ant.* 19. cap. vi. §. 4.   (d) Et reciperare Armeniam, ni VIBIO MARSO Syriae legato bellum minitante cohibitus foret. *Tacit.* Ann. xi. cap. 10.   (e) About A.U. 795, vid. Pagi; Crit. in Bar. A. D. 42, n. viii.

Syria.

Syria. There is therefore no abſurdity at all in ſuppoſing that *Cyrenius* was ſent by *Auguſtus* with extraordinary power at the later end of *Herod*'s reign to make a ſurvey in *Judea,* and that about ten or twelve years afterwards he came as the ordinary governour into *Syria,* and then made a Cenſus in that province and in *Judea* annexed to it.

2. I T is objected, that none of the *Roman* or *Greek* hiſtorians, though *Cyrenius* has been ſpoken of by ſeveral of them, have taken any notice of this Cenſus.

I ANSWER, that this is no difficulty at all. I ſuppoſe, that no one will make any queſtion, but that *Cyrenius* made an aſſeſſement in *Syria* and *Judea,* when he was ſent preſident into *Syria,* becauſe we have *Joſephus*'s authority for it. And yet none of the *Roman* or *Greek* authors have ſaid any thing of this Cenſus.

THOUGH *Tacitus* has in the paſſage cited above reckoned up divers of *Cyrenius*'s exploits and honours, and others have made mention of him and of ſome of his Services; yet *Florus* (a) has taken notice of a conſi-

(a) Marmaridas atque Garamantas Curinio ſubigendo dedit (*Auguſtus*). Potuit & ille redire Marmaricus; ſed modeſtior in aeſtimanda victoria fuit. *Florus* lib. iv. cap. 12.

derable

derable action of his, omitted by all the reft: If indeed he means our *Cyrenius*.

3. BUT it will be faid: It may be certainly concluded from the account which *Jofephus* has given of the Cenfus made (A) by *Cyrenius* after *Archelaus's* banifhment, that *Cyrenius* had never been in *Judea* or enrolled the *Jews* before. If he had, *Jofephus* could not well have omitted to take notice of it then.

I OWN, that at firft fight this muft appear a very confiderable difficulty.

(1.) BUT it ought to be obferved, that *Jofephus* does not particularly name any of *Cyrenius's* honours or fervices, befide thofe which relate to the City of *Rome.* *Jofephus* knew of divers others, but he does not exprefle them. And among thofe omitted or referred to in the general only, may be that of the firft furvey in *Judea.*

(2.) I THINK it is plain, that either *Jofephus* did not care to give any particular account of that oath taken by the *Jews* to *Auguftus* in the later end of *Herod's* reign, or elfe that he found but a flight account of it in thofe Memoirs or hiftories which he made ufe of. He had faid nothing of it,

(A) See the account above p. 103.

had

had it not been for a moſt remarkable diſturbance in *Herod*'s court and family, with
which it had a connexion.

AND any one may perceive, that it is
then touched upon very ſlightly. Is it not
ſtrange that *Joſephus* ſhould not name the
officer who took the oath for *Auguſtus?*
No one can make any doubt, but there was
ſome Perſon of eminence deputed by the
Emperour for that work. As *Joſephus* did
not mention him then, I ſhould never expect to find his name afterwards. And who-
ever can account for *Joſephus's* omiſſions
relating to the affair of the oath, may account
for his ſilence in this paſſage, though *Cyrenius*
had been once before in *Judea.*

(3.) I THINK that arguments formed
upon the omiſſions of Hiſtorians are of very
little weight. There are in *Joſephus* other
omiſſions as remarkable as this. I deſire to
conſider the account he gives, in his *War of
the Jews,* of the reducing *Judea* to a province. ' *Archelaus's* country being reduced to
' a province, *coponius* a man of the *equeſtrian*
' rank among the *Romans* was ſent Procurator,
' being inveſted with the power of life and
' death. In his time [ἐπὶ ʒʒʒ] a certain *Galilean,*
' whoſe name was *Judas,* excited the people
to

to a rebellion, telling them, That they were
' of a mean spirit, if they could endure to pay
' tribute to the *Romans*, and acknowledge
' mortal men for their Lords after God had
' been their King.   This man was the head
' of a distinct Sect, in nothing like (*a*) the
rest.   This is all he says.   He does not say
there was now any census made, has not one
word of *Cyrenius* or his coming into *Judea*.

I T is true that *Josephus* has, in two other
places in the War of the *Jews* (*b*), occasionally mentioned *Cyrenius*, and in the later
of those places, his census also.   But it must
be allowed to be a very great omission, not to
do this in the proper place, in the account of
the reduction of *Judea* to the state of a province.   This might have been reasonably expected in a history of the War, when this af-
sessement made by *Cyrenius* and the principle broached at that time were main foun-
dations of it.

I F it be said, that *Josephus* passed over
this affair slightly in *the War*, because he intended to write his *Antiquities* and mention
it more particularly then : I answer, this is
said without ground.   And I might as well

(*a*) *De Bell.* Lib. ii. cap. 8. §. 1.   (*b*) Ibid. c. 17.
§. 8. & l. 7. c. 8. §. 1.

N   say,

say, that *Josephus* omitted in his *Antiquities* the particular account of *Cyrenius's first* assessment, because he intended to write afterward another book of the history of the *Jews*, and go over their affairs once more, as he expresly assures us at the conclusion of his *Antiquities*.

JOSEPHUS informs us in his *Life*, writ after the *War*, and the *Antiquities*, that the *Jews* had a battle with *Gessius Florus* their last Procurator, and killed him and a good many of his men; and that this victory was fatal to them: Forasmuch as this determined them to the war with the (*a*) *Romans*. Is it not strange that *Josephus* should say nothing of this in the history of the *War*, where he has made so frequent mention of *Florus*, and ascribed the *jewish* uneasinesse under the Roman Government to the cruelties and other irregularities of this man? For this instance I am indebted to (*b*) Monsieur *Le Clerc*.

(*a*) Ὁ δ᾽ ἐπελϑὼν κỳ συμβαλὼν μάχη ἐνικήϑη, πολλῶν ℱ μετ᾽ αὐτῆ πεσόντων: κỳ γίνεται τὸ Γεσσίε πταῖσμα, συμφορὰ ℥ παιδὸς ἡμῶν ἔϑνες· ἐπήρϑησαν ℱ ἐπὶ τῆτο μᾶλλον οἱ τὸν πόλεμον ἀγαπήσαντες, κỳ νικήσαντις τὰς Ῥωμαίες εἰς τελ℗ ἠλπίσαμεν. in Vit. §. 6.   (*b*) Hist. Ecc A. D. 66. n. 12.

THERE is another omiffion appears to me very remarkable. *Pheroras, Herod's* youngeft brother, is often mentioned by *Jofephus.* He has particularly informed us, that when *Auguftus* was in *Syria,* he gave this *Pheroras* a Tetrarchy (*a*) at the requeft of *Herod.* And we are informed by *Jofephus,* of *Pheroras's* retirement into his Tetrarchy, of *Herod's* vifiting him there, and of *Pheroras's* dying (*b*) at home, and of his being brought afterwards from thence to be buried. But yet, if I miftake not, he has never once faid what this Tetrarchy was, whofe it had been before, nor where it lay. It is true, that whereas in the *Antiquities* (*c*) *Jofephus* fays *Pheroras* went to his Tetrarchy; in his *War* (*d*) he fays, he went to *Peraea,* (or as in fome copies *Petraea*): but *Peraea* properly fo called, could not be this Tetrarchy, becaufe *Peraea* belonged all along to *Herod.* But this Tetrarchy of *Pheroras* was given him by *Auguftus,* and was diftinct from that eftate or revenue which (*e*) had

(*a*) Antiq 15. c. 10. §. 3, de B. J. l. i. c 29.
(*b*) Ibid. l. 17. c 3.
(*c*) Φεράραν δ' ἐπὶ τῆς αὐτᾶ τετραρχίας· p. 756. v 37.
(*d*) Φεράρας ꝑ ὑπεχωρήσειν εἰς τὴν Περαίαν p. 1031. v. 41. vid. & p 1032. v. 20.
(*e*) Τῶ ᾦ ἀδελφῷ Φερώρᾳ παρὰ Καίσαρꝋ ᾐτήσατο τετραρχίαν, αὐτὸς ἀπονείμας ἐκ τῆς βασιλείας πρόσοδον ἑκατὸν ταλάντων κ. λ. Antiq. 15. c. 10. §. 3.

N 2   been

been fettled upon him by *Herod.* Thefe particulars may convince us, that, though *Cyrenius* was in *Judea* in the time of *Herod,* *Jofephus* was capable of omitting to take notice of it.

4. AGAIN, it will be faid: It may be fairly concluded from another place in *Jofe-phus,* that *Cyrenius* was but once in *Judea.* For he fays, that ' *Maffada* was then held ' by *Eleazar,* the chief man of the *Sicarii,* ' a defcendent of *Judas,* who perfwaded ' not a few of the *Jews* not to enrole ' themfelves, as I have faid (*a*) above, when ' *Cyrenius* the Cenfor was (*b*) fent into ' *Judea*.

I OWN it, this is a difficulty, but the argument is not conclufive. It is true, that *Judas* made this difturbance when *Cyrenius was fent into Judea,* or in the time of *Cy-renius:* but it does not follow that *Cyre-nius* was fent but once into *Judea.* The *New Teftament* will afford us an inftance upon this very fubject which will be of ufe to

(*a*) Vid. *de Bell.* l. 2. c. 17 §. 8.   (*b*) Καλεῖται ἢ τὸ μὲν φρύριον Μασάδα, προσσήκει ἢ τ̄ κατειληφ́σιων ἀυτὸ σικαρίων δυνατὸς ἀνὴρ Ἐλεάζαρ⊙, ἀπόγον⊙ Ἰύδα τ̄ πεισαντ⊙ Ἰεδαίων ἐκ ὀλίγες, ὡς πρότερον δεδηλώκαμεν, μὴ ποιεῖαϊ τὰς ἀπογραφὰς, ὅτε Κυρήνι⊙ τιμητὴς εἰς τὴν Ἰεδαίαν ἐπέμφθη. *de B.* l. 7. c. 8. §. 1.

US

us. *Gamaliel* fays: *After this man rofe up* Judas *of* Galilee, *in the days of the taxing, and drew away much people after him.* ^{Acts v. 37.} If we had in our hands this book only of St. *Luke*, namely the *Acts of the Apoftles*, it is not unlikely that many would have fuppofed, that St. *Luke* knew of no other taxing made in *Judea*, but that, in the time of which *Judas* rofe up. But we are affured from his *Gofpel*, that this conclufion would have been falfe : for there, he has fpoke very particularly of another, which he calls the *firft*, or at left diftinguifhes very plainly from fome other.

I MUST be allowed to repeat here once more, that arguments formed upon the filence of writers are very feldom of much moment. *Jofephus* is the only *jewifh* writer of thofe times, in whom we have the hiftory of that country : And it cannot be juftly conclud-that any particular thing was not done, or that fuch or fuch a circumftance did not attend it, becaufe he has not mentioned it. All writers have their particular views, and fome things we are very defirous to know might for fome reafon or other, which we are ignorant of, lie without the compafs of their defigns. Befides, the moft accurate and

N 3 care-

careful hiftorians have omitted many facts or incidents, that might be very properly men- tioned, through forgetfulneffe or overfight. I take the omiffion of the defcription of the Tetrarchy that belonged to *Pheroras* to be a remarkable inftance of this fort.

5. B u t it will be faid, that *Tertullian* is pofitive, the cenfus in *Judea* at the time of our Saviour's birth was made by *Sentius Saturninus* (*a*).

I a n s w e r to this : (1.) It ought to be confidered, that the Heretic *Marcion*, with whom *Tertullian* difputes in this place, did not admit the authority of the firft chapters (*b*) of St. *Luke's* Gofpel. And it was the cu- ftom of *Tertullian* to argue from thofe parts of fcripture, which the Heretics he was dealing with (*c*) acknowledged. Poffibly there- fore *Tertullian* having, or fuppofing he had reafon to think, that this cenfus was made, when *Saturninus* was prefident of *Syria*, he

(*a*) Sed & cenfus conftat actos fub Augufto nunc in Judaea per S.ntium Saturrinum. Apud quos genus ejus inquirere potuiffent. *Contr. Marc.* l.b. 4. c 19.   (*b*) Accedit his Cerdon quidam.———Su'um evangelium Lucae, nec ta- men totum recipit. Poft hunc difcipulus ipfius emerfit Mar- cion.———Haerefin Cerdonis approbare conatus eft. *de praef- crip. Haeret.* cap. 51.   (*c*) Quam & argumentationibus earum, & fcripturis quibus utuntur, provocavimus ex abundanti. *de carne Chrifti,* cap. 25.

might

might choose to mention the ordinary officer
as a thing certain : but yet might not intend to affirm that the census was made by
him, but only that it happened in his time.
Isaac Casaubon judged it not unreasonable
so to understand *Tertullian*, who often uses
words (*a*) improperly. I thought it not fit
to deprive the reader of this answer of this
learned man. But I do not adopt his interpretation of *Tertullian*.

(2.) *TERTULLIAN*'s authority
ought not to outweigh the testimony of
more ancient writers who were nearer the
event. *Justin Martyr*, in his first apology,
presented to the *Roman Emperour* sixty years
before *Tertullian* wrote his books against
Marcion, says, this Census was performed in
Judea by *Cyrenius*; and all other writers
agree with *Justin*, as has been shewn already.

(3.) *TERTULLIAN*'s authori-
ty is of the less weight in this point, because
he has made very gross blunders in history, of

(*a*) Tertullianus cum adversus Marcio. scribit, *Sed & co stat*,
——ad majorem fidem magistratum ordinarium potius nomi-
nat, quam extraordinarium. Ait autem *per Sentium Saturninum*
durè & Tertullianice, hoc est, improprie pro ἐπὶ Σεντίε Σατερνίε,
ε, vel ἡγεμονεύοντ῎Θ- τῆς Σ. Κ. *Casaub. Exercit.* 1. n. 31.

N 4   which

which I fhall fay fomewhat more in the *third* chapter.

(4.) I IMAGINE fome account may be given of this miftake of *Tertullian*. It has been obferved, that *Marcion*, whom *Tertul- lian* was now arguing with, did not own the firft chapters of St. *Luke's* Gofpel. *Ter- tullian* therefore not having his eye particular- ly upon St. *Luke*, and fuppofing that this Cenfus was made in *Judea* when *Saturninus* was prefident of *Syria*, fays, it was made *by* him.

JUDEA having been afterwards a branch of the province of *Syria*, he con- cluded that it was fo at this time, and that therefore the Cenfus muft have been made by the Prefident of *Syria*. But this was argu- ing from later to more early times, as men not throughly verfed in hiftory are apt to do.

AFTER the banifhment of *Archelaus*, *Judea* was annexed to *Syria*. But whilft *Herod* was living, the prefident of *Syria* had not any proper authority in *Judea*. The Prefident of *Syria* was always the moft con- fiderable officer in the Eaftern part of the Empire. When the *Romans* had any

war

war (a) in that part of the world, the neighbouring Kings were obliged to follow his directions, to furnish those sums of money, or those troops which he required, and to send these to the places he appointed. When any differences happened between these Kings and Tetrarchs, they were bound to refer them to him, nor could they march any forces out of their territories without his consent.   But he seems not, especially in a time of peace, to have had any proper authority within their dominions.

Nor do I think, that I here impute to Tertullian any very gross mistake.   The state of dependent kingdoms and provinces in the Roman Empire underwent frequent changes. And a person had need to have made history his peculiar study, and to have aimed at some uncommon accuracy, in order to understand the state of all the Roman provinces for a couple of Centuries.

I have now gone through all the difficulties which are of any moment in this point.

(a) Tum intellecto Barbarorum irrisu, qui peterent quod eripuerant, consuluit inter primores civitatis Nero, bellum anceps an pax inhonesta placeret, nec dubitatum de BELLO—— scribitur tetrarchis ac regibus praefectisque ac procuratoribus, —jussis Corbulonis obsequi. Tacit. Ann. 15. c. 25.

I HAVE

I HAVE nothing farther to add to those evidences which I have already produced, except these two observations: 1st. that it seems to me highly probable from the manner in which *Eusebius* speaks of this matter in his chronicles, that it was originally the common opinion of Christians, that *Cyrenius* was sent into *Judea* on purpose to make this Census: ' In the thirty third year of ' *Herod, Cyrenius* being sent by the Roman ' Senate made a Census (or *enrolments*) of ' goods and persons (*a*)'. This does very much confirm the opinion of those learned men who think, that *Cyrenius* was sent with extraordinary power : Though why *Eusebius* mentions the *Senate* instead of the *Emperour*, I know not.

POSSIBLY some may be disposed to set aside *Eusebius*'s authority, because, in his Ecclesiastical History, he has confounded the two surveys. But I must confesse, I ascribe that, not to ignorance, but to somewhat a great deal worse. It is impossible, that a man of *Eusebius*'s acutenesse, who had the *New Testament* and *Josephus* before him, should think a Census made after *Archelaus*'s banishment was the same with that made before

(*a*) Chron. pag. 76.

Herod

Herod died. But *Eusebius* was resolved to have St. *Luke's* history confirmed by the express testimony of the *jewish* Historian, right or wrong. Here *Eusebius* was under a biasse. In his Chronicle we have a simple unbiassed account of what was the opinion of Christians and others at that time.

Secondly, I t seems to me in the nature of the thing most probable, that some person was sent with extraordinary power to make this Enrolment. There is no evidence in *Josephus,* that *Augustus* had any intention to take away the Kingdome from *Herod* and make *Judea* a province. A Census in his dominions was a very great disgrace. But to have ordered it to be performed by the President of *Syria* would have been an additional affront. It would have looked like making *Herod* subject to *Syria.* Since *Judea* was to continue a distinct Kingdome, as hitherto, and only to be reduced to a more strict dependence, the only method of making this Census could be that of sending some person of honour and dignity, like *Cyrenius,* to enrole the subjects of *Herod,* and value their estates, that for the future, tribute might be paid according to this Census. And this does admirably suit the nature

ture of the oath mentioned in *Jofephus*, the fubftance of which was to be faithful to *Cefar* and *Herod*.

I conclude therefore, that it is upon the whole moſt probable, that the firſt affeffement, of which St. *Luke* here writes, was performed by *Cyrenius*, as well as the fecond. This appears to me a very natural meaning of St. *Luke*'s words, and the external evidences for this fuppofition feem to me to outweigh the objections.

I f any are ſtill of another opinion, I wiſh they would fupport *Herwaert*'s interpretation by at leſt two or three unexceptionable examples from fome good *Greek* writers.

W e have now got through the affair of the Cenfus. If I have not been fo happy, as to remove every difficulty attending this text of St. *Luke* ; yet I hope the reader will allow at leſt, that I have not concealed or diffembled any.

CHAP.

C H A P. II.

Two objections taken from the Silence of *Josephus*.

§. I. *He has not mentioned the slaughter of the Infants of* Bethlehem : §. II. *Nor of the* Galileans, *whose blood* Pilate *had mingled with their Sacrifices.*

§. I. **S**t. *Matthew* says : *Then* Herod, *when he saw that he was mocked of the wise men, was exceeding wroth, and sent forth, and slew all the children that were in* Bethlehem, *and in all the coasts thereof, from two years old and under, according to the time which he had diligently enquired of the wise men* *.

* Mat. ii. 16.

I t is objected to this, That if there had been so cruel a slaughter made by *Herod*, of innocent infants at *Bethlehem*, a place not far from *Jerusalem*, it is very unlikely it
should

fhould have been omitted by *Jofephus*, who has writ the Hiftory of the *Jews*, and particularly of the reign of *Herod*.

To this I anfwer : 1. This appears to me to be at the beft an objection of a very extraordinary nature. The moft exact and diligent hiftorians have omitted many events that happened within the compafs of thofe times of which they undertook to write. Nor does the reputation which any one hiftorian has for exactneffe invalidate the credit of another, who feems to be well informed of the facts he relates. *Suetonius, Tacitus,* and *Dio Caffius,* have all three written of the reign of *Tiberius* : but it is no objection against the veracity of any one of them, that he has mentioned fome things of that Emperour, which have been omitted by the reft. No more is it any objection against St. *Matthew,* that he has related an action of *Herod,* not mentioned by *Jofephus*.

2. THERE have been as great cruelties committed by many Eaftern Princes: nor was there ever any man more likely than *Herod* to give the orders here mentioned by St. *Matthew*. When he had gained poffeffion of *Jerufalem* (a) by the Affiftance of

(a) *Jofeph. Antiq.* l. 14. c. 16. §. ult.

the

the *Romans,* and his rival *Antigonus* was taken prifoner, and in the hands of the *Roman* General *Sofius,* and by him carried to *Mark Antony, Herod* by a large fum of Money perfwaded *Antony* to put him to death. *Herod's* great fear was, that *Antigonus* might fome time revive his pretenfions, as being of the *Afmonean* family. *Ariftobulus,* brother of his wife *Mariamne,* was murdered (*a*) by his directions at eighteen years of age, becaufe the people at *Jerufalem* had fhewn fome affection for his perfon. In the feventh year of his reign from the death of *Antigonus,* he put to death *Hyrcanus,* grandfather of *Mariamne,* then eighty years of age, and who had faved *Herod's* life when he was profecuted by the Sanhedrim ; a man, who in his youth, and in the vigour of his life, and in all the revolutions of his fortune, had fhewn a mild and peaceable difpofition (*b*). His beloved wife, the beautiful and virtuous *Mariamne* had a public execution (*c*), and her mother *Alexandra* followed foon after (*d*). *Alexander* and *Ariftobulus,* his two Sons by *Mariamne,* were ftrangled in prifon by his order (*e*)

(*a*) *Antiq.* xv. c 3. §. 3. *de Bell* L. i. c. 22.   (*b*) *Antiq.* 15. c. vi *de Bell.* ubi fupra.   (*c*) *Antiq* 15. c. vii. §. 5. 6. (*d*) Ibid. §. 8.   (*e*) *Antiq.* 16. c. xi. §. 6. *de Bell.* L. i. c. 27.

upon groundleſſe ſuſpicions, as it ſeems, when they were at man's eſtate, were married and had children. I ſay nothing of the death of his eldeſt Son *Antipater.* If *Joſephus*'s character of him be juſt, he was a miſcreant, and deſerved the worſt death that could be inflicted.

I n his laſt ſickneſſe, a little before he died, he ſent orders throughout *Judea,* requiring the preſence of all the chief men of the nation at *Jericho.* His orders were obeyed, for they were enforced with no leſs penalty than that of death. When theſe men were come to *Jericho,* he had them all ſhut up in the *Circus,* and calling for his Siſter *Salome* and her husband *Alexas,* he told them : My life is now but ſhort, I know the diſpoſitions of the *jewiſh* people, and nothing will pleaſe them more than my death. ' You ' have (*a*)theſe men in your cuſtody, as ſoon ' as the breath is out of my body, and be- ' fore my death can be known, do you let ' in the ſoldiers upon them and kill them. All ' *Judea* and every family will then, though ' unwillingly, mourn at my death'. Nay, *Jo-*

(*a*) Τὲς ἢ τὲς φρκεκμένκς ἄνδρας, ἐπειδὰν ἐκπνένσω, τάχιϛα κτείνατε περιϛήσαντες τὲς ϛρατιώτας, ἵνα πᾶσα 'Ικδαία κ̓ πᾶς οἶκ☮, ἄκων ἐπ' ἐμοὶ δακρύσῃ· *de Bell* i. c. 33. § 6.

fephus fays, ' That with tears in his eyes he ' conjured them by their love to him and their ' fidelity to God, not to fail of doing him ' this honour: And they promifed (*a*) they ' would not fail.

THESE orders indeed were not executed. But, as a modern hiftorian of very good fenfe obferves, ' The hiftory of this his moft wick- ' ed defign takes off all objection againft the ' truth of murdering the innocents, which ' may be made from the incredibility of fo ' barbarous and horrid an act.   For this ' thoroughly fhews, that there can nothing ' be imagined fo cruel, barbarous, and hor- ' rid, which this man was not capable of ' doing (*b*)'.

IT may alfo be proper to obferve, that al- moft all the executions I have inftanced in were Sacrifices to his ftate jealoufy, and love of empire. And the flaughter which St. *Matthew* has given an account of, was made up- on the occafion of tidings brought to *Jerufalem*, of the birth of one who was *King of the* Jews.

(*a*) Καὶ ὁ μ̃ μετὰ δακρύων ποτνιώμεν⊙, κ̃ τῶ συγγενῶς τὴν ἐυνόιαν κ̃ πίςιν τῶ Θεῖκ προσκαλῶν, ἐπίσκηπτε μὴ ἠτιμῶας ἀξιῶν· κἀκεῖνοι ὡμολόγυν ἃ παραβίσαϊ· *Antiq.* 17. c. vi. §. 5.
(*b*) *Prideaux Conn*. Part. ii. p. 655.

3. *JOSEPHUS* has given us an account of a terrible execution made in *Herod's* court, and at *Jerusalem* about this very time, upon the occasion of some predictions that God was about to take away the kingdome from *Herod*. I think it was made at the very same time with the slaughter of the infants. St. *Matthew* relates only what was done at *Bethlehem*, *Josephus*, what happened at *Jerusalem*. The Silence of *Josephus* about the former, and of St. *Matthew* about the later, may be in a good measure accounted for by these two or three considerations.

(1.) S*t*. *Matthew* was not concerned to relate state matters, but barely to give the history of Jesus Christ, and therefore all that he was obliged to take notice of upon this occasion was the attempts made upon the life of Jesus. *Josephus's* is a political history of the *jewish* nation, and therefore the executions at Court might be more suitable to his design.

(2.) A*ll* writers of good sense and candour, who have wrote the history of such jealous and cruel princes as *Herod*, have been obliged, both out of a regard to themselves, and their readers, to omit some of

5   their

their odious and offensive actions, and to pass
by some parts or circumstances of those transactions which they mention (*a*).   And I
cannot help paying a particular respect to the
Evangelists for the many instances of their
candour and goodnesse, and for this in particular, that they have none of them sought
to brand the memory of *Herod,* who sought
the life of Jesus, with the many cruelties of
his reign, nor the dreadful circumstances of
his death; and that *Matthew,* who alone
has informed us of the murder of the infants,   confined his narration to that, and
passed by all the other tokens, which, I doubt
not, *Herod* shewed at this time of a most
odious jealousy.

N o r would I blame *Josephus* barely for
the omission of the barbarities committed at
Bethlehem.   He has related many cruel actions of *Herod.*   To have related them all
would probably have appeared spite and ill
will, rather than faithfulnesse or impartiality.
It is evident there were many put to death
at *Jerusalem,* beside those he names in the
account of that execution.   Possibly the

(*a*) Neque sum ignarus, a plerisque scriptoribus, omissa
multa tum pericula & poenas, dum copia fatiscunt; aut
quae ipsis nimia & maesta fuerant, ne pari taedio lecturos ad-
ficerent, verentur. *Tacit. Ann,* l. vi. c. 7.

O 2   omission

omiſſion of the murder of the Infants may be owing to thoſe reaſons I have here hinted, namely, a fear of being charged with a deſign to load *Herod* unreaſonably, or a fear of rendering his hiſtory diſagreeable by too particular a detaile of cruel actions.

(3.) I HAVE thus far endeavoured to account for *Joſephus*'s ſilence in the way of apology for him, and ſhould be glad to leave the matter here : but his ſtrange way of ſpeaking, and that in two (A) places of his works, of an execution at *Jeruſalem* about this time, though according to his own account and acknowledgement it was very ſevere and terrible, will not permit me to conclude here. Suppoſing then that that execution was made on account of diſcourſes which happened at *Jeruſalem* upon the rumour of the birth of Jeſus, I think, that ſince *Joſephus* was determined in the main to vindicate *Herod* upon that occaſion, he was obliged for his own honour to ſay nothing of what was done at *Bethlehem*. The ſlaugh-

(A) One of thoſe paſſages with obſervations upon it may be ſeen above, p. 70.-86. It is the paſſage I referred to Vol. 1. p 278, as deſerving a *particular attention*. If the reader has not yet obſerved it, I would now recommend it to his peruſal. The other paſſage will be found toward the later end of §. 1. of the next chapter to this.

ter

ter of all the infants from two years old and
under, of a whole City, town, or village,
and the diſtrict round about it, whatever co-
lours an hiſtorian might have put upon it,
would have appeared to all mankind, but
prejudiced and hardened *Jews*, an horrid
inhumanity.

4. S T. *Matthew*'s account is confirmed
by the teſtimony of ancient Chriſtian Authors. I give one paſſage from *Juſtin Martyr*, who wrote before the middle of the
ſecond Century. ' But, ſays he, *Herod*,
' when the *Arabian* wiſe men did not come
' back to him as he had deſired them, but
' according to a command given them re-
' turned by another way into their own coun-
' try, and when *Joſeph* together with *Mary*
' and the young child were gone into *Egypt*,
' according to directions given to them alſo
' by a divine revelation, not knowing the
' child whom the wiſe men had come to
' worſhip, commanded all the children
' in *Bethlehem* without exception to be
' killed (*a*). This was propheſied of by *Je-*
' *remiah*, the ſpirit of God ſaying by him
' thus: *A voice was heard in Rama.----*

(*a*) Πάντας ἁπλῶς τὰς παῖδας τὰς ἐν Βηθλεὲμ ἐκέλευσεν ἀναι-
ρεθῆναι, Dialog. Part. ii. p. 304. *Pariſ.* (p. 307. *Thilb.*)

O 3　　　　　THIS

THIS is all I offer by way of anfwer to this objection.

THERE is however a noted paffage in *Macrobius*, a Heathen Author, who flourifh-ed in the later end of the fourth century, who among other jefts of *Auguftus* has this: ' When he [*Auguftus*] had heard that a-' mong the children within two years of ' age, which *Herod* King of the *Jews* com-' manded to be flain in *Syria*, his own fon ' had been killed, he faid : *It is better to be* ' *Herod's hog than his fon* (a).

I LAY little or no ftreffe upon this paffage, partly becaufe it comes too late, partly be-caufe there is reafon to fuppofe *Macrobius* has been miftaken about the occafion of the jeft. No early chriftian writers have faid any thing of *Herod's* having had a young child of his own killed in the flaughter at *Bethlehem*. If *Auguftus* did pafs this jeft upon *Herod*, it might be occafioned by the death of *Antipater*, or rather of *Alexander* and *Ariftobulus* (b).

(a) Cum audiffet inter pueros, quos in Syria Herodes Rex Judaeorum intra bimatum juffit interfici, filium quoque ejus occifum: ait, *Melius eft Herodis porcum effe quam filium.* Macrob. Sat. lib. 2. c. 4.   (b) See Doctor *Whitby's* An-not. on *Matt.* ii. 16, 17.

§. II. An objection of the like fort with that we have been considering, may be made against St. *Luke*, who says, *There were pre-sent at that season, some that told him of the Galileans, whose blood Pilate had mingled with their Sacrifices.* It has been ^{Luke xiii.} thought strange by some, that *Josephus* has made no mention of this event.

In answer to this objection, I shall trans-cribe a passage of *Josephus*. ' *Judas* the ' *Galilean* introduced a fourth sect among ' the *Jews*. In all other things they agree ' with the *Pharisees*, but they have an in- ' vincible love of liberty, and acknowledge ' God alone their Lord and Governour. Nor ' can any kind of death, or any punishments ' of their friends and relations make them ' call any man Lord. As many have been ' witnesses of their immoveable firmness, ' I shall say no more upon this head: Not ' out of a fear, lest my accounts should be ' thought incredible, but rather because it is ' not easy fully to represent their contempt ' of all kinds of sufferings (*a*).

(*a*) Ὁυ ρ̃ δέδοικα μὴ εἰς ἀπιϛίαν ὑποληφθῇ τι ϛ̃ λεγομένων ἐπ᾽ αὐτοῖς, τἐναντίον ἢ μὴ ἐλασσῶνως ϛ̃ ἐκείνων καταφρονήματ☉, δεχομένε τὴν ταλα.πωρίαν τῆς ἀλγηδόν☉, ὁ λόγ☉ ἀφρηῆται. *Antiq.* L. 18. C. 1. §. 6.

PERHAPS the *Galileans* mentioned by St. *Luke* were some of the followers of the before mentioned *Judas*. *Josephus* says he has omitted the greatest part of the sufferings of that Sect. I think it is not difficult to guesse the reason. *Judas's* principles were very popular among the *Jews*, but in the opinion of the *Romans* they were criminal, as being inconsistent with Subjection to their government. And it was next to impossible for *Josephus* to give a particular account of all transactions in *Judea* relating to this matter, without offending the *Jews* his countrymen on the one hand, or the *Romans* on the other.

BUT whether the *Galileans* mentioned by St. *Luke* were men of this principle is not certain, nor is it material. For though they were not, the passage just transcribed from *Josephus* may satisfie us, that many remarkable events have been omitted by him upon some account or other.

CHAP.

CHAP. III.

An objection againſt the Fifteenth year of the Reign of *Tiberius* compared with the age of Jeſus at his Baptiſm.

§. I. *The Obj. ſtated.* §. II. *The firſt Solution: That St.* Luke, *by the fifteenth of* Tiberius, *might intend the fifteenth of his Proconſular power, not of his ſole empire after the death of* Auguſtus. §. III. *The conſiſtence of other notes of time in the Goſpels with this Suppoſition.* §. IV. *The ſecond Solution: That the age of thirty years aſcribed to* Jeſus *at his baptiſm may be underſtood with latitude.*

S T. *Luke* ſays: *Now in the* FIF-TEENTH YEAR OF THE REIGN OF TIBERIUS CESAR, *Pontius Pilate being governour of* Judea.----*the word*

of

of God came unto John the son of Zacha-

rias in the wildernesse *.---- Now when all the people were baptized, it came to passe, that Jesus also being baptized, and praying the heaven was opened: And the Holy Ghost descended in a bodily shape like a dove upon him, and a voice came from heaven, which said, Thou art my beloved Son, in

thee I am well pleased. And Jesus himself
----BEGAN TO BE ABOUT THIRTY YEARS OF AGE.

AGAINST this account of St. *Luke* this objection may be formed.   St. *Matthew* says expresly, that Jesus was *born in Bethlehem of Judea in the days of Herod the king.*   But, though Jesus was born but a month or two before the death of *Herod*, he would be at left thirty one years of age at his baptism. But if Jesus was born above a year, much more, if above two years before *Herod's* death, then the age of *thirty years* here ascribed to him at his baptism is absolutely inconsistent with the notes of time mentioned at the commencement of *John* the *Baptist's* ministry: even allowing, that *the word of God came to John* in the very beginning of the *fifteenth year of Tiberius*, and that Jesus was baptized a few months after.

BEFORE

BEFORE I state this objection at length, I would observe, that the true genuine meaning of these words, *Jesus himself* (a) *began to be about thirty years of age*, is not that he then *entered* the thirtieth year of his age, but Jesus was about thirty years of age when he began his ministry : or *when* (b) *he thus began to shew himself publickly*. This, I think, is now the general opinion of (c) learned men.   So the *Greek* word of this text is used by St. *Luke* in other places. Thus the High Priests and others charge Jesus before *Pilate, saying, He stirreth up the people, teaching throughout all Jewry,* Lukexxiii BEGINNING [ἀρξάμενⓍ *having begun*] *from* 5. *Galilee to this place.*   St. *Peter* in the debate concerning the choice of an Apostle in the room of *Judas* says : *Wherefore of these men which have accompanied with us* ALL THE TIME *that the Lord Jesus went in and out among us,* BEGINNING *from the bap-*

(a) Καὶ αὐτὸς ἦν ὁ Ἰησᾶς ὡσεὶ ἐτῶν τριάκοντα ἀρχόμενⓍ, ὤν, κ. λ.   (b) Dr. *Clarke*'s Paraphrase.   (c) Lucae mentem Janfenius [Conc. cap. 14] optimè affecutus eft, quam fic exprimit: *Senfus erit, & ipfe Jefus erat fere tri-g.nta annorum, cum jam fufcepto baptifmo aufpicaretur deinde munus fuum.* Bafnage Annal. Pol. Ecc. ant. D. 5. n. 28. vid. & *Anton. Cappell.* de coenâ Chrifti fupremâ. Sect. 12. c. 23. Mr. *Whifton*'s fhort view of the harmony, &c. p. 136.

tifm

tifm (c) of *John*, unto the fame day that he was taken up from us, muſt one be ordained to be a witneſſe with us of his refurrection.

Acts i. 21. 22.

I COME now to the objection : *Auguſtus* died and *Tiberius* ſucceeded him the 19th. of *Auguſt*, A. U. 767, *Julian* year 59, A. D. 14. Therefore the fifteenth of *Tiberius* began the 19th. *Aug.* A. U. 781, A. D. 28. *Herod* died (A) before the Paſſover in A. U. 750, *Julian* year 42, or elſe before the Paſſover in A. U. 751, *Jul.* year 43. If then *John* the *Baptiſt* began to preach in the beginning of the fifteenth of *Tiberius*, in the later end of A. U. 781, and Jeſus be ſuppoſed to have been baptized by *John* a few months after, on the 6th of *January* of the year following, *viz.* A. U. 782; Jeſus muſt have been in the 32d. year of his life, if *Herod* died in the Spring A. U. 751, and if Jeſus was born the 25th *Decemb.* preceeding, *viz.* A. U. 750. But if *Herod* died A. U. 750, and Jeſus was born the 25th *Decemb.* before, *viz.* A. U. 749, then he would be at his baptiſm in the 33d. year of his age.

(a) 'Εν ᾧ ἐισῆλθε κỳ ἐξῆλθεν ἐφ' ἡμᾶς ὁ Κύρι☉ 'Ιησῦς, ἀρξάμενω☉ ἀπὸ τῦ βαπτίσματ☉ 'Ιωάννȣ·

(A) See the Appendix.

BUT

BUT it may be made appear feveral ways, that Jefus was born above a year, probably above two years before *Herod* died.

1. THIS may be inferred from the Evangelifts themfelves. For it is very probable that *Herod* lived a year or more after the murder of the infants. The wife men having worfhiped Jefus, when they were departed, *Behold the angel of the Lord appeared to Jofeph in a dream, faying, arife, and take the young child and his mother and flee into Egypt,* AND BE THOU THERE UNTIL I BRING THEE WORD: *for Herod will feek the young child to deftroy him. When he arofe, he took the young child and his mother by night, and departed into Egypt.* And *was there* UNTIL THE DEATH OF HEROD. The direction given to *Jofeph* by the angel, may afford ground to fuppofe, that *Jofeph* was to make fome ftay in *Egypt*, at leaft fome months, or more than a few weeks or days: which, from what follows, appears to have been *till the death of Herod.*

Matth. ii. 13.—15.

MOREOVER St. *Matthew* fays, that *when Herod was dead, Behold, an angel of the Lord appeared to Jofeph in a dream in Egypt, faying, Arife, take the young child*

and

and his mother, and go into the land of Ifrael: FOR THEY ARE DEAD WHICH SOUGHT THE YOUNG CHILDES LIFE.

v. 19, 20.

I T being known from *Josephus*, that *Antipater* died but five days before his father *Herod*, it may be inferred from the use of the plural number, that *Antipater* is meant by the angel as well as *Herod*, and that he had been concerned in the defign to put Jefus to death, and that his cruel intentions were one caufe of *Joseph's* removal out of *Judea* into *Egypt*. But *Antipater* could have no influence on his father's counfels for ten months or more before *Herod* died, as will appear prefently : therefore the murder of the infants happened, moft probably, a year before the death of *Herod*.

I T may likewife be concluded from Saint *Matthew's* account, that Jefus was born near two years before the murder of the infants. For thus he fays : *Now when Jefus was born in Bethlehem of Judea, in the days of Herod the king : Behold there came wife men from the eaft to Jerufalem, faying, Where is he that is born king of the Jews? for we have feen his ftar in the eaft, and* Matt. iii. 1 2. *are come to worfhip him.------Then Herod, when he had privily called the wife men,*

en-

enquired of them diligently what time the star appeared *.

* v. 7.

T H E wife men having been to worſhip the child, and departing into their own country without coming back to Jeruſalem, *Then Herod when he ſaw that he was mocked of the wiſe men, was exceeding wroth, and ſent forth, and ſlew all the children that were in Bethlehem and in all the coaſts thereof, from two years old and under, according to the time which he had diligently enquired of the wiſe men †.*

†—v. 16.

JESUS was born before the wiſe men came, for their queſtion was: *Where is he that is born?* They knew he was born, becauſe they had ſeen his ſtar in the eaſt. *Herod* enquired what time the ſtar appeared, and ſlew all the children from two years and under, according to that time. Therefore the ſtar had appeared two years before, and Jeſus was born at or near that time.

N o r can the ſuppoſed diſtance between the appearing of the ſtar and the arrival of the wiſe men weaken this calculation. There might be many reaſons to hinder their undertaking the journey immediately: Poſſibly, they apprehended no neceſſity of ſetting out ſooner. For allowing the truth of the fact,

that

that they had feen a ftar by which they underftood the birth of a King in *Judea*, they
could not well make any doubt of his living,
or of their having an opportunity to worfhip him, though they delayed a year or two.
But, whatever were the reafons of their delay, we have no right to depart from the
words of St. *Matthew*, who intimates very
plainly, that it was *two years* from the appearing of the Star to the time in which
Herod ordered the children to be flain.

ADD thefe two years to the forementioned year which *Herod* lived after the
flaughter of the children; and it will appear, that according to St. *Matthew*, Jefus
was born three years before *Herod*'s death.

2. IT may be proved from *Tertullian* that
Jefus was born above two years before the
death of *Herod*, for he fays, that the cenfus
or tax made in *Judea*, at the time of which
Jefus was born, was made (*a*) by *Sentius
Saturninus*. But *Jofephus* affures us, that
Quintilius Varus was come into *Syria* as
Succeffor to *Saturninus*, before (*b*) the death
of *Herod*. It may not be eafy to determine
exactly from *Jofephus* the time of *Varus's*

(*a*) Adv. *Marc.* lib. 4. c. 19. See above P. 182. (*b*) Antiq.
17 c. 5. § 2. & alibi.

arrival

arrival in *Syria* : But there are in being some
ancient Coins (*a*) or Medals of the City of
Antioch, the Capital of that Province, that
demonstrate the time of his government.
One of these coins has on the reverse a figure
representing the City of *Antioch*, and the
name of *Varus* with a date in *Greek* numerals xxv. And there are others with the
same figure and inscription, with the numerals xxvi, xxvii. The first of these coins
assures us, that *Varus* was in *Syria* before
September A. U. 748. For the Era which
the *Antiochians* used at that time was that
of the Actiac Victory, which was obtained
A. U. 723 (*b*). The 25th year of this Era
ended the second of *September* A. U. 748. It
is therefore manifest that Jesus was born before *September* in that year, if *Saturninus*

(*a*) Scripsit ad me Card. Norifius, extare in Scrinio illustrissi-
mi Marchionis Riccardi nummum minimae magnitudinis
caput jovis in antica repraesentantem, in cujus postica habetur,
ΕΠΙ ΟΥΑΡΟΥ ΑΝΤΙΟΧΕΩΝ, mulier sedens pede super figu-
ram Orontis fluminis, tenens dextrâ palmam : & in medio EK.
id est. Anno xxv. Pagi *appar. ad Bar.* n. 136. vid. omnino.
Norif. Epoch. Syromaced. Dissert. 3. c. 7. & Memoires de
l'Academie des Inscrip. Tom. 4. p. 181. ed. Amst.

(*b*) Doctor *Allix* supposes the *Antiochian* Era of the Actiac
Victory does not begin till A. U. 724. Vid. Dissert. de J. C.
Anno & Mense natali, p. 102. It is not my business to enter
into dispute upon this head. The other opinion seems to me
most probable. vid. *Norif.* ubi supra. *Pagi* Apparat. n. 103, 104.

P   made

made the Cenſus of which St. *Luke* ſpeaks, or if it was made in his time. And if it be ſuppoſed, that Jeſus was born on the 25th day of *December*, then his nativity muſt neceſſarily be placed as far back as the 25th. *Decemb.* A. U. 747.

3. I EXPECT likewiſe to be here reminded of ſome things advanced by me in the fiſt chapter of this Book; and that it will be urged: If the oath which *Joſephus* ſays was taken by all the *Jews* to *Auguſtus* and *Herod* relate to the Cenſus or enrolment which St. *Luke* ſpeaks of, then Jeſus muſt have been born about three years before the death of *Herod.*

POSSIBLY the objection may be ſtated in this manner.

IT cannot be leſs than ten months from the commencement of the enquiries made by *Herod* into the cauſe of *Pheroras's* death and the crimes of *Antipater* to the death of *Herod.* When the firſt diſcoveries were made, *Antipater* was at *Rome*. *Herod* ſent for him in a very preſſing but kind manner, diſſembling all ſuſpicions concerning him, that he might not delay to return to *Judea*. *Joſephus* ſays, that when *Antipater* returned, he knew nothing of the ac-

cuſations

cusations which had been brought against him, though (a) *seven months* had then passed from the first discoverie of his crimes. In a day or two after *Antipater's* return to *Judea Herod* calls a council, in which (b) he himself and *Varus*, Governour of *Syria*, presided. *Antipater* is brought before them, convicted and remanded to prison. But *Herod* not daring to pronounce sentence on *Antipater* without leave from *Augustus*, Expresses were sent to *Rome* with an account of what had passed. After that these messengers were sent away from *Judea*, a letter was intercepted, which was written to *Antipater* by *Acme* a jewish woman at *Rome* in the Service of the Empresse *Livia*, in which letter were fresh proofs of *Antipater's* designs. Hereupon *Herod* sent away fresh dispatches from *Rome*. These return to *Judea*, and bring word, that *Acme* had been put to death by *Augustus*, and that the Emperour left it to *Herod* to do with *Antipater* as he thought fit. Soon after this, *Antipater* was put to death, and in five days after *Herod* died (c).

(a) Καίτοι μεταξὺ ᾧ ἐλέγχων κỳ τῆς ἐπανόδȣ διελθόντων ἑπτὰ μηνῶν. *De Bell.* lib 1. cap. 31. p.1034. v 27.
(b) Ibid. cap. 32.   (c) Vid. *Joseph. de Lell.* lib.i. cap. 30; — 33. *Ant.* l. 17. cap. 3.——8.

As there was a fecond Ambafly fent to *Rome* after the trial of *Antipater*, and this returned before *Herod* died, with an account that *Acme* had been put to death, upon informations they had carried with them to *Rome*, it is impoffible to affign lefs than three months for the interval between the arrival of *Antipater* in *Judea* and *Herod's* death, which added to the former *feven* make *ten* months.

It being fuppofed in the *firft* chapter, that the execution which *Herod* made in his own family, happened at the fame time with the flaughter of the children at *Beth-lehem*, it muft next be confidered how long time that execution preceded the firft enquiries into *Antipater's* defigns. The facts mentioned by *Jofephus* in this interval ftand thus.

HEROD having put to death feveral of his courtiers and fervants, calls his friends together, charges *Pheroras's* wife with creating difturbances, and infifts upon it that *Pheroras* put her away. *Pheroras* loving his wife too well to comply with this demand, the two brothers fall out. *Pheroras* leaves *Herod* and goes to his Tetrarchy, withal fwearing folemnly never to come to *Herod*

Herod more. About this time, as it feems, *Antipater* with his father's confent left *Judea* and went to *Rome.* Soon after *Pheroras* was gone home, *Herod* fell fick. But though *Herod* fent for *Pheroras,* he would not come to him. Not long after, *Pheroras* is fick, *Herod* goes to fee him, they are reconciled, *Pheroras* dies. *Herod* has him brought to *Jerúfalem* and buried there (*a*).

WHEN *Pheroras* was buried, fome of his fervants made applications to *Herod,* defiring him to enquire into the manner and caufes of *Pheroras*'s death. Thefe enquiries open a horrid fcene of wickedneffe. And it appears, that a confpiracy had been formed by *Antipater* to poifon his father *Herod;* and that he had committed the execution of this defign to *Pheroras,* and fervants of his own whom he had left behind him when he went to *Rome,* and who were to obey *Pheroras*'s directions (*b*).

IT will not be eafie to allot lefs than three months for the facts juft now mentioned in the interval between the execution in *Herod*'s family and the firft enquiries into the

(*a*) *Jofeph. de Bell.* lib.i. cap. 29. §. 4. *Ant.* 17. cap. 3.
(*b*) *De Bell.* ibid. c. 30. *Ant.* ibid. 4.

caufe

caufe of *Pheroras's* death. Three months added to the former *ten* make *thirteen.*

THE execution fpoken of by *Jofephus* and the flaughter of the children mentioned by St. *Matthew* being allowed to have happened both at the fame time, the interval between the birth of Jefus and this execution is already computed. It cannot be lefs than a year and nine or ten months, that is, near two years; confequently, we have a frefh argument that Jefus was born *three* years before the death of *Herod.* But how inconfiftent this is with Jefus being *about thirty years of age* in the *fifteenth* year of *Tiberius,* appears from what has been faid already.

HAVING now ftated thefe objections and given them their full force, as I imagine, before I proceed to offer at a reply, I would make two or three reflexions upon fome particulars contained in them.

I DO allow, that it appears to me highly probable, that *Herod* did live a year at left after the flaughter of the infants.

BUT as for *Tertullian's* teftimony, that the Tax in *Judea* was made by *Saturninus,* I think it is not of much weight; fince he is the only perfon that has faid this, and he
flourifhed

flouriſhed not till about two hundred years after the event. Beſides, though *Tertullian* was well skilled in the Roman Laws and Cuſtoms, he has committed many groſs blunders in hiſtory. The reader may ſee ſeveral of them collected by (*a*) *Dodwell* in his Diſſertations upon *Irenaeus*. One of them is the computation *Tertullian* has made of the time from the nativity of Jeſus to the taking of *Jeruſalem* (*b*) by *Veſpaſian*; which, according to him, was not full fifty three years. And in reckoning up the reigns of the ſeveral Emperours he has quite omitted that of *Claudius,* and allotted not quite ten years to the reign of *Nero*. He, who could make ſuch miſtakes in the hiſtory of the Roman Emperours, might very eaſily be ignorant who was Preſident of *Syria* at the time of our Saviour's Nativity.

N o r am I ſatisfied with the proofs offered in theſe objections, that Jeſus was born near two years before the ſlaughter of the children at *Bethlehem*. Dr. *Whitby* (*c*) queſtions whether ἀπὸ διετὲς ϰ ϰατωτέρω ſhould not be rendered from *one year old* and under rather than from *two years* old and under.

(*a*) Diſſer. iii. §. xiii.   (*b*) Vid. *Tertul.* adverſ.
Jud. cap. 8.   (*c*) *Matth.* ii. 16.

         But

But let διετης fignifie two years, yet I think
no conclufion can be made about the
precife time of the birth of Jefus from
Herod's orders. It is moft likely, that this
ftar appeared fome time before the birth
of Jefus, and that it was underftood by the
wife Men to prefignifie it. Hereby they
were prepared for their journey, and it is
highly probable that thefe Wife men came into *Judea* to worfhip this King, as foon as
they could after they concluded he was born,
and that they arrived at *Jerufalem* in a very
few months after his birth. But fince their
enquiry was : *Where is he that* IS BORN
King of the Jews? *Herod,* whofe cruelty
had in a manner no bounds, orders all chil_
dren near *Bethlehem* to be flain who had been
born fince the appearing of the Star, or
perhaps even for fome fpace before the
time, at which, after an exact enquiry of
the wife men, he perceived it had appeared.

As there appears not to be any proof from
St. *Matthew,* that Jefus was born two years,
or near two years before the flaughter of the
infants ; fo, I think alfo, that there are no
proofs in *Jofephus* that the Oath taken by
the

the *Jews* had preceded two years or near two years the execution made in *Herod's* court. The Oath and the Execution are related by *Josephus* both together. The reader is referred to that paſſage, as alſo to the charge brought againſt *Pheroras's* wife immediately after that execution was over. A mong other things in that charge *Herod* ſays,-----*That ſhe did all ſhe could to create a difference be-tween him and his brother; that the fine impoſed upon the Phariſees had been evaded by her means; and that in the preſent af-fair nothing had been done without her. This preſent affair* I ſuppoſe to relate to the *predictions given out by the Phariſees, that God would take away the kingdome from Herod and his children.* The payment of the fine is the laſt crime ſhe is charged with be-fore this affair, which had preceded the exe-cution. It certainly therefore is not a crime of two years ſtanding. *Herod* in ſo long a time might have found out ſome new fault in a woman, he was ſo much offended with. We may be pretty well aſſured from this ac-count, if I miſtake not, that this Oath had preceded the ſaid execution and predictions but ſome few months only.

SUP-

SUPPOSING then the Execution to be truly dated, in the objection, at about thirteen months before the death of *Herod*, we may infer, that the *Oath* in *Jofephus*, and the *defcription* in St. *Luke* was made, and that Jefus was born about a year and fix or feven months before *Herod's* death.

IF indeed *Antipater* had been at *Rome* two years before he was recalled by his father, as fome learned men have thought, then this execution muft have been made above thirteen months before *Herod's* death; becaufe it is likely, or rather certain, that *Antipater* was in *Judea* at the time of that execution. But I think it is a miftake to fuppofe he had been fo long out of *Judea*. *Antipater* ftayed fome time in *Judea* after his brothers *Alexander* and *Ariftobulus* were (*a*) dead, and took a great deal of pains to defeat and fet afide the advantageous marriages which *Herod* defigned for their children : He alfo entered into cabals with *Pheroras* and his wife in order to fecure the Succeffion for himfelf. Moreover, *Saturninus* was got to *Rome* a good while before *Antipater* went from home. *Jofephus* fays in his *Antiquities*, that *Antipater* having refolved, if pof-

(*a*) Antiq. 17. c. 1.

fible,

fible, to haften his father's death, and being
defirous to ftrengthen and fecure his own intereft that he might reign after him, ' He re-
' mitted large fums of money to his father's
' friends at *Rome*, that he might gain their
' good will, but efpecially that he might have
' the favour of *Saturninus* the governour of
' *Syria*. (*a*) *Saturninus* is not here called
governour of *Syria*, becaufe he was then
actually in that Poft, for he is manifeftly
at *Rome* ; but to diftinguifh him from others
of that name, of which there were many.
And it appears from the parallel place in the
War of the Jews, that one favour which
Antipater defired of thefe perfons at *Rome*
who had influence on his father was, that
they would write to *Herod* that his [*Antipater's*] prefence at *Rome* would be fervice-
able to him in the prefent pofture of affairs.
Antipater had now fettled all things with
Pheroras for the poifoning of *Herod*, as
foon as an opportunity offered. But *Antipater*, fo long as he ftaid in *Judea*, could
not forbear converfing with *Pheroras* and
his wife, which was extremely difagreeable

(*a*) Καὶ μάλιϛα τὰς ἐπὶ Ῥώμης φίλας ΠΟΜΠΑΙΣ μεγάλων
δωρεῶν ἰώνας καθιϛάμενΘ-, πρὸ πάντων δὲ Σατυρνῖνον, τὸν τῆς Συρίας
ἐπιμ.λητήν. ibid. p. 7,50, v. 10.

to *Herod.* ' Therefore *Antipater* (a) con-
' trived by the intereſt of friends at *Rome*
' to procure leave for a voyage thither. Theſe
' writing, that it would be very proper for
' *Antipater* to be ſent to *Ceſar* without de-
' lay, he [*Herod*] immediately ſent him
' thither, having furniſhed him with a ſump-
' tuous equipage and large ſums of money,
' giving him alſo his Will to carry with him
' to the Emperour.'

I T is true, that after *Antipater*'s journey
to *Rome,* mention is made of *Saturninus* as
in *Syria:* but then it is, becauſe *Joſephus* relates a faĉt that had happened before *Antipater* went from *Judea. Joſephus,* giving
an account of what *Antipater* did at *Rome,*
mentions (b) ſome accomplices of *Syllaeus*
ſent thither by *Saturninus* to anſwer for
themſelves. But this might have been done
by *Saturninus* ſome time before.

A G A I N, if *Antipater* had been two years
out of *Judea, Herod,* who wanted plauſible
reaſons to induce him to return, could not
have failed to put this, of his long abſence,

(a) Πραγματίνεται, διὰ τ̃ ἐπὶ τῆς 'Ιταλίας φίλων, τὴν ἐις
'Ρώμην ἀποδημίαν αὐτῷ. γραψάντων ρ̃ ἐκείνων, δεῖν 'Αντίπατρον
πεμφθῆναι διὰ χρόνε πρὸς Καίσαρα, ὁ ἡ ἔτι μελλήσας ἐξέπεμψε,
χ. λ. de B. l. 1. c. 29. §. 2.   (b) De B. ibid. §. 3.
Antiq. 17. c. 3. §. 2.

into

into his letters, as a very cogent and unexceptionable argument, which yet he does not appear (a) to have done.

IT may be farther argued, that *Antipater's* journey to *Rome* did not precede the death of *Herod* two years. The very commencement of the enquiries into the death of *Pheroras* could not be above ten months before the death of *Herod*, as has been shewn already. A great progreſſe had been made in thoſe examinations, *Doris, Antipater's* mother, had been detected and put out of (b) *Herod's* houſe; *Mariamne* the High Prieſt's daughter (c) was alſo put away, and her ſon ſtruck out of a new Will *Herod* had made. ' When theſe things were doing, ' ſays *Joſephus, Bathyllus Antipater's* freed-' man arrived from *Rome.* And being put ' to the queſtion was diſcovered to have ' brought with him a freſh quantity of poy-' ſon to be given to his [*Antipater's*] mo-' ther and *Pheroras,* that if the former had ' failed to diſpatch the King they might try ' this (d) upon him.' Before *Antipater* had

gone

(a) See the ſubſtance of theſe letters, *De B.* l. 1. c. 31. §. 3. *Antiq.* 17. c. 5. §. 1.   (b) *Antiq.* 17. c 4. §. 2.   (c) Ibid
(d) Ἐν τέτῳ ᵟ ʹ κϳ Βάθυλλος ἐκ Ῥώμης ἀπελεύθερος Ἀντιπάτρε παρῶν, κϳ βασανισθεὶς εὑρίσκεται φάρμακον κομίζων τῇ τε αὐτῦ
μητρὶ

gone to *Rome* he had provided (*a*) poyſon for *Pheroras* to give his father. It is plain, that when *Bathyllus* was ſent from *Rome*, *Antipater* did not know whether *Pheroras* had made any uſe of the firſt poyſon or not, and that he had ſtill a full confidence in him. But if *Antipater* had been gone from *Judea* two years, and had heard nothing of the effect of that poyſon, ſuch a delay would have created ſuſpicions. Moreover this ſecond preparation appears to be ſent to back the former ; ſo that we may be aſſured, we are to go backward, not years, but only ſome months for the true time of *Antipater*'s leaving *Judea*.

ONCE more, the firſt opening of the en-quiries into the cauſes of *Pheroras*'s death has been laid at about ten months before the death of *Herod*. That *Antipater* was then but newly ſet out for *Rome*, may be inferred from hence. *Pheroras* being dead, *Herod* had him brought to *Jeruſalem*, honoured him with a funeral, and made great lamenta-tions for him. 'This, *ſays Joſephus*, was 'the beginning of ſorrow to *Antipater*

μητρί κ̀ Φερώρα, ὡς ἐι τὸ πρότερον μὴ ἄπτοιτο ϛ̄ βασιλέως, τότω γῶν μεταχειρίζοντο αὐτόν. ibid. §. 3. *de B.* 1. c. 31. §. 1.

(*a*) *Antiq.* ibid. §. 3. *De Bell.* ibid. c. 30. § 5.

'though

' though (a) he was then ſailed to *Rome*.
' God requiring of him the blood of his
' brothers. I ſhall give a particular relation
' of this whole affair, that it may be an ad-
' monition to all mankind to adhere to the
' practiſe of virtue.' If *Antipater* had
been then any long time out of *Judea*, *Joſephus* would have ſaid, though he was *then
at Rome*, or though he *had been ſome time
there*. It is poſſible, *Antipater* might have
been gone from home a month or two: but the phraſe here uſed by *Joſephus* ſeems
to me to import, that there were not yet
come to *Jeruſalem* any tidings of *Antipater*'s arrival at *Rome*.

I HOPE it will be excuſed, that I have
inſiſted ſo long upon this point. The ſuppoſition, that *Antipater* was gone to *Rome* before the removal of *Saturninus*, and two
years or more before the death of *Herod*, has
cauſed much confuſion in the chronology of
many learned men about this time.

THERE is in *Joſephus* another paſſage,
not yet obſerved by any one upon this occaſion, that I know of, which may help to
determine the time of the execution made

(a) Καὶ πένθος μέγα ἐπ' αὐτῷ προέθετο· τῦτο Ἀντιπάτρῳ κỳ τοίγε ἐπὶ Ῥώμης πεπλευκότι κακῶν ἐγένετο ἀρχὴ, τῆς ἀδελφοκτονίας αὐτὸν τινυμένε ễ Θεῦ. κ. λ. Antiq. 17. c. 3. §. 3.

by *Herod* in his court and at *Jerusalem*, and
which will confirm my opinion about it.
Josephus, having given the history of *Herod's*
putting to death his two Sons *Alexander* and
Aristobulus, makes divers reflections upon
that action. It might have been sufficient,
says he, even supposing them guilty of the
crimes laid to their charge, to have condemned them to perpetual imprisonment, or
to have banished them, but to take away
their lives was a piece of downright cruelty.
‘ Nor does the delay extenuate the crime,
‘ for after deliberation, having been resolved
‘ at one time and in suspense at another, to
‘ commit such a fact, is an argument of a
‘ bloody disposition, and of a mind obsti-
‘ nately bent upon wickednesse : Which
‘ same temper he shewed afterward upon
‘ another occasion, when he spared not others
‘ [or *the rest*] persons who seemed to be the
‘ most dear to him of any. The justice of
‘ their punishment abates our compassion
‘ for their ruine, but yet his cruelty was a-
‘ like here also, in that he spared not even ·
‘ them. But of these more in course (*a*)
‘ by and by’. HIS

(*a*) Ἐν ἐπιςάσει ἢ, ὃ πολλάκις μ̃ ὁρμηθέντα πολλάκις ἢ μελλή-
σαντα, τὸ τελευταῖον ἢ ὑποςῆναι κ̃ διαπράξαμ̃, φονώσης κ̃ δυσ-
μετακινήτ8

THIS laſt piece of cruelty I take to mean the execution made by *Herod* in his court, and which *Joſephus* relates afterward in the next book of theſe *Antiquities*. It cannot refer to the death of *Antipater*, becauſe he is but one ; nor to the deſign upon the *chief men of Judea* ſhut up in the *Circus*, becauſe they had committed no offenſe, and that deſign was never executed ; nor to the *Rabbies*, becauſe they do not appear to have ever been dear to *Herod*. But it muſt be the before mentioned *execution*, of which I hope the reader has a clear idea. Then *Herod* put to death all of his own family that adhered to the things ſaid by the *Phariſees*, and to other perſons that appear to have been favourites with him. And it is obſervable, that as in that account *Joſephus* is pleaſed to divert himſelf with thoſe executions ; ſo, here alſo, even when he is aggravating the cruelty of *Herod*, he betrayes the ſame good will toward thoſe who then ſuffered under the rage of this inhumane tyrant.

μεταχινῆτε ψυχῆς ἀπὸ τ̄ χειρόνων ἐδήλωσε ᾗ κỳ τοῖς αὖθις ἐκ ἀποχόμενος ὐδὲ τ̄ περιλοίπων ὅσες ἐδόκει φιλτάτες, ἐφ' οἷς τὸ μ̄ δίκαιον ἔλαττον ἐπόιει συμπαθείᾳ τὰς ἀπολυμένες, τὸ ᾗ ὠμὸν ὅμοιον ἦν, τῷ μηδὲ ἐκείνων φεισαμένῳˑ διεξίμεν ᾗ ὑπὲρ αὐτῶν ἑξῆς ἀφηγέμενοι· Antiq 16. c. ult. ad fin.

Q   IT

I T would be desirable here to settle exactly the time when these two sons of *Herod*
were put to death. Dr. *Allix* (*a*) places the
council of *Berytum,* before which they
were tried, and by which they were condemned, in the month of *May,* A. U. 749,
about ten months before *Herod* died. But if
Herod died in the Spring A. U. 750, as the
Doctor supposes, this council is certainly placed
by him too late. It is evident from particulars insisted on in the objection, and since allowed or mentioned by me, that it must have
preceded the death of *Herod* above ten
months. Moreover, *Saturninus* was one of
this council, and if the first Medal and the
epocha above mentioned be allowed, *Saturninus* was gone from *Syria* before *Sept.*
748. It may be, however, supposed, I think,
that this Council was not held long before
the removal of *Saturninus :* And it is certain from the passage just transcribed, that
the execution of the *Pharisees* and others
at *Jerusalem* happened some considerable
time after the death of *Alexander* and *Aristobulus.*

(*a*) —Conventum Berytensem qui habitus est in causa Alex-
andri & Aristobuli Maio mense A. U. 749. ibid. p. 18. vid. &
p. 13. & alibi.

IF

IF any ſhould object, that according to the account I have given of the *Oath* or Enrolment, that it was owing to the diſpleaſure of *Auguſtus* againſt *Herod*, it cannot be placed ſo near the end of *Herod's* reign as I here ſuppoſe, but muſt have happened a conſiderable time before the removal of *Saturninus* ; becauſe *Auguſtus* appears to have been reconciled to *Herod* before *Saturninus* left the province, and before the Council at *Berytum* in which *Alexander* and *Ariſtobulus* were condemned : I anſwer, that the enrolment is not placed by me too late at all. It might be reſolved upon by *Auguſtus* before, and yet not be executed till after *Saturninus* went away. And though *Auguſtus* might be in ſome meaſure pacified, yet he might think fit to have the aſſeſſement made. Beſides, though *Joſephus* ſays, that upon the applications *Nicolas* of *Damaſcus* had made to *Auguſtus* at *Rome*, the Emperour was reconciled to *Herod*, that *Syllaeus* was ordered home, required to pay the money he owed, and give all proper ſatisfaction, and was afterward (*a*) to be puniſhed : Yet it is certain, that

(*a*) Και πέρας εἰς τᵘτο κατέςη Καῖσαρ, ὡς ᵊ μ̅ Συλάιᵘ καταγνῶναι θάνατον, Ἡρώδη ᴐ διαλλάττεϑ —— τὸ ᴐ σύμπαν, ὁ μ̅ Σύλλαιος ἀνεπέμπετο, τὰς δίκας ᴐ τὰ χρέα τοῖς δεδανεικόσιν ἀποδώσων, ἔιτα ὅυτω κολασθησόμενος. Antiq. 16. c. 10. §. 9.

Syllaeus

Syllaeus did not give *Herod* or any one elfe fatisfaction. And it may be from thence inferred. that *Herod* was not fully reinftated in *Auguftus*'s favour, for then *Syllaeus* would have been more fubmiffive. *Jofephus* relating *Antipater*'s voyage to *Rome*, of which we have made frequent mention, fays:
' *Syllaeus* the *Arabian* (a) alfo went thither
' at the fame time, not having performed
' any of thofe things which *Cefar* enjoined.
' And *Antipater* accufed him to *Cefar* upon
' the fame heads he had been before accufed
' of by *Nicolas*.' From what has been faid concerning the time of *Antipater*'s journey it appears, that this accufation muft have been brought againft *Syllaeus* in the laft year of *Herod*'s life.

IT is evident, that *Herod*'s affairs were not in a good. pofture at this time at *Rome*. If they had, *Antipater* could not have made the ftate of them, and the fervice he might do his father there, a pretenfe for his journey. Moreover, *Antipater* (b) charged *Herod* with a fum of two hundred talents, laid out

(a) Συνεξορμᾶ ᾽ Ἀντιπάτρῳ ᾽ Σύλλαιος ὁ Ἄραψ, μηδὲν ὧν προσέταξε Καῖσαρ διαπεπραγμένος· ᾽ Ἀντίπατρος αὐτῶ κατηγορεῖ ἐπὶ Καίσαρος, περὶ ὧν πρότερον Νικόλαος. ibid. l. 17. c. 3. §. 2.

(b) Διακίσια γὰ ἀναλώματος ἀνήνεγκε τάλαντα, ᾽ τύτων μεγίστη πρόφασις ἦν ἡ πρὸς Συλλαῖον δίκη· De B. 1. c. 31. §. 2.

chiefly

chiefly, as he pretended, in the caufe againft *Sylla us*, his father's great enemy. From all which it is reafonable to conclude, that *Nicolas* had, in his hiftory, out of regard to his mafter and himfelf, magnified the fucceffe of his negociations at *Rome*. Nor can it be juftly expected from an Hiftorian, that, when he comes down to the affairs of his own time, he fhould be perfectly indifferent toward thofe in which he acted a part himfelf.

HAVING now cleared the way, I would lay down two or three conclufions.

1. I APPREHEND it appears from what has been here offered, that there is no neceffity of placing the birth of Jefus above a year and fix months before the death of *Herod*. If *Herod* died in *March* A.U.750, I fhould be inclined to place the nativity of Jefus in *September* or *October* A U. 748. If *Herod* died in *March* 751, then the nativity of Jefus might very well be placed in *September* or *October* 749. As I am not able fully to determine the time of *Herod*'s death, I fhall for the future have fome regard to both thefe dates of our Saviour's Nativity.

2. THE account that has been given above of the time of *Saturninus*'s removal,

and

and *Varus*'s arrival in the province of *Syria* does also incline us to one of these dates. It is not improbable, that the oath was taken or the assessment made much about the same time that *Varus* came into *Syria*. And it is supposed by many learned men, that the Roman Governours usually came from *Rome* into these Eastern Provinces at the later end of the summer. It is certain, that upon the removal of *Archelaus*, when *Cyrenius* came Governour into *Syria*, there was an assessment made in *Syria* and *Judea*. I am the rather inclined to think this the time of the Oath, because *Josephus* in his history does not relate it when it was taken, but mentions it only upon occasion of a disturbance at *Jerusalem* which had a connexion with it. And it is observable, that he has said nothing of *Varus*, nor of the concerns of *Syria*, till we hear of *Varus* being at *Jerusalem* when *Antipater* returned home. But, if those Medals are to be relied on, *Varus* had now been a good while in *Syria*. There is therefore in *Josephus* a long gap in the concerns of *Syria*, and also in the publick concerns of *Judea* from the council at *Berytum* to the Execution at *Jerusalem*. During this time of *Josephus*'s silence, I sup-

pose

pofe the affeffement was made. According
to the firft of the *Antiochian* Medals, *Varus*
came into *Syria* before *Sept.* 748. If this
be fuppofed the moft likely date of his government, and if it be alfo moft probable
that *Herod* died A. U. 750, thefe may ftrongly difpofe us to place the nativity of Jefus in
September or *October* 748.

3. T H E later part of the Summer, or
Autumn feafon feems to be the moft likely
time of the year for the birth of Jefus. There
is no particular reafon to determine us to the
25th of *December*. The very depth of
Winter is not a very proper feafon for a furvey
and affeffement, when people are to enter
themfelves according to their tribes or families. The Autumn, when Harveft and
Vintage are over, is a time of general leifure.
When Jefus was born at *Bethlehem*, *There*
were in the fame country fhepherds abiding
in the field, keeping watch over their flocks Lu!e ii.8.
by night. In fome very mild climates fheep
may be abroad in the night time in *Decem-*
ber. But it is not very likely, they fhould
be fo in thofe countries, where they muft be
attended with Shepherds. This circumftance is not very favourable to the fuppofition, that Jefus was born the 25th *Dec.*

and

and we are at liberty to place it in autumn, a more likely feafon.

I t is not improbable then, that Jefus might be born fome time between the middle of *Auguft* and the middle of *November*. *Cyrenius*, we may fuppofe, came into *Judea* at the time, or foon after the time that *Varus* came Governour into *Syria*, and publifhed the Decree of *Auguftus*, requiring all people to enter themfelves, their dependents, and eftates. *Judea* was a country of a narrow compaffe, and the affeffement might very well be made in two or three months. *Cyrenius* coming into the country, and being a man of difpatch in all his undertakings, being defirous alfo to haften to *Rome* to receive the honours decreed him for the Victory over the *Homonadenfes*, being alfo concerned to fet fail before the bad weather came on, appointed all people to enrole themfelves with all expedition within a certain limited time, which they did accordingly. *And all went to be taxed every one in his own city.* The fhort time appointed for this work may be fairly concluded from St. *Luke*'s hiftory of it. If the fpace of time allotted for it had been of any confiderable length, it cannot be thought but that *Jofeph* would

ver. 3.

would have taken an opportunity to go to
Bethlehem some while before the time of the
Virgin's delivery, or else have deferred the
journey till that was over. There is not the
left hint, that this journey was taken just at
this feason in obedience to a divine admoni-
tion. It is given us as the pure refult of o-
bedience to this decree of *Augustus*.

W E will now lay together a few events
of this time, in the order in which it may be
fuppofed they happened.

A B O U T a year and fix or feven months
before the death of *Herod*, foon after the arrival of *Varus* in the province of *Syria*, in
August or *September*, A. U. 748, or
749, *Julian* year 40, or 41, *Cyrenius* [or
fome other perfon of eminence] came into
Judea, an affeffement was made there, and
in the time of it, Jefus was born at *Bethlehem* in the month of *September* or *October*.
After the term of forty days was expired Jefus
was prefented at the Temple at *Jerufalem*,
and *Mary* made her offering according to the
Law. When thefe things were finifhed, they
went from *Jerufalem* and dwelt in fome
City of *Judea*, poffibly at *Bethlehem*. In
the year following, *viz.* A. U. 749, or 750,
about the beginning of *February*, came *wife
men*

Matt. ii. 2. *men from the eaſt to Jeruſalem, ſaying, where is he that is born king of the Jews?* They, being guided by the ſtar which they had ſeen in the eaſt, went and worſhipped him. After their departure, the Virgin and the child Jeſus being now fit for travelling, *Joſeph* was admoniſhed by *an angel to take the young child and his mother and flee into* v. 13. *Egypt,* which he did. *Herod* ſoon perceiving from the wiſe men's not returning to him, that he had been *mocked* by them, and being much enraged thereat, *ſent forth and ſlew all the children that were in Bethlehem, and in all the coaſts thereof, from two years* v. 16. *old and under, according to the time which he had diligently enquired of the wiſe men.* He alſo put to death at the ſame time divers *Phariſees,* and other perſons at *Jeruſalem,* ſome of his own family and attendants; who, being before in expectation of the coming of a great Prince who was to riſe up from among them, and by the arrival of the wiſe men had been confirmed in the belief that this event was now at hand, expreſſed themſelves in terms, which *Herod* and his ſon *Antipater* and their flatterers termed ſeditious. Immediately after theſe executions *Pheroras's* wife was called to an account alſo; as being
ſuppoſed

supposed to have entertained the same principles and expectations with these *Pharisees*, to whom she had lately shewn great favour in paying the fine imposed upon them for not entering themselves and taking the appointed Oath in the time of the forementioned assessment. *Pheroras* not submitting to the orders given him by *Herod* in council to put away his wife, *Herod* and *Pheroras* fell out. Hereupon, in the later end of *February*, or beginning of *March*, the same year *Pheroras* retires with his wife to his Tetrarchy. And *Antipater* having, before (*a*) this by various practices, and particularly by letters procured from *Rome*, disposed his father to consent to his making a Journey into *Italy*; and supposing, that by the execution now just over, all turbulent spirits had been awed and peace and quiet might ensue, sets sail for *Rome*. In the later end of *April* or the beginning

---

(*a*) The account of *Antipater*'s sending letters and presents to *Rome* is Antiq. 17. c. 1. §. 1. Of *Herod*'s last quarrel with *Pheroras*, his forbidding *Antipater* to converse with *Pheroras*, or his wife, of *Antipater*'s journey to *Rome*, and *Pheroras*'s retirement is ibid. c. 3. In the *War*, [l. 1. c. 29. §. 2.] *Antipater*'s letters to *Rome* and his journey are mentioned together: but as his journey is here also represented as the effect of advice brought from *Rome*, it is supposed that these letters were sent by him some time before. And *Pheroras*'s retirement is the thing next mentioned.

of

of *May* following, *Pheroras* dies, is brought to *Jerusalem* and buried. No sooner was the Mourning for him over, but his Servants apply to *Herod* to make enquiry into the causes of his death : and now in the middle of *May*, or soon after, the Examinations into this matter began; and though *Antipater* was sailed from *Judea* for *Rome*, and got at a distance from the place in which justice ought to be executed on him, and therefore, according to the ordinary course of things, it might have been supposed he was in safety; yet from this time the divine vengeance began to prepare itself against him, till at last it fell upon him for all his horrid crimes. The evidence was at first obscure and imperfect, but opened continually more and more. *Herod* in his letters to *Antipater* dissembled his resentments, but earnestly pressed his return to *Judea*. About the middle of *December*, seven months after the first enquiry into the cause of *Pheroras*'s death, *Antipater* arrived at *Jerusalem* : And is tried there before *Herod*, and *Varus* President of *Syria*, and condemned to death. *Herod* however, not daring to proceed to execute the Sentence without express leave from *Augustus*, sent Ambassadors to *Rome* with a

full

full account of what had paffed, and foon
after, a fecond Ambaffy, new evidence having been found after the departure of the
former. Thefe laft Ambaffadors return to
Judea with full power from *Auguftus* about
the middle of *March* A. U. 750, or 751:
foon after which *Antipater* was executed,
and in five days time *Herod* himfelf died,
about a year and five or fix months after the
birth of Jefus.

Upon the whole, I prefume it appears,
we lie under no neceffity of dating the
birth of Jefus before the later end of the
year of *Rome* 748, or 749. We hereby
in part abate the objection, as ftated above;
but ftill we have before us, undoubtedly, a
very great difficulty. We will now enquire
what can be faid to it.

§. II. 1. WHEN St. *Luke* fays, *Now in
the fifteenth year of the reign of Tiberius,--
the word of God came unto John*, he may
intend fome computation of the reign of
Tiberius, different from that of his fole empire after the death of *Auguftus*. It is no
unufual thing for the reigns of Princes to be
computed from feveral dates. There were
two computations of *Nebuchadnezzar's*
reign. For, as Dr. *Prideaux* obferves,
‘ *Nabo-*

' *Nabopollasar* King of *Babylon* being old
' and infirm took his son *Nebuchadnezzar*
' into partnership in the Empire, and sent
' him with an army into those parts [*Syria*
' *and Palestine*]. And from hence the *jewish*
' computation of the years of *Nebuchadnez-*
' *zar's* reign begins.---But according to the
' *Babylonians* his reign is not reckoned to
' begin till after his father's death, which
' happened two years afterwards. And both
' computations being found in scripture, it
' is necessary to say so much here for the re-
' conciling of them (*a*).' And there were
two or three ways of computing the reign
of (*b*) *Cyrus*.

B u t to come nearer to our time, there
were many computations of the reign of
(*c*) *Augustus*. Some computed the beginning of his reign from the year in which
Julius Cesar was killed, as (*d*) *Josephus*:
who says: *Augustus* reigned fifty seven years
six months and odd days. Some from the year
after, and reckoned his reign fifty six years.
Others computed from the year in which the

(*a*) Conn. Part. 1. p. 60.　　(*b*) *Marshall's* Treatise
of the 70 weeks, p. 44.　　(*c*) Vid. *Petav.* Rationarium
Temp. Part 2. l. 3. c. 15. *Pagi* appar. n. 66.---73. 103. 114.
(*d*) *Antiq.* 18. c. 2. §. 2. *De Bell.* 2, c. 9. §. 1.

victory

victory was obtained at (*a*) *Actium*, and say he reigned reigned forty four years; others from the year after, as *Ptolomee*, in his Canon, and St. *Clement* (*b*) of *Alexandria* ; and give him only forty three years. And *Herod* reigned thirty four years from the death of *Antigonus*, thirty seven from the time he was declared King of *Judea* by the (*c*) Roman Senate.

2. THERE seems to be very good reason to conclude from divers passages of the Roman historians and the most ancient Christian writers, that there were two different computations of the beginning of *Tiberius*'s reign, one from the time he was made Collegue with *Augustus*, and the other from his sole empire after the death of *Augustus*.

SEVERAL very learned men and very eminent chronologers (*d*) are of opinion, that St. *Luke* intends the former of these

---

(*a*) Atque ab eo tempore exercitibus comparatis, primum cum M. Antonio, Marcoque Lepido, dein tantum cum Antonio, per duodecim fere annos, novissime per quatuor & quadraginta solus Rempublicam tenuit. *Sueton.* in *August.* c. 8. vid. *Dio.* l. 51.   (*b*) Strom. p. 339. A Edit. *Parif.*

(*c*) *Joseph.* de B. 1. c. ult. §. 8 1. *Antiq.* 17. c. 8. §. 1.

(*d*) *Herwartus* in nova & vera chronologia cap. 248. *Uffer.* Ann. A. M. 4015. *Joann. Cleric.* Differtatio de Ann. vitae Christi. *Prideaux* Conn. Part. ii. Book 9. A. D. xii. *Pagi* Critic. in Baron. A. Chr. 11. 71.

two

two computations. I fhall give a brief account of the grounds there are for this fuppofition, taken chiefly from Doctor *Pagi*; who appears to have beftowed a great deal of pains upon this argument, and muft be allowed to have treated it with great accuracy and judgment.

(1.) T н а т *Auguftus* did in part lay afide government fome time before he died, may be inferred from the words of an uncertain author of a Panegyrick, in which, in the name of the City of *Rome* he diflwades *Maximianus Herculeus* from refigning the Empire. ' Is it fit, *fays he*, that you fhould ' now give your felf a difcharge, and do that ' fo foon, which *Auguftus* did not do till after ' the feventieth year of his age, and the fif- ' tieth of (*a*) his reign?'

(2.) S е v е r a l of the Roman hiftorians have exprefly mentioned *Tiberius*'s being taken into partnerfhip in the Government with *Auguftus*.

(*a*) Quoufque hoc Maximiane, patiar, me quati, te quiefcere, mihi libertatem adimi, te ufurpare tibi illicitam miffionem? An quod Divo Augufto poft feptuaginta aetatis, quinquaginta imperii, non licuit annos, tam cito licuit tibi? Panegyr. cap. 11. laudat. a *Pagio*. Critic. *A.* Ch. 11. n. iii.

VELLEIUS

VELLEIUS PATERCULUS, who lived in the reigns of these two Emperours, says, ' that at the desire of *Augustus* there ' was a law passed by the Senate and People ' of *Rome,* that *Tiberius* might have equal ' power with him in all the provinces and (*a*) ' armies'. *Suetonius* says, ' There was a ' Law made, that *Tiberius* should govern ' the provinces jointly with *Augustus,* and ' make the Census with (*b*) him'. *Tacitus* says ' That *Tiberius* was made collegue in ' the Empire (with *Augustus*) taken into ' partnership with him in the Tribunician ' power, and recommended (*c*) to all the armies'.

(*a*) Cum res Galliarum maximae molis, accensasque plebis Viennensium dissensiones, coercitione magis quam poenâ molliffet, & Senatus Populusque Rom. (postulante patre ejus) aequum ei jus in omnibus provinciis exercitibusque effet, quam erat ipsi, decreto complexus effet.——in urbem reversus, jampridem debitum, sed continuatione bellorum dilatum, ex Pannoniis Dalmatiifque egit triumphum. *Vellei.* lib ii. cap. 121.

(*b*) A Germania in urbem post biennium regreffus, triumphum quem distulerat egit———Dedicavit & Concordiae aedem: item Pollucis & Castoris, suo fratrifque nomine, de manubiis. Ac non multo post lege per Coff. lata, ut provincias cum Augusto communiter administraret; simulque censum ageret, condito lustro in Illyricum profectus est. *Suet.* in *Tiber.* cap. 20. 21.

(*c*) Drufoque pridem extincto, Nero solus è privignis erat : illic cuncta vergere: filius, collega imperii, confors tribunitiae

' armies'. And there are in this laſt mentioned
(*a*) Hiſtorian frequent references to *Tiberius*'s
partnerſhip in the empire with *Auguſtus.*

I MUST be allowed to be particular in
the account of ſome things ſaid by *Dio.* In
his hiſtory of the affairs A. U. 765, A.D.
12. he ſays : ' *Auguſtus* (*b*) now advanced
' in years, recommended in a writing *Ger-*
' *manicus* to the Senate, and the Senate to
' *Tiberius.* He did not however read the
' writing himſelf (not being able) but *Ger-*
' *manicus*, as he had been wont to do.----
' But yet he did not lay aſide the care of
' the public.'---Under the next Year, A. U.
766. A. D. 13. the ſame hiſtorian ſays :
' *Auguſtus* then accepted (*c*) for the fifth

poteſtatis adſumitur, omniſque per exercitus oſtentatur. *Tacit.
An.* lib. 1. cap. 3.

(*a*) Etenim Auguſtus, paucis ante annis, cum Tiberio Tribuniciam poteſtatem A PATRIBUS RURSUM poſtularet, &c.
id. ibid. c. 10 Verſae inde ad Tiberium preces. Et ille variè
differebat, de magnitudine imperii, ſua modeſtia : ſolam Divi
Auguſti mentem tantae molis capacem: ſe in PARTEM CURARUM
VOCATUM, experiendo didiciſſe, quam arduum,---regendi cuncta
onus. ibid. c.-11.

(*b*) Ὁ ϳ δὴ Ἀύγυϛος ἐκειϳόν τε, ὡς ϰ ἐπὶ γήϱως ὼν, τῇ βυλῇ,
ϰ ταύτην τῷ Τιβεϱίῳ παϱακατέϑετο· ἀνέγνω ϳ τὸ βιβλίον ὐκ ἀυϳὸς
(ὐ γὰϱ οἱός τε ἦν γεγωνίσκειν) ἀλλ' ὁ Γεϱμανικὸς, ὣςπεϱ ἐιώϑει.
---ὐ μέντοι ἑ τἄλλα ἧτϳόν τι παϱα τῦτο διώκει. Dio. l. 56.
p. 587. B. C.   (*c*) Τήν τε πϱοϛασίαν ῆ κοινῶν τὴν
δεκέτιν, τὴν πέμπτην ἄκων δὴ ὁ Ἀύγυϛος ἔλαβε, ϰ τῷ Τιβεϱίῳ τὴν
ἐξυσίαν τὴν δημαϱχικὴν ἀυϑις ἴδωκε. ibid. p. 588. B.

time,

' time, though unwillingly, the government
' of the ſtate for ten years, and renewed alſo
' the Tribunician power to *Tiberius*.' He
ſays alſo, ' That *Auguſtus* (a) on account
' of his great age (which likewiſe hindered
' his coming to the Senate, except very rare-
' ly) deſired he might have twenty annual
' counſellors.----And a decree was paſſed, that
' whatever was enacted in council by him,
' together with *Tiberius*, and thoſe ſaid
' counſellours, and the Conſuls in being, and
' the Conſuls elect, and his Grandſons adop-
' ted by him, and any others whom he
' ſhould call to his council, ſhould be ratified,
' and deemed of the ſame authority, as if
' enacted by the authority of the whole
' Senate.' This mention of *Tiberius*, and
of him only by name , in this Decree of
the Senate, next after *Auguſtus*, appears to
me remarkable. I do not obſerve that any
of theſe paſſages of *Dio* have been quoted
by *Pagi*. For what reaſon he omitted them
I do not know. He has however inſiſted

(d) Καὶ συμβάλας, ὑπὸ ᵗ γήρως (ὑφ' ἅπερ ἐδὲ ἐς τὸ βαλευτήριον
ἔτι, πλὴν σπανιώτατα, συνεφοίτα) εἴκοσιν ἐτησίας ᾐτήσατο——ᵏ
προσεψηφίσθη, πάνθ' ὅσα ἂν αὐτῷ μετά τε ᵗ Τιβερία ᵏ μετ'
ἐκείνων, ᵗ τι ἀεὶ ὑπατευόντων, ᵏ ᵗ ἐς τῦτο ἀποδεδειγμένων, ᵗ
τι ἐγγόνων αὐτᵘ ᵗ ποιητῶν δηλονότι, ᵗ τε ἄλλων ὅσας ἂν ἑκάστοτε
προσπαραλάβῃ, βαλευομένῳ δόξῃ, κύρια, ὡς ᵏ πάσῃ τῇ γερυσίᾳ
ἀρίσαντα, ἶναι. ibid. C. D.

R 2   upon

upon another paſſage of this historian taken from the preceding year, *viz.* A. U. 764. A.D. 11. But his argument from it ſeems to me to be founded upon a forced and arbitrary conſtruction of *Dio :* and therefore I content my ſelf with referring the reader for it to (*a*) him, and (*b*) Monſieur *Le Clerc*, who alſo lays a ſtreſſe upon it.

ONCE more, *Dio* ſays, that upon the death of *Auguſtus* ' *Tiberius* immediately ' (*c*) ſent away letters from *Nola* to the ar- ' mies and all the provinces, as Emperour : ' but yet did not call himſelf ſo, though ' that, with other titles, had been given him ' by a decree'.

(3.) THERE is a particular fact related of *Tiberius* by ſeveral Hiſtorians, ſaid to be done by him when *Prince*, which yet muſt have been done before *Auguſtus* died. *Plinie* ſays, that *Tiberius* was much given to drinking : ' And that it was thought, that ' for this reaſon *Lucius Piſo* had been choſen ' by him to be Prefect of *Rome*, becauſe he ' had continued two days and two nights

(*a*) A D. 11.n. 13, 14, 15.   (*b*) Ubi ſupra.

(*c*) Τοιȣτος ȣν δη τις ων, ἐς τε τὰ ςρατόπεδα κỳ ἐς τὰ ἔθνη, πάντα, ὡς Ἀυτοκράτωρ, ἐυθὺς ἀπὸ τῆς Νώλης ἀπέςειλε, μὴ λέγων ἀυτοϗάτωρ ἐιναι· ψηφισθὲν ᷅ ἀυτῷ κỳ μιτὰ Ϯ ἄλλων ὀνομάτων, ἐκ ἰδέξατο. Dio. l.57. p.602. D.

' drinking

' drinking with him (a) when *Prince*'.
Suetonius fays, that *Tiberius* in his firft cam-
paines, was much reflected on for his exceffe
in drinking, and that, ' Afterwards when
' Prince, in the very time of the Correction
' of the public manners he fpent a night and
' two days in eating and drinking with
' *Pomponius Flaccus* and *Lucius Pifo*, to the
' former of which he gave immediately the
' province of *Syria*, and to the other the
' prefecture of the City *(b)*'.

IT may be worth while to obferve with
Pagi, that thefe two writers who tell us the
ftory of this drunken bout of *Tiberius*, and
the confequences of it, feem not to have
had their accounts from one and the fame
fource. They differ from each other in two

(a)———Tribus congiis (unde & cognomen illi fuit) epotis
uno impetu, fpectante miraculi gratia Tib. principe, in Senecta
jam fevero atque etiam faevo alias, fed ipfa juventa ad merum
pronior fuerat: eaque commendatione credidere L. Pifonem
urbis Romae curae ab eo delectum, quod biduo duabufque
noctibus perpotationem continuaffet apud ipfum jam PRINCIPEM.
Plin. Nat. Hift. lib. 14. cap. 22.

(b) In caftris tiro etiam tum, propter vini aviditatem pro
Claudio, *Caldius*, pro Nerone *Mero* vocabatur. Poftea PRIN-
CEPS in ipfa publicorum morum correctione cum Pomponio
Flacco & L. Pifone noctem continuumque biduum epulando
potandoque confumpfit: quorum alteri Syriam provinciam,
alteri praefecturam urbis confeftim detulit. *Suet.* in Tib.
cap. 42.

of

or three particulars: One fays, that this piece of exceffe lafted *two days and two nights*; the other, *one night and two days.* *Plinie* mentions only the preferment of *Pifo,* *Suetonius* adds that of *Flaccus* alfo. But they both agree in faying, that *Tiberius* was *then Prince*; and *Suetonius* adds a very particular circumftance as to the time, that it was during the correction of the public manners, which may very naturally lead us to what he had faid of the Law paffed, that *Tiberius* fhould govern the provinces jointly with *Auguftus* and make the Cenfus with him; one part of which at *Rome* was the Correction of manners.

B u t we muft enquire fomewhat more particularly into the time of this act of intemperance. It may be eafily inferred from *Tacitus :* who relating the affairs of the year in which *Domitius Aenobarbus* and *M. Furius Camillus* were Confuls, fc. A. U. 785, A. D. 32. fays: ' Then *Pifo* had the ' honour of a public funeral by decree of ' the Senate, having behaved in his office to ' general fatisfaction for (*a*) twenty years'.

(*a*) Dein Pifo viginti per annos pariter probatus, publico funere ex decreto Senatus celebratus eft. *Tacit. Ann.* lib. vi. cap. 11.

' If

If we go back twenty years, we are brought
to the 12th year of the Chriſtian Era, and the
765th of the City; in which year, according to *Tacitus*, *Piſo* muſt have been prefect
of *Rome*, which is two years before the
death of *Auguſtus*.

THERE are however ſome objections to
this ſtory, which muſt be conſidered before
we leave it. Several (*a*) learned men would
read in *Tacitus* X. inſtead of XX. But to
this Doctor *Pagi*'s reply is ſufficient, that
this emendation is without the authority of
any Manuſcripts. It is likewiſe objected,
that *Pomponius Flaccus* was not Prefect of
Syria till long after the year of the City 765 :
conſequently, neither was *Piſo* then made
Prefect (*b*) of *Rome*. Dr. *Pagi* (*c*) allows
very readily, that *Pomponius* did not at this
time go Prefect into *Syria* ; but then he
gives ſeveral inſtances of men who have been
nominated governours of provinces, who
yet never went into them; one is *Aelius*

─────────

(*a*) Lipſius in loc. *Noriſ. Cenot. Pil. Diſſ.* ii. p.324.

(*b*) Sed hoc amplius ex Suetonio colliges, factum Piſonem
Praefectum, ſub idem tempus quo Pomponius Syriae Praetor.
Ille autem Syriae non ante annum 773 praeponi potuit (Maeſiam
enim provinciam adminiſtrabat, A.772.uti ex *Tacit.* lib. ii. clarum:)
non ergo tot annos Piſo Praefectus urbi. *Lipſius* ubi ſupra.
vid. etiam *Noriſium* ibid.

(*c*) A. Chr. 11, n. v.

Lamia,

Lamia, who by this very fame Emperour had been nominated prefect of the fame province likewife, namely of *Syria,* but yet never went thither. The fact is taken notice of by (*a*) *Tacitus,* and (*b*) *Dio,* which laft obferves, that this was a common practife with *Tiberius. Tacitus* has mentioned another like inftance in the reign of *Nero* (*c*).

ANOTHER objection againft *Pifo's* being made prefect of the City A. U. 765, is this: *Suetonius* fays, that this exceffe of *Tiberius* was committed during the public correction of manners: By which he has been fuppofed to refer to *Tiberius's* being made Cenfor with *Auguftus.* But Cardinal *Noris* objects, that the Cenfus was not made by *Auguftus,* A. U. 765, but 767. And

(*a*) Extremo anni [A. U. 786. A. D. 33] Mors Aelii Lamiae funere cenforio celebrata, qui adminiftrandae Suriae imagine tandem exfolutus, urbi praefuerat. *Tacit. Ann.* lib. vi. c. 27.

(*b*) Τότε Πείσωνα τὸν πολίαρχον τελευτήσαντα δημοσίᾳ ταφῇ ἐτίμησε, κ̀ Λύκιον (legendum Λάμιον, id eft Lamiam) ἀντ' αὐτῦ ταμίαν ἀνθείλετο, ὃν πρόπαλαι τῇ ϛρατιᾷ (legendum Συρίᾳ) Muretus in Tacit. An. vi.) προςάξας κατεῖχεν ἐν τῇ Ῥώμη. τῦτο δ κ̀ ἐφ' ἑτέρων πολλῶν ἐποίει, ἔργῳ μ̄, μηδενὸς αὐτῶν δεόμενος, λόγῳ δ̀, τιμᾶν αὐτὺς προσποιύμενος· Dio. lib. 58. p. 633 D.

(*c*) Syria P. Anteio deftinata, & variis mox artibus elufus, ad poftremum in urbe retentus eft. *Tacit. Ann.* lib. 13. cap. 22.

he

(a) he is of opinion, that the *public correction of manners* which *Suetonius* here speaks of intends the Edicts which *Tiberius* published against Luxury A. U. 775. For my own part, I cannot see, but that the words of *Suetonius* may very well refer to the time in which *Tiberius* was decreed Censor with *Augustus*, which might be done A. U. 765 : though the Census was not made, or at left not finished, till the year 767.

B U T that this *correction of manners*, which *Suetonius* here speaks of, is not that which he has himself mentioned in another (b) place ; and which *Tacitus* says was made A. U. 775 (c), may be made evident from two or three passages not particularly insisted on by *Pagi*. *Seneca* says, that *Tiberius* gave secret directions of importance to *Piso*, when he went into *Campania*, at which time there were divers uneasinesses and dis-

---

(a) Sed Suetonius si *censorem* Tiberium significaret, annum U. C. 767. designasset, quo *ipsa publicorum morum correctio* a censoribus peracta est. Itaque designat tempus, quo Tiberius publicis edictis urbano luxui Modum ponebat, A. U. 775. ibid. p. 324. vid. eund. p. 329.   (b) In Tib. cap. 34.
(c) Caius Sulpicius, D. Haterius consules sequuntur. Inturbidus externis rebus annus, domi suspecta severitate adversum luxum. *Ann.* L. iii. cap. 52.

contents

contents in the City (*a*). This Journey of
Tiberius was made in the beginning of the
year before that, in which the Edicts were
published for the suppressing of luxury,
namely in the year of the City 774, as appears from *Tacitus* *b*). It is plain therefore, that *Piso* was Prefect of *Rome* in 774,
and in the very beginning of it: and it may
be supposed, that *Tiberius* had had considerable experience of *Piso's* fidelity and ability
in that post before that, since he relied upon
him in a very critical conjuncture.

CARDINAL *Noris* objects (*c*) farther: It is
true *Tiberius* had proconsular power in the
provinces two years before *Augustus's* death:
all the authority he had in the city was owing to his Tribunician power, but that included

(*a*) L. Piso, urbis custos, ebrius ex quo semel factus est,
fuit, majorem partem noctis in convivio exigebat. usque in
horam sextam fere dormiebat: hoc erat ejus matutinum.
Officium tamen suum, quo tutela urbis continebatur, diligen-
tissime administravit. Huic & Divus Augustus dedit secreta
mandata, cum illum praeponeret Thraciae, quam perdomuit,
& Tiberius proficiscens in Campaniam, cum multa in urbe &
suspecta relinqueret & invisa. *Seneca* ep. 83.

(*b*) Sequitur Tiberii Quartus, Drusi secundus consulatus.
ejus anni principio Tiberius, quasi firmandae valetudini, in
Campaniam concessit: longam & continuam absentiam paula-
tim meditans. *Tacit. Ann.* lib. iii. cap. 31.

(*c*) His accedit, Tiberium in provinciis biennio ante mortem
Augusti imperium obtinuisse; intra urbem vero non habuisse,
nisi

cluded only a right of interceding or forbidding, but could not give the power of appointing a Prefect.

I THINK it is undoubted, that *Tiberius* might call the Senate by virtue of the Tribunician power (*a*), and it is likely do several other things. But there is no need of contending about this point. Perhaps *Tiberius* did not nominate and appoint *Pifo* Prefect of the City : He might however recommend him fo effectually to *Auguftus*, his Collegue, that he might appoint him. Dr. *Pagi* obferves, that *Plinie*, fpeaking of this matter, ufes the word *choofing*, not appointing (*b*).

I IMAGINE, that this fact is now cleared up and vindicated againft the feveral objections which have been made to it, and that *Pifo* was *appointed* or *chofen* to be Prefect of the City of *Rome* by *Tiberius, then Prince,* two years before the death of *Auguftus,* namely, in A. U. 765.

BUT before I quite leave this ftory, I would ftrengthen the argument founded up‑

---

nifi jus intercedendi ob tribuniciam poteftatem. Quare unus Auguftus Urb's praefecti defignandi poteftatem habebat. *Norif.* ibid. p. 324.

(*a*) Vid. *Uffer. Ann.* A. M. 4015. & 4017.

(*b*) Eàque commendatione credidere L. Pifonem Urbis Romae curae ab eo *delectum.* vid. *Pagi. Crit.* ad an. Ch. 11. n. iv.

on it by a remark or two upon the Title of *Prince* given here to *Tiberius* by *Plinie* and *Suetonius.*

I⊤ is well known that *Prince* was the foft title, which *Auguftus* chofe rather than that of (*a*) King or Dictator. This title therefore, when ufed abfolutely, is equivalent to Emperour : And *Dio* fays, that *Tiberius* had the title of Emperour given him by a decree, before *Auguftus* died, as has been obferved already. Moreover this title of Emperour is frequently given by *Roman* and *Greek* Authors to *Titus* and *Trajan* on accounts of their tribunician and proconfular power, which they enjoyed, the former in the life-time of his father *Vefpafian*, the later, of *Nerva.* Doctor *Pagi* thinks, this title of Emperour which was given to thefe Collegues in the Empire was founded particularly on the perpetual proconfular power in all the provinces (*b*). But however that

(*α*) Qui cuncta difcordiis civilibus feffa, nomine Pʀɪɴᴄɪᴘɪs fub imperium accepit. *Tacit. Ann.* lib. 1. cap. 1. Non regno tamen, neque dictatura, fed ᴘʀɪɴᴄɪᴘɪs nomine conftitutam Rempublicam. *id. ibid.* cap. 9.   (*b*) Titus enim, quemadmodum & ante eum Tiberius, ac poft eum Trajanus, imperii Collega fuit, ideoque imperatoris titulo exornatus. Imperii collegae Tribunicia poteftate, & imperio proconfulari donabantur, ratione cujus imperatores nuncupati. *Pagi.* A. D. 71. n. iii. *in Crit. ad Bar.*

be,

be, it is certain, they are often called Emperours. *Jofephus* in his defcription of *Vef-pafian*'s and *Titus*'s triumph at *Rome* after the *jewifh* war, fays, That the (a) Emperours lodged the night before near the temple of *Ifis*. *Plinie* the elder in his dedication of his Natural Hiftory to *Titus*, written before the death of *Vefpafian*, calls *Titus Emperour* (b) more than once. *Philoftratus* fays, that *Titus* was declared Emperour at *Rome*, and admitted to equal power in the government (c) with his father. It is in vain therefore to fay, that *Titus* was called Emperour in his father's life-time purely on account of his having been faluted Emperour by his Soldiers in the Camp, or in the Senfe in which this word was ufed under the Commonwealth, fince *Philoftratus* fays he was declared Emperour at *Rome*.

(a) Ἐκεῖ γὰρ ἀνεπαύοντο τῆς νυκτὸς ἐκείνης οἱ αὐτοκράτορες. *Jofeph.* de Bell. lib. vii. cap. v. p. 1305. v. 2.

(b) Jucundiffime Imperator——Sciantque omnes quam ex aequo tecum vivat imperium. Triumphalis & Cenforius tu, fexiefque conful, ac Tribuniciae poteftatis particeps. *Plin.* in Praefat.

(c) Ἀναρρηθεὶς ἢ Αὐτοκράτωρ ἐν τῇ Ῥώμῃ, κὴ ἀριστείων ἀξιωθεὶς τούτων, ἀπῄει μὲν ἱσομοιρήσων τῆς ἀρχῆς τῷ πατρί κ. τ. λ. Cumque imperator Romae effet appellatus, omnibus ornatus dignitatibus, Romam iter ingreffus, ut patris collega fieret. *Philoft.* vit. Appollonii lib. vi. cap. 30. p. 269. *Lipfiae.* 1709.

More-

Moreover *Capitolinus* (*a*) calls *Vespasian* and *Titus Princes* without any diftinction. All thefe paffages thus laid together may fatiffie us, that *Prince* and *Emperour* are equivalent in thefe writers; and that *Tiberius* had a right to the title of Prince, even during the life-time of *Augustus*, after he was made his Collegue in the Empire. I fhalt refer the reader to but one paffage more, in which *Plinie* the younger affures us, that *Trajan* was declared Emperour (*b*) by *Nerva* in his life-time. And it feems very ftrongly to fupport Doctor *Pagi's* opinion, that the title of Emperour given to thefe Collegues was founded rather on their Proconfular empire than their Tribunician power.

(4.) T H E R E are two or three verfes of *Dionyfius* the geographer, which Doctor *Pagi* efteems a very remarkable teftimony to the Proconfular Empire of *Tiberius* (*c*).

It

(*a*) Avus Annius Rufus, item Conful & praefectus urbi adfcitus in patricios a PRINCIPIBUS Vefpafiano & Tito cenfo- ribus. *in Marc. Antonin Philof.*

(*b*) Simul filius, fimul Caefar, mox IMPERATOR, & confors Tribuniciae poteftatis, & omnia pariter & ftatim factus es, quae proxime parens verus tantum in alterum filium con- tulit. *Plin. Paneg.* cap. 8.

(*c*) 'Εκ διὸς 'Αυσονίης ἀεὶ μέγα κοιρανέοντες· v. 78. A Jove Aufonii femper longe lateque dominantes.

Ῥώμη

It appears from the two laſt of theſe verſes, that in *Dionyſius*'s time *Rome* was governed by more than one Prince.   It has been queſtioned indeed, when *Dionyſius* lived, and who are the *Princes* he ſpeaks of.   Some have thought, they were the two *Antoninies* : others have thought, he intended *Severus, Caracalla* and *Geta.*   (*a*) Cardinal *Noris,* I think, hath put it beyond all doubt by a paſſage alleged from (*b*) *Plinie,* that *Dionyſius* lived in the time of *Auguſtus.*   The Cardinal indeed ſuppoſes, that the Princes here referred to are *Caius* and *Lucius Caeſar, Auguſtus*'s adopted Sons.   Doctor *Pagi* ſeems to me to have ſhewn, that the title of ἄνακτες cannot belong to them ; and that *Auguſtus* and *Tiberius* are the Princes which *Dionyſius* means : But for the particulars I muſt refer the reader to the Doctor himſelf (*c*).

> Ῥώμην τιμήεσαν, ἐμῶν μέγαν εἶκον ἀνάκτων,   355
> Μητέρα πασάων πολίων, ἄφνειον ἰδέθλον.   356

De amne Tiberi loquitur ; aitque, Qui amabilem ſecat in duaſ partes Romam, Romam honorabilem, meorum magnam domum Principum vel Dominorum. *Dionyſ.* orbis deſcript.

(*a*) Cenotaph. Piſ. Diſſ. ii. p. 193. '   (*b*) Hoc in loco [Arabia nempe] genitum eſſe Dionyſium, terrarum orbis ſitus recentiſſimum auctorem,   quem ad commentanda omnia in orientem praemiſit Divus Auguſtus, ituro in Armeniam ad Parthicas Arabicaſque res Majore filio. *Plin. Hiſt. Nat.* lib. vi. cap. 27.

(*c*) Critica in Baron. A. D. 11. n. vi. vii.

THERE

(5.) THERE were two different computations of *Tiberius*'s reign in the time of St. *Clement* of *Alexandria*. For having first said, that *Augustus* reigned forty three years and *Tiberius* twenty two (*a*), he adds: ‘ But some reckon the reigns of the Roman ‘ Emperours thus.---*Augustus* reigned forty ‘ six years four months and one day. Then ‘ *Tiberius*, twenty six years, six months, ‘ nineteen days (*b*).

HAVING laid before the reader the chief arguments that have been produced for the Proconsular or joint Empire of *Tiberius* with *Augustus*, I will consider also some of the objections there are against this opinion.

1. IT is objected, That *Spartian* says, that *Marcus Aurelius* and *Lucius Verus* (*c*) were the two first *Augusti* that governed the *Roman Empire* together. But to this it is answered, that none of the Patrons of this opinion ever said, that *Tiberius* had the title of *Augustus*, whilst *Augustus* lived, but only that he was Collegue with him

(*a*) Ἀύγυςος, ἔτη τεσσαράκοντα τρία· Τιβέριος, ἔτη κβ. *Clement.* Strom. lib. 1. p. 339. A. Parisis 1629.

(*b*) Τινὲς μ̄ τοι τᾶς χρόνας τ̄ Ῥωμαϊκῶν βασιλέων ὕτως ἀναγράφυσι——Ἀύγυςος ἐβασίλευσεν ἔτη μϛ, μῆνας δ, ἡμέραν μίαν. Ἔπειτα Τιβέριος, ἔτη κϛ, μῆνας ϛ, ἡμέρας ιθ· id. ibid. C.

(*c*) Hi sunt, qui postea duo pariter Augusti, primi rempublicam gubernaverunt. *Spartian.* in Hadrian. cap. 24.

3

in

in the Empire. Thefe words of *Spartian*
are no more an objection againft *Tiberius*'s
Proconfular Empire, than they are againft
Titus's and *Trajan*'s, who certainly enjoyed
this honour, the one with his father *Vef-*
pafian, and the other with *Nerva*.

Nor indeed did the title of *Auguftus*
give any new power. It was only a title of
honour (*a*), which fort of Titles were ufually taken gradually. *Tiberius* ever refufed
that of Father of his country. And would
not permit that of *Auguftus* to be given him
by any Decree, though he accepted of it
from fome perfons, and made ufe of it himfelf in his letters to (*b*) foreign Princes. And
Dio takes notice of it as a fingularity in *Ca-*
ligula, that in one day he accepted all thofe
titles which *Auguftus* had received throughout his long reign, and had fuffered to be
given him only one by one (fome of which
Tiberius never would accept of) except only
that of father of his country; which he

(*a*) Vid. *Dio.* lib. 53. p. 507.

(*b*) Τό τε τȣ̃ πατρὸς τ̂ πατρίδος πρόσρημα παντελῶς διεώσατο,
τὸ τȣ̃ Ἀυγȣ́σȣ ȣκ ἐπέθετο μ̃ (ȣδὲ ϑ̃ ψηφισθῆναι ποτὲ ἴασε)
λεγόμενον δ' ἄκȣων, κ̃ γραφόμενον ἀναγινώσκων, ἔφερε· κ̃ ὁσάκις
γε βασιλεῦσι τισὶν ἐπίςελλε, κ̃ ἐκεῖνο προσενέγραφε. *Dio* lib. 57.
p. 607. A.

took upon him alfo in a fhort time after (*a*).

2dly, I t is objected : If *Tiberius* had been made Collegue in the empire with *Auguftus,* there could have been no reafon for thofe fears about the Succeffion of *Tiberius*, which *Livia* fhewed upon the death (*b*) of *Auguftus*. Nor would *Tiberius* have hefitated to accept the empire when offered to him by the Senate : Or indeed, what occafion could there have been for any new inveftiture at all ?

B u t to this, I think it is eafy to anfwer, that it is no furprifing thing, that *Livia* fhould be under fome pain, when the fettlement of her fon in the Empire was at ftake. Though *Tiberius* had been partner in the empire, yet certainly the death of *Auguftus* made a great change. *Germanicus* was very popular, and at the head of a numerous army (*c*). And as for *Tiberius's* hefitation, he had been hitherto but partner in the empire, and fome kind of new inveftiture was needful. It is

---

(*a*) Ὥςε πάντα ὅσα ὁ Ἀύγυςος ἐν τοσ·τῳ τ̃ ἀρχῆς χρόνῳ μόλις κỳ καθ᾽ ἓν ἕκαςον ψηφισθέντα οἱ ἐδέξατο (ὧν ἔνια Τιβέριος ὄδ᾽ ὅλως προσήκατο) ἐν μιᾷ ἡμέρᾳ λαβεῖν. κ. τ. λ. *Dio.* lib. 59. p 64ι. D.

(*b*) Actibus namque cuftodiis domum, & vias fepferat *Livia.Tacit. Ann.* lib. 1. cap. 5.

(*c*) *Tacit. Ann.* lib. i. cap 33.—35. *Dio.* lıb. 57. pag. 603.

true,

true, he carried his diffimulation very far: but *Auguſtus* himſelf never renewed a freſh term of government (which he did ſeveral times) but with much difficulty; and not till he had been overcome by impòrtunity and the conſideration of the neceſſity of affairs.

HOWEVER, this diffimulation of *Ti.beriuſ* has afforded a new proof, that he had been Collegue with *Auguſtus*. For, as *Tacitus* and *Dio* intimate very plainly the fears which *Tiberius* had of *Germanicus*; ſo *Suetonius* in particular ſays, ' He pretend' ed a bad ſtate of health, that *Germanicus* ' might entertain hopes of a ſpeedy Succeſſi-' ' on, or at leſt (*a*) a parrnerſhip in the empire'. But ſuch an expectation had been ridiculous in *Germanicus*, and this pretenſe of *Tiberius* could never have had the effect he deſigned, if no one had been partner in the empire before.

3. BUT the chief objection againſt the ſuppoſition, that St. *Luke* has computed the reign of *Tiberius* from the time of his Proconſular empire ſeems to be this; That it does not appear that any writers have com-

(*a*) Simulavit & valitudinem, quo aequiore animo Germanicus celerem Succeſſionem vel certè ſocietatem principatus operiretur. *Suet.* in Tiber. Cap. 25.

puted

puted the reign of thofe who were Collegues in the empire by the epocha of their Pro-confular empire, and that in particular there are no traces of this computation of *Tiberius*'s reign (*a*).

To this I anfwer: There is reafon to think, that people did often compute according to the epocha of the Proconfular empire. *Pagi* mentions a Medal which has this infcription: *In the* xi. *new facred year of the Emperour Titus Cefar Vefpafian* (*b*) *Auguftus.* Now *Titus* reigned alone after his father's death but a little above two years.

I T will not be expected, I fhould here at-tempt to explain the meaning of the epocha of the *new facred Year.* All that I fhall ob-ferve, is, that it appears not to have been ufed upon the coins of any Emperours befide thofe of *Vefpafian, Titus, Domitian* and

(*a*) Eft autem inauditum in omni memoria, *Titi* annos ab alio initio fuiffe deductos quam a morte Vefpafiani. S. *Bafnage* Annal. Pol. Ecclef. A. D. 11. n. iv.

(*b*) Sic in nummo Graeco apud Occonem pag. 166. legitur ΑΥΤ. ΤΙΤΟΥ. ΚΑΙΣΑΡΟΣ. ΟΥΕΣΠΑΣΙΑΝΟΥ. ΣΕΒ. ΕΤΟΥΣ. ΙΕΡΟΥ. ΙΑ. id eft, Imperatoris Titi Caefaris Vefpafiani Augufti anno novo Sacro xi. Quo ex Titi nummo manifefte apparet, deceptos viros eruditos qui negant annos Tiberii, Titi, aliorum-que Imperii Collegarum numeratos fuiffe. Haec porro epocha non nifi in Vefpafiani, Titi, Domitiani & Nervae nummis oc-currit. *Pagi. Crit. in Baron.* A.D. 81. n. iii.

S

Nerva :

Nerva : And that it does not begin at any
one common period, such as the building or
dedication of any one particular Temple,
but that the numbers answer exactly to the
years of the several emperours on whose
coins it is found (*a*).   And Doctor *Pagi* is of
opinion, that it was an epocha chiefly used
by the people of *Syria* and *Egypt*, because
the epithet *sacred* is more common upon
their coins than any others (*b*).

A N D I cannot but think, that there were
for some time different computations of the
length of *Nerva's* and *Trajan's* reigns; and
that they were owing to this, that *Trajan*
was for some time *Nerva's* Collegue in the
empire.   *Dodwell* (*c*) was of opinion,
that *Nerva* did actually resign the empire to
Trajan before his death.   And so (*d*) *Au-*

(*a*) Nisi enim hoc modo in nummis Titi, Domitiani &
Nervae epocha haec explicetur, impossible est nummos inter
se posse convenire; cum eorum imperii annos non excedat,
sed ad amussim iis respondeat. *Pagi.* ibid.

(*b*) Et nullibi sacri nomen frequentius, quam in nummis in
Syria & Ægypto percussis, usurpatum. *Pagi.* ibid. n.iv.

(*c*) Vid. Append. ad Dissert. *Cypr.* n. 39, 40.

(*d*) Quid enim Nerva Cretensi prudentius?—Qui cum ex-
trema aetate apud Sequanos, quo Tyranni defecit metu, imperium arbitrio legionum cepisset; ubi prospexit, nisi a superiori-
bus robustioribusq; corpore, animoque geri non posse, mense Sexto
ac Decimo semet eo abdicavit. *Aurel. Vict. de Caesar. in Nerva.*

relius

relius Victor, and (*a*) *Lactantius* feem to
fay. I think indeed that *Nerva* did not
refign, not only becaufe *Eutropius* (*b*) fays
that *Diocletian* was the firft of all the Roman Emperours that did fo, but efpecially
becaufe the younger *Plinie*, who ferved under *Nerva* and *Trajan*, and knew them both
very well, fays nothing of it, though he
often (*c*) mentions their joint empire.
But I think, that the notion which the forementioned Authors had of *Nerva*'s refigning
may be very well accounted for upon the Suppofition, that they had met with different
computations of the time of thefe two Princes
reigns, in fome ancient writers : And their
miftake is not eafie to be accounted for
otherwife.

(*a*) Simul & exemplum Nervae proferebat, qui imperium
Trajano tradidiffet. *De Mort.* Perfecut. cap. 18.

(*b*) Diocletianus privatus in villa, quae haud procul a Salonis
eft, praeclaro otio fenuit, inufitata virtute ufus ; ut folus
omnium poft conditum Romanum imperium ex tanto faftigio
fponte ad privatae vitae ftatum civilitatemque remearet. *Eutrop.*
lib. ix. cap. 28.

(*c*) Affumptus es in laborum curarumque confortium.
Plin. Paneg. cap. 7. Inde QUASI depofito imperio qua fecuri-
tate, qua gloria laetus ? (*Nerva nempe*). Nam quantulum re-
fert deponas an PARTIARIS imperium, nifi quod difficilius
hoc eft? ibid. cap. 8. Magnum hoc tuae moderationis indi-
cium, quod non folùm fucceffor imperii, fed PARTICEPS etiam
fociufque placuifti. cap. 9.

As

As for *Tiberius*, I take it for granted that it has been fully proved, that he was for some time partner in the empire with *Augustus* ; and particularly that it has been made appear that *Piso* was Prefect of *Rome* twenty years, and that he was put into that Post by the appointment or procurement of *Tiberius.* (Thus much I think Monfieur *Basnage* allows) (a). And *Suetonius* and *Plinie* both say that *Tiberius* was *then* Prince.

And it is highly probable, that the firft Chriftians had a perfwafion that there were two different epochaes of the beginning of *Tiberius*'s reign : Otherwife, when they faid, that Jefus was crucified in the fifteenth year of *Tiberius*, when the two *Gemini* were Confuls, namely A. D. 29. (as they did almoft univerfally) after he had preached above (b) two years, or a (c) whole year including two

(a) Ubi fupra. A. D. 11. n. ii. b) Tricefimo enim juxta Evangeliftam Lucam anno aetatis fuae coepit in carne Dominus Evangelium praedicare, & juxta Johannem Evangeliftam, per tria pafchata duos poftea implevit annos: & inde fex Tiberii fupputantur anni &c. *Apollinarius Laodicenus* apud *Hieron.* Comment. in Dan. c. 9. Ὁ δὲ Ἰούδας παρὰ τῷ Ἰησοῦ ὧδε τρία διέτριψεν ἔτη· *Orig* cont. Celf. l. 2. p. 67.

(c) Καὶ ὅτι ἐνιαυτὸν μόνον ἔδει αὐτὸν κηρῖξαι, καὶ τοῦτο γέγραπται οὕτως——πεντεκαιδεκάτῳ ἔν ἔτει Τιβερίου, καὶ πεντεκαιδεκάτῳ Αὐγούςου· οὕτω πληροῦται τὰ τριάκοντα ἔτη ἕως ὃ ἔπαθεν. *Clem.* *Alex.* Stom. l. 1. p. 340. A.

pafſovers,

paffovers, or a year and fome (*a*) few months; they muſt have been ſenſible that they contra-dicted St. *Luke*; who ſays, that the *word of God came* to *John* the *Baptiſt* in the *fifteenth year of Tiberius*; ſince alſo they muſt neceſſarily have allowed fome time for the miniſtry of *John*, diſtinct from that of Je-ſus.

THAT we have ſo few examples of this way of computing the reign of *Tiberius* is not to be wondered, conſidering how few ancient writers who lived near his time are come down to us, and eſpecially ſuch as lived in the Provinces, where this epocha muſt have been chiefly uſed. The diſtinct com-putation of *Auguſtus's* reign to the time of his death, and of *Tiberius's* after him was undoubtedly moſt commodious : and for this reaſon, probably, the computation of *Ti-berius's* reign from the time of his Procon-ſular Empire was ſoon dropped. Beſides, *Tiberius* ſeems to have taken pains to obli-terate this date of his government: inaſmuch as he was unwilling to have it thought that he owed his greatneſſe to the adoption of *Auguſtus*, or the intrigues of his mother

(*a*) Ἐνιαυτὸν γάρ πε κ̀ μῆνας ὀλίγες ἐδίδαξιν Orig. *Philoc.* p. 4.

Livia;

Livia ; but would have it afcribed folely to the free choice of the people after *Auguftus's* death (*a*), that is, to his own merit, as *Dio* exprefly fays (*b*).

TIBERIUS then having had for fome time before the death of *Auguftus* equal power with him in all the provinces and armies, and having been made thereby partner with him in the empire, it is not impoffible, but that St. *Luke* might compute the reign of *Tiberius* by this epocha.

WE fhould now, if poffible, fettle the exact time when *Tiberius* was made partner with *Auguftus*. It may be concluded, that he was fo A. U. 765, two years before *Auguftus* died, becaufe in that year *Pifo* was made prefect of *Rome*, *Tiberius* being *Prince*. And Arch-bifhop *Ufher* and Dr. *Prideaux* place the beginning of this government of *Tiberius* in this year.

THERE is however a confiderable difficulty attending this matter, becaufe *Velleius*

(*a*) Dabat & famae, ut vocatus electufque potius a Republica videretur, quam per uxorium ambitum & fenilem adoptionem inrepfiffe *Tacit. Ann.* lib. 1. cap. 8.

(*b*) Ἤδη μ γ̀ ἤκουσα ὅτι ἐπειδὰν ἡ Λιϰία ἄϰοντος ὧ 'Αυγούσου τὴν ἀρχὴν αὐτῷ περιπεποιηϰέναι ἐλίγετο, ἔπλαττεν ὅπως μὴ παρ' ἐϰείνης ἀλλὰ παρὰ τῆς βουλῆς ἀναγϰασός ὡς Ϲ ϰατὰ ἀρετὴν σφῶν προήϰων δόξειεν αὐτὴν ἰιληφέναι· *Dio.* lib. 57. p. 603 D.

and

and *Suetonius* differ about the time in which
the Law was paſſed by the Senate decreeing
Tiberius equal power with *Auguſtus* in the
provinces and armies. According to *Suetonius* this law was not paſſed till after *Tiberius*'s triumph, which certainly happened
A. U. 765. A. D. 12. But according to
Velleius (*a*) this law was paſſed at the deſire
of *Auguſtus* before *Tiberius* returned to
Rome from *Germany* to make his triumph.
Doctor *Pagi* (*b*) is inclined to prefer the
teſtimony of *Velleius Paterculus* before that
of *Suetonius*, becauſe *Velleius* was contemporary with *Tiberius*. But yet he dares not
be poſitive in this matter, becauſe St. *Clement*'s numbers are different from both.
However, as *Tiberius* was Conſul in the 21ſt,
and 31ſt years of our Lord, he judges this
piece of reſpect to the tenth and twentieth
years from the 11th year of our Lord to (*c*)

(*a*) *Sueton.* in *Tiber.* cap 21, 22. *Velleius* Pat. L. ii. cap.121.
Their words are tranſcribed above, p. 241.

(*b*) Vid. Crit. A. Ch. 11. n. x.

(*c*) Quia tamen Tiberius anno Chriſti xxi. rurſuſque anno
Chriſti xxxi. Conſul proceſſit, exiſtimandum, utrumque con-
ſulatum ob Decennalia & Vicennalia Imperii Proconſularis
Tiberii geſtum, ideoque & illum anno Chriſti xi. Imperio
Proconſulari donatum: quamquam uterque conſulatus anno
Chriſti xii. quo rem actam narrat Suetonius, reſpondere etiam
poſſit, etiamſi quinquennalia legitimo tempore celebrata fuerint.
id. ibid.

be

be a confirmation of the Suppofition that *Tiberius*'s proconfular power commenced A. D. 11. He obferves alfo marks of honour fhewn to the Quinquennals of this epocha, fuch as the dedication of temples by himfelf or the people of the provinces, the founding of cities by dependent princes, and fuch other the like things, with which the *Quinquennals* and *Decennals*, that is, the fifth and tenth years of remarkable events were wont to be celebrated.

As he thinks it moft probable, that *Tiberius*'s Proconfular Empire began A. U. 764. A. D. 11 ; fo he is pretty well fatisfied as to the month and day of the month; which he thinks was the 28th of *Auguft*, or vth. of the Kalends of *September*. One reafon for it is, that from the 725th year of the City, *Auguftus* feems to have had a particular refpect for the vth. of the Kalends of months. Moreover, according to the fecond computation which *Clemens Alexandrinus* mentions of the reign of *Tiberius*, it muft have begun on the 28th. of *Auguft*. Saint *Clement* fays, that *Tiberius* reigned twenty fix years, fix months, nineteen days. Now *Tiberius* died the 16th. of *March* A.D. 37. From the 28th. of *Auguft* A,D. 10 to the
16th.

16th. of *March* A. D. 37ᵉ are exactly (according to Doctor *Pagi's* reckoning) fo many
years, months, and days as St. *Clement* mentions. So that though St. *Clement* has been
in the wrong as to the year, fince he begins
this computation of *Tiberius's* reign A. D.
10; yet he has helped us to the month and
day of the month on which it commenced (*a*).

I HAVE reprefented the Doctor's fenfe
of this matter, as well as I can, in a few
words. But I cannot fay, that this reafoning
is altogether convincing. I muſt acknowledge, that I fee not how any argument can
be drawn from St. *Clement's* teſtimony,
either for the year or month of this epocha,
if his numbers have been altered, as the
Doctor allowes they have been in many
places, and particularly in this very paffage.

THERE appears to me fome weight in
the Doctor's obfervation upon the Quinquennals and Decennals of this epocha: But
yet it is not fully concluſive. There might
be fome other reafon, befide that here fuppofed, for *Tiberius's* taking the confulſhip

(*a*) Quare Clemens Alexandrinus rei geſtae diem nobis con-
fervavit, fed numeri annorum corrupti, quod in eo auctore
non infequens. *Pagi. Critic.* A.D. 11. n. ix.

A.D.21.

A. D. 21. and 31. The 22d. and 26th. years of the Chriſtian Era are as remarkable as any other for the founding of Cities, dedicating temples, and erecting of monu-ments. Though indeed, if this epocha be-gan in the midle of any year, it is obvious at firſt ſight, that theſe honours may be divided betwixt two years.

AND perhaps *Velleius Paterculus* and *Sue-tonius* may be reconciled by ſuppoſing only, that there was ſome time between *Auguſtus*'s propoſing *Tiberius*'s partnerſhip with him to the Senate, and the paſſing of the Act.

UPON the whole, I think there is good reaſon to believe, that *Tiberius* was Collegue in the Empire with *Auguſtus*, and that this epocha of *Tiberius*'s empire was followed for ſome time by ſome perſons, in the pro-vinces at leſt : but it appears to me uncertain, when this Proconſular empire began, whether about *two* years, or about *three* years before *Auguſtus* died.

LET us however adjuſt the numbers in St. *Luke* to this computation of the reign of *Tiberius*, which commenced either about two years, or about three years before his ſole empire after the death of *Auguſtus*.

And

And we will have an eye to the two dates of our Saviour's nativity abovementioned, *fc.* *September* or *October* A. U. 748, and 749·

IF *Tiberius*'s Proconsular Empire began about *three* years before *Augustus* died, *fc.* the 28th. of *Aug.* A. U. 764, A. D. 11. then this 15th. of *Tiberius*'s reign (according to this computation of it) began *August* 28. A. U. 778. A. D. 25. Suppoling that *John* the *Baptist* began his miniltry *November* following, in the fame year; and that Jefus was baptized by him the 6th. of *January* following in, A. U. 779. A. D. 26 : Then upon the fuppofition that Jefus was born in *September* A. U. 748, he would be at his baptifm thirty years of age and fome months over.

IF *Tiberius*'s Proconfular empire commenced about *two* years before the death of *Augustus*, *fc.* A. U. 765. A. D. 12, then the fifteenth of the reign of *Tiberius* began in A. U. 779. A. D. 26. And fuppofing that *John* the *Baptist* began his miniltry in *November* of that year, and that Jefus was baptized by him the 6th. of *January* following, A. U. 780. A. D. 27, then, upon the fuppofition that Jefus was born in *September* A. U. 749, he would be at the time of his

baptifm

baptifm thirty years of age and fome months over: Or, if born A. U. 748, he would be fomewhat more than thirty one years of age.

WE will put this matter one way more. If *John* the *Baptift* began his miniftry in the fifteenth of *Tiberius* A. U. 778. A. D. 25. (as in the firft ftating of this queftion) but did not baptize Jefus till the 6th. of *January* A. U. 780. A. D. 27, after he had preached fomewhat above a year, then Jefus would be at his baptifm thirty years of age and odd months, if he was born A. U. 749; thirty one years of age and fome odd months, if born the later end of the year 748.

I SEE not but that we have a very good right to take thofe dates of thefe events which appear moft favourable to St. *Luke*; fince it is not abfolutely certain when *Herod* died, or when *Tiberius*'s Proconfular Empire began: Nor have any of the writers of harmonies determined, that I know of, beyond contradiction, the fpace of time between the commencement of *John* the *Baptift*'s miniftry and our Saviour's baptifm. But if we allow on each hand the dates the left favourable to St. *Luke*'s numbers, *viz.* that Jefus was born A. U. 748. and that he was

not

not baptized till *January* A. U. 780. A. D.
27 ; yet even then Jesus would be little more
(as has been shewn) than thirty one years of
age ; at which time a person may be said
very properly to be ABOUT *thirty years of
age,* as will appear by and by.

I IMAGINE I have now shewed, that
there is nothing improbable in the suppofition, that St. *Luke* computed the reign of
Tiberius, not from his sole empire after the
death of *Auguftus* but from the time of his
proconfular empire, when he had equal power with *Auguftus* given him in all the provinces and armies, and that upon this suppofition, there lies no objection againft the age
afcribed to Jefus at his baptifm.

§. III. HOWEVER, in order to compleat
this Solution of this difficulty, it will be proper to confider some other notes of time,
which we find in the Evangelifts, and to enquire, whether thefe likewife agree with this
fuppofition.

ST. *Luke* fays : *Now in the fiftcenth
year of the reign of Tiberius Cefar,* PON-
TIUS PILATE BEING GOVERNOUR OF JUDEA
----*the word of God came unto John the*
Luke iii. *Son of Zacharias.*
I, 2.

IT

IT has been the opinion of some learned men, that *Pilate* did not come into *Judea* so soon as the 15th year of *Tiberius*'s Proconsular empire, the 12th of his sole empire, A. U. 778. A. D. 25.

THAT every one may judge of this matter, I shall set down the account *Josephus* has given of *Pilate*'s leaving *Judea*, from which we shall be able to conclude, when he came into it.

THE Senate of the *Samaritans* sent complaints against *Pilate* to *Vitellius*, President of *Syria*. And *Josephus* says: ' *Vitellius*, sending his friend *Marcellus* to administer the affairs of *Judea*, commanded ' *Pilate* to go to *Rome* to answer to the ' Emperour for those things of which he ' was accused by the *Jews*. And *Pilate* ' having spent TEN YEARS IN JUDEA, hastened away to *Rome*, in obedience to the ' commands of *Vitellius*, not daring to refuse. But before he got to *Rome*, *Tiberius* ' was dead.

' MOREOVER *Vitellius* came into *Judea*, and went up to *Jerusalem*. It was then a ' Feast time. The Feast is called the PASSOVER. *Vitellius* being received there with ' great magnificence, abolished entirely the

T   tax

'tax upon vendible fruits, and granted to
'the Priests the right of keeping in the
'temple the Vestment of the High-Priest
'and all its ornaments as they had done for-
'merly.----- Having conferred these favours
'upon the nation, he also took away the
'Priesthood from the High-Priest *Joseph*,
'who is likewise called *Caiaphas*, and sub-
'stituted in his room *Jonathan* the Son of
'*Ananus* the High-Priest. And then re-
'turned to *Antioch* (*a*).

JOSEPHUS immediately after this
says, that *Tiberius* sent orders to *Vitellius* to
to go and make a league with the King of
the *Parthians*; that *Vitellius* having had a
meeting with the King at the river *Euphrates*,
and executed his commission, returned again
to (*b*) *Antioch*.

(*a*) Καὶ 'Ουϊτέλλιος, Μάρκελλον τὸν αὐτῷ φίλον ἐκπέμψας
ἐπιμελητὴν τοῖς 'Ιεδάιοις γινσόμενον, Πιλάτον ἐκέλευσεν ἐπὶ 'Ρώμης
ἀπίναι, πρὸς ἃ κατηγοῖεν 'Ιεδαῖοι διδάξοντα τὸν αὐτοκράτορα· καὶ
Πιλάτος, δέκα ἔτεσιν διατρίψας ἐπὶ 'Ιεδαίας, εἰς 'Ρώμην ἠπείγετο,
ταῖς 'Ουϊτελλίᾳ πειθόμενος ἐντελῶς, ἐκ ἐν ἀντειπεῖν πρὶν ἢ τῇ 'Ρώμῃ
προσχεῖν αὐτόν, φθάνει Τιβέριος μετασάς. 'Ουϊτέλλιος δ', εἰς τὴν
'Ιεδαίαν ἀφικόμενος, ἐπὶ 'Ιεροσολύμων ἄνεισι, καὶ ἦν αὐτοῖς ἑορτὴ,
Πάσχα ἡ καλεῖτα· δεχθεὶς ἡ μεγαλοπρεπῶς 'Ουϊτέλλιος, τὰ τέλη
τῶν ὠνημένων καρπῶν ἀνίησιν εἰς τὸ πᾶν τοῖς ταύτην κατοικῶσι καὶ
τὴν στολὴν τῶ ἀρχιερέως, καὶ τὸν πάντα αὐτῶ κόσμον συνεχώρησεν
ἐν τῶ ἱερῷ κείμενον ὑπὸ τοῖς ἱερεῦσιν ἔχειν τὴν ἐπιμέλειαν, καθότι
καὶ πρότερον ἦν αὐτοῖς ἐξεσίω· κ. τ. λ. *Joseph.* Ant. lib. 18. cap·
v. §. 2, 3. pag 801. 802.   (*b*) Id. Ibid. p. 802. 803.

AFTER

AFTER this *Vitellius* received orders from *Tiberius* to go and make war with *Aretas* King of *Petra*.

' *Vitellius* then having got all things
' ready for the war with *Aretas*, haftened
' away for *Petra* with two legions, and
' other auxiliary forces, and was come as far
' as *Ptoloma·s*. But as he was about to
' march his army through *Judea*, the chief
' men met him, entreating him not to go
' through their country; ---He complied
' with their requeft. And having ordered
' his army to take their rout through the great
' plain, he himfelf with *Herod* the Tetrarch
' and their friends went up to *Jerufalem*, to
' worfhip God, a Feaft of the *Jews* being
' at hand (*a*). He was received by the people
' of the *Jews* with great refpect. Having
' been there three days, he took away the
' High-Priefthood from *Jonathan* and gave it
' to his brother *Theophilus*. And on the
' fourth day after his arrival, receiving let-
' ters which brought an account of the death
' of *Tiberius*, he took an oath of the peo-
' ple to *Caius* (*b*)'.

(*a*) Ἑορτῆς πατρίϐ τοῖς Ἰϐδαίοις ἐνεστηϰυίας.
b) Id. ibid. cap. vi. §. 3.

A FEW

A few remarks on this account will suffice.

I t is not exprefly faid, which Feaft of the *Jews* the laft mentioned Feaft was : But there can be no doubt, but that it was the Paffover A. D. 37. I think this is not contefted by any one. *Tiberius* died the 16th of *March*, A. D. 37. The news of his death might eafily reach *Judea* by the Paffover of that year, and could not be retarded to the Feaft of *Pentecoft*.

T h e Paffover firft mentioned in this account muft have been the Paffover A. D. 36. It is evident, that the fummer following *Vitellius* went as far as the river *Euphrates*, and returned to *Antioch*: and the next fpring he was to go and make war with *Aretas*. But whilft his troops marched towards *Petra*, he went up to *Jerufalem* at the Paffover in the year thirty feven, as has been obferved. Nothing can be plainer, I think, than that *Pilate* was removed before the Paffover in thirty fix. And he muft have been out fome time before. *Vitellius* did not go to *Jerufalem* immediately after he had fent away *Pilate*, but firft ordered his friend *Marcellus* to take care of affairs there.

It

I т is not said here, how long *Pilate* had been out, before *Vitellius* went up to *Jerusalem* ; but it is probable, it was half a year. This may be concluded from hence. *Josephus* says, that *Vitellius*, when he was at *Jerusalem*, the first time here spoken of, put the High-Priest's vestment into the Priest's hands to be kept by them in the Temple. *Josephus* is very expresse, that this favour was conferred by *Vitellius* upon the nation at this time, and that having done so, he put out *Caiaphas* and returned to *Antioch*. Now in another place *Josephus* says : ' This Vest-
' ment King *Herod* kept here [*in the Castle*
' *of Antonia*]. And after his death it was
' kept in the same place by the *Romans* till
' the times of *Tiberius Cesar*. In his reign
' *Vitellius* president of *Syria*, having come
' to *Jerusalem*, and the people receiving
' him in a very honourable manner, he being
' willing to make them a suitable return,
' since they had desired that the sacred vest-
' ment might be in their own custody, wrote
' to *Tiberius Cesar* about it, and he grant-
' ed their request (*a*).' From this passage it

appears,

(*a*) Ταύτην ὁ βασιλεὺς Ἡρώδης ἐφύλαξεν ἐν τῷ τόπῳ, ἡ μετὰ τὴν ἐκείνε τελευτὴν ὑπὸ Ῥωμαίοις ἦν μίχρι ᵗ Τιβερίε Καίσαρος

T 3   χρόνων

appears, that *Vitellius* did not put the High-Prieft's Veftment into the hands of the *Jews* without leave from *Tiberius*. If *Vitellius* actually made this grant when he was at *Jerufalem* at the Paffover A. D. thirty fix, (as *Jofephus* fays exprefly in the firft paffage) it is likely the *Jews* had fent their requeft to him about the time that *Pilate* was removed. And confidering the flowneffe of *Tiberius* in all his proceedings, it will not be thought ftrange, that we allow half a year between the *Jews* prefenting their requeft to *Vitellius* in *Syria*, and the return of an anfwer from the Emperour: It is rather furprizing it fhould have come back fo foon.

I T is poffible that fome may except againft this argument, and fay, that the grant was not made by *Vitellius*, when he was at *Jerufalem*; but that he there received the *Jews* requeft, then wrote to *Tiberius*, and fometime after this put the facred Veftment into their cuftody. But though *Jofephus* does in this laft paffage feem to place things in this order; yet I fhould think that fince

χρόνων· ἐπὶ τότε ὃ Ουιτίλλιος ὁ τῆς Συρίας ἡγεμὼν, ἐπιδημήσας τοῖς Ἱεροσολύμοις, διαμένε ἧ πλήξες αὐτὸν λαμπρότατα πάνυ, θέλων αὐτὸς τῆς εὐποιίας ἀμείψαθς, ἐπεὶ παρεκάλισαν τὴν ἱερὰν ςολὴν ὑπὸ τὴν αὐτῶν ἐξουσίαν ἔχειν,ἔγραψε περὶ τότων ᵀ ι ε ἰῳ Καίσαρι, κἀκεῖνος ἐπέτρεψε. *Ant.* lib. xv. cap xi §.4.

in the paſſage firſt cited, he ſays, *Vitellius* be-
ſtowed this favour upon the *Jews*, whilſt at
Jeruſalem at that time; it may be inferred,
that the petition had been preſented to him
whilſt in *Syria*, and that he brought *Tiberius*'s
grant to *Jeruſalem* with him.

HOWEVER, though this argument ſhould
not be allowed me, yet ſince upon *Pilate*'s
removal *Marcellus* was ſent to govern in
Judea, it is plain there was ſome time between *Vitellius*'s iſſuing his orders to *Pilate*
to go to *Rome*, and his own Journey to
Jeruſalem. This time might be the ſpace
of five or ſix months, and I apprehend that
the probability at leſt of my reaſoning a-
bove, that *Vitellius* received the *Jews* petition for keeping the High-Prieſt's Veſtment
in *Syria*, then wrote to *Tiberius*, and delivered it to them, when he was at *Jeruſalem*, may very much diſpoſe us to admit
the ſuppoſition of this ſpace.

AND though it ſhould be thought, that
at the Paſſover next after *Pilate*'s removal
Vitellius did not give the High-Prieſt's
Veſtment into the *jewiſh* hands, but only
received their petition for that favour; yet
this does fully overthrow the opinion of
thoſe, who have thought, that *Pilate* was

removed

removed but a few weeks before the death of *Tiberius*. *Vitellius*, after the removal of *Pilate*, was at *Jerusalem* at a Passover, and having been magnificently received by the *Jews*, in requital of their civilities wrote to *Tiberius* (so we will suppose at present) that they might have the keeping of the High-Priest's garment, and *Tiberius* granted it. This Passover then was not that Passover, at which *Vitellius*, being at *Jerusalem*, heard of the death of *Tiberius*. We are therefore fully assured that the passover which followed the removal of *Pilate* was not the passover A. D. 37, before which *Tiberius* died, but the passover preceding, *viz.* that in A. D. 36.

I t is certain then, that *Pilate* was removed before the Passover, A. D. 36, and probable, that he was removed about five or six months before it, namely, about *September* or *October*, A. D. 35. about a year and a half before the death of *Tiberius*.

S i n c e *Josephus* says, that *Pilate* spent *ten* years in *Judea*; he came thither about *October* A. D. 25, or at least before the Passover A. D. 26, in the twelfth year of *Tiberius's* sole empire, which twelfth year began the nineteenth of *August* A. D. 25. This

alfo

also is perfectly confiftent with what *Jofe-phus* fays of *Valerius Gratus*, the firft Procurator of *Judea* under *Tiberius*, that he 'fpent eleven years in *Judea*, and was then 'fucceeded by *Pontius Pilate (a)*'.

So that though we fhould fuppofe that *Tiberius's* Proconfular Empire began three years before the death of *Auguftus*, as Dr. *Pagi* is inclined to do, fc. 28. *Auguft.* A.U. 764. A.D. 11; yet *Pontius Pilate* would even then be in *Judea* in the fifteenth of that Empire, which began *Aug.* 28. A.U. 778. A.D. 25.

THERE is one difficulty, and but one in all this matter. *Jofephus* fays, that ' *Pi.* ' *late* ---- haftened away to *Rome* in obe-' dience to the commands of *Vitellius*, not ' daring to refufe. But before he got to ' *Rome*, *Tiberius* was dead'.

IT will be beft to take the objection from Mr. *Whifton*. ' Now it is known from *Jo.* ' *fephus* that *Pontius Pilate* was Procurator ' of *Judea* but ten years ; and that he was ' put out fo little a while before the death ' of *Tiberius*, that the Emperour was actual-' ly dead before *Pilate* arrived at *Rome* to

(*r*) Καὶ Γρᾶτ☉ μ̃ ταῦτα πεάξας ἰις Ῥώμην ἰπαναχωρῖι, ἔνδεκα ἔτη διατρίψας ἐν Ἰεδαίᾳ. Πόντιος ἡ Πιλάτ☉ διάδοχος αὐτῷ ἔκειν· Antiq. 18. c. 2. §. 2.

answer

' anfwer for himfelf. *Tiberius* died *March*
' 26th. (*a*) A. D. 37. And *Pilate* might
' be out of his office a month, or fix weeks
' before, fuppofe it *February*, from thence
' we muft count ten years backward for
' for the beginning of *Pilate*'s government,
' which will therefore fall into *February*
' A. D. 27. (*b*).'

THIS is the difficulty: But I think, it
would be very wrong to be determined by
one fingle Sentence againft all the evidence
which arifes from the whole feries of a narration. It is extremely evident, that the
Feaft time, in which, *Vitellius*, being at
Jerufalem, heard of the death of *Tiberius*,
is not the Paffover which followed next after *Pilate*'s removal. I fhall not repeat
particulars, but content my felf with referring the reader to *Jofephus*'s account, already tranfcribed.

AND if this one fentence about the time
of *Pilate*'s arrival at *Rome* be inconfiftent
with the reft of the ftory, it is more reafon-

(*a*) I fuppofe that Mr. *Whifton* herein follows *Dio* (unlefs
it be a fault of the prefs) : But according to *Suetonius* and
Tacitus, *Tiberius* died the 16th. of *March*. vid. *Pagi. Crit.
in Baron.* A. D. 37. n. ii.

(*b*) *Whifton*'s fhort view of the harmony of the four Evangelifts, pag. 139.

able

able to suppose, that *Josephus* was mistaken in this particular, than in every thing else. He might be mis-informed about the time when *Pilate* got to *Rome*, but he could not well be ignorant of some of the most remarkable events in his own country, that is, when *Pilate* left *Judea*, when *Caiaphas*, and his Successor *Jonathan* were put out of the High-Priest's Office.

B u t there is no reason to suppose this particular is inconsistent with the other circumstances mentioned in this relation. Mr. *Whiston* indeed can allow but a *month* or *six weeks* between the time of *Pilate's* removal out of his office and his arrival at *Rome*. But it ought to be considered, that *Pilate* was not sent to *Rome* in order to take possession of a kingdome or some new ample province, but to answer for his conduct in his late government. Nor was he sent express: Nor was he recalled by the Emperour himself. But he was sent away by *Vitellius*, a fellow subject, though a superior officer. *Josephus* says, that *Pilate* *hastened away to Rome*. I have given his words the strongest sense in the translation: but I think, the meaning is no more than that he went away out of *Judea*. And

Josephus

Josephus intimates very plainly the reluctance
with which *Pilate* obeyed *Vitellius,* when
he fays, that he went, not *daring to refuse.*

THERE was, if I miftake not, fome
Law under the Commonwealth, which required the Governours of provinces to be at
Rome in three months time after their term
of government was expired: But whether
that law was in force now, I cannot fay.
However it is plain it was not obferved:
Pifo's conduct is a proof of it. *Germanicus*
died in *November* or (a) fooner: As may be
inferred from a paffage of *Suetonius,* who fays,
' that the publick forrow for his death at
' *Rome* continued even through the Holy
' Days of *December* (b)': meaning, I fuppofe, the *Saturnalia*, which were celebrated in the middle of that month. And
as *Germanicus* died in *Syria,* fome time
muft be allowed for the carrying the news

(a) *Bafnage* [Ann. Polit. Ec. Vol. 1. p. 221.] fuppofes he
died in *July. Decimo quinto* Julii Germanicum vitam cum morte
commutaffe ex Tacito conjecturam facimus: *Equefter ordo inftituit, uti turmae idibus Juliis imaginem ejus fequerentur.*
Ann. l. 2. c. 83. (b) Sed ut demum fato functum
palam factum eft, non folatiis ullis, non edictis ullis inhiberi
luctus publicus potuit, duravitque etiam per feftos Decembris
menfis dies. *Sueton.* in *Calig.* cap. 6.

of

of his death from thence to *Rome*. *Piso* was gone from the Province of *Syria* before the death of *Germanicus*. It is moſt probable, that he was turned out by *Germanicus* (*c*). And yet he was not come to *Rome* at the time of the *Megalenſian* games of the next year, which were kept on the fifth of *April* (*b*). It is true, the people of *Rome* were very uneaſy at theſe delays of *Pſo*, becauſe they wanted to have him brought to his trial for the death of *Germanicus*, whom he wasthought to have poyſoned. But yet I do not perceive that when (*c*) his trial came on, his long abſence from *Rome* is reckoned up amongſt his other crimes.

AND to add no more, the ſlowneſſe of *Tiberius* in all his proceedings may help us to account for *Pilate*'s delays in going to *Rome*,

(*a*) Addunt p'erique juſſum (*Piſonem*) provinciae decedere. *Tacit. Ann.* lib. ii. cap. 70.

(*b*) Et quia Ludorum Megalenſium ſpectaculum ſuberat, *etiam voluptates reſumerent.* Tum exuto juſtitio, reditum ad munia; & Druſus Illyricos ad exercitus profectus eſt, erectis omnium animis petendae a Piſone ultionis, & crebro queſtu, *quod vagus interim per amoena Aſiae atque Achaiae, adroganti & ſubdola mora ſcelerum probatiores ſubverteret.* *Tacit. Ann.* lib III. cap. 6, 7.

(*c*) Id. ibid. cap. 13.

though

though it be fuppofed that he made a year and a half of it.

JOSEPHUS fays, that *Tiberius* was the moft dilatory Prince that ever lived (*a*). His conduct towards *Herod Agrippa* affords a ftrong proof it. A Servant of *Agrippa* waited upon the Prefect of *Rome*, affuring him he had fome informations of great confequence to give to the Emperour relating to his mafter. The Prefect fent him to *Tiberius*, but he, without making any particular enquiry into the matter, only keeps the man fafe in cuftody. *Agrippa* lying under the Emperour's difpleafure was forced to make intereft to have his fervant heard. And though he then informed the Emperour of words fpoken by *Agrippa* which were little lefs than treafon, and *Agrippa* was immediately thereupon confined; yet he was never called for again, though *Tiberius* lived fix months (*b*) after. *Tacitus* has mentioned another inftance well nigh, or quite as remarkable (*c*). This flow way of thinking

---

(*a*) Μελλητης ἐι καὶ τις ἑτέρων βασιλέων ἢ τυράννων γενόμενος· Antiq. lib. 18. pag 811. v. 3.

(*b*) *Jofeph.* Ant. 18. cap. vii.

(*c*) Confultufque Caefar *an fepeliri fineret*, (*De Afinio Gallo loquitur*) non erubuit permittere, ultroque incufare cafus, qui *reum*

ing and acting was visible in *Tiberius* in his very youth (*a*).   And no historian of those times is silent about it.   *Pilate*, who had served *Tiberius* ten years, could not be ignorant of what all the world knew.   He might have many probable reasons to think, that, if he did not come in the Emperour's way, he should never be called for.   If enquiry was made for him, an excuse might be found out that would serve for some time. Sicknesse might be pretended, as a reason for his stay in *Asia*, *Achaia*, or some other place where he was got.   Perhaps this was really the case.   To be put out of his Government by *Vitellius*, upon the complaints of the people of his province,   must have been a very grievous mortification. *Eusebius* assures us, that not long after this *Pilate* made away with himself out of vexation for his many misfortunes (*b*).

reum *abstulisset antequam coram convinceretur.*   Scilicet medio triennio detuerat tempus subeundi judicium consulari seni tot consularium parenti.   *Tact. Ann.* lib. vi. cap. 23.

(*a*) Saeva ac lenta natura ne in puero quidem latuit. *Sueton.* in *Tiber.* cap. 57.   Sed mitigavit Sejanus, non Galli amore, verum ut cunctationes principis aperirentur; gnarus eum lentum in meditando. *Tacit. Ann.* lib. iv. cap. 71.

(*b*) Πόντιος Πιλᾶτος ἐπὶ Γαίᾳ Καίσαρος ποικίλαις περιπεσὼν συμφοραῖς, ὥς φασιν οἱ τὰ Ῥωμαίων συγγραψάμενοι, αὐτοφονευτὴς ἑαυτῷ ἐγένετο· *Euseb.* Chron. p. 78.

THERE is another note of time mentioned in St. *John's* Gospel, which ought also to be confidered. *Then faid the Jews, Forty and fix years was this temple in building : and wilt thou rear it up in three days ?*

John ii. 20.

I SUPPOSE, that the objection to be formed upon this text is to this effect. Thefe words were fpoken by the *Jews* at the firft Paffover of our Saviour's public miniftry, and the next after his Baptifm by *John*. The Temple which the *Jews* fpoke of, was the Temple then before their eyes, and which *Herod* had rebuilt or repaired. But *Herod* did not make the propofal for rebuilding it till the eighteenth year of his reign, reckoning from the death of *Antigonus*. Therefore, if the fifteenth of *Tiberius's* reign mentioned by St. *Luke* be the fifteenth of his Proconfular Empire, and not of his fole empire after the death of *Auguftus*, this temple could not have been fo long as *forty fix years* in building, at the time thefe words were fpoken.

To this I might anfwer, That an objection taken from *Jofephus's* account of the time when *Herod* repaired the temple can be of little moment : becaufe in one place

place he fays, that *Herod* repaired the temple in the fifteenth (*a*), and in another the eighteenth year (*b*) of his reign. As the fifteenth year from the death of *Antigonus* is fuppofed to be coincident with the eighteenth year from the time in which *Herod* was declared King of *Judea* by the Senate of *Rome*, fome may be difpofed to conclude, that, when *Jofephus* fays *Herod*'s propofal to rebuild the Temple was made to the *Jews* in the eighteenth year of his reign, he computes from the time in which *Herod* was declared King by the Roman Senate.

BUT I do not infift upon this, and am willing to allow, that *Herod* made the propofal to the *Jews* of building their temple in the eighteenth year of his reign from the death of *Antigonus*.

AND I think it is as likely that the *Jews*, in thefe words recorded by St. *John*, refer to the time of *Herod*'s propofal, as to the time in which he began actually to repair the temple. It is moft probable, that *Herod* made this offer to the *jewiſh* people, when affembled together at one of their great Feafts. This therefore would be the moft folemn and

(*a*) De Bell. lib. i. cap. 21. init.
(*b*) Ant. lib. xv. cap. xi. init

U   remark-

remarkable Epocha of rebuilding the temple, which work undoubtedly he set about as soon afterwards as he could.

AND it is very common to say, that men do things, when they propose to do them, or begin to do them. Thus *Josephus* says in his *War of the Jews* : 'In the fifteenth year ' of his reign he [*Herod*] repaired the tem- ' ple it self, and enclosed a spot of ground ' about it, of double the compass with that ' which surrounded it before. This was done ' at a vast expence, and is a proof of his uncom- ' mon magnificence (*a*). We will allow that the fifteenth year in this place ought to be corrected by his *Antiquities*, where he says, that ' in the eighteenth year of his reign ' *Herod* projected [or undertook] the re- ' building the Temple, which was the great- ' est of all his works (*b*)'. But then it ap_ pears from hence, that *Herod* is said by *Jo-sephus* in one place to *do* what in another he is only said at the same time to *propose* or begin.

(*a*) Πεντεκαιδεκάτῳ γῦν ἔτει τῆς βασιλείας, αὐτόν τε τὸν ναὸν ἐπεσκεύασε, κỳ τὴν περὶ αὐτὸν ἀνετειχίσατο χώραν, τῆς ἄσης διπλασίαν, ἀμέτροις μ̃ χρησάμενος τοῖς ἀναλώμασιν, ἀνυπερβλήτῳ ⳝ τῇ πολυτελείᾳ· De Bell. lib. i. cap. 21. init.

(*b*) Τότε γῦν ὀκτωκαιδεκάτῳ τῆς Ἡρώδȣ βασιλείας γεγονότος ἐνιαυτȣ,——ἔργον ȣ τὸ τυχὸν ἐπεβάλετο, τὸν νεὼν ⳝ Θεȣ δὶ αὐτȣ κατασκευάσασϑ· *Ant.* lib. xv. cap. xi. init.

SUPPO-

SUPPOSING that the *Jews* in this text of *John* refer to the time in which *Herod* made the proposal of rebuilding the temple, we will see how this term of forty six years will agree with the Supposition that St. *Luke's* fifteenth year of *Tiberius* is the fifteenth of his Proconsular Empire.

IF the fifteenth of *Tiberius's* Proconsular Empire began the 28th of *August* A.U.778. A.D.25. (according to Dr. *Pagi's* opinion) and if *John* the *Baptist* began to preach in *November* that year, but did not baptize Jesus till after he had preached a year and some months, then the Passover at which these words were spoken was the Passover A. U. 780. A.D. 27.

OR if the fifteenth of *Tiberius's* reign began A. U. 779, A. D. 26, and *John* began then to preach, and Jesus was baptized by him, some time before the passover next following; still these words would be spoke by the *Jews* at the Passover A.U.780, A.D.27.

THE eighteenth year of *Herod's* reign, from the death of *Antigonus*, is supposed to have begun some time in A. U. 734. *Herod* might make his offer to the *Jews* of rebuilding the Temple at the Feast of Tabernacles, in *November* that year. From *November* A. U. 734. to the Passover A.U.

U 2   780. A D.

780, A. D. 27, is almoſt forty five years and an half. At this time therefore the *Jews* might not improperly ſay, the temple had been *forty ſix years in building.* The forty ſixth year was then current. And it was to the purpoſe of the *Jews,* rather to add to, than to diminiſh the time which had been ſpent in that work. So that there is no time more ſuitable to theſe words of the *Jews* than the Paſſover A. D 27. Though there is no manner of inconſiſtence between underſtanding the fifteenth of *Tiberius,* of his Proconſular Empire, and ſuppoſing that theſe words were ſpoken at the Paſſover A. D. 28. And then the Temple might have been above forty ſix years in building.

WHAT has been here ſaid, may be ſufficient to ſhew, that St. *Luke* might compute the reign of *Tiberius* from the epocha of his Proconſular Empire; that if he did, Jeſus might be ſaid, with great exactneſſe and propriety, to be *about thirty years of age* at his baptiſm ; and that there is nothing in this ſuppoſition inconſiſtent with any other notes of time mentioned in the Goſpels.

§. IV. ANOTHER way of ſolving this difficulty is this. Theſe words of Saint *Luke : And Jeſus himſelf began to be about*
thirty

thirty years of age, may be understood with ^{Luke iii.} some latitude. Jesus might be thirty (*a*) two ^{23.} years of age or more at this time. The word *about* (ὡσεὶ) is often uſed, where a pre- ciſe exactneſſe is not intended or expected. *Matth.* xiv. 21. *And they that had eaten were* ABOUT *five thouſand* [ὡσεὶ πεντακισχί- λιοι], *beſide women and children.* And the other Evangeliſts, in ſpeaking of this Mira- cle, uſe the ſame phraſe *. St. *Luke* ſays, ^{* Mark vi.} *Act.* ii. 41. *And the ſame day there* ^{44.} ^{Luke ix.} *were added unto them about* [ὡσεὶ] *three* ^{14.} *thouſand ſouls.* And with a like latitude ^{John vi.} ^{10.} does this phraſe; ſeem to be uſed in many other places †. ^{† Luke i.} ^{56.}

IT is *Kepler's* opinion, that round and ^{xxii. 41.} decimal numbers may be uſed with great ^{xxiii. 44.} ^{John i. 49.} latitude: And that a perſon may be very truly ^{Act. v. 36.} ſaid to be about thirty years of age, if he be above five and twenty and under thirty five: But that, if a perſon be ſaid to be about eight and

(*a*) Ex noſtrâ quidem Chronologia, ſequitur Chriſtum jam annum xxxii. evaſiſſe cum ad baptiſmum acceſſit. Nil tamen in ea, vel abſurdi, vel pugnae aliquid cum Lucâ intelligi- mus, cùm de viro annos duos & triginta nato, cujus aetas dubitanter profertur, non incongrue dici poſſit, eſt annorum circiter triginta——Iterum iterumque monemus, ex phraſi Lucae, Joſephi de ſupremo Herodis anno chronologia damna- ri nequit. *Baſnage* Ann. Pol. Ec. Ante Dom. 3. n, vi. vid. etiam ad A. D. 30. num. iv.

twenty

twenty or two and thirty years of age, it is to be suppofed he is exactly fo old, or not above a month or two more or lefs. (*a*).

AND indeed many examples of this ufe of round numbers may be found in the (*b*) beft writers, even without the particle ὡσεὶ, *about*, which of it felf feems to be a hint, that the writer does intend to be underftood with fome latitude.

(*a*) Hic receptus mos eft linguis omnibus ut circiter 5000 dicamus quicquid eft inter 4500 & 5500. Quare fic etiam in noftro exemplo quicquid eft inter 25 & 35, id omne circiter 30 dici poteft. Alia effet voculae ratio, fi praefixiffet numero non rotundo. Ut fi dixiffet circiter 28 annos, vel circiter 32 annos. Quae enim infra decem nominatim exprimuntur, iis appofita vocula *circiter* raro unum annum folidum in dubio ponat, fed fere menfes tantum aut dies aliquot numero paucos & infra quantitatem anni folidi. *Keplerus de Anno C. Natali.* Cap. xii. p. 140, 141.

(*b*) Ab illo enim profectu viribus datis tantum valuit, ut in QUADRAGINTA deinde annos tutam pacem haberet. *Livius*, Lib. i. cap. xv. n. 7. This refers to *Numa*'s reign, of which afterwards *Livie* fays——Romulus feptem & triginta regnavit annos, Numa TRES ET QUADRAGINTA. ibid. cap. xxi. When the City of *Rome* was taken by the *Gauls* and the remnant of the people were entering into the Capitol, *Livie* ufes thefe words: Verfae inde adhortationes ad agmen juvenum; quos in Capitolium atque in arcem profequebantur, *commendantes virtuti eorum juventaeque urbis per* TRECENTOS SEXAGINTA *annos omnibus bellis victricis,*——*fortunam.* id. lib v. cap. 40. *Camillus* not long after in the very fame year, in his fpeech to diffwade them from removing to *Veii*, fays; TRECENTESIMUS SEXAGESIMUS QUINTUS *annus urbis, Quirites, agitur.* ibid. cap. 54. vid. eundem Lib. vi. cap. 28. n. 7. & *Joan. Cleric.* notas.

IF

IF we may take St. *Luke*'s words in this manner, there is scarce any need that I should trouble the reader with any calculation, to shew the agreement of his numbers with the time of our Saviour's nativity.

THE fifteenth of *Tiberius*'s sole empire began A. U. 781. A. D. 28. If Jesus was baptized the 6th *January* A. U. 782, A.D. 29, he would be but some months above thirty three years of age, though he was born so soon as *September* A. U. 748. And if he was born A. U. 749, then, though his baptism be placed in the beginning of A. U. 783, A. D. 30, still he would be little more than thirty three years of age.

ALL the other notes of time in the Gospels are also very easily reconciled with this fifteenth of *Tiberius*'s sole Empire. *Pontius Pilate* came into *Judea* before the Passover in the 12th year of *Tiberius*'s sole Empire, A. U. 779, A. D. 26. (as has been shewn) : And continued there *ten* years. Therefore he was undoubtedly Governour of *Judea* at the commencement of *John* the *Baptist*'s ministry, and till after our Saviour's crucifixion.

As for those words of the *Jews* spoken by them at the first Passover of our Saviour's

ministry,

miniftry, *Forty fix years has this temple been building*, it is but to fuppofe that they referred, not to the time when *Herod* made the propofal of repairing the Temple in the 18th year of his reign, but to the time when in purfuance of that propofal he actually fet about the work, after he had got all things in a readineffe for it, and it will be eafily perceived that thefe words are agreeable to truth.

I do not prefume to determine, which of thefe two Solutions is the jufteft: or whether St. *Luke* intended the fifteenth of *Tiberius's* Proconfular Empire when he was made Collegue with *Auguftus*, or the fifteenth of his fole Empire. In order to do this, it would be needful, as I apprehend, to confider the time allotted by the Evangelifts to the miniftry of *John* the *Baptift* and our Saviour, the Chronology of the *Acts* of the *Apoftles*, compared with fome paffages in the Epiftles, and alfo the teftimonies of the ancient Chriftian writers. As I have not here room for all thefe premifes, it may be beft to wave the conclufion. All I fhall fay at prefent is, that the Suppofition, that St. *Luke* intended the former of thefe two epochaes, feems to be very much favoured by the firft Chriftians,

ftians, who generally place the crucifixion of Jefus at the Paffover of the 15th of *Tiberius*'s fole Empire, when the two *Gemini* were Confuls of *Rome*, A. D. 29 : And that their teftimonies are of great weight with me. I fubjoin in the Margin *(a)* a few of them, for the fake of thofe who may happen to be unacquainted with thefe matters.

I APPREHEND that each of thefe is a very good Solution of the objection ftated at the beginning of this chapter, though I believe many will think it is there ftated by me in a manner very favourable to an objector. Nay, I imagine I have faid what is fufficient to fatisfy any reafonable perfon, that there does not lie any objection againft any notes of time mentioned by the Evangelifts

(a) Hujus [*Tiberii*] quinto decimo anno imperii paffus eft Chriftus ——Quae paffio hujus exterminii intra tempora lxx. hebdomadarum perfecta eft fub Tiberio Caefare, Coff. Rubellio Gemino & Rufio Gemno, menfe Martio, temporibus Pafchae. *Tertul.* adverf. Jud. c 8. Atque exinde ufque ad annum quintum decimum Tiberii Caefaris, quando paffus eft Chriftus, numerantur anni fexaginta. *Africanus* apud *Hieron.* Dan. C.ix. Qui fuit fub imperio Tiberii Caefaris; cujus anno quinto decimo, id eft, duobus Geminis confulibus ——Judaei Chriftum cruci affixerunt. *Lactant.* Inft. l.4. c. 10. Extremis temporibus Tiberii Caefaris, ut fcriptum legimus, Dominus nofter Jefus Chriftus a Judaeis cruciatus eft,————duobus Geminis confulibus. de *Mort. Perfecut.* c. 2.

from

from the Chronology of other ancient writers. This is fufficient to my prefent purpofe.

I HAVE nothing farther to add here, befide this one obfervation.

I T is no difparagement to the facred Hiftorians, that we are fomewhat at a lofs to fettle precifely the very year of fome of thofe events which they have related. Many important facts related by the beft hiftorians are attended with Chronological difficulties. I fhall give but one inftance, an inftance which we are nearly concerned with. *Jofephus* was a man of a learned education, is a profeffed writer of hiftory, of the civil and facred hiftory of his country: and is generally allowed to be an accurate writer. He has exprefly mentioned two epochaes of the commencement of *Herod*'s reign, and has given an account of his death, and the duration of his government. He has writ the hiftory of the whole reign of this Prince. He has related the Series of events, and the Succeffion of the Princes and Governours of *Judea* before and after *Herod*. He has put down the years of the *Olympiads*, and the names of the Confuls, when fome of the moft remarkable of thefe events happened. Nor have all *Roman* and *Greek* hiftorians been

been silent about *Herod* or his defcendents, and the *jewifh* Affairs, near this time: Not to mention *Talmudical* or other *jewifh* Authors. And yet, notwithftanding all thefe advantages, whether through prejudice or want of fufficient light, it has happened, that learned men have differed widely about the time of *Herod*'s death, and are not yet come to a full agreement.

C H A P. IV.

Of *Annas* and *Caiaphas.*

§. I. *The difficulty relating to their being both high-priests at the same time considered.* §. II. *Of Caiaphas being high-priest* that year, *in which Jesus was crucified.*

I. WE have another objection against the account St. *Luke* gives of the Government *Judea* was under, when *John* the *Baptist* began to preach. *Now in the fifteenth year of the reign of Tiberius Cesar, Pontius Pilate being governour of Judea, and Herod being Tetrarch of Galilee.*-----ANNAS AND CAIAPHAS BEING THE HIGH-PRIETS *the word of* *God came unto John* *.

*Luke iii. 1, 2.

I T is objected, that it appears from the books of the *Old Testament*, the writings of *Josephus* and other *Jews*, that there was

but

but one High-Prieſt among the *Jews* at a time. St. *Luke* therefore has been miſtaken in ſaying, that *Annas* and *Caiaphas* were both High-Prieſts.

MUCH has been writ upon this ſubject, and learned men (*a*) have been of divers opinions. I hope I may be excuſed, if in this place I depart from the method I uſually take in conſidering theſe objections, and do not ſet down all the Sentiments of writers upon this point.

I SHALL here therefore do little more than deliver my own Sentiments concerning this matter in a few particulars, which, I hope, will contain a ſufficient anſwer to the objection.

1. IT would be extremely unreaſonable to impute to St. *Luke* ſo great a miſtake as the ſuppoſing, that there were properly two High-Prieſts among the *Jews* at the ſame time. He appears in the reſt of his hiſtory well acquainted with *jewiſh* affairs. It is plain, that he knew very well there was one who was in the office of High-Prieſt: ch. xxii. 50. *And one of them ſmote the Ser-*

(*a*) Vid. *Baron.* Ann. A. D. 31. num. 8.——*Caſaubon* in *Baron.* Exerc. xiii. Num. v. *Selden* de Succeſſ. in Pontif. Lib. i. cap. 12. *Hammond.* Annot. cum multis aliis.

vant

vant of the HIGH-PRIEST.---- 54. *Then took they him and led him, and brought him to the* HIGH-PRIEST's *houſe.*

2. I т is likely, that the power which the *jewiſh* people were poſſeſſed of under the *Romans* was lodged chiefly in the hands of two perſons: and it may be ſuppoſed, the *Jews* choſe to have it ſo. When they had reſolved upon the War with the *Romans*, *Joſephus* ſays: ' They aſſembled in the tem-
' ple, and appointed ſeveral Generals. And
' *Joſeph* the Son of *Gorion*, and the High-
' Prieſt *Ananus*, were choſen to be ſupreme
' governours (*a*) of all things in the City.'
I have not obſerved this paſſage quoted by any upon this occaſion : Whether it be material or not, the reader will judge. But it has inclined me to ſuppoſe, that about this time there were uſually among the *jews* two perſons, to whom the government was chiefly committed. I muſt however advertiſe the reader, that *Ananus*, here called High Prieſt, was not then in the office of the Prieſt-hood.

(*a*) Καὶ συναθροισθέντες εἰς τὸ ἱερὸν, ςρατηγὸς ἀπέδειξαν ᾧ πολέμε πλέιονας· ἡρέθη ϳ 'Ιώσηπ۞ υἱὸς Γωρίων۞, ᵹ ὁ ἀρχιερεὺς 'Αναν۞, ᵹ τε κατὰ τὴν πόλιν ἁπάντων αὐτοκράτορες, ᵹ μάλιςα τὰ τείχη τῆς πόλεως ἀνεγείρειν· De Bell. 2. c. 20. §. 3.

3. SINCE *Caiaphas* was now properly High-Prieſt, and *Annas* had been ſo ; if the latter was now in ſome poſt of authority, they might be both ſaid very properly to be High-Prieſts at this time. *Joſephus* often calls *Saturninus* and *Volumnius* Preſidents or Governours of *Syria* (*a*), though *Saturninus* only was Preſident, and *Volumnius* the Emperour's Procurator, that is, the officer that took care of the revenue.

THERE happened a diſturbance between the *Jews* and the *Samaritans* in the reign of *Claudius*. *Cumanus* the Procurator of *Judea* was not able to compoſe it : appeals were made to *Quadratus* Preſident of *Syria*. He having puniſhed ſeveral ' ſent two others of ' the moſt powerful men of the *Jews*, as ' alſo THE HIGH PRIESTS *Jonathan* and ' *Ananias,* and *Ananus* the Son of this laſt ' mentioned perſon, and ſome other conſide- ' rable men to *Ceſar* (*b*)'. I take this paſſage of *Joſephus* (which has been often cited by

(*a*) Πολλάκις μ̅ ἐπὶ Σατυρνῖνον ἐλθόντα & 'Ουολύμνιον τὰς Συρίας ἡγεμόνας· Ant. lib. 16. cap. x. p. 741. v. 1, 2. Τοῖς Καίσαρ& ἡγεμόσιν Σατυρνίῳ τε κ̕ 'Ουολυμνίῳ——ἐπί τε Σατυρνίν8 κ̕ 'Ουολυμνί8 τ̅ Συρίας ἐπιστατύντων. ibid. cap.ix. p.734. v.25. & 37.

(*b*) Δύο δ̕ ἑτέρυς τ̅ δυνατωτάτων, κ̕ τὰς ἀρχιερεῖς 'Ιυνάθην κ̕ Ανανίαν, τόν τε τύτυ παῖδα "Ανανον —— ἀνέπεμψεν ἐπὶ Καίσαρα. De Bell. lib. ii. cap. xii. §. 6.

learned

learned men) to be very near parallel with
St. *Luke's.*

JONATHAN had been High-Prieſt,
but had been put out long before now by
Vitellius (a): *Ananias* was (b) now High-
Prieſt. In like manner, in the caſe in queſtion,
Annas had formerly been High-Prieſt, but
Caiaphas was now in that office.

I am the more inclined to think *Joſephus's* ſtile here parallel with St. *Luke's,*
becauſe it appears from another place, where
Joſephus mentions this affair, that *Ananus,*
the third perſon named, was then Captain
of the Temple (c). From whence I conclude, that the Three perſons here mentioned
were then in the three chief poſts of the
jewiſh civil and ſacred Government. He
ſpeaks indeed of two others, whom he calls
the *moſt powerful of the Jews.* But I apprehend they were ſo only in reſpect of their
influence. It is reaſonable to ſuppoſe, that
the perſons named were in the moſt eminent
Stations.

T here is another particular, in which
theſe two paſſages are parallel: *Jonathan,*

(a) Ant. 18. cap. 6. §. 3.
(b) Ibid. 20. cap. 4. p. 886. v. 41.
(c) Ant. 20. c. 5. p. 889. v. 36.

who had been High-Prieft, is named before *Ananias*, then in office: The two
names ftand in the fame order in Saint
Luke.   I fuppofe, that thefe propofitions
may afford a clear Solution of this difficulty.

THE learned *Selden* conjectures, that
Annas and *Caiaphas* are not mentioned in
this place by St. *Luke* on account of any
Sacred function they difcharged, but as they
were the two perfons who had then the chief
authority under the *Romans* in the *Civil* adminiftration of the *jewiſh* affairs : that *Annas*
was now Prince of the *Sanhedrim*, and
Caiaphas the father of it; and that therefore *Annas* is firft named, as being in the
more honourable ftation of the civil government. He fuppofes that thefe two pofts might
then be annual, that *Annas* was Prince of
the *Sanhedrim* when *John* the *Baptift* began his miniftry, and that *Caiaphas* was
Prince when our Saviour was crucified.
And therefore St. *John* fays particularly,
that *Caiaphas* was High-Prieft *that fame
year* *. But that afterwards when *Peter* * *Joh.* xi.
and *John* were called before the council, 49. 51.
Annas, who is firft † named, was *Prince*, † *Acts* iv.
6.

X   and

and *Caiaphas*, *Father* of the *Sanhe-drim* (*a*).

SELDEN offers thefe thoughts, as conjectures only. I hope therefore, it will not be deemed prefumption, to be of another mind, or to offer fome different thoughts upon this fubject.

As *Caiaphas* was now in the office of the Prieſthood when *John* the *Baptiſt* be-gan his miniſtry, I fuppofe that *Caiaphas* is mentioned by St. *Luke* on the account of

---

(*a*) Hinc, fi conjecturae venia detur, exiſtimarim, Annam & Caiapham Pontifices fimul a D. Luca dictos, non qua facrae functionis dignitas illo nomine denotatur, fed qua civilis eorum adminiſtratio, ut & ceterorum quibufcum conjunguntur, ad ipfum annum, de quo verba ibi fiunt, indicandum denotaretur. Scilicet Annam tunc fuiſſe Synedrii Principem, Caiapham verò ejufdem Patrem.——Ita demum cur Caiaphas, quem facram dignitatem ipfam velut Aharonis fucceſſorem geſſiſſe inter-vallo illo ex Jofepho docemur, Annae poſtponatur, ratio non inepta reddi poteſt. Etenim Principi Synedrii Pater Synedrii erat femper fecundarus. Sed vero nec Principis nec Patris Synedrii munus femper perpetuum erat, fed ab alio ad alium, pro re nata tranſlatum. Quod ex titulo Talmudico Horaijoth, cap. iv. alufque Magiſtrorum commentariis elicitur. Et forfan tunc temporis annuum erat. ——— Atque illinc forfan altera illa quaeſtio de Caiaphae pontificatu fuo anno apud D. Joannem defignato folvenda——Adeo ut Anno Tiberii xv, feu in loco D. Lucae, Annas eſſet Princeps Synedrii, Caiaphas Pater, anno vero Paſſionis Annas Pater, Caiaphas Princeps; poſtmodum vero Annas, inter fuos utpote eminentiſſimus, itidem Prin-ceps, & Caiaphas Pater, ut in Actorum quarto. *Selden.* de Succ *In Pontif.* lib. i. c. xii.

the

the High Priesthood, and the Civil Authority
joined with it; and that, the *jewish* government being at this time under the *Romans*
Ariftocratical, *Annas* is mentioned together
with *Caiaphas*, as being the other chief perfon in the *jewish* adminiftration. But I am
of opinion, that we have not fufficient light
at prefent to determine, what Poft of honour *Annas* was in, though that of Prince
of the *Sanhedrim* be as likely as any. However, I cannot eafily perfwade my felf, that
during the *Jews* fubjection to the *Romans*,
the Prince of the Sanhedrim, or any other
Jew, not in the High Priefthood, was equal,
much lefs fuperior to him who enjoyed that
Office: unlefs, when there was fome *jewish*
Prince appointed Governour of the Temple
by the Roman Emperour. If *Jofephus*'s
authority be fufficient to decide this matter,
it is plain the High-Prieft had the chief power in the *jewish* nation under the *Romans*.
This may be concluded from hence, that he
has preferved the Succeffion of the High-
Priefts, and of them only, to the deftructi-
on of the Temple. But if there had been
after the removal of *Archelaus* any perfons
in an office of fuperior authority to the High-
Prieft, he would have alfo given us their

X 2
names.

names. We should also in all probability have met with some accounts in his history, of the putting out of these Officers by the Roman Governours, when they did not behave to satisfaction. And indeed *Josephus* seems to me expresly to say, that the High-Priest was the chief person in the *jewish* nation under the *Romans*. Having at the conclusion of his Antiquities reckoned up the *jewish* High-Priests he says : ' Some ' of these administered affairs under *Herod* ' the King and his Son *Archelaus :* after ' their death the administration was *Ari-* ' *stocratical,* but the Presidentship of ' the nation was committed to the High- ' Priests (*a*).

FARTHER, I apprehend no mystery at all in the order in which these two persons are named by St. *Luke.* Ancient writers seem not to be very solicitous about the order in which they name persons who are pretty near equal (*b*). I suppose that
Caiaphas

(*a*) Καί τινες μ̃ αὐτῶν ἐπολιτεύσαντο ἐπί τε Ἡρώδȣ βασιλεύον-τ⊙, ϗ ἐπὶ Ἀρχελάȣ ᵹ παιδὸς αὐτȣ· μετὰ δὲ τὴν τȣτων τελευτὴν, ἀρισοκρατία μ̃ ἦν ἡ πολιτεία, τὴν ʝ προςασίαν ᵹ ἔθνȣς οἱ ἀρχιερεῖς πεπίσευντο· Joseph. Antiq. xx. c. 9. fin.

(*b*) Thus *Herodotus* says, that *Cambyses* was the Son of *Cyrus* and *Caffandana :* and presently after, that he was Son of this woman and *Cyrus.* Παρέλαβε τὴν βασιλη̃ην Καμβύσης, Κύρȣ

Caiaphas was at this time chief in dignity and authority in the government : But that neverthelesse, there is no abfurdity or impropriety in naming *Annas* firft, inafmuch as he was father-in-law to *Caiaphas*, and was paft the Priefthood.

§. II. I T will perhaps be expected I fhould here fay fomewhat to a Text of St. *John*, which has a relation to this matter, and which does appear at firft to be a very difficult place. *And one of them named Caiaphas, being* HIGH-PRIEST THAT (a) SAME YEAR, *faid unto them, ye know nothing at all, nor confider that it is expedient for us, that one man fhould die for the people, and that the whole nation perifh not. And this fpake he, not of himfelf : but being (b)* HIGH-PRIEST THAT

Κύρε ἐὼν παῖς ᾗ Κασανδάνης————ταύτης ᷍ τῆς γυναικὸς ἐὼν παῖς ᷍ Κύρε Καμβύσης· *Euterp.* init. *Jofephus* fay·, *Herod* had two Sons by a *Samaritan* woman, namely, *Antipas* and *Archelaus.* Soon after, *Archelaus* is mentioned firft, ἣν ᷍ κἀκ ᷍ Σαμαρίαν ἔθνες μία, ᷍ παῖδες αὐτῇ Ἀντίπας ᷍ Ἀρχέλαῷ——Ἀρχέλαῷ ᷍ ᷍ Ἀντίπας ἐπὶ Ῥώμης παρά τινι ἰδιώτη τροφὰς εἶχον· *Antiq.* 17. c. 1. § 3. *Jofephus* fays again, that *Herod* called to the Council at *Berytam Salome* and *Pheroras, De Bell.* l. 1. c. 27. §. 3. Afterwards *Tero* the old Soldier complains to *Herod*, that he hearkned to *Pheroras* and *Salome* againft his own Sons, *ibid.* §. 4.

(a) Ἀρχιερεὺς ὢν ᷍ ἐνιαυτῆ ἐκείνε ὢν ᷍ ἐνιαυτῆ ἐκείνε, προεφήτευσεν.

(b) Ἀλλὰ ἀρχιερεὺς

YEAR, HE PROPHESIED *that Jesus should die for that nation: and not for that nation only, but that also he should gather* John xi. 49—52. *together in one the children of God that were scattered abroad.*

THERE are here two things which need to be explained; *first*, Why *Caiaphas* is said to be High-Priest *that same year* : And *secondly*, What is meant by his *prophesying*, being *High-Priest*.

SOME have thought that the Phrase, *being High-Priest that year*, implies that St. *John* supposed the High Priesthood was annual. And upon this account they have been willing to charge him with a great mistake. For *Pontius Pilate* was Governour of *Judea* ten years, and *Caiaphas* was put into the Priesthood by *Valerius Gratus*, *Pilate's* Predecessor; and continued in it, till after *Pilate's* removal. *Selden* thought that by High-Priest is meant the chief man of that nation, and particularly the Prince of the Sanhedrim, which post might be at that time annual. For my own part, I think, *that year* (as it ought to have been rendered, and as the same phrase is render'd *v.* 51, and not that *same year*) denotes no more than at *that time*. It is
very

very common to put *years* and *days* in the plural number, for time. *After many* DAYS *thou shalt be visited: In the latter* YEARS *thou shalt come into the land that is brought back from the sword*, &c. *Then shall the* Ezek.
xxxviii. 8. *offerings of Judah be pleasant unto the Lord, as in the* DAYS *of old, and as in* Malach.
iii. 4. *former* YEARS. There are other texts perhaps more apposite to our purpose. *And thou shalt go unto the priest that shall be in* Deut.
xxvi. 3. THOSE DAYS. *And he shall dwell in that City, until the death of the high-priest that* Josh. xx.
6. *shall be in* THOSE DAYS. *Philo* uses the word *day*, in the singular number, in the same manner: Speaking of the trial of Jealousy, he says, the man and the woman shall go up to the temple, ' and the man standing before the ' altar shall declare the cause of his jealousy ' in the presence of him who is Priest at that ' (*a*) day'. All that St. *John* says therefore is, that *Caiaphas* was High Priest at that time, or the High-Priest of that time. And if we ought to suppose any thing emphatical in the expression, which yet I cannot see, I apprehend it arises from the distance between the

---

(*a*) Καὶ ὁ μ̄ ἀνὴρ τὰς ἀντικρὺ δ̄ βωμῦ, παρόντος δ̄ κατ᾽ ἐκείνην τὴν ἡμέραν ἱερωμένȣ, δηλȣ́τω τὴν ὑπόνοιαν ἅμα· κ. λ. De Legibus special. p. 785. C.

time,

time of the event and the writing. Saint *John* writing his Gospel a considerable time after the crucifixion of Jesus, when many might be supposed to be ignorant who was then High-Priest, and there having been under the *Romans* frequent removals made in that office, it was natural enough for him to expresse this circumstance with some peculiar emphasis, or to mention it more than once.

THE other difficulty to be considered lies in these words : *Being High-Priest that year he prophesyed.* Here I cannot perceive the sense of this observation, supposing, with *Selden*, High-Priest to stand for Prince of the Sanhedrim. By *prophesying* I understand in this place, declaring the event, which it was in a peculiar manner the office of the Priest to do, when he was enquired of, or when God was enquired of (A) by him concerning any important matters under deliberation. Thus

(A) *Then the king sent to call Ahimelech the* PRIEST *the Son of Ahitub* ——*And Saul said unto him, Why have ye conspired against me, thou and the Son of Jesse,*——*and hast* ENQUIRED *of God for him?* 1 Sam. xxii. 11 13. *And David said to Abiathar the* PRIEST, *Bring hither the Ephod. Then said David, O Lord God of Israel*——*Will the men of Keilah deliver me into his hand? Will Saul come down, as thy servant hath heard?*——*And the Lord said he will come down,* 1 Sam. xxiii. 10.—12. *And when Saul enquired of the Lord, the Lord answered him not, neither by dreams, nor* BY URIM, *nor by prophets,* ch. xxviii, 6.

Josephus

Josephus says: ' But the *Philistines*, when
' they heard that the *Hebrews* had made
' *David* King, brought forth their army
' against him.----------But the (*a*) King of
' the *Jews* (for he allowed not himself to
' do any thing without prophesy, and the
' command of God, and assurance of the
' event from him) required the High-Priest
' to foretell him, what was the will of God,
' and what would be the issue of the battle.
' When he had prophesied victory and pow-
' er, he led out his forces against the *Phi-*
' *listines*'. And presently after : ' The (*b*)
' King of the *Israelites* enquiring again of
' God, concerning the event of the battle,
' the High-Priest prophesyed', that he should
do so and so, and then would have a sure
and easy victory : referring to the story told,
2 *Sam*. v. 22---25.

LET us now apply these remarks in a general paraphrase of this text of St. *John*.
Some of the council, of a different opinion

(*a*) Ὁ ὃ τ̄ Ἰυδαίων βασιλεὺς, ἐδὲν ᵹᷓ ἄνευ προφητείας, κϳ τ̄
κελεῦσαι τὸν Θεὸν, κϳ περὶ τ̄ ἐσομένων λαβεῖν ἐγγυητὴν ἐκεῖνον,
ἑαυτῷ ποιεῖν ἐπέτρεπεν. ἐκέλευσε τὸν ἀρχιερέα, τί δοκεῖ τῷ Θεῷ, κϳ
ποδαπὸν ἔσαι τὸ τῆς μάχης τέλ⊙, προλέγειν αὐτῷ· προφητεύ-
σαντ⊙ ὃ νίκην κϳ κράτ⊙, ἐξάγει τὴν δύναμιν ἐπὶ τὰς Παλαιϛί-
νας· *Antiq.* 7. c. 4. §. 1.

(*b*) Πάλιν ὃ τ̄ βασιλέως τ̄ Ἰσραηλιτῶν ἐρομένε τὸν Θεὸν, περὶ
τῆς περὶ τὴν μάχην ἐξόδε, προφητεύει ὁ ἀρχιερεὺς, κ. λ. ibid.

from

from thofe whofe words are recorded v. 48, having, as may be fuppofed, from confiderations taken from the difpofitions of the people, the temper of the Roman Governour, and other circumftances of their affairs, exprefled fome doubts about the fucceffe of a profecution of Jefus, and the confequences of taking away his life: ' *Caiaphas,* who
' was the High-Prieft at that time, when it
' came to his turn to deliver his opinion,
' faid : You have hitherto talked very weak-
' ly and ignorantly. You may proceed in
' the cafe before you without hefitation. The
' taking (*a*) away the life of this man will
' be fo far from being ruinous to the whole
' nation in this country and in other parts,
' as fome of you fear, that it will be much
' for the advantage of the people of God
' every where. This however he faid, not
' merely of himfelf: but being then High-
' Prieft, he foretold the iffue and event of
' their counfels and of the death of Jefus :
' And that it (*b*) would come to paffe that
' Jefus would die for that nation, and not

(*a*) Ὑμεῖς ἐκ οἴδατε ἐδὲν ἐδὲ διαλογιγίζεσθε ὅτι συμφέρει ἡμῖν ἵνα εἷς ἄνθρωπ@- ἀποθάνῃ ὑπὲρ ̃$ λαᾶ, κỳ μὴ ὅλον τὸ ἔθν@- ἀπόληται.

(*b*) Προεφήτευσεν ὅτι ἔμελλεν ὁ Ἰησᾶς ἀποθνήσκειν ὑπὲρ ̃$ ἔθνες, κ. λ.

' for

' for that nation only, but that through his
' death he would alſo gather together in one
' the children of God which were ſcattered
' abroad.'

CHAP. V.

Of the different names given to *Herodias*'s firſt husband by the Evangeliſts and *Joſephus*.

I COME now to conſider the difficulty hinted above (A) ariſing
from the different names given by
the Evangeliſts and *Joſephus* to the firſt huſband of *Herodias :* whom they call *Philip* *, *Matth.
Joſephus, *Herod*. I need not tranſcribe xiv. 3.
here the paſſages of the Goſpels, or of *Jo-* 17.
ſephus, relating to this affair. If the reader 19.
will be pleaſed to look back (B) he will
find what is ſufficient for the purpoſe.

(A) Vol. 1. p, 14. note c.
(B)—p. 12.———15.

As

As *Josephus*, speaking of this unlawful marriage of *Herod* the Tetrarch and *Herodias*, calls her first husband *Herod*; so it is certain that according to him, *Philip*, whom Saint *Luke* stiles *Tetrarch of Iturea and the region* *of Trachonitis*, could not be the person:

Luke iii.1.

for *Josephus* says, that *Herodias's daughter Salome was married to Philip, Herod's Son, the Tetrarch* (a) *of Trachonitis*. Nor is there any mention made in *Josephus* of any other Son of *Herod* the Great, who was called *Philip*, beside the forementioned Tetrarch of *Iturea* and *Trachonitis*.

I HAVE no reason to say any thing more of *Philip* the Tetrarch than I have done already, having shewn in another place (c), that St. *Luke* has given a just account of him. But I will here give a brief history of *Herod*, to whom *Josephus* says *Herodias* was first married; because I apprehend it may be needful for some readers, and it will be of great use to us upon this occasion.

HEROD was the Son of *Herod* the Great by *Mariamne* daughter of *Simon* the High-Priest. After *Herod* the Great had

(a) Ἡ ἢ θυγάτηρ αὐτῆς Σαλώμη Φιλίππῳ γαμεῖται, Ἡρώδῃ παιδὶ τῷ Τετράρχῃ τῆς Τραχωνίτιδ℗· Antiq. 18. c. vi. §. 4.
(c) Vol. i, p.12.

killed

killed his two Sons *Alexander* and *Aristo-bulus*, he repented of what he had done, and refolved to take fpecial care of their children. And in particular, he contracted *Herodias*, daughter of *Ariftobulus*, to the above mentioned *Herod* (*a*). There happened indeed afterwards fome alterations in the difpofitions made by *Herod* the Great at this time, but however this (*b*) contract remained good, as may be concluded from hence : that this contract is not mentioned among thofe alterations, and becaufe in the account *Jofephus* gives of *Herod* the Tetrarch's unlawful marriage with *Herodias*, her firft husband, whom fhe left in his lifetime, is exprefly faid to be *Herod* Son of *Mariamne* the High-Prieft's daughter.

HEROD the Great in one of his wills, made after this contract, appointed the faid *Herod* his Succeffor in cafe *Antipater* fhould die before him. But afterwards, in the enquiries concerning *Antipater*'s defign to poyfon his father, it appeared that *Mariamne*, mother of *Herod*, had been con-

(*a*) Ἐνεγγυητό τε εἰς γάμον——την ἢ ἑτέραν Τ̅ Ἀριϛοββλȣ θυγατέρων, Ἡρώδη παιδὶ τῷ αὐτῷ· γίνεται ἢ τῷ βασιλῖι ἐκ τῆς Τ̅ Ἀρχιερέως θυγατρός· Ant. lib. 17. c. i. p.751. v. 1. vid. & p.1027. v. 36.

(*b*) Vid. *Jofeph.* p. 751. v. 20. p. 1028. v. 35.

cerned

cerned in the fame defign : whereupon *Herod* the Great put away *Mariamne*, altered the claufe of his Will relating to her Son, and took away the Priefthood from her father (*a*) *Simon*. After this we hear no more of *Herod*, till we have the account of *Herodias*'s leaving him.

HERE then lies our difficulty. The Evangelifts call *Herodias*'s firft husband *Philip*. It is objected that they muft mean *Philip* the Tetrarch. But it is plain from *Jofephus*, that *Philip* the Tetrarch was not her firft husband, but *Herod*, fon of *Herod* the Great by *Mariamne* the High-Prieft's daughter.

IN anfwer to this : 1. It has been faid by fome, that *Jofephus* was miftaken. Mr. *Bafnage* (*b*) of *Flottemanville*, whom I have

often

(*a*) Καὶ διὰ τάδε Ἡρώδης ἐκείνην τε ἐξέβαλε κỳ τὸν υἱὸν αὐτῆς ἐξήλειψε ᵗ διαθηκῶν, ἐις τὸ βασιλευσαι μεμνημένων ἐκείνȣ· κỳ τὸν πενθερὸν τὴν ἀρχιερωσύνην ἀφείλατο Σίμωνα τὸν ᵗ Βοηθȣ· Antiq. 17. c.iv. p.757. v.43. vid. & p. 1033. v. 30.

(*b*) Nulla ergo excufatio Jofepho parari poteft. Cujus narrationi, illa Evangeliftarum, miflâ vel eorum ἀναμαρτησία dubio procul eft anteponenda, cum teftes & plures, & antiquiores fuerint, & rationes longè graviores habuerint diligentius inquirendi in caufas mortis illatae Joanni, quas ducunt ex Herodiadis, Philippo Legitimo viro, contra jus & fas, ab Antipae ereptae odio, in Joannem, fceleftas nuptias damnantem.
Equi-

often quoted, is fully perſwaded, that *Philip*, Tetrarch of *Iturea* and *Trachonitis*, was *Herodias's* firſt huſband. Beſide that the Evangeliſts lived nearer the time of the Event than *Joſephus*, he ſays, they had more reaſon to be well informed in this matter than *Joſephus*, and they are three to one. Mr. *Baſnage* does not deny *Herod's* having had a ſon of his own name by the High-Prieſt's daughter: but he ſays, this ſon died before his father. And he thinks, that *Joſephus* ſays as much, and has aſſured us that after *Antipater* was dead, *Herod* had no ſons left, beſide *Archelaus, Herod Antipas*, and *Philip*, betwixt whom he divided his kingdome. And therefore *Joſephus* is guilty of a moſt flagrant ſelf-contradiction in making the Son of the High-Prieſt's daughter, *Hero-*

Equidem Joſephus tenetur ἐπ' αὐτοφόρῳ deprehenſus, cum ipſe docuerit, Herodi Magno poſt mortem Antipatri, nil filiorum fuiſſe, praeter Archelaum, Herodem Antipam, & Philippum, quos inter, regnum diviſerat ſuum. Nec vero ſimile eſt in teſtamento, hujus Herodis, Herodiadi, ut ait Joſephus, matrimonio conjuncti, parentem non meminiſſe, ne expers partis eſſet, de bonis ejus; eo magis, quo multa Salomi ſorori ſuae praedia moriendo dederat Herodes. Id faciles Joſepho largiemur, ex Simonis Pontificis filia procreatum Herodi regi filium fuiſſe, paterno nomine donatum. Parenti ſuperſtitem fuiſſe, negabimus, ex alto hiſtoriae Judaicae ſilentio, in qua vir ille partes egiſſet ſuas.——— Erravit igitur Joſephus——— *Baſnage. Ann. Polit. Eccleſ.* A. D. 29. n. iii.

dias's

dias's husband.　Besides there is no mention of this Son in *Herod* the Great's laft will, which would be very ftrange, if he was then alive, efpecially confidering that *Herod* left his Sifter *Salome* a very good eftate in land.

THIS is Monfieur *Bafnage*'s Solution: but, in my opinion, a very poor one.　I will not be pofitive that *Jofephus* has made no miftake in the accounts of *Herod*'s family: becaufe where a man has iffue by feven or eight wives, as *Herod* had, perhaps a writer had need to have a head peculiarly turned for genealogy to be fecure from all errors in giving an account of his children and all their marriages; efpecially confidering how much the (D) female defcendents of *Herod* in-

(D) Befide *Herodias*, her three nieces, daughters of her brother *Herod Agrippa*, would employ the attention of an Hiftorian.　*Bernice*, the eldeft, after the death of her firft husband *Herod* King of *Chalcis*, married *Polemon* King of *Cilicia*, [or as fome read it *Lycia*].　'But this marriage lafted not long, ' for *Bernice* left Polemon.'　Ὀυ μὴν ἐπὶ πολὺ συνέμεινεν ὁ γάμ⊙, ἀλλὰ Βερνίκη δἰ ἀκολασίαν, ὡς ἔφασαν, καταλείπει τὸν Πολέμωνα· *Antiq.* 20. c. 6. §. 3. *Mariamne* [the fecond daughter] ' about ' the fame time, having divorced *Archelaus* the Son of *Helchias*, married *Demetrius* the *Alabarch* of the *Jews* at *Alexandria*.τῷ ἀυτῷ ἣ καιρῷ κỳ Μαριάμμη,παραιτησαμένη τ̃ Ἀρχέλαον, συνῴκησε τῷ Δημητρίῳ—τότε δὴ κỳ τὴν ἀλαβαρχίαν ἀυτὸς εἶχε. ibid. *Drufilla*, the youngeft, left *Azizus* King of the *Emefenes* and married *Felix*: as has been fhewn already, V.I. p. 33.

have

increafed the task in a fhort time by leaving or divorcing their husbands. But I can never perfwade my felf, that *Jofephus*, a profefied writer of *jewifh* hiftory, could be guilty of fo many miftakes as are included in a miftake about *Herodias's* firft husband. If he was not furnifhed with the events of all *Herod's* children, yet he muft certainly know the marriages of the laft princes in the land of *Ifrael*, his own country. Could he be ignorant who was *Philip* the Tetrarch's wife? who was the firft husband of *Herod* the Tetrarch's fecond wife, and of *Agrippa* the

have put down here all thefe inftances for the fake of a remark. Our Saviour fays : *Whofoever fhall put away his wife, and marry another, committeth adultery againft her. And if a woman fhall put away her husband, and be married to another fhe committeth adultery.* Mark x. 11, 12. It may be inferred from hence, that the *jewifh* women, as well as the men, did then practife Divorces, and after that marry to others. Thefe inftances from *Jofephus* confirm the inference. We may be affured thefe Lad es were not fingular. Their examples would be followed by others: and, it is likely, were fupported by many precedents. If the women took this licence, what wou'd not the men do! Our Hiftorian *Jofephus* afiords us a double example of this practice. His firft wife left him, *vit.* §. 75. And he married another. Her he divorced after he had had three children by her, becaufe he was not pleafed with her Manners. And then he married a third, by whom alfo he had children. καθ᾽ ὃν δὴ καιρὸν κỳ τὴν γυναῖκα, μὴ ἀρισκόμενΘ- αὐτῆς τοῖς ἤθεσιν, ἀπεπεμψάμην,τριῶν παίδων γενομένην μητέρα. §. 76.

Y   Great's

Great's Sister? Was not *Herodias*'s leaving her firſt husband, in all reſpects a moſt notorious action? Was not *Joſephus* well acquainted with her nephew, *Agrippa* the younger?

Mr. *Baſnage* ſays, *Joſephus* has aſſured us *Herod* had but three ſons left after the death of *Antipater*. I think, *Joſephus* has never ſaid any ſuch thing. If he had, he would be a writer of no weight, ſince he has afterwards expreſly ſaid that *Heroridas*'s firſt husband was *Herod* the ſon of the High-Prieſt's daughter. And if *Joſephus* had aſſured us *Herod* the Great had but three ſons left after *Antipater* was dead, Mr. *Baſnage* might have ſpared his arguments from the omiſſion of *Herod* the High-Prieſt's daughter's ſon, and the large eſtate left to *Salome*, in *Herod* the Great's laſt will.

Indeed, there is no reaſon to conclude that *Herod*, ſon of the High-Prieſt's daughter, died before his father: but a great deal of reaſon to ſuppoſe he ſurvived him, beſide the expreſſe mention made of him long afterwards as the husband of *Herodias*. For in the will his father made after the enquiries into *Antipater*'s conſpiracy, and there:

therefore in the laſt year of his life, this ſaid *Herod*'s ſucceſſion was ſtruck out, as *Joſe-phus* expreſly ſays (a).   And though there be no mention made in *Herod*'s laſt will, of any other ſons by name, beſide thoſe to whom he left a part of his territories; yet it is very likely, there were others to whom he left preſents (b).   It is not ſtrange that *Herod* ſhould leave no towns or Lordſhips to this ſon (though living) in his laſt will, ſince his mother had been lately detected in a great crime.   Nay, it is not ſtrange, that Three ſons only of *Herod* had Tetrarchies, and the reſt, though never ſo many, only ſums of money or revenues.   As for the Towns bequeathed by *Herod* to his ſiſter *Salome* ; ſhe had been always faithful to him, and it was fit ſhe ſhould have ſome extraordinary teſtimony of his affection. *Joſephus* himſelf (c) aſſigns this as the

(a) See before, p. 221.   (b) *Joſephus*'s account of *Herod*'s laſt Will is, that he gave to *Herod Antipas*, Galilee, *&c.* to *Philip*, *Gaulonitis*, &c. to *Archelaus* the Kingdome, to *Salome* his Siſter, *Jamnia*, &c. and that he took care of all the reſt of his family, leaving them handſome legacies of mony or ample revenues. πρυνόησε ϳ κϳ τ̃ λοιπῶν ὁπόσοι συγγενεῖς ἦσαν αὐτῷ, χρημάτων τε δόσεσι κϳ προσόδων ἀναφοραῖς, ἑκάςυς ἐν εὐπορίᾳ καθιςάμενⒸ. Antiq. 17. c. 8. §. 1.

(c) Σαλώμην τε ἐπὶ μέγα ἐπλύτιζεν τὴν ἀδελφὴν, ἕυνεν τε ἐν πᾶσι πρὸς αὐτὸν διαμεμενηκυῖαν κ. τ. λ. Antiq. 17. c. vi. §. 1.

reaſon

reafon of that regard fhewed to her in *He-rod*'s wills.

AND *Philo* fays, that when *Pilate* dedicated fhields and placed them in *Herod*'s palace at *Jerufalem* (a), the *Jews* got four (b) of the Kings fons, and other his defcendents to make ufe of their intereft with *Pilate* to remove the fhields. If *Philo* may be relied upon in this matter, and if we may underftand the word *Sons* in the moft proper fenfe, (which it feems moft reafonable to do) and not for Grandchildren or other defcendents; then *Herod* muft have left behind him at left two Sons, befide thofe three betwixt whom he divided his dominions : For *Archelaus* certainly was not one of the *four* fons whom *Philo* fpeaks of, becaufe he had been banifhed into *Gaul* long before *Pilate*'s government. Suppofing then that *Herod* Tetrarch of *Galilee* and *Philip* Tetrarch of *Trachonitis* were two of the four, there muft have been two other Sons of *Herod*, befide them and *Ar-chelaus*.

(a) Ἀνατίθησιν ἐν τοῖς κατὰ τὴν ἱερόπολιν Ἡρώδε βασιλείοις· *Philo de legat. in Cai. p.* 1034. A,   (b) Προςησάμενοι τὰς τε βασιλέως υἱεῖς τέτταρας —— ϗ τὰς ἄλλες ἀπογόνες· id. ibid.

BUT

But however *Philo* ought to be understood, I can never think it a fair way of getting rid of this difficulty to charge *Josephus* with a great many grossblunders.

2. I proceed therefore to lay before the reader another Solution which has been in the main approved of already by many learned men.

(1.) The Evangelists and *Josephus* are in the right, and none of them have committed any mistake in this matter. I have just shewn, that there is no reason to think *Josephus* was mistaken. And it is as unreasonable to suppose, that the Evangelists are mistaken. They all agree in calling *Herodias*'s first husband *Philip*. And they appear to be fully master of the history of *Herod* the Great's family. One or other of them have told us, that *Archelaus* succeeded his father in *Judea*, that *Herod* (who was also called *Antipas*) was Tetrarch of *Galilee*, *Philip* of *Trachonitis*. If they had not been well informed, some errors would have appeared here. St. *Luke* has given the proper titles and characters to all the other descendents of *Herod* whom he hath mentioned afterward, *Herod* the King, *Agrippa*, *Bernice*, *Drusilla*.

THEY speak of this unlawful marriage of *Herodias*, as a matter they were well acquainted with; and *Josephus* concurs with them in the main.

(2.) THE Evangelists do not intend *Philip* the Tetrarch, but the same person that *Josephus* does. If they had intended *Philip* the Tetrarch, when they speak of *Herodias*'s husband, they would have given him his title. This is their constant method. St. *Matthew* says, that Jesus was born *in the* Matth. ii.
1.
Luke i. 5. *days of Herod the king*. St. *Luke*, that the vision of *Zacharias* was *in the days of Herod the king of Judea*. In the account of our Saviour's return from *Egypt* St. *Matthew* says, that *Joseph* heard that *Archelaus* did reign, in *Judea, in the room of* Matth. ii.
22. *his father Herod*. St. *Luke* gives the proper titles to all the princes whom he mentions at the beginning of *John* the *Baptist*'s Luke iii. 1. ministry. In the account of *Pilate*'s sending our Saviour to *Herod* it appears plainly, Luke xxiii.
6.--8. that he was the Tetrarch of *Galilee*, to whom he was sent. When St. *Luke* begins the history of *Herod Agrippa*, he calls him Act xii. 1.
Act.xxv.
13. *the king*. He gives also the title of *King* to *Agrippa*.

INDEED

INDEED the church at *Jerufalem* in their prayer to God give *Herod* and *Pontius Pilate* no titles. And I believe none would have them there at length. In the account of the death of *John* the *Baptift*, and this marriage, all the Evangelifts do ever give *Herod* his title: But not one of them have given the *Philip* whom they mention any title, but that *Herod had laid hold of John, and put him in prifon for Herodias fake, his brother Philip's wife,* or bound him in prifon *for Herodias fake, his brother Philip's wife.* Again: *H rod the Tetrarch being reproved by him for Herodias his brother Philip's wife.* I make no doubt therefore but that *Philip, Herodias's* firft husband, was a private perfon who lived in all probability at *Jerufalem,* and that *Herod* the Tetrarch in his way to *Rome* there fell in love with her and made the contract. *Philip* then, whom the Evangelifts fpeak of, as the firft husband of *Herodias,* was a private perfon, invefted with no titles or dignities: and fo is *Jofephus's Herod*, as appears from the hiftory I have given of him: And it is not unlikely, that this was one reafon, among others, why *Herod* the Tetrarch's propofal of mar-

Act.iv. 27.

Matth.xiv. 1. Mark vi. 14. Luke iii. 19. xi. 7. Matth.xiv. 3. Mark vi. 17. Luke iii.

riage.

riage was fo foon accepted by *Herodias,* an ambitious woman.

THE only difficulty therefore concerning this matter arifes from the name. *Jofephus* calls this perfon *Herod,* the Evangelifts *Philip* : Moreover *Philip* was the name of the Tetrarch of *Iturea* and *Trachonitis,* therefore it may be thought ftrange, that *Herod* the Great fhould have another fon called *Philip.*

THIS difficulty will be cleared by the following confiderations. It is not at all ftrange that *Herod* the Great fhould have two fons called by the fame name, when he had children by feven or eight wives. Even according to *Jofephus,* the eldeft fon was called *Antipater,* and another, who was the youngeft, *Antipas* or *Herod Antipas,* the Tetrarch of *Galilee.* Thefe are but one and the fame name, only a different termination. *Jofephus* mentions three of of *Herod's* fons of the name *Herod,* without any other addition (*a*). But yet it is highly probable, they had fome other names by which they were diftinguifhed,

(*a*) Vid. *Jofeph. Antiq.*L. 17. C. i, L. 18, C. vi. §. 4. *De Bell.* L. i. C. xxviii. & Genealog. Herod. in *Reland. Paleft. Illuftr.*

though

though *Josephus* has not mentioned them. *Grotius* (*a*) thinks it very probable, there was a *Philip* among the anceftors of *Herod* the Great, after whom two of his fons were named *Philip*: as there were two of them, who bore the name of *Antipater* or *Antipas* from his father.

THOUGH there was another brother by the fame father, namely *Philip* the Tetrarch, called by the fame name with *Herodias*'s husband; yet it was not neceffary for the Evangelifts to take notice of it. When writers relate a well known fact, near the time in which it happened, whilft there is no danger of perfons making a miftake, this precaution is often neglected. *Dio*'s account of *Archelaus*'s removal is thus: ' *Herod* of *Paleftine* being accufed by his ' brothers was banifhed to the other (*b*) ' fide the *Alps*'. *Herod* was the name by which the Tetrarch of *Galilee* was ufually called. And he alfo was afterwards banifhed to the other fide the *Alps*. Yet I believe no one ever charged *Dio* with a miftake here as to the perfon he fpeaks of, or fuf-

(*a*) In *Matth*. xix. 3.

(*b*) Ὅ, τε Ἡρώδης ὁ Παλαιϛηνὸς, αἰτίαν τινὰ ἀπὸ Ṫ ἀδελφῶν λαβὼν, ὑπὸ τὰς Ἄλπεις ὑπερωρίσθη. lib. 55. p. 567. B.

pected

oected that he thought the Tetrarch of *Ga-lilee*, was banished from his dominions A.U. 759. I will transcribe here an observation of the learned and judicious Dr. (*a*) *Prideaux.*
' He [*Ptolomy Lathyrus*] was succeeded
' by *Cleopatra* his daughter, and only le-
' gitimate child. Her proper name was
' *Berenice*, and so *Pausanias* calls her. For
' it is to be noted that as all the males of this
' family had the common name of *Ptolomy,*
' so all the females of it had that of *Cleo-patra,* and besides had other proper names
' to distinguish them from each other.
' Thus *Selene* was called *Cleopatra,* and so
' were also two other of her Sisters. And
' in like manner this daughter of *Lathyrus,*
' whose proper name was *Berenice* bore also
' that of *Cleopatra,* according to the usage
' of her family. The observing of this will
' remove many obscurities and difficulties
' in the *Egyptian* History'.

THE Evangelists do all agree in calling *Herodias*'s first husband *Philip:* and they appear fully masters of their story. It is therefore highly reasonable to suppose he was called *Philip* as well as *Herod.* I shall put a case resembling this. *Josephus* al-

(*a*) Conn. Part. ii. year before Christ 81, p. 396:

ways

ways calls *Livia*, *Augustus*'s wife, (*a*) *Julia*, though that was the proper name of *Augustus*'s daughter, without ever giving the left hint of his reason for it. It is true, that though the Roman historians do generally call her *Livia*; yet they have told us, that she had also the name of *Julia*, and have informed us of the reason of it; which was, that *Augustus* in his last will adopted his wife into the *Julian* family, and appointed that she should bear the name of *Julia* (*b*). And there are medals, on which she bears this name. But if nothing of this had appeared in any of the Roman authors, or inscriptions that are extant; yet since *Josephus* appears to be well acquainted with the Roman affairs from *Julius Cesar* down to his own time, I believe, most men would have allowed that he had some good reason for calling the wife of *Augustus Julia*. And for the same reason a like supposition ought to be made in behalf of the Evangelists in the case before us.

(*a*) Vid. *Joseph.* p. 1028. not. h.

(*b*) Tiberium & Liviam heredes habuit. Livia in familiam Juliam nomenq; Augustae adsumebatur. *Tacit. Ann.* Lib. i. c 8. vid. & *Sueton. Aug.* cap. 101. *Dion.* p. 600. A.

It

I t was exceeding common among the ancients, *Jews* and others, for perfons to have two names, and to be called fometimes by the one, and fometimes by the other. There are feveral inftances in the *New Teftament.* *Simon, who is called Peter; Lebbeus, whofe furname was Thaddeus : Thomas, which is called Dydimus : Simeon, that was called Niger ; Saul* who was alfo called *Paul.*

Matt. x. 2, 3.

John xi. 16. *Act.* xiii.1.

· *JOSEPHUS* calls *Caiaphas,* the High-Prieft, *Jofeph.* He has indeed told us that he was alfo called *Caiaphas* (a). If man-kind would have been as equitable to the writers of the *New Teftament,* as they ufual-ly are to other authors, to fome who are far from giving equal tokens of fkill or probity with them, this would have created no dif-ficulty, though *Jofephus* had never fubjoined the name of *Caiaphas* to that of *Jofeph.* But if any had been difpofed to give the Evangelifts unfair and unequal treatment, it is likely, they would have pretended that here was a notorious blunder; and that *Caiaphas* was fo far from being High-Prieft when *John Baptift* began his miniftry, and when Jefus was crucified, that there never

, (a) P. 795. v. 23. 802. v. 28.

was

was any such person High-Prieſt among the *Jews*.

I HOPE what is already ſaid may be ſufficient to convince all reaſonable men, there is no juſt ground to ſuſpedt the Evangeliſts of any miſtake in the name of *Herodias*'s firſt huſband. However, there is ſomewhat farther to be offered. There are other writings extant in which he is called *Philip*. I ſhall tranſcribe here the account of it in Dr. *Whitby*'s words. ' *Gorionides* ſaith, ' *Herodias* was firſt married to *Philip*, and ' then taken away from him by *Herod An-* ' *tipas*. The old *Hebrew* chronicle ſaith, ' *Uxorem fratris ſui Philippi ipſo vivente* ' *junxit ſibi matrimonio, quae liberos ex* ' *fratre ejus ſuſceperat, & tamen is eam* ' *duxit uxorem* ' (chap. 36). And an old ' *Chronicle* of the ſecond Temple, ſaith, ' *Antipas Philippi fratris ſui uxorem ac-* ' *cepit, ex qua ille liberos ante genuerat* ' (F. 54. c. 4.) *i. e. Antipas* married the ' wife of his brother *Philip*, he being yet ' living, and having had children by her (*a*).

(*a*) *Whitby* on *Matth.* xiv. 3.

CHAP.

C H A P. VI.

Of *Zacharias* the Son of *Barachias.*

THERE are some difficulties attending the prophetical repre-
sentation, given by our Lord, of
those judgments which he fore-
saw, would soon befall the *jewish* nation.
This we have in two of the Evangelists, in
St. *Matthew*, and St. *Luke*. One account
will illustrate the other, and we may have
some occasion to refer to each of them : and
therefore I shall set them both down here
at once.

THE account of this matter, as it stands
in St. *Matthew*, is thus: *Woe unto you
Scribes and Pharisees, hypocrites, because
ye build the tombs of the Prophets, and
garnish the sepulchres of the righteous ; and
say, if we had been in the days of our fathers,
we would not have been partakers with
them in the blood of the Prophets. Wherefore*

fore ye be witnesses unto your selves, that ye are the children of them that killed the Prophets. Fill ye up then the measure of your fathers. Ye Serpents, ye generation of vipers, how can ye escape the damnation of hell? Wherefore, behold, I send unto you Prophets, and wise men and Scribes, and some of them ye shall kill and crucifie, and some of them shall ye scourge in your Synagogues, and persecute them from city to city: that upon you may come all the righteous blood shed upon the earth, from the blood of righteous Abel, unto the blood of ZACHARIAS, SON OF BARACHIAS, whom ye slew between the temple and the altar. Verily, I say unto you, all these things shall come upon this generation *.

THE parallel place in St. Luke is in these words: Wo unto you, for you build the sepulchres of the Prophets, and your fathers killed them. Truly ye bear witness that ye allow the deeds of your fathers, for they indeed killed them, and ye build their sepulchres. Therefore also said the wisdom of God, I will send them Prophets and Apostles, and some of them they shall slay and persecute; that the blood of all the Prophets, which was shed from the foundation

* Matth. xxiii. v. 29.—36.

dation

dation of the world, may be required of this generation ; from the blood of Abel, unto the BLOOD OF ZACHARIAS, *which perished between the altar and the temple : verily, I say unto you, it shall be required of this generation*.*

* *Luke* xi.
47—51.

HERE the Evangelists may be charged with a mistake several ways. They who would suppose, that the *Zacharias* here referred to, is *Zacharias*, one of the twelve lesser *jewish* prophets, will say, they must have been mistaken, because in the time of this *Zacharias*, the temple is supposed to have been in ruins: and therefore it is impossible, he should have been killed *between the temple and the altar*. And others, who suppose the *Zacharias* here intended, is the *Zacharias*, whose death is related in 2 *Chron.* xxiv, may say, that St. *Matthew* mistook the name of his father. For his name was *Jehojada*, and not *Barachias*.

THERE is another *Zacharias*, whose death is related by *Josephus*. But that happened not till long after the time, in which our Saviour is supposed to have spoken these words. This seems to afford the most formidable objection. I shall therefore state

and

and confider it particularly. And in an-
fwering this I hope to anfwer alfo the other
two.

BEFORE I ftate this objection, I fhall
here tranfcribe the paffage of *Jofephus*, on
which it is founded. I muft abridge it indeed, but I fhall omit nothing that's material to the point before us.

'THE zealots, *fays Jofephus*, were ex-
'ceedingly enraged againft *Zacharias* (*a*)
'the fon of *Baruch*: for he was a man who
'detefted all wickedneffe, was a lover of
'liberty, and moreover was very rich. They
'call (*b*) together therefore by a decree feven-
'ty of the chief of the people, and form
'a kind of Council deftitute of all autho-
'rity. They then brought *Zacharias* be-
'fore them, and accufed him of a confpiracy
'with the *Romans*: and in particular charg'd
'him with fending meffengers to *Vefpafian*,
'the better to concert meafures for betray-
'ing them into his hands'. But they had no
witneffes. The facts were not proved.
Zacharias in a fpeech he delivered before the
Council confuted all the calumnies of the

(*a*) Ζαχαρίαν υἱὸν Βαρέχε.

'(*b*) Συγκαλᾶσιν ἐξ ἐπιτάγματ⊙ ἑβδομήκεντα ᾦ ἐν τέλει
δημοτῶν.

Z   zealots,

zealots, and warmly reproved them for their wickednesse ' The seventy then acquitted ' him, choosing rather to die with him, than ' to bring upon themselves the imputation ' of his death. He being thus absolved, the ' zealots raised a loud clamour against these ' Judges, as not understanding the design for ' which they had been invested with autho-' rity. And two of the most daring of the ' zealots, falling upon *Zacharias* in the middle ' of the Temple, slew him there *(a)*.

It may be said then : From hence it appears, that the writers of these books were not acquainted with the affairs of those times. These writings therefore don't come from St. *Matthew* or St. *Luke.* At left the authors of them did not live at the time they are supposed to have lived : possibly not till long afterwards. How else could they have committed such a blunder, as to make Jesus tell the *Jews* of his time, in the reign of *Tiberius,* that they had killed *Zacharias* the son of *Barachias,* or *Baruch;* when *Josephus* informs us, that he was not killed till the latter end of *Nero's* reign,

(a) Δύο 5 τῶν τολμηροτάτων, προσπεσόντες ἐν μέσῳ τῷ ἱερῷ, διαφθείρεσι τὸν Ζαχαρίαν. De Bell. l. 4. c. 5. § 4.

above

above thirty years after thefe words are faid
to have been fpoken by Chrift?

I. T o this I anfwer, in the *firft* place,
that the fact related by *Jofephus* does not
fuit the words of Chrift in the Evangelifts.

F o r (1.) the name of the father of *Zacharias* feems to be different. Dr. *Whitby*
(a) obferves ' that as *Baruch* in *Jeremiah*,
' and the *Apocrypha* is always called by
' the Septuagint Βαρὲχ (*Baruch*) fo ברכיה
' (*Barachiah*) is rendered by them Βαραχίας
' (*Barachiah*) *Ifa.* viii. 2. *Zach.* i. 1. 7.
' And in *Neh.* iii. we find Βαραχίας (*Ba-
' rachias*) *v.* 4. and Βαρὲχ (*Baruch*) *v.* 20.
' which fhows they were not the fame
' name'.

(2.) T h e i r characters are not the
fame. The defign of our Saviour's difcourfe
obliges us to fuppofe, that the *Zacharias* he
mentioned was a *prophet*: Whereas the
Zacharias in *Jofephus* has not that character from him.

(3.) T h e place, in which they are faid
to have been flain, is not the fame. The
Zacharias in the gofpels perifhed *between
the temple and the altar*, according to both
St. *Matthew* and St. *Luke*. But there is

(a) On *Matth.* xxiii. 35.

no

no reafon to fuppofe, that *Jofephus's Zacharias* was flain in the inner court, in
which the altar ftood. The council was not
held within that Court : and *Zacharias*
feems to have been flain immediately after
his abfolution by the council. If he was
flain in any part of the (ἱερὸν) temple, that
is perfectly agreeable to the words of *Jofephus*; for under that name were comprehended the temple and all the courts
and buildings belonging to it.

THESE feveral inftances of difagree-
ment, I fhould think, muft incline moft
perfons to conclude, that the fame *Zacharias*
was not intended by the Evangelifts and
Jofephus.

BUT perhaps this is more than is reafonable to expect fhould be allowed by an Objector. He can eafily believe of writers who
are in little credit with him, that they may
run far wide of the truth ; and really intend a fact that has but a fmall refemblance
with their relation. With fuch what hath
been faid hitherto will have little weight.

I PROCEED therefore to fome other
confiderations.

II. I SAY then, that our Lord in the
words we are now confidering, inftanceth

in

in facts suppofed to have been done a confiderable time before. The whole tenour and
defign of his difcourfe affure us of it.

THE *Zacharias* he mentions is not one
whom they of that age had themfelves flain,
but rather one of thofe prophets whofe
tombs they built.

THE fum of what our Saviour fays (if
I miftake not) is this: Ye fay, *If we had
been in the days of our fathers, we would
not have been partakers with them in the
blood of the prophets.* This you fay; but,
as hereby you own, that you *are the children of them that killed the prophets*; fo by
your conduct, by your malice, your pride,
your hypocrify, your obftinate difobedience
to God, you make it appear that you allow
the deeds of your fathers, and are their genuine off-fpring. You even exceed them in
wickedneffe. You are now filling up, and
you will ftill go on to fill up the meafure
of their iniquity. I am come among you
in my fathers name, and have done works
which no man ever did; but you do not
hearken to me. My words you do not receive, and me you will crucifie. God will
ftill fend among you, as he did to your fathers, prophets and wifemen, to inftruct you

in

in the moſt excellent doctrine, to admoniſh and reclaim you: but ye will kill and crucifie them, ſcourge them in your Synagogues, and perſecute them from City to City. Hereby you will make the wicked deeds of your fathers your own, and bring the guilt of 'em upon your ſelves: You will hereby deſerve, that all the righteous blood, ſhed from the foundation of the world, from the blood of righteous *Abel* to the blood of *Zacharias*, ſhould be required of you: and verily I ſay unto you, *it ſhall be required of this generation.*

Our Lord ſeems to me to remind them of inſtances of diſobedience and cruelty, which they were well acquainted with, *which they avowedly condemned*, and pretended to ſee the evil of; but yet did, and would imitate in a moſt notorious manner: and. hereby would bring the guilt of them upon themſelves. And the concluſion of all obliges us to ſuppoſe, that the death of the *Zacharias* he had mentioned, was an act of cruelty committed by their fathers. This is the ſenſe of the words in both the Evangeliſts.

This appears to me ſo evident, that if there had been no event recorded in any of
their

their ancient writings which anſwered to the
death of *Zacharias* here deſcribed ; yet I
ſhould have ſuppoſed that there was ſome
ſuch event, that had happened ſome time
before, and which they were then well acquainted with.

III. HOWEVER, we have (*a*) a fact
recorded in the *Old Teſtament* which exactly anſwers the words of our Saviour. It
is in 2 *Chron.* xxiv. 17.---22. *Now after
the death of Jehojada-- -they left the houſe
of the Lord God of their fathers------and
wrath come upon Judah and Jeruſalem----
yet he ſent prophets unto them to bring
them again unto the Lord, and they teſtifid
againſt them : but they would not give
ear. And the ſpirit of God came upon
Zachariah, the ſon of Jehojada the prieſt,
which ſtood above the people, and ſaid unto them, Thus ſaith God, Why tranſgreſſe
ye the commandment of the Lord? And
they conſpired againſt him, and ſtoned
him with ſtones at the commandment of
the king in the court of the houſe of the
Lord. Thus Joaſh the king remembered
not the kindneſs which Jehojada his father had done to him, but ſlew his ſon :*

(*a*) Vid. *Whitby*, *Matt.* xxiii. 36.

and

and when he died, he said, the Lord look upon it and require it.

This fact is exactly parallel with that described by your Lord. (1.) This *Zachariah* spoke in the name of the Lord (*the spirit of God came upon him*). It was suitable to our Lord's design to instance in the death of a prophet. *Ye say, if we had been in the days of our fathers, we would not have been partakers with them in the death of the* PROPHETS ---- *I send unto you* PROPHETS, *and wisemen and scribes.* *Abel* was a *righteous man,* and this *Zacharias* a *prophet.*

(2.) THE place, in which this *Zacharias* is said to have been killed, answers the description in the Evangelists. He was slain in the *court of the house of the Lord,* that is, in the court of the priests, the inner court of the temple. In both the Evangelists the same place is specified, *between the temple and the altar.* This particular circumstance of so remarkable an event was, doubtless, handed down to them by tradition. According to the account in the *Chronicles,* he was in the inner court when he delivered his message from God to them : *He stood above the people.* The ground of the inner court was raised above the rest. He stood at

the

the extremity of that, and spoke to the people standing in the next court below him. *At the commandment of the King*, they rushed in upon *Zachariah*. He retired, they pursued him and *stoned him with stones*, so that he fell down in the space between the altar of burnt-offerings and the temple.

(3.) OUR Lord subjoins : *whom* YE SLEW. The death of *Zacharias* in the *Chronicles* was the act of the nation, of King and People. This particular is added to this instance with the highest propriety. The death of *Abel* was the death of a *righteous man*, but not committed by them. The death of *Zacharias* was the act of their ancestors, that is, of that people to whom our Lord was speaking. For a nation is in all ages reckoned the same people. *And he answered and said unto them, what did Moses command* YOU *? Verily I say unto you, Moses gave* YOU *not that bread from heaven. Did not Moses give* YOU *the law ?*

Mark x. 3.
Joh. vi. 32.
--vii 19.
see--- 22.

(4.) EXPRESSIONS made use of in the history of *Zacharias* in the *Chronicles*, and by our Saviour in his discourse to the *Jews* put it past doubt that he intended this fact,

fact, and alluded to this very account in that book. *Behold I fend unto you prophets and wife men and fcribes.* The hiftory in the *Chronicles* begins thus : *Yet he fent unto them prophets to bring them again unto the Lord, and they teftified againft them,*&c. It concludes thus: *And when he died, he faid, the Lord look upon it and require it.* Our Saviour tells the *Jews, that the blood of all the prophets would be required of that generation.*

(5.) As the fact related in the *Chronicles* does in all its circumftances anfwer that defcribed by our Lord, fo there is a fuitablenefle in the order in which it ftands in our Lord's difcourfe. *Abel* is the firft *righteous man* flain, and the death of this *Zacharias* is the laft act of cruelty to a *prophet* related in the *Jewifh* facred writings.

IV. It ought to be obferved, that there is an exact harmony between the Evangelifts, in the account they have given of this difcourfe of our Saviour, though there is no reafon to think that one has copied the other. This ought to fatisfy us that no miftake has been made.

In one particular indeed there is a difference. In St. *Matthew Zacharias* is ftiled
the

the son of *Barachias,* whereas in St. *Luke's* account it is not said who was his father.

AND in this particular the person whom our Saviour speaks of seems not to answer to him mentioned in the Chronicles. For there he is called the son of *Jehojada.*

THERE is therefore but one objection against supposing, that our Saviour meant the *Zacharias* in the *Chronicles.* But it is such an objection as deserves consideration.

IT has been observed by (*a*) divers learned men, that many persons among the *Jews* were called by two names, especially when their true name happened to have some of the letters of the word *Jehovah* in it. For this reason *Barachias* may have been used for *Jehojada,* since likewise these two names have much the same meaning.

OTHER learned men suppose, that *Barachias* was very early inserted into Saint *Matthew's* Gospel by some transcriber. There is the more reason for this supposition, because it is wanting in St. *Luke* : Or else *Jehojada* might have been originally in St. *Matthew,* but some Christian transcriber not well acquainted with the *Jewish* history nor knowing who *Jehojada* was, and there-

(*a*) Vid. *Grot.* & *Whitb.* in loc.

fore

fore fufpecting that to be a miſtake, might
pretend to correct it by putting *Barachias* in
the room of *Jehojada*. *Zachariah* the ſon
of *Barachias*, whoſe prophecies form one
of the books of the *Old Teſtament*, was
certainly better known among the Chriſtians
than *Zacharias* the ſon of *Jehojada*. It is
not at all unlikely therefore, that our not
having this name in St. *Matthew* may be
owing to the ignorance and raſhneſſe of ſome
tranſcriber. This ſuppoſition ſeems to be
favoured by what St. *Jerome* ſays, who informs us, that in the *Goſpel of the Nazarenes*
Zachariah is called *the Son of* (a) *Jehojada.*

S o m e have thought, that there is a like
inſtance in *Matth.* xiii. 35, where we have
theſe words : *That it might be fulfilled*
which was ſpoken by the prophet ſaying, I
will open my mouth in parables, &c. The
the words of this quotation are in *Pſ.* 78. 2.
the title of which is *Maſchil of Aſaph.* Saint
Jerome (b) ſays that in ſome copies of
St. *Matthew* it was written : *That it might*
be fulfilled which was ſpoken by the prophet
Eſaias. He thinks it was originally : *which*

(a) In evangelio quo utuntur Nazareni, pro filio Barachiae,
filium Jojadae reperimus ſcriptum. S. *Hieron.* comment. *Matth.*
xxiii. 36.   (b) In loc.

was spoken by the prophet Asaph. But some transcriber, not knowing *Asaph* to be a prophet, put *Esaias* in his room. Afterward, others, perceiving there were no such words as those which follow here to be found in *Esaias,* left out his name. And from thence forward in most copies it was written: *which was spoken by the prophet,* saying, &c.

I CRAVE leave to mention an observation, that may support the former of these two suppositions, *viz.* that originally *the son of Barachias* was wanting in St. *Matthew,* as well as in St. *Luke.* The ancient Christians seem to have been very much divided in their opinion who the *Zacharias* here spoken of was. Many Christians in St. *Jerome's* time thought he was *Zacharias* the father of *John* the *Baptist,* borrowing this notion (as he *(a)* adds) from some Aprocyphal books of no authority. In the copies of St. *Matthew's* Gospel in his time, he was stiled the son of *Barachias,* as in ours: But the *Nazarene* Christians, being *Jews* by birth, and understanding the history of their own nation, had it in their Gospel, *Zacharias the son of Jehojada.* This in-

(a) Com. in *Math.* xxiii. 36.

deed

indeed was the truth, but it seems to have been an insertion.

B u t this is left to the reader to judge of as he thinks fit. It is highly probable, that one of these may be the case; either that *Johojada* not being well known, *Barachias* was put in his room: or else, that *the Son of Barachias*, was added.

T h e r e being so probable an account of this reading, I hope there remains no farther scruple about this text.

There is another interpretation of these words which some have inclined to, namely, that the *Zacharias* here mentioned is the *Zacharias* whose death *Josephus* has given us the history of : and that our Saviour spoke of him by way of prophecy. But as there can be no objection which I am concerned with formed against the Evangelists from this sense of the words, I have taken no notice of it.

Besides, I think it is by no means the true sense of the place. Dr. *Whitby* observes very well, that ' Christ speaks ' here of the Prophets whom they had slain, ' not of one who was to be slain a little be- ' fore the destruction of *Jerusalem* ; for ' then

‘ then none of the people could have un-
‘ derftood his meaning’.

By the whole tenour of our Saviour's
difcourfe, the *Zacharias* he fpeaks of is
excluded from the number of thofe that
were to be flain. If the *Zacharias* whom
Jofephus fpeaks of was as good a man as he
reprefents him, and did faithfully reprove the
wickedneffe of the prevailing party of his
nation, he might be one of thofe *holy and
wife men,* whom our Saviour forefaw would
be flain by the *Jews.* But he can never be
the *Zacharias* whom our Saviour mentioned
by name, for he is one of thofe *prophets*
which had been flain before, and whofe
blood would be required of them.

CHAP.

C H A P. VII.

Of *Theudas.*

T will be proper in the next place to
consider the objection relating to
Theudas. The Apostles were
brought before the council at *Jerusalem*:
And when they took counsel to slay them,
Gamaliel commanded to put the Apostles
forth a little space; and said unto them,
Ye men of Israel take heed to your selves,
what ye intend to do as touching these
men. FOR BEFORE THESE DAYS ROSE UP
THEUDAS, *boasting himself to be some body,*
to whom a number of men, about four hun-
dred, joined themselves : who was slain,
and all as many as obeyed him, were scat-
tered and brought to nought. AFTER THIS
MAN *rose up Judas of Galilee, in the days*
of the taxing, and drew away much people
after him : and all, even as many as obeyed
Act. v. 34. *him, were dispersed.*
36.

THIS

THIS ſpeech of *Gamaliel* was made not long after our Saviour's aſcenſion. *Ludovicus Cappellus* places it in the beginning of (*a*) *Caligula's* reign. Dr. *Whitby* (*b*) and others three or four years ſooner, in the 20th of *Tiberius* A. D. 34. And *Gamaliel* here ſpeaks of *Thendas* as having given diſturbance before *Judas* of *Galilee*, who in the days of the taxing drew away much people. This refers doubtleſs to the aſſeſſement made by *Cyrenius* after *Archelaus* was depoſed, when *Judea* was reduced to a Roman (*c*) Province: which happened in the ſixth or ſeventh year of the Chriſtian Aera. It was at this time that *Judas*, whom *Joſephus* calls *Judas Gaulanites*, and likewiſe *Judas* the *Galilean*, rais'd diſturbances in that country.

BUT *Joſephus* gives us an account of an Impoſtor, called *Theudas*, when *Cuſpius Fadus* was Procurator in *Judea*; and therefore not before the fourth year of *Claudius* the Roman Emperor A. D. 44. that is, ſeven years after *Gamaliel's* ſpeech was made,

(*a*) *Spicileg.* in Act. cap. v. 36. (*b*) *Whitby* Par. upon this text. (*c*) *Joſ. Antiq.* Lib. xvii. cap. ult. xviii. cap. 1. *De B. Jud.* Lib. vii. cap viii. §. 1.

accord-

according to *Cappellus's* computation, and ten years after it, according to Dr. *Whitby's.*

    J O S E P H U S's words are these: ‘ Whilst *Fadus* was Procurator of *Judea,* ‘ a certain Impostor called *Theudas* per- ‘ swaded a very great multitude, taking their ‘ effects along with them to follow him to ‘ the river *Jordan.* For he said he was a ‘ prophet, and that causing the river to di- ‘ vide at his command, he would give them ‘ an easie passage over. By these speeches ‘ he deceived many. But *Fadus* was far ‘ from suffering them to go on in their ‘ madnesse : for he sent out a troop of horse, ‘ who, coming upon them unexpectedly, ‘ slew many, and took many prisoners. ‘ *Theudas* himself was among the latter. ‘ They cut of his head, and brought it to ‘ *Jerusalem.* These things happened in ‘ *Judea,* while *Cuspius Fadus* was Pro- ‘ curator (*a*).’

It

(**a**) Φάδε ἢ τ' Ἰεδάιας ἐπιτροπέυοντος, γόης τίς ἀνὴρ, Θευδᾶς ὀνόματι πείθει τ' πλεῖσον ὄχλον, ἀναλαβόντα τὰς κτήσεις ἕπεσθαι πρὸς τὸν Ἰορδάνην ποταμὸν ἀυτῷ. προφήτης ᵹ ἔλεγεν ἔιναι, ἡ πρόσάγ- ματι τὸν ποταμὸν αίσας, διοδον ἔφη παρέξειν ἀυτοῖς ῥαδίαν· ἡ ταῦτα λέγων πόλλες ἐπάτησεν. ὀ μὴν ἔιασεν ἀυτὲς, τῆς ἀφροσύνης ὄναδξ Φάδες, ἀλλ' ἐξέπεμψεν ἴλην ἱππέων ἐπ' ἀυτὲς, ἥτις ἀπροσ- δόκητος ἐπιπεσῦσα, πόλλες μὲ ἀνῖλε, πόλλες ᵹ ζῶντας ἔλαβεν. ἀυτὸν

IT may therefore be pretended, that Saint *Luke* has made a miftake. The *Theudas* whom *Jofephus* mentions appeared not till feveral years after *Gamaliel's* fpeech was made. Nor has *Jofephus* faid any thing of any other. The perfon *Gamaliel* fpeaks of is of the fame name. He likewife *boafted himfelf to be fome body*, that is, *a prophet.* He was flain, and his followers were fcattered. In thefe particulars *Gamaliel* and *Jofephus* agree. Therefore they mean the fame perfon, but they differ moft widely about the time. For which reafon St. *Luke* muft have been miftaken.

DIVERS folutions have been offered of this difficulty.

1. SOME fay, St. *Luke* might put the affair of *Theudas* into *Gamaliel's* fpeech by way of anticipation. He knew very well, that *Theudas* did not appear till after this time; but this being a very proper inftance, and fuitable to the main fcope and defign of the fpeech which *Gamaliel* made, He inferted it himfelf. But this is not at all agreeable to the fimplicity of

αὐτόν τε τὸν Θευδᾶν ζωγρήσαντες ἀποτέμνουσι τὴν κεφαλὴν, κỳ κομίζουσιν εἰς Ἱεροσόλυμα· τὰ μ̃ ἐν συμβάντα τοῖς Ἰεδαίοις κατὰ τὸς Κυσπίε Φάδε τῆς ἐπιτροπῆς χρόνες, ταῦτα ἐγένετο. *Ant.* 20. c. 4. §. 1.

St. *Luke's*

St. *Luke's* narration, especially considering how particular he is as to the number of *Theudas's* followers: *To whom a number of men, about four hundred joined themselves.* And one would think *Valesius* was at a loss for examples of anticipation, when the only one he produces is out of a Poet, and that has scarce any resemblance with this before us (*a*).

2. SOME think that *Josephus* has been mistaken, and has misplaced *Theudas's* insurrection. This Solution *Valesius* prefers before the former; and it is approved likewise by Monsieur (*b*) *Le Clerc.* They understand *Gamaliel* to say: *Before these days* (*c*) that is, a *little while ago* rose up *Theudas,* boasting himself to be some body. And if you look farther back (*d*), *before this man*
(not

(*a*) Alia quoque conciliandi ratio excogitari potest; si dicamus B. Lucam in eo loco κατὰ πϱόληψιν locutum esse. Quae quidem figura occurrit interdum apud antiquos scriptores exempli causa apud Virgilium cum dicit
———*portusque require Velinos.*
Atqui cum haec dicerentur Aeneae, nondum condita erat Velia. *Valef. Annot. in Eufeb.* H. E. L. ii. c. xi.

(*b*) Clerici Hiftor. Eccl. A.D. 28. n.60.

(*c*) Πϱὸ γ̃ τέτων τ̃ ἡμεϱῶν ἀνέςη Θευδᾶς. Quae verba rem nuper ac novissimè factam demonstrant. *Valef.* ubi fupra.

(*d*) Sed quoniam Casaubonus negat Graecos unquam i locutos fuisse, producendus est testis omni exceptione major.

Is

(not *after this man*, as we render it) rofe up
Judas of *Galilee*.------Thus, according to
Valefius, *Jofephus* has not mifplaced this
event of *Theudas* above twelve years ; but
according to Mr. *Le Clerc*, the errour is greater, for he fuppofes he *rofe up* A. D. 28.

BUT this kind of Solution appears to me
perfectly arbitrary, and not to be untying,
but cutting the knot. And I freely own, I
have no right to them. It is very unlikely,
that *Jofephus* fhould have been miftaken a-
bout the time of that *Theudas*'s infurrection
which he gives an account of. He may have
made miftakes in chronology : but *Jofephus*
is very exprefs here, that this affair happened
in the time of *Fadus*, when he himfelf muft
have been feven years of age.

AND in my opinion thefe learned men
give a wrong meaning to two expreffions in
Gamaliel's fpeech. It is not neceffary to un-

?s eft Clemens Alexandrinus, qui in lib. 7 Stromat. fub finem,
eodem prorfus modo locutus eft quo B. Lucas—*Nam Marcion
i'fdem quidem temporibus vixit quibus Bafilides & Valentinus.
Verum tanquam fenior cum illis adhuc junioribus verfatus eft.*
addit deinde, μεθ' ὅν Σίμων ἐπ' ὀλίγον κηρύσσοντος ϒ̃ Πέτρѕ
ὑπήκυσεν. *Poft quem Simon praedicantem Petrum audivit aliquamdiu.* Quis non videt in hoc Clementis loco *poft hunc* idem
Valere atque *ante hunc*—fed & geographiae fcriptores, quoties
terrarum fitum & populorum nomina defcribunt, eodem loquuntur modo. Dicunt enim μετὰ τѕ́τѕς ἰσὶν ἐκεῖνοι. *id. ibid.*

der

derftand thofe words, *Before thefe days rofe up Theudas*, of a *little while ago*, two or three years before. Thefe common phrafes are loofe and undetermined in all languages, and fignifie fometimes, a fhorter, at others, a longer fpace of time. And the fubjcct matter of the difcourfe, or the coherence of things, or fome light from abroad can alone determine what the fpace of time intended is. It is faid : *But Saul increafed the more in ftrength, and confounded the Jews which were at Damafcus.*----AND AFTER THAT MANY DAYS *were fulfilled, the Jews took counfel to kill him.* By thefe *many days* can be meant but a fhort fpace of time, as appears from *Gal.* i. 17. 18. St. *Paul* tells *Felix: Forafmuch as I know that thou haft been of many years a judge unto this nation, I do the more chearfully anfwer for my felf.* Though it is likely, *Felix* had not then been in *Judea* above five years. And yet it might be faid very properly, that he had been there *many years:* fince in five years time, a Governour may be fuppofed to gain a good infight into the laws and cuftoms of his province, and the temper of the people ; as alfo, becaufe very often Governours were removed in a fhorter fpace of time.

Acts ix. 22. 23.

Act. xxiv. 10.

time. When *Pilate's* Soldiers had marched into *Jerusalem* with Ensigns, the *Jews* went
from thence in a great body to *Pilate* at
Cesarea, and there made *Supplications, Josephus* (a) says, *many days.* But it appears
presently afterwards, that on the (b) *sixth day*
from their arrival *Pilate* seated himself on
his Tribunal, and granted their petition.
So *Josephus* relates this in his Antiquities.
In his *War* these earnest Supplications continued *five whole days* (c) *and nights.*

THUS these phrases that seem to import
a long duration, are much limited by the connexion of a discourse, or by the nature of
the things spoken of. And other phrases
that denote ordinarily a shorter duration, must
be understood sometimes with great latitude. There is an example in *Jeremiah* ch.
xxxi. 31. *Behold* THE DAYS COME *saith
the Lord, that I will make a new covenant
with the house of Israel, v. 33.* AFTER
THOSE DAYS, *saith the Lord, I will put my
law in their inward parts.* I suppose no
one thinks, these promises or predictions were
to be accomplished presently. *Porphyry* says

(a) Ἱκετείαν ποιέμενοι ἐπὶ πολλὰς ἡμέρας. Antiq. 18. cap.4.
§, 1.   (b) Κατὰ ἕκτην ἡμέραν———αὐτὸς ἐπὶ τὸ βῆμα
ἧκε ibid.   (c) Ἐπὶ πέντε ἡμέρας κὴ νύκτας ἴσας ἀκίνητοι
διεκαρτέρων, lib. 2.c. 9. §. 2.

A a 4   ‘ that

' that many of the ancients had been fup-
' pofed to underftand the founds of birds
' and other animals, and *Apollonius* (*a*) of
' *Tyana* not long ago.' *Apollonius* died
before the end of the firft century of the
Chriftian Aera. *Porphyry* was not born till
the 232d, or 233d year (*b*) of the fame
Aera. Every one muft be fenfible, with
what latitude *Porphyrie's not long ago* is to
be underftood.

I s e e no neceffity therefore of reftraining
the fenfe of the phrafe in this text, *before
thefe days*, to two or three years. It may as
well intend twenty or thirty years. It is
plain it does fo here, fince it was not till
after Theudas that *Judas* rofe up.

W h i c h brings me to the other phrafe
mifunderftood by thefe learned men : *After this man*, μετὰ τῦτον. The inftances
of the ufe of this prepofition by Geogra-
phers for a remoter diftance are not to the
point, becaufe here it imports time. And
as for *Valefius's* quotation from St. *Clement*,
I think it not worth while to confider here,
whether he underftand it aright or not. At
the beft St. *Clement's* paffage is very ob-

. (*a*) Ὡς ἐπὶ μ̅ τ̅ παλάιων ὁ Μελάμπⱺ,——κ̣ ὁι τοῖϛοι, ξ̣
πρὸ πόλλⱴ ϳ Ἀπολλώνιος ὁ Τυανέυς. *Porphyr. de Abſt.* lib. 3. c. 3.
(*b*) Vid. *Luc. Holſten. de V.t. & Script. Porphyr.* cap. 2.

fcure

fcure and perplexed. St. *Luke's* phrafe is
one of the moſt common phrafes in all the
Greek language, and is ever underſtood as it
is rendered in this place by our tranſlators.
It would be unreafonable to affix a new meaning to a very common phrafe upon the
fingle authority of one obfcure paſſage. This
is faid upon the fuppofition that the phrafe
in St. *Clement* was the fame with that in
St. *Luke*, and that the fenfe affigned by *Valefius* to St. *Clement's* paſſage was the moſt
likely fenfe of any. But indeed the phrafe in
St. *Clement* is not the fame, and for that
reafon is of the lefs weight here.

I SUPPOSE then that our tranſlation is
juſt, and that the fubſtance of this part of
Gamaliel's fpeech is this: Not long fince
rofe up *Theudas*. It might be thirty years
or more. The perfons he fpoke to knew
very well how long. And after this man,
in the time of the celebrated aſſeſſement,
when *Judea* was made a Roman province,
rofe up *Judas* of *Galilee*. Both thefe men
periſhed, and their adherents were fcattered.

3. AND the Solution, already offered
by divers learned (a) men, of the difficulty
under confideration, appears to me perfectly

(a) Cafaub, Exercit. in Baron. ii. n. 18. Grot. & Hamm. in
Act. v. 36.

juſt.

juſt. There were two *Theudas's* in *Judea* that were impoſtors, one before *Judas* of *Galilee,* and another in the reign of *Claudius.* There is no miſtake upon this head in *Joſephus,* nor in St. *Luke,* who has given us an exact and true account of *Gamaliel's* ſpeech.

It is not at all unlikely that there ſhould be two impoſtors in *Judea* of the ſame name in the compaſs of about forty (A) years, and that they ſhould both come to the ſame end. Theſe are the two chief difficulties in this matter, and they may be both cleared up.

(1.) It is not at all ſtrange that there ſhould be two impoſtors in *Judea* of the *name Theudas,* in the ſpace of forty years. There were ſeveral impoſtors named *Simon.* Beſide *Simon Magus,* mentioned in the *New Teſtament,* and often ſpoken of by the firſt Chriſtian writers, there was one *Simon* a ſervant of *Herod,* who, after his maſter's death, had the impudence to ſet himſelf up

(A) The interval cannot be ſhorter. *Joſephus's Theudas* could not appear before the year 44. *Gamaliel's Theudas* roſe up before *Judas* of *Galilee,* who made his diſturbance in the 6th or 7th year of the Chriſtian Æra.

for

for King, and put (*a*) on a diadem. After a long and obstinate engagement with *Gratus*, he was defeated, and his men were dispersed. He was taken prisoner, and by *Gratus's* order his head was (*b*) cut off. There was another *Simon*, son of *Judas* of *Galilee*, who was crucified in the (*c*) reign of *Claudius* by *Tiberius Alexander*, governour of *Judea* after *Fadus*. There was in the time of *Felix* one *Simon* of *Cyprus*, who pretended to Magic. I have already mentioned him in another place (B).

THERE were likewise several *Judas's* who gave disturbance to this country in a very short time. *Judas* of *Galilee* was a noted person, mentioned here by *Gamaliel*, and oftentimes by *Josephus*. He rose up in the time of the taxing presently after the removal of *Archelaus*. There was (*d*) another *Judas* (c), son of *Ezechias*, who soon af-

ter

(*a*) Ἦν ἢ κỳ Σίμων δȣλος μ̄ Ἡρὠδȣ ȣ̄ βασιλέως.—ȣτος ἀρθεὶς τῇ ἀκρασίᾳ τ̄ πραγμάτων, διάδημά τε ἐτόλμησε περιθίαϑ. *Antiq.* 17. c. 12. §. 6. (*b*) Γρᾶτος ἐντυχὼν τὴν κεφαλὴν ἀποτέμνει ibid. (*c*) Ibid. l. 20. c. 4. §. 2. (B) Vol. I. p. 34. (*d*) Ἰȣδας ἢ ἦν Ἐζεκίȣ υἱός, κ. λ. *Antiq.* 17. cap. 12. §. 5. (c) Archbishop *Usher* thinks this *Judas* to be *Gamaliel's Theudas*. ‘ For whereas *Jehudah* of the *Hebrews* is the same with *Theudah* of the *Syrians*, from whence *Judas* and *Thaddeus* [compare *Luke* vi. 16. with *Mark* iii. 18.] and much rather *Theudas*, the same name plainly comes. This

Judas

ter *Herod's* death affected regal authority, and did a great deal of mifchief. There was one *Judas,* fon of *Sepphoraeus,* a man in great reputation for his skill in the law, who with fome others raifed a Sedition during *Herod's* laft ficknelfe. He and fome of his confederates (a) were burnt alive. So that there were three men of the fame name, who in the fpace of about ten years raifed commotions in *Judea.*

(2.) Nor is the agreement of *character* and *circumftances* mentioned by *Gamaliel* and *Jofephus* a proof they fpeak of one and the fame perfon. There are but two particulars of this fort: That they pretended to be extraordinary perfons, and that they were flain and their followers fcattered or brought to nought. But in this there is nothing extraordinary. Though there had been yet more circumftances, in which they had agreed, this would have been no proof that one and the fame perfon is fpoken of.

GAMALIEL fays: *Theudas boafted himfelf to be fome body,* and he *was flain: Jofephus,* that *Theudas faid he was a prophet,* and *his head was cut off.*

‘ *Judas* feems to be no other than *Theudas,* of whom *Gamaliel*
‘ fpeaks *Acts* v. 36.’ *Annals* p. 797.

(a) *De Bell.* l. 1. c. 33. §. 2.———4.

JOSEPHUS

JOSEPHUS has informed us, concerning the *Theudas* he fpeaks of, that he got a good number of people to follow him to *Jordan*. Though *Gamaliel* and *Jofephus* had concurred in fo particular a circumftance as this (which they do not) yet it would not have been a fufficient reafon for our fuppo-fing that they intended the fame perfon.

I SHALL give an inftance. Of *Simon* (a) above-mentioned, fervant of *Herod*, *Jofephus* fays, that he plundered and burnt the palace at *Jericho*. And that he burnt feveral royal houfes in divers parts, having firft given them to be plundered by his followers. He fays alfo, that the people with *Simon* were chiefly (b) *Peraeans*, or people that lived on the other fide of *Jordan*. Afterward, even while he is fpeaking of affairs that paffed in *Judea* foon after the death of *Herod*, he fays that ' at *Amatha* near *Jordan* ' a Royal Palace was burnt down by a num-' ber of men very much like thofe who were ' with (c) *Simon*.'

(a) Τὸ ἐν Ἰεριχῶντι βασίλειον πιμπρησι δι' ἁρπαγῆς ἄγων τὰ ἐγκαταλελειμμένα. Antiq. 17. c. 12. 6.

(b) Τό τε πολὺ τ Περάιων· ibid.

(c) Κατεπρήσθη ἡ κ τὰ ἐπὶ τῷ Ἰορδάνη ποταμῷ ἐν Ἀμαθοῖς βασίλεια ὑπὸ τινῶν συστάντων ἀνδρῶν Σίμωνι παραπλησίων. ibid.

IF *Josephus* had omitted this laft fact, and fome other hiftorian had related it, together with the name of the leader of this body of men, and given them their character; which, if true, muft have refembled that of the men with *Simon* ; unlefs the reputation of this hiftorian had been very well eftablifhed, it would have been thought that he was miftaken, and the perfon he meant. was *Simon*, though he called him by another name. A palace burnt down at *Amatha* by *Jordan*. Who could thefe be but *Simon*'s people, who, *Josephus* fays, were moftly *Paraeans*? Then the time agrees exactly: Both facts in the abfence of *Archelaus* from *Judea* after his father's death. This writer therefore muft have been grofly miftaken in the name of the perfon to whom he afcribes the conduct of this action.

Or, it is not unlikely, that Critics, might have been divided : Some would have vindicated *Josephus*, and fome the other writer. And yet they would have been all miftaken, unlefs they had allowed two different bodies of men, and two different matters to be fpoken of, and that both the hiftorians were in the right.

IF

I T is certain, that thefe impoftors about this time had a refemblance in their pretenfions and their fates : one boafted he would give his followers a paffage over *Jordan*, as *Jofephus's Theudas :* another promifed his people they fhould fee the walls of *Jerufalem* fall down before them, as the *Egyptian* Impoftor. The great fcene of expectation was the (a) wilderneffe. But in this they agreed univerfally, the company was routed and difperfed, and ufually the leaders executed. This, we may be certain was the cafe, or elfe the government had been overturned.

T H E S E few circumftances then, in which *Gamaliel's Theudas* refembles him mentioned by *Jofephus* are no good argument that one and the fame perfon is intended.

B E S I D E S, there is one material circum-ftance in which they differ. *Gamaliel* fays : *before thefe days rofe up Theudas,----to whom a number of men, about four hundred joined themfelves.* But *Jofephus* fays of his *Theudas,* that he *perfwaded a very great multitude to follow him.* And that *many were flain,* and *many taken prifoners. Jofephus's Theudas* therefore muft

(a) *Matth.* xxiv. 26. *Jofeph. Antiq* 20. cap. 7. 6. & alibi.

have

have had with him a much larger company than the former.

(3.) I t has been very well obſerved by (*a*) Dr. *Whitby*, that the ancients generally agreed there was a *Theudas* before the coming of our Lord, though *Joſephus* has taken no notice of him. *Beza* (*b*) was of opinion that the *Theudas*, of whom *Gamaliel* ſpeaks, did not ariſe before our Saviour's nativity, but ſoon after *Herod*'s death, in that ſort of interregnum, which there was in *Judea*, whilſt *Archelaus* was at *Rome*. Which was alſo Archbiſhop *Uſher*'s opinion, as I have ſhewn above.

It is certain that this was a time of the utmoſt confuſion. *Joſephus* has mentioned ſeveral by name who then gave diſturbance in that country, and hinted at miſchiefs done by others, whoſe names he has not put down. It is plain he has paſt by many more than he has mentioned. For he ſays: ' At that ' time (*c*) there were innumerable diſtur- ' bances in *Judea*'.

(*a*) Ἐρᾶμεν ὅτι Θευδᾶς πρὸ τῆς γενέσεως Ἰησῦ γέγονέ τις παρὰ Ἰεδαίοις, μέγαν τινὰ ἑαυτὸν λέγων. Orig. cont. Celſ. p. 44. See more citations in *Whitby* upon the place.   (*b*) In loc.   (*c*) Ἐν τέτῳ ᵓ κὴ ἕτερα μύρια θορύβων ἐχόμενα τὴν Ἰεδαίαν κατελάμβανε. Antiq. 17. c. 12. §. 4. vid. & de B. l. 2. c. 4.

CONSIDERING all these things, that there had been before this many pretenders in *Judea*; that *Josephus* has been far from mentioning all that rose up in the later end of *Herod's* reign, and in that remarkable time of confusion which succeeded his death; since there had been in this country in a very short time divers adventurers for power and authority of one and the same name ; and since *Theudas* (*a*) was no uncommon name among the *Jews*; and since these leaders of parties and factions very much resembled each other, and that sometimes in more particulars than those specified by *Gamaliel*, it is not at all unlikely that there were two *Theudas's* who were impostors. We may depend upon it there were. *Gamaliel* speaks of one who was before *Judas* of *Galilee*, and *Josephus* of another in the time of *Claudius*.

INDEED I am somewhat surprized that any learned man should find it hard to believe, that there were two Impostors in *Judea* of the name of *Theudas* in the compass of forty years (*b*).

BATRICI.

(*a*) Frequens erat id nomen apud Hebraeos. Itaque non mirum est diversis temporibus plures extitisse factiosos homines ejusdem nominis. *Grot.* in loc. (*b*) Duos enim Theudas fuisse, qui se prophetas esse mentiti, alter post alte-

B b rum

BATRICIDES, Patriarch of *A-lexandria* about the middle of the eighth century, fuppofed that the High-Prieft *Simon,* firnamed the *Juft,* and who according to other Hiftorians (*a*) died abont 290 years before the Chriftian Aera, and *Simeon,* who took our Saviour into his arms when he was prefented at the temple, were one and the fame perfon, and that he was then 350 years of age (*b*). I do not fay, thefe two miftakes are equal ; but the pretence for thus confound-ing two perfons is juft the fame, in both thefe cafes, which is the agreement in name and character.   For the High-Prieft's name is fometimes writ *Simeon :* He was called *the juft :* And the Evangelift fays, that *Simeon* was JUST *and devout.*

rum Judaeos ad fpem rerum novarum concitaverint, nunquam adduci poffum ut credam, *Valef.* ubi fupra.

(*a*) See *Prideaux* Conn. Part. 1. Book 8. year before Chrift 292.   (*b*) *In feptuaginta autem fuit vir, qui nun-cupatus eft Simeon Juftus; is qui excepit ulnis Dominum no-ftrum Chriftum e Templo.—Produxit autem Deus ei vitae ter-minum, adeó ut viveret* CCCL *annos, & videret Dominum noftrum Chriftum. Quem cum vidiffet, dixit, nunc dimitte fervum tuum O Domine,* &c. apud *Selden.* De Succ. in Pontif, L. 1. c. vii.

CHAP.

CHAP. VIII.

Of the *Egyptian* Impostor.

T HERE is yet another particular, in which it has been thought by some that *Josephus* contradicts St. *Luke*. In the xxi. of the *Acts of the Apostles* is the account of the *uproar* at *Jerusalem*, when the *Jews* apprehended *Paul* and would have *killed him*. When the chief captain had taken him from the *Jews*, and had got him in his own custody, it is said, he put this question to him : *Art not thou that Egyptian, which before these days madest an uproar, and leddest out into the wildernesse* FOUR THOUSAND *men that were murderers?*

Acts xxi. 38.

THE objection lies against the number here mentioned. For *Josephus*, speaking of this same *Egyptian*, says : he gathered together *thirty thousand men*.

We have the ftory twice told in *Jofephus*, in his *Antiquities*, and in his Hiftory of the *jewifh War*. I fhall fet down *Jofephus*'s words, and leave it to the reader to judge, whether an objection of any weight can be formed againft St. *Luke* from the account we have of this affair in *Jofephus*. I fhall in the firft place tranfcribe the account in the *jewifh War*, becaufe that was firft writ.

'But the *Egyptian* falfe prophet
' brought a yet heavier difafter upon the *Jews*.
' For this impoftor coming into the country
' and gaining the reputation of a prophet,
' gathered together thirty thoufand men who
' were deceived (*a*) by him. Having brought
' them round out of the wildernefle up to
' the mount of Olives, he intended from
' thence to make his attack upon *Jerufalem*,
' and having beaten the Roman Guard, to
' bring the people into fubjection to him,
' and govern them by the help of the men
' whom he had got with him. But *Felix*
' coming fuddenly upon him with the Ro-
' man Soldiers, prevented the attack: and

(*a*) Μείζονι ἢ ταύτης πληγῇ Ἰυδαίας ἐκάκωσεν ὁ Ἀιγύπτι☉· ψευδοπροφήτης· παραγενόμενος γὸ εἰς τὴν χώραν, ἄνθρωπος γόης, κὴ προφήτη πίςιν ἐπιθεὶς ἑαυτῷ, περὶ τρισμυρίες μ̃ ἀθροίζει τ̃ ἠπατη-μένων· περιαγαγὼν ἢ αὐτὲς ἐκ τῆς ἐρημίας εἰς τὸ Ἐλαιῶν καλύμενον ὅρος κ. λ.

' all

' (a) all the people joined with him in their
' own defense, so that, when they came to
' engage, the *Egyptian* fled, followed by a
' a few only. A great number of those
' that were with him were either slain or
' taken prisoners. The rest of the multi-
' tude being scattered shifted for them-
' selves as they could.'

THE account he gives of this affair in
the *Antiquities* is thus : ' About the same
' time (*he had been speaking of some other
events in the beginning of Nero's reign*)
' there came (b) a person out of *Egypt* to
' *Jerusalem*, who pretended to be a Prophet,
' and having perswaded a good number of
' the meaner sort of people to follow him to
' the Mount of Olives, he told them, that

(a) Καὶ πᾶς ὁ δῆμος συνεφήψατο τῆς ἀμύνης· ὥςε συμβο-
λῆς γενομένης, ᾗ μ̃ Αἰγύπτιον φυγεῖν μετ' ὀλίγων, διαφθαρῆναι
ᾗ κͅ ζωγρηθῆναι πλείςυς σὺν αὐτῷ. τὸ ͅ λοιπὸν πλῆθος σκεδασθὲν
ἐπὶ τὴν ἑαυτῶν ἕκαςον διαλαθεῖν· De Bell. 2. c. 13. §. 5.

(b) Ἀφικνεῖται ͅ τὶς ἐξ Αἰγύπτυ κατὰ τȣτον τὸν καιρὸν εἰς τὰ
Ἱεροσόλυμα, προφήτης ἶναι λέγων, κͅ συμβȣλεύων τῷ δημοτικῷ
πλήθει σὺν αὐτῷ πρὸς ὄρος τὸ προσαγορευόμενον Ἐλαιῶν ἔρ-
χεᾳ——θέλειν ͅ ἔφασκεν αὐτοῖς ἐκεῖθεν ἐπιδεῖξαι, ὡς, κελεύσαντος,
αὐτȣ, πίπτοι τὰ τῶν Ἱεροσολύμων τείχη, δι' ὧν τὴν εἴσοδον ἀυτοῖς παρέξειν ἐπηγγέλλετο· Φῆλιξ ͅ, ὡς ἐπύθετο ταῦτα, κελεύει τὰς
ςρατιώτας ἀναλαβεῖν τὰ ὅπλα, κͅ μετὰ πολλῶν ἱππέων τε κͅ πεζῶν
ὁρμήσας ἀπὸ τῶν Ἱεροσολύμων προσβάλλει τοῖς περὶ τ̃ Αἰγύπτιον· κͅ
τετρακοσίȣς μ̃ αὐτῶν ἀνεῖλε, διακοσίȣς ͅ ζῶνͅας ἔλαβεν ὁ ͅ Αἰγύπτιος
ἀυτὸς διαδράσας ἐκ τῆς μάχης ἀφανὴς ἐγένετο· Antiq. 20. c. 7 §. 6.

Bb 3 ' from

' from thence he would let them fee the walls
' of *Jerufalem* fall down at his command,
' and promifed through them to give them
' entrance into the City. But *Felix* being
' informed of thefe things ordered his fol-
' diers to their arms. And marching out of
' *Jerufalem* with a large body of horfe and
' foot, fell upon thofe who were with the
' *Egyptian:* killed four hundred of them,
' and took two hundred prifoners. But the
' *Egyptian* getting out of the fight, efcap'd'.

THE reader, if he thinks it needful,
may confult the commentators and other
writers who (*a*) have confidered this difficulty. *Grotius* fuppofes, that they were
at firft but *four thoufand*; but that at length
they increafed to the number of *thirty thoufand*. *Valefius* reckons there were *four thoufand* only that were *murderers* or *Sicarii*, tho'
the whole company amounted to the number
Jofephus mentions. Dr. *Whitby* thinks, that it
is likely the number in *Jofephus* was originally *three thoufand*. And certainly none of thefe
folutions are contemptible. But, for my
own part, I think there is more need of re-

(*a*) Grot. *Whitby* in loc. *Jofeph.* p. 1075. not. p. *Valef.*
in *Eufeb.* Hift. L. ii. cap. 21.

conciling

conciling *Josephus* with himself, or at least one of these accounts with the other, than to reconcile St. *Luke* with *Josephus*.

IF indeed we had any good reason to think, that the number in *Josephus* was originally three thousand, the disagreement would be small. The number of a multi‐ tude got together in a short time, and soon dispersed, might not be exactly known : the chief captain at *Jerusalem* might com‐ pute them at four thousand, and *Josephus* think they were but three thousand.

DR. *Aldrich* has proposed another very ingenious conjecture: that originally the number of the whole company in *Josephus's War of the Jews* was four thousand, and that the number of *two hundred* said in the *Antiquities* to be taken prisoners was ori‐ ginally *two thousand*: Both which errors might happen only by a very small altera‐ tion (*a*).

BUT I choose not to insist upon any of these Solutions, which rely on emendations made without the authority of any Manuscripts.

(*a*) Suspicamur interim pro διακοσίας scriptum olim δισχιλίας, permutatis λ & δ, vel etiam Λ. & Δ. ex τετρακισχιλίας factum esse τρισμυρίας ne dubitamus quidem. *Aldr.* in *Joseph.* p. 1075. Not. p.

The

The numbers in *Jofephus* are at prefent plainly faulty. In the firft account he fays they were thirty thoufand in all, and that a *great number of thefe were either flain or taken prifoners.* I might have rendered the words, *the moft of them.* But though I do not give them that fenfe, yet certainly the *four hundred flain* and *two hundred taken prifoners*, in the other account, cannot be reckoned a *great number* or a *large part* of thirty thoufand.

But then, as I do not infift on thefe conjectural emendations for reconciling *Jofephus* with St. *Luke*; fo, on the other hand, would be very unfair, firft to take it for granted that the number of thirty thoufand in *Jofephus* is right, and then arbitrarily to reform all the other numbers in him, in order to form an objection againft the *New Teftament.*

I think therefore there can be no objection brought againft the numbers in Saint *Luke* from what *Jofephus* has faid of this affair, becaufe his two accounts are not confiftent one with another in this point : And that is fufficient.

But yet I cannot leave the Hiftory *Jofephus* has given us of this *Egyptian*,
with-

without making two or three obfervations.

1. THE chief captain here asks Saint
Paul: *Art not thou that Egyptian which*
(*a*) LEDDEST OUT *into the wildernesse?*....
which feems to imply, fince the queftion was
asked at *Jerufalem*, that thefe men, or a
good number of them at left, were drawn
out of *Jerufalem*: And *Jofephus* fays exprefly in the later account, that this impoftor
came *out of Egypt to Jerufalem; and perfwaded a good number of the meaner fort of
people,* (*i, e.* who were there) to *follow
him.*

2. THE chief captain fpeaks of their
being *led out into the* WILDERNESSE. This
circumftance *Jofephus* has mentioned in the
firft account, where he more particularly relates their march, and the compaffe they
took, than in the other.

3. THIS *Egyptian* efcaped. *Jofephus*
has put down this in both places, and undoubtedly this is fuppofed in the queftion
put to St. *Paul* by the chief captain. The
agreement in this particular deferves to be
taken notice of, becaufe it was the com-

(*a*) Ὁ ἐξαγαγὼν.

mon

mon fate of thefe impoſtors to periſh them-
ſeves with a good number of their followers

4. This *Egyptian* cauſed this diſturbance, according to *Joſephus*, when *Felix*
was Governour of *Judea*. This impoſtor
therefore did not ariſe any long time before the ſeiſure of St. *Paul* at *Jeruſalem*.
He might be ſtill living therefore: In this
reſpeƈt there was no abſurdity in this queſtion of the chief captain.

5. Another particular, which we are
obliged to *Joſephus* for, is, *that all the people* (*ſc.* at *Jeruſalem*) favoured, or joined
with *Felix*, upon this occaſion, in their
own defenſe : That is, all but ſome very
mean people. If *Joſephus* had not mentioned this, perhaps it would have been ſaid :
Since conſiderable numbers uſually joined
theſe impoſtors, and it is likely more favoured
them ; how was it poſſible, that the chief
captain ſhould ask *Paul*, when he ſaw the
whole city was in an uproar, and the people were ready to tear him to pieces : *Art not
thou that Egyptian ?* That pretended prophet, that *before theſe days* madeſt *an uproar ?* A man of a favourite charaƈter at this
time among the *Jews !*

I THINK

I THINK indeed, that if *Josephus* had omitted this circumstance, it would have been a very good reply, to say, that the chief captain did not yet know what was the matter : And though there was a loud cry in the multitude, of *away with him*; Yet the confusion was such, *some saying one thing*, and *some another*; that the chief captain had yet no notion what the case was. However we have now no occasion to have recourse to this reply. *Josephus* has told us, that all the people favoured *Felix* in his enterprize against this man : whether it was because he came from *Egypt*, or what was the reason, is of no importance.

6. THERE is a remarkable agreement between the chief captain in the *Acts* and *Josephus*, in the description they give of this man. The chief captain says : *Art not thou that Egyptian?* And it is observable, that *Josephus* has not mentioned this man's name in either of the accounts. In the first he calls him the *Egyptian false prophet*, and *the Egyptian*. In the other, he says, *there came one* (or a certain person) *out of Egypt* : And again, *Felix* fell upon those who were *with the Egytian* : But the E^{tian} *n* escaped.

WE

W E have therefore in the *Acts* the exact manner, in which the *Jews* about this time fpoke of this impoftor. This is with me a proof, that St. *Luke* lived and wrote about this time: that is, at the time he is fuppofed to write. We have here undoubtedly the chief captain's queftion in the very words in which it was put. St. *Luke* muft have received this account from St. *Paul*, or fome one elfe who was prefent, if he was not by himfelf.

A F T E R all thefe points of agreement we may be allowed to fuppofe, that, if we had *Jofephus*'s original numbers (the only material particular in which his two accounts differ the one from the other and from St. *Luke*) they would have been exactly, or very near the fame with thofe in the *Acts*.

THE
CONCLUSION.

I HAVE now performed what I under-took, and have ſhewn that the account given by the Sacred Writers of perſons and things is confirmed by other ancient authors of the beſt note. There is nothing in the books of the *New Teſtament* unſuitable to the age in which they are ſuppoſed to have been writ. There appears in theſe Writers a knowledge of the affairs of thoſe times not to be found in authors of later ages. *We are hereby aſ-ſured, that the books of the New Teſta-ment are genuine, and that they were writ by perſons who lived at or near the time of thoſe events of which they have given the hiſtory.*

ANY one may be ſenſible, how hard it is for the moſt learned, acute, and cautious man to write a book in the character of ſome perſon of an earlier age ; and not betray his own time by ſome miſtake about the affairs of the age in which he pretends to place him-

himfelf, or by allufions to cuftoms or principles fince fprung up, or by fome phrafe or
expreffion not then in ufe. It is no eafy
thing to efcape all thefe dangers in the fmalleft
performance, though it be a treatife of theory
or fpeculation. Thefe hazards are greatly
encreafed, when the work is of any length,
and efpecially if it be hiftorical, and be concerned with characters and cuftoms. It is
yet more difficult to carry on fuch a defign in
a work confifting of feveral pieces, writ to
all appearance by feveral perfons. Many indeed are defirous to deceive, but all hate to
be deceived. And therefore, though attempts
have been made to impofe upon the world
in this way, they have never or very rarely
fucceeded, but have been detected and ex-
pofed by the skill and vigilance of thofe
who have been concerned for the truth.

THE Volume of the *New Teftament* con-
fifts of feveral pieces. Thefe are afcribed to
eight feveral perfons. And there are the
ftrongeft appearances that they were not all
writ by any one hand, but by as many
perfons as they are afcribed to. There are
leffer differences in the relations of fome
facts, and fuch feeming contradictions as
would never have happened, if thefe books
had

had been all the work of one perfon, or of
feveral who writ in concert. There are as
many peculiarities of temper and ftile, as there
are names of writers : divers of which fhew
no depth of Genius, or compaffe of knowledge. Here are reprefentations of the titles,
pofts, behaviour of perfons of higher and
lower rank in many parts of the world.
Perfons are introduced, and their characters
are fet in a full light. Here is a hiftory of
things done in feveral cities and countries,
and there are allufions to a vaft variety of
cuftoms and tenets of perfons of feveral nations, fects, and religions. The whole is
writ without affectation, with the greateft
fimplicity and plainneffe, and is confirmed
by other ancient writers of unqueftioned
authority.

IF it be difficult for a perfon of learning
and experience to compofe a fmall treatife,
concerning matters of fpeculation, with the
characters of a more early age than that in
which he writes ; it is next to impoffible,
that fuch a work of confiderable length,
confifting of feveral pieces, with a great
variety of hiftorical facts, reprefentations of
characters, principles, and cuftoms of feveral nations and diftant countries, of perfons

of

of all ranks and degrees, of many interests and parties, should be performed by eight several persons, the most of them unlearned, without any appearance of concert.

I MIGHT perhaps have called this argument a demonstration, if that term had not been often misapplied by men of warm imaginations, and been bestowed upon reasonings that have but a small degree of probability. But though it should not be a strict demonstration, that these writings are genuine : or though it be not absolutely impossible in the nature of the thing, that the books of the *New Testament* should have been composed in a later age than that to which they are assigned, and of which they have innumerable characters; yet, I think, it is in the highest degree improbable, and altogether incredible.

I F the books of the New Testament were writ by persons who lived before the destruction of Jerusalem, that is, if they were writ at the time in which they are said to have been writ, the things related in them are true. If they had not been matter of fact, they would not have been credited by any persons near that time, and in those parts of the world in which they

are

are faid to have been done, but would have
been treated as the moft notorious lies and
falfhhoods. Suppofe three or four books
fhould now appear amongft us in the language moft generally underftood, giving an
account of many remarkable and extraordinary events which had happened in fome
kingdome of Europe, and in the moft noted
cities of the countries next adjoining to it;
fome of them faid to have happened between
fixty and feventy years ago, others between
twenty and thirty, others nearer our own
time : Would not they be looked upon as
the moft manifeft and ridiculous forgeries
and impoftures that ever were contrived?
Would great numbers of perfons, in thofe
very places, change their religious principles
and practifes upon the credit of things repor-
ted to be publickly done which no man had
ever heard of before? Or rather, is it poffible
that fuch a defign as this fhould be conceived
by any fober and ferious perfons, or even
the moft wild and extravagant?

IF *the hiftory of the New Teftament
be credible, the Chriftian Religion is true.*
If the things here related to have been
done by Jefus, and by his followers, by virtue of powers derived from him, do not

prove

prove a perſon to come from God, and that his doctrine is true and divine, nothing can⸗ And as Jeſus does here in the circumſtances of his birth, life, ſufferings, and after exaltation, and in the ſucceſſe of his doctrine anſwer the deſcription of the great perſon promiſed and foretold in the *Old Teſtament*, he is at the ſame time ſhewed to be the Meſſiah.

FROM the agreement of the writers of the New Teſtament with other ancient writers we are not only aſſured that theſe books are genuine, but alſo that they are come down to us pure and uncorrupted, without any conſiderable interpolations or alterations. If ſuch had been made in 'em, there would have appeared ſome ſmaller differences at leſt between them and other ancient writings.

THERE has been in all ages a wicked propenſity in mankind to advance their own notions and fanſies by deceits and forgeries. They have been practiſed by *Heathens*, *Jews*, and *Chriſtians*, in ſupport of imaginary hiſtorical facts, religious ſchemes and practiſes, and political intereſts. With theſe views ſome whole books have been forged, and paſſages inſerted into others of undoubted

ed authority. Many of the Chriſtian writers of the ſecond and third centuries, and
of the following ages appear to have had
falſe notions concerning the ſtate of *Judea*
between the nativity of Jeſus and the deſtruction of *Jeruſalem*, and concerning many
other things occaſionally mentioned in the
New Teſtament. The conſent of the beſt
ancient writers with thoſe of the *New
Teſtament* is a proof, that theſe books are
ſtill untouched, and that they have not been
new modelled and altered by Chriſtians of
later times in conformity to their own peculiar Sentiments.

T H I S may be reckoned an argument,
that the generality of Chriſtians have had
a very high veneration for theſe books ; or
elſe, that the ſeveral ſects among them have
had an eye upon each other, that no alterations might be made in thoſe writings to
which they have all appealed.   It is alſo
an argument, that the Divine Providence
has all along watched over and guarded
theſe beſt of books (a very fit object of
an eſpecial care) which contain the beſt of
principles, were apparently writ with the
beſt views, and have in them inimitable
characters of truth and ſimplicity.

A N

APPENDIX

Concerning the time of *Herod*'s death.

N all enquiries concerning the chronology of the *New Testament*, and particularly concerning the true time of our Saviour's nativity, and the commencement of his miniftry, it is very needful to take into confideration the time of *Herod* the Great's death. Indeed it is very defirable in the firft place to fettle exactly the date of this event. But to do this is a very hard task. Nor has any one yet been fo happy, as to remove all difficul-

ties

ties and give univerſal ſatisfaction upon this head.

THAT none may be quite at a loſſe in judging of the difficulty conſidered in the *third* chapter of this Volume, I ſhall here give a brief account of this matter.

THE chief opinions at preſent concerning the time of *Herod's* death are theſe three. Some think he died a little before the paſſover of A. U. 750, *Julian* year 42. others, on *Novemb.* 25, that ſame year: others, a ſhort time before the Paſſover, A. U. 751.

§. I. THE *Engliſh* reader may ſee all, in a manner, that can be ſaid for the ſecond opinion, in Mr. *Whiſton's ſhort View of the Harmony of the four Evangeliſts, Prop.* 12. But, though ſeveral very learned men have embraced this opinion, it appears to me a meer hypotheſis without foundation. The only ground of it is a *jewiſh* account of their Feaſts and Faſts, in which that day is noted as a Feaſt ; becauſe on it *Herod* died. But (*a*) this book appears to be of no authority.

(*a*) See *Whitb.* Annota. *Matth* ii. 23. *Lamy* Apparat. Chronol. Part. i. cap. 9. §. 5.

C c 3 §. II. THAT

§. II. THAT *Herod* died but a short
time before some one of the *jewish* Pass-
overs, is evident from (*a*) *Josephus.* If
we reject entirely his authority, it is in vain
to talk about the time of *Herod's* death.
Archelaus kept a Passover in *Judea* after
his father's death, before he went to *Rome* ;
which he would not have done, if it had
not been near. He had good reason to
hasten to *Rome.* He had many enemies.
Herod Antipas had been appointed his father's successor in a former Will, and he pretended that Will ought to take place. When
the *Jews* at the Temple made their de-
mands of *Archelaus,* he gave them fair
words, that they might not make any disturbance and retard his journey (*b*), he
being in haft to go to *Rome.* This haft is
expressed by *Josephus* in the *War,* and in
the *Antiquities* in very strong terms. *Archelaus,* in his way to *Rome,* at *Cesarea,*
met *Sabinus* the Emperour's Procurator in

(*a*) *De Bell.* l. 2. c. 1. *Antiq* 17. c. 9.

(*b*) Πρὸς ἃ ταρωξύνετο μὲ 'Αρχέλαۛ, ἀπείχετο ἣ τὴν ἀμύναν
ὑπὸ τ' περὶ τὴν ἔξοδον ἐπείξεως, κ. λ. De Bell. 2. c. 1. §. 3. Τέτοις
'Αρχέλαος, καίτερ δεινῶς φέρων τὴν ὁρμὴν αὐτῶν, ἐπένευε, ἔχων
τὴν ἐπὶ 'Ρώμης ὁδὸν ἀνύεϛ προκειμένην αὐτῷ τάχος, ἐπὶ περισκο-
πήσει τ' δοξάντων τῷ Καίσαρι. Antiq. 17. c. 9. §. 1.

Syria,

Syria, who was going (*a*) in all haſt to *Je-rusalem* to ſecure *Herod*'s treaſure for *Au-guſtus*. By help of the interceſſions of *Va-rus*, preſident of *Syria* (who was then likewiſe at *Ceſarea*) *Archelaus* prevailed up-on *Sabinus* to promiſe, that he would not proceed any farther. But notwithſtanding that, when *Archelaus* was gone away, he went up to *Jeruſalem* ; and there ordered all things, according to his own will and pleaſure. This was all managed without any orders from *Rome*. If *Herod* had been dead two or three months, they would have had directions from thence upon this matter. Nay, if *Herod* had been dead one month, this vigilant Procurator would have been at *Jeruſalem* before now. I think this has not been inſiſted on by any before. But I take it to be a demonſtration, that, according to *Joſephus*, *Herod*'s death happened but a very ſhort ſpace before ſome Paſſover.

§. III. THAT *Herod* died a little before the Paſſover A. U. 750, *Jul.* year 42, is argued in this manner. His diſtemper had made great progreſſe before the pulling down

---

(*a*) Ὑπαντιάζει δ᾽ ἐν Καισαρεία τὸν Ἀρχέλαον Σαβῖνος, Καίσαρος ἐπίτροπος τ῅ ἐν Συρία πραγμάτων, εἰς Ἰυδαίαν ὡρμη-μένος ἐπὶ φυλακῇ τ῅ Ἡρώδυ χρημάτων. Antiq. ib.d. §. 3. vid. & De B. ibid. c. 2. §. 2.

the

the Golden Eagle at the Temple. The
jewiſh Rabbies excited their Scholars to this
action, *News being brought that Herod
was* (*a*) DYING, as it is in the *War;* (*b*)
DEAD, as it is in the *Antiquities.* Theſe
Rabbies were taken up and carried to *Jericho,* where *Herod* was. A council was
called, and they were tried. *Herod* was ſo
ill that he could not ſtand, and notwithſtanding the new ſtrength (*c*) which rage
gave him upon this occaſion he was carried
(*d*) to the council in a chair. Soon after this
theſe Rabbies were burnt to death, and that
very (*e*) night there was an eclipſe of the
moon. This eclipſe, according to aſtrono-
mical computations, happened (*f*) the 13th
March, A. U. 750. After this, *Herod*
grew worſe and worſe. It is plain, he could
not live long. The Paſſover (*g*) of this
year happened the 11th of *April.* From

(*a*) Διηφημίσθη ϰỳ θνήσκειν ὁ βασιλεύς. de Bell. 1. c. 33. §. 1.
(*b*) Καὶ οἱ μ̃ τοιούτοις λόγοις ἐξῆραν τὰς νέας· ἀφικνεῖται ͻ
λόγ☉ εἰς αὐτὰς τεθνᾶναι φράζων τ̃ βασιλέα, ϰỳ συνέπϛαττε τοῖς
σοφιϛαῖς. *Antiq.* 17. c. 6. §. 3. (*c*) Ἐπὶ τότοις ὁ βασιλεύς,
δι᾽ ὑπερβολὴν ☞ ὀργῆς ϰρείττων τ̃ νόσα γενόμεν☉, πρόεισιν εἰς
ἐκκλησίαν, ϰ. λ. de Bell 1. c. 33. §. 4. (*d*) Καὶ
παραγενομενων, ἐξεκκλησιάσας εἰς τὸ αὐτὸ θέατρον ἐπὶ κλινιδίς
ϰείμενος ἀδυναμία ☞ ϛῆναι. *Antiq.* ibid. (*e*) Καὶ ἡ
ϛελήνη ͻ τῆ αὐτῆ νυκτὶ ἐξέλιπεν. ibid. §. 4. (*f*) *Petav.*
Doctri. Temp. l. xi. c. 1. (*g*) Vid. *Lamy* App. Chron.p.58.

the 13th of *March* to the 11th of *April* is a
sufficient space of time for all that *Josephus*
has related concerning *Herod's* illness, his
settling his affairs, the execution of *Antipater, Herod's* death and funeral ; which are
the things placed between the Eclipse and
Archelaus's coming to *Jerusalem* at the
Passover.

In the *War*, (*a*) *Josephus* says that *Archelaus* was banished in the ninth year of his
reign : In the Antiquities, that he was accused before *Augustus* by the *Jews* and
Samaritans in the (*b*) tenth year of his
government. In his *own life Josephus*
says, that his father was born in the (*c*) tenth
year of *Archelaus's* reign. From whence
one would be apt to conclude, that *Archelaus* reigned *nine* years compleat ; and that
the *tenth* year was current, when he was banished. *Dio* (*d*) places *Archelaus's* banishment in the 759th year of *Rome*. If *Herod* did not die till the beginning of A. U.

(*a*) Ετει της αρχης εννατω φυγαδευεται μεν εις Βιενναν. de B. l. 2.
c 7. § 3.   (*b*) Δεκάτω] ετει της αρχης Αρχελάε, οι
πρωτοι———κατηγορεσιν αυτε επι Καισαρ. l. 17. c. 15. 2.
(*c*) Και [γίνεται] Ματθίας βασιλευοντ Αρχελάε το δέκατον.
§. 1.   (*d*) Ο, τε Ηρώδης ο Παλαιστινός,———υπο τας
Αλπεις υπερωρίσθη· η το μέρ της αρχης αυτε εδημοσιώθη. l. 55.
p. 557. B.

751, the

751, the ninth year of *Archelaus*'s reign could not be compleated in the 759th year of *Rome*. But if *Herod* be suppofed to have died the beginning of A. U. 750, *Jofephus* and *Dio* agree. Moreover, *Jofephus* fays that (*a*) *Cyrenius* feiled *Archelaus*'s eftate, and finished the Affeffement in *Judea* in the *thirty feventh year after the defeat of Antony at Actium by Cefar Auguftus.* The victory at *Actium* was obtained the 2d· *Septemb.* A. U. 723. Therefore the 37th year from it begins 2d. *Sept.* A. U. 759, and ends 2d. *Sept.* 760. Suppofing then, that *Herod* died the beginning of A. U. 750, there is in this particular alfo a very good harmony between *Jofephus* and *Dio*.

THERE is however one great difficulty attending this opinion. For *Jofephus* has faid in two places, that *Herod* reigned *thirty four years* after the death of (*b*) *Antigonus*; and *thirty feven years* after he was

(*a*) Κυρήνι⊙ ἤ τὰ Ἀρχελάȣ χρήματα ἀποδόμεν⊙ ἤδη, κ̓ τ̀ ἀποτιμήσεων πέρας ἐχȣσῶν, ἃι ἐγένοντο τριακοςῷ κ̓ ἑβδόμῳ ἔτει μετὰ τὴν Ἀντωνίȣ ἐν Ἀκτίῳ ἧτταν ὑπὸ Καίσαρ⊙· Antiq. l. 18. c. 2. §. 1.

(*b*) — Τελευτᾷ βασιλεύσας ἀφ' ȣ̓ μ̀ ἀποκτείνας Ἀντίγονον ἐκράτησε τ̀ πραγμάτων, ἔτη τέσσαρα κ̓ τριάκοντα, ἀφ' ȣ̓ ἢ ὑπὸ Ῥωμαίων ἀπεδείχθη βασιλεὺς, ἑπτὰ κ̓ τριάκοντα· de B. J. l. 1. c. ult. §. 8. vid. & Antiq. 17. c. 8. § 1.

declared

declared King by the Roman Senate. And
he places this declaration of (*a*) the Senate
in A. U. 714, the death of (*b*) *Antigonus*
in the year 717. If indeed at the beginning
of A. U. 750, *Herod* had reigned thirty
six years compleat from the firſt date of his
reign, and thirty three from the later ; ſo
that the 37th of the one epocha, and the
34th of the other were to be current at the
time of his death ; then *Herod* might be
ſaid not improperly to have reigned, with
reſpect to the one, thirty ſeven years, and
to the other, thirty four. It is ſuppoſed by
ſome learned men that *Herod* was declared
King by the Senate, (*c*) toward the very
end of the year 714, by others (*d*) the
later end of *October* or beginning of *November*, by others (*e*) in *September* or *October*, by others (*f*) about the middle of *July*,
that year. But then, at the beginning of
the year 750, *Herod* could not have reigned
from this date thirty ſix years compleat, nor
was the 37th year current. *Herod* took *Je-*

(*a*) *Antiq.* 14. c. 14 §. 5. *de B.* 1. c. 14. §. 4.   (*b*) *Antiq:*
14. c. *ult.* §. 4.   (*c*) Alix de J. C. Anno & menſe natali.
p. 75.   (*d*) *Baſnage Ann. Polit.* E. Vol. 1. p. 17. n. 16.
(*e*) *Noriſ. Cenot. Piſ.* p. 139. *Pagi Appar.* p. 80.   (*f*) *Whiſton's
ſhort view.* p. 150.

rufalem as fome (*a*) think in *September* A.U. 717, others (*b*), about the end of *June*, Archbifhop *Ufher* (*c*), on the firft of *January* this year. If the Archbifhop's fuppofition could be allowed, we fhould have here no difficulty. But if any of the others are followed, then from this date of *Herod's* reign, *viz.* the taking of *Jerufalem*, or the death of *Antigonus* (which are all one) to the beginning of the year 750, we have not quite thirty three years compleat, nor is the thirty fourth current.

IN anfwer to this difficulty it is faid (*d*) by learned men, that the years of the *jewifh* Kings were computed from the beginning of the Month *Nifan*, which ufually anfwers pretty near to our *March.* Infomuch that, if a King began to reign in any part of the year before, even in *February*, another year of his reign would begin with *Nifan*, that is, *March.* So *Jofephus* relates, that *Jerufalem* was taken (*e*) by *Pompey* when

(*a*) Alix ubi fupra. p. 117.   (*b*) *Whifton* ibid. p. 152. B. *fnage* ibid. p 30. n. 9. (*c*) Annals. P.J. 4677.   (*d*) Inde etiam anni regum Hebraeorum fupputabantur, ita ut fi quis Rex in Adar regnaret, a Nifan alter annus imperii ejus inciperet. *Reland.* Antiq. Heb. de Temporib. facris, c. 1. init. vid. & *Kep-ler.* de ann. natal. J. C. cap. 7. p. 46.   (*e*) *Antiq* 14. c. 4. §. 3.

Antony

Antony and *Cicero* were Conſuls, by *Herod,* when *M. Agrippa* and *Caninius Gallus* were conſuls, *on the very anniverſary of the ſame calamity from Pompey, it having been taken by him on the ſame* (*a*) *day twenty ſeven years before:* Though there were but twenty ſix years compleat between theſe two events. And from the taking of *Jeruſalem* by *Herod* to its deſtruction by *Titus, Joſephus* computes (*b*) one hundred and ſeven years, though it was but one hundred and ſix compleat. But, in my opinion, theſe inſtances are not home to the point. For in them the year named is current. Whereas, in the caſe before us it is not ſo. If *Herod* died in the beginning of the year 750, the thirty third and thirty ſixth years of his reign were not compleat.

§. IV. OTHER (*c*) learned men ſuppoſe that *Herod* died a ſhort time before the Paſſover A. U. 751. This they argue from the number of years aſſigned to *Herod's* reign in the places above mentioned. They do not allow the truth of the *Talmudical* account of computing the Reigns of the *jewiſh*

(*a*) Ibid. c. 16. §. 4.　　　(*b*) Ibid. 20. c. 9. vid. *Kepler* ibid.　　　(*c*) Vid. *Lamy* Appar. Chron. Part i. c. ix. *Baſnage* Annal. Pol. Ecc. Vol. i. p 156. n. v.

Kings

Kings from the beginning of *Nifan* or from the Paffover. If *Jofephus* had followed fuch a kind of computation, he would have given fome hint of it in his books writ in the *Greek* language and for the inftruction of ftrangers. They fay alfo, that *Herod's* was a flow lingring diftemper; and that it is not likely he fhould die fo foon after the execution of the Rabbies and their accomplices, as is fuppofed by the Patrons of the former opinion. Laftly, they obferve the (A) agreement of all the other numbers in *Jofephus* concerning the dates of the reign of *Archelaus* and other fons of *Herod*.

Th is opinion however labours under feveral very great difficulties. *Dio's* account of the removal of *Archelaus* is entirely rejected. But to do this (*b*) is not very reafonable. Farther, the fupporters of this opinion muft allow of the Eclipfe abovementioned; or they muft fay it was no real eclipfe, but only fome obfcurity that was taken for an Eclipfe. If they allow the Eclipfe, then *Herod* muft have lived a year

---

(A) *Note*, the learned men, who efpoufe the former opinion, fuppofe alfo that *Jofephus's* numbers in all other places agree with them. (*b*) Vid. *Norif. Cenot. Pil.* p. 147.

after

after the execution of the Rabbies, provided he died (*a*) but a few days before the Passover A. U. 751. But it is incredible that *Herod* should live so long, considering the description *Josephus* gives of the distemper. Besides, it is evident that the Mourning of the *jewish* people for the Rabbies, at the Passover next after *Herod's* death, was (*b*) very fresh, which it could not have been, if the Rabbies had been dead above a year before. Moreover, it is evident, that *Herod's* Ambassadors were sent away to *Rome* to know *Augustus's* pleasure concerning *Antipater*, some time (*c*) before the disturbance at the Temple, when the Golden Eagle was taken down. And it is very plain, that *Herod* lived not (*d*) many days after the arrival of the Ambassadors. So that according to this opinion these Ambassadors must have spent above a year in their journey from *Judea*

(*a*) Quae aptis temporibus tribui non possunt, nisi haec mors contigerit jam aliquibus mensibus promoto Anno U. C. 751, in quo comprobavimus mortuum fuisse Herodem. Quoquo autem anno mortuus sit, NON MULTIS ANTE PASCHA DIEBUS mors illa obtigit, ut testatur Josephus, cui fidem adhibemus. *Lamy ubi supra.* §.

(*b*) Ἦν δὲ τὸ πένθος οὐχ ὑπεσταλμένον, ἀλλ' οἰμωγαὶ διαπρύσιοι, καὶ θρῆνος ἐγκέλευστος, κοπετοί τε περιηχοῦντες ὅλην τὴν πόλιν. de B. 2. c. 1. §. 2. vid. & Antiq. 17. c. 9. §. 1. (*c*) De B. 1. c. 32. fin. Antiq. 17. c. 5. fin. (*d*) De B. ibid. c. 33. §. 7, 8. Antiq. ibid. c. 7. & c. 8. §. 1.

to *Rome* and back again, though they were sent upon very preffing bufineffe, which is also incredible. Or they muft reject the account of the Eclipfe and fay, as Father *Lamy* (*a*) does, that it was only a paleneffe or obfcurity which was no real Eclipfe of the Moon; which, I believe, will appear very unreafonable to all Aftronomers.

THESE are the three principal opinions concerning the time of *Herod*'s death. And thefe the main arguments for, and objections againft them. I prefume it appears to the reader from particulars alledged from *Jofephus* and *Dio*, That *Herod* did not die before the year 750, nor furvive the year 751: And that he died a fhort time before the *jewifh* Paffover, of one of thefe years. It follows that if *Herod* died in 750, he died three years and nine months before the Vulgar Chriftian Æra, which commences *January* 1. A. U. 754. If at the time abovementioned in the year 751, then he died about two years and nine months before the faid Æra. Which is the truth I dare not determine.

(*a*) Ubi fupra. §. 6.

F I N I S.

INDEX

TO THE

SECOND VOLUME.

Caiaphas

INDEX.

INDEX.

INDEX.

A CATALOGUE of BOOKS Printed for and Sold by *A. Bettefworth*, at the *Red-Lion* in *Pater-Nofter-Row*.

	l.	s.	d
A			
ATalantis, 4 Vol. 12ves.	00	09	00
Apuleius's Golden Afs, 2 Vol. 12ves.	00	06	00
Atlas Manuale: Or, A Sett of fmall Maps. By Moll. 8vo.	00	05	00
Athenian Oracle, now in the Prefs, 8vo.			
Acta Regia: Or, An Abridgment of Mr. Rymer's Fœdera. Publifh'd Monthly, at 1 s. each.			
Apollo's Feaft, 12ves.	00	01	00
Art of Pleafing in Converfation, in French and Englifh. By Cardinal Richlieu. 12ves.	00	03	00
Agreeable Variety, 8vo.	00	03	06
Art of Thinking Tranflated by Ozell. 12ves.	00	03	06
Arabian Nights Entertainment, Compleat, 6 Vol. 12ves.	00	15	00
Abridgment Statutes, 6 Vol. 8vo.	01	10	00
Addifon's Travels, 12ves.	00	03	00
Works, 3 Vol. 12ves.	00	09	00
Works, 4 Vol. 4to.	03	00	00
Accomplifh'd Conveyancer, 3 Vol. 8vo.	00	18	00
B			
BRidgman's Conveyancer, Folio.	01	10	00
Bifhop Blackhall's Works, 2 Vol. Folio.	01	12	00
Bifhop Burnet on the Thirty nine Articles, Folio.	00	12	00
Abridgment of his Hiftory of the Reformation, 3 Vol. 12ves.	00	09	00
Dr. Barlow's Works, 2 Vol. Fol.	02	02	00
Book of Homiles, Folio, 1726.	00	12	00
Boyce on the Thirty nine Articles, Folio.	00	09	00
Burnet's Theory of the Earth, 2 Vol. 8vo.	00	12	00
Dr. Bates Works, Folio, 1724.	01	07	06
Burnet's (Dr. Thomas) Sermons at Boyle's Lectures, for the Years 1724, 1725, 2 Vol.	00	09	00
Effay upon Government, 8vo.	00	01	06
Scripture Trinity, 8vo.	00	02	00
Blackmore's (Sir Richard) Effays, 2 Vol. 8vo.	00	11	00
Creation, a Poem, 12ves.	00	02	00
Redemption, a Poem; being a Supplement to the Creation, 8vo.	00	04	00
Buchanan's Hiftory of Scotland, 2 Vol. Englifh, with curious Cuts, 8vo.	00	11	00
Boyer's French and Englifh Dictionary, 8vo.	00	07	00
Telemachus, 2 Vol. 12ves.	00	05	06
Bailey's Etymological Englifh Dictionary	00	07	00
Tranflation of Erafmus Colloquies.	00	05	06
Bruyere's Works, 2 Vol. Tranflated from the French, 8vo.	00	09	00
Betterton's Life with the Amorous Widow.	00	03	06
Behn's Novels, 2 Vol. 12ves.	00	05	00
Plays, 4 Vol. 12ves.	00	12	00
Boerhave's Aphorifms, Tranflated into Englifh, 8vo.	00	05	06
Mrs. Barker's Novels, 2 Vol. 12ves.	00	05	00
Patchwork Screen, 2 Vol. 12ves.	00	05	00
Britifh Apollo, 3 Vol. 12ves. containing two Thoufand Anfwers to Curious Queftions in moft Arts and Sciences, 12ves.	00	09	00

Britifh

	l.	s.	d.
British Compendium: Containing the Descents of the English, Scotch, and Irish Nobility, with their Arms curiously Engraven, 3 Vols. 12ves.	01	02	06
Builders Dictionary, 8vo.	00	04	00
Dr. Brown of Cold Baths. 12ves.	00	01	06
Boileau's Art of Poetry, 4 Canto's, 12ves.	00	01	06
Lutrin: An Heroi-Comical Poem.	00	01	06
Bulstrode (Whitlock) Essays, 8vo.	00	04	06
Bridges of Fractions, 12ves.	00	01	00
Bradley's New Improvements in Planting and Gardening, 8vo.	00	06	06
Byshe's Art of Poetry, 2 Vol.	00	05	00
Blackmore's Ecclesiastical Antiquity, abridg'd from Bingham, 2 Vol.	00	11	00
Ball's Astrology improv'd	00	02	00
Burkett of the New Testament, Folio.	01	03	00
Beveridge's Private Thoughts, 8vo.	00	09	06
Ditto, 12ves.	00	01	06
Prayer, 8vo.	00	03	06
Ditto, 12ves.	00	01	06
Blackmore on Consumptions, 8vo.	00	03	06
on the Spleen	00	05	06
on the Gout and Rheumatism	00	03	06
on the Vapours.	00	04	06
Bingham's Antiquities, 2 Vols. Folio.	02	10	00
Brown (Tho.) Works, 5 Vols. 12ves.	00	12	06
Bishop's Sermons at Lady Moyer's Lecture, 8vo.	00	05	00
Baynard of Hot and Cold Baths, 8vo.	00	05	06

C

	l.	s.	d.
CAssandra: A fam'd Romance, 5 Vols. 12ves	00	15	00
Cook of Forest Trees, 8vo.	00	03	06
Bishop Cumberland, De Legibus Naturæ, 8vo.	00	06	00
Cato's Letters, 4 Vols. 12ves	00	10	00
Cave's Primitive Christianity, 8vo.	00	04	06
Calamy's (Benj.) Sermons, 8vo.	00	04	06
Clark's Body of Divinity, 2 Vol. 8vo.	00	09	00
Cocker's English Dictionary, 8vo.	00	02	00
Decimal Arithmetick, 8vo.	00	03	06
Countess of Morton's Devotions, 24s.	00	00	06
Dr. Comber's Companion to the Altar, 8vo.	00	04	06
Christian Pattern, Translated from the Latin of Tho. a Kempis, 24o.	00	01	00
Culpeper's English Physician Enlarg'd	00	02	06
Midwife, 12ves.	00	02	06
Dispensatory, 12ves.	00	02	06
Courtier, Translated from the Italian.	00	05	00
Cap of Gray Hairs for a Green Head, 8vo.	00	01	06
Croxall's Æsop's Fables, 12ves.	00	03	00
Cox's History of Carolina, 8vo.	00	02	06
Cruso's Life abridg'd, in a neat Pocket Volume, 12ves.	00	02	06
Cambray's Private Thoughts upon Religion, 12ves.	00	02	06
Cornelius Nepos, Englifh'd by several Hands, 12ves.	00	02	00
Cockman's Tully's Offices, 12ves.	00	02	06
Christian's Companion to the Closet and Altar, 12ves.	00	02	06
Chevalier de Vaudray, a Novel, 12ves.	00	02	00
Cole's Latin and English Dictionary, 8vo.	00	06	00
Cæsar ex Recensione, Tho. Parsell, 12ves.	00	02	06
Cum Notis Delphini, 8vo.	00	06	06
Constitutions, Canons, and Articles, of the Church of England, 8vo.	00	02	06

Clark's

	l.	s.	d.
Clark's Anſwer to the Religion of Nature delineated, 8vo.	00	01	00
Ditto, againſt Hutchinſon's Ideas of Beauty, 8vo.	00	01	06
Clarendon's (Lord) Hiſtory of the Rebellion, 6 Vols. 8vo.	01	10	00
Caſes againſt the Diſſenters, 3 Vols. 8vo.	00	15	00
Clark, (Dr. Samuel) on the Attributes, 8vo.	00	06	00
Seventeen Sermons at St. James's, 8vo.	00	06	00
on the Goſpels, 2 Vols. 8vo.	00	11	00
Cheyne (Dr.) on Health and Long Life, 8vo.	00	04	06
Congreve's Plays and Poems, 3 Vols. 12ves.	00	09	00
Critical Hiſtory of England, 2 Vols. 8vo.	00	11	00
Cheſelden's Anatomy, 8vo.	00	06	00
Cambden's Britannia 2 Vols. Folio.	03	10	00
Churches no Charnel Houſes, proving the Indecency of Burying in Churches and Church-Yards.	00	01	
Carcaſe's Book of Rates Folio 1726.	01	05	
Comical Hiſtory of Francion, 2 Vols. 12ves.	00	05	06
Chambers's Dictionary of Arts and Sciences, 2 Vols. Folio.			
Chillingworth's Works, Folio, 1726.	00	12	06
Chandler (Biſhop) Defence of Chriſtianity, 8vo.	00	05	06
Collier's Sacred Interpreter, 2 Vol. 8vo.	00	10	00
Cambray of the Being and Exiſtence of God, 12ves.	00	03	00
Clarendon and Whitlock compared, 8vo.	00	05	00
Collier's Antoninus, 8vo.	00	04	06

D

	l.	s.	d.
Domat's Civil Law in its Natural Order, Tranſlated by Dr. Strahan, 2 Vols. Fol.	02	02	00
Dupin's Method of Studying Divinity, 8vo.	00	05	00
Dionis's Midwifry, Engliſh, 8vo.	00	04	06
Devout Chriſtian's Companion, 2 Vols. 12ves.	00	06	00
Dacier's Abridgment of Plato's Works. Tranſlated from the French, 2 Vols. 12ves.	00	05	00
Drelincourt of Death, 8vo.			
Dictionarium Ruſticum & Urbanicum: Or, A Dictionary of Country Affairs, 2 Vols. 8vo.	00	05	00
	00	09	00
Defoe's Works, 2 Vols 8vo.	00	10	00
Drexelius's Hourly Companion, 12ves.	00	01	00
Derham's Phyſico-Theology, 8vo.	00	06	00
Aſtro-Theology, 8vo.	00	04	06
Dupin's Hiſtory of the Church, abridg'd, in four neat Pocket-Volumes, 12ves.	00	10	00
Dryden's Plays, in 5 Vols. 12ves.	01	00	00
Miſcellanies, 6 Vols. 12ves.	00	18	00
Virgil, with Cuts, 3 Vols. 12ves.	00	11	00
Juvenal, 12ves.	00	03	06
Fables.	00	03	06
Ditton, on the Reſurrection, 8vo.	00	05	00
on Fluids, 8vo.	00	03	00
Defence of the Female Sex.	00	03	00
Dalton's Country Juſtice, with large Additions, by W. Nelſon, Eſq, Folio, 1726.	01	05	00
Danois's Tales of the Fairies, 3 Vol. 12ves.	00	07	06
Dictionary of all Religions, 8vo.	00	04	06
Degolls on Worms, 8vo.	00	01	06
Ductor Hiſtoricus, 2 Vo's. 8vo.	00	10	00

England's

ENgland's Intereft : Or, The Gentleman and Farmer's Friend.   00 01 06

English Liberties : Or, The Free-born Subjects Inheritance. ⎱ 00 04 06
By W. Nelfon, Efq,   ⎰

Effay on the Tranfmutation of the Blood, 8vo.   00 01 00

Eutropius, in Ufum Delphini, 8vo.   00 02 06

Echard's Hiftory of England, Folio.   01 16 00

     Roman Hiftory, 5 Vols. 8vo.   01 05 00

     Ecclefiaftical Hiftory, 2 Vols. 8vo.   00 09 00

     Gazetteer, in Two Parts, 12ves.   00 03 06

     Terence, 12ves.   00 02 06

     Hiftory of the Revolution, 8vo.   00 04 06

Eufebius's Ecclefiaftical Hiftory, Englifh, Folio.   01 00 00

Etheridge's Plays, 12ves.   00 03 00

Englifh Expofitor, 12ves.   00 01 00

Echard's (Dr.) Works, 8vo.   00 04 06

England's Black Tribunal, 12ves.   00 02 06

Everard's Gauging, 12ves.   00 02 06

Eikon Bafilike : To which is added, The Life of King Charles ⎱ 00 05 06
the Firft, by Perinchief.   ⎰

F

FLavell's Works, 2 Vol. Folio.   02 00 00

     Husbandry Spiritualiz'd, 12ves.   00 02 00

     Navigation Spiritualiz'd, 8vo.   00 01 06

Bifhop Fleetwood's Relative Duties, 8vo.   00 04 06

Fifher's Arithmetick, 12ves.   00 02 06

Farrier's and Horfeman's Dictionary, 8vo.   00 05 06

Familiar Letters of Love and Gallantry, in Two neat Pocket ⎱ 00 05 00
Volumes, 12ves   ⎰

Florus in Ufum Delphini, 8vo.   00 04 06

Frauds of the Romifh Priefts and Monks, in Two Volumes, 12ves.   00 05 06

Fable of the Bees, 8vo.   00 05 06

Friend's Hiftory of Phyfick, 2 Vols. 8vo.   00 10 00

Freeholder, 12ves.   00 03 00

Fuller's Pharmacopœia Extemporanea, 12ves.   00 03 00

     The fame in Englifh, 8vo.   00 05 06

Fidde's Sermons, Folio.   00 17 06

Farquhar's Plays and Poems, 2 Vols. 12ves.   00 06 00

G

GOodman's (Dr.) Penitent pardoned, 8vo.   00 04 06

     Winter Evening Conference, 8vo.   00 04 00

     Old Religion, 12ves.   00 02 06

Glanvill of Witches, 1726. 8vo.   00 05 06

Gordon's (Patrick) Geographical Grammar, 8vo.   00 05 00

     (George) Introduction to Geography, Aftronomy, Dyal- ⎱ 00 04 06
ling, and Chronology, 8vo. 1726.   ⎰

Gerhard's Meditations. By Rowell.   00 03 00

     Ditto, fmall Edition.   00 01 00

Gentleman Angler, 12ves.   00 01 06

Gaftrell's Chriftian Inftitutes, 12ves.   00 02 06

Gentleman Inftructed, 8vo.   00 02 06

Guillim's Difplay of Heraldry, Folio.   02 02 00

Gentleman Jockey, 8vo.   00 01 06

Gibfon's Farrier's Guide, 8vo.   00 05 00

     Farmer's Difpenfatory, 8vo.   00 04 00

     Method of Dieting Horfes, 8vo.   00 03 06

	l.	s.	d.
Gay's Paftorals,	00	01	06
Gedde's Tracts, 3 Vols. 8vo.	00	18	00
Guardian, 2 Vols. 12ves.	00	05	00
Gardner's Dictionary, 2 Vols. 12ves.	00	12	00
Gibfon's Anatomy of Human Bodies, 8vo.	00	05	06

H

	l.	s.	d.
HENRY, (Matthew) on the Bible, 6 Vols.	06	06	00
Works, Collected into One Volume.	01	07	06
Hooker's Ecclefiaftical Polity, 1724, Folio.	01	01	00
Horneck's (Dr.) Crucified Jefus, 8vo.	00	05	06
on Confiseration, 8vo.	00	04	06
Beft Exercife, 8vo.	00	04	06
Fire of the Altar, 12ves.	00	01	00
Handley's Mechanical Effays on the Animal Oeconomy, 8vo.	00	05	00
Colloquia Chirurgica: Or, The Whole Art of Surgery, 8vo.	00	02	06
Hawney's Trigonometry, 8vo.	00	06	00
Compleat Meafurer. 12ves.	00	02	06
Hiftory of England, 4 Vols. 8vo. With the Heads of all the Kings and Queens curioufly Engrav'd.	01	02	00
Howell's (Lawrence) Hiftory of the Bible, 3 Vols. With 150 Copper Plates, 3 Vols. 8vo.	01	00	00
Howell's (James) Familiar Letters, 8vo.	00	05	00
Harris's (Dr.) Lexicon Technicum, 2 Vols. Folio.	02	10	00
Hudibras, in Three Parts; with a new Sett of Cuts.	00	03	00
Hiftory and Prefent State of the Kingdom of France, 2 Vols. 12ves.	00	06	00
Hatton's Pfalter, 12ves.	00	02	06
Howard's Neweft Way of Cookery, 12ves	00	02	06
Hiftory of Englifh Martyrs in Queen Mary's Reign, 8vo.	00	04	06
Hatton's Comes Comercii, 8vo.	00	02	00
Hiftory of Hungary, 12ves.	00	02	06
Hewit's Tables of Intereft, engraven on Copper Plates, 12ves.	00	02	06
Hiftory of Tryals and Attainders, 2 Vols. 12ves.	00	05	06
Hutchinfon's Enquiry into our Ideas of Beauty and Virtue, 8vo.	00	04	06
Hanover Tales: Or, The Secret Hiftory of Count Fradonia, and the Unfortunate Beritia, 12ves.	00	01	06
Henley's Heathen, an Hiftorical Poem	00	01	06
Horatius in Ufum Delphini, 8vo.	00	06	06
Haywood's Novels, 4 Vols. 12ves.	00	10	00
Hook's Experiments, publifh'd by Derham.	00	05	06
Hiftoria Sacra: Or, Hiftory of the Feafts and Fafts of the Church of England.	00	05	00
Hope's Compleat Horfeman, Folio.	01	02	06
Howard's Plays, 12ves.	00	03	00
Hiftory of Herodotus, Englifh'd by Littlebury, 2 Vols. 8vo.	00	10	00
The Hive: Or, A Collection of Songs, 3 Vols. 12ves.	00	07	06
Hiftory of the Devil, 8vo.	00	05	00

J

	l.	s.	d.
Johnfon's (Samuel) Works. Folio.	00	10	06
Jones's Poetical Mifcellanies, 12ves.	00	01	00
Juftinius in Ufum Delphini, 8vo.	00	05	06
Englifh'd, by Brown, 12ves.	00	02	06
Jenks's Devotions on feveral Occafions	00	03	00
Juvenalis in Ufum Delphini, 8vo.	00	05	06
Jenkins of the Chriftian Religion, 2 Vols. 8vo.	00	10	00
Journey through England, 3 Vols. 8vo.	00	15	00
Inquiry into the Original of our Ideas of Beauty and Virtue, 8vo.	00	04	06

Jackman

	l.	s.	d.
Memoirs of Anne of Auſtria, 5 Vols. 12ves.	00	15	00
Moyle's Works 2 Vols. 8vo.	00	11	00
Montaigne's Eſſays, 3 Vols. 8vo.	00	15	00
Miſſon's Travels over England, 8vo.	00	04	06
Mauger's French Grammar, 8vo.	00	02	00
Martial in Uſum Delphini, 8vo.	00	06	06
Miſcellanea Aurea : Or, Golden Medley.	00	04	00
Medulla Hiſtoriæ Anglicanæ, 8vo.	00	06	00
Motteaux's Don Quixot, 4 Vol. 12ves.	00	10	00
Morgan's Principles of Medicine, 8vo.	00	06	00
Moreland's Vade Mecum, 8vo.	00	02	00
Maſter-Key to Popery, 3 Vols. 12ves.	00	09	00
Milbourn's Legacy to the Church of England, 2 Vols.	00	09	00
Mandey, of Meaſuring, 8vo.	00	05	00
Maſhmer's Husbandry, 2 Vols. 8vo.	00	09	00
Mangey, on the Lord's Prayer, 8vo.	00	03	06
Muſæ Anglicanæ, 2 Vols.	00	05	06
Moor (Biſhop of Ely) his Sermons, 2 Vols. 8vo.	00	09	00

N

	l.	s.	d.
Nicholls's Conference with a Theiſt, 2 Vols. with large Additions, 8vo.	00	10	00
New Voyage round the World by a Courſe never fail'd before, 8vo.	00	04	06
Nelſon's (Robert) Works, Abridg'd and Methodiz'd, 2 Vol. 12ves.	00	06	00
Noble Slaves, a Novel, 12ves.	00	02	00
New Miſcellaneous Poems, with Five Love Letters from a Nun to a Cavalier, and the Cavalier's Anſwer, in Verſe.	00	02	00
Nelſon of the Feaſts and Faſts of the Church of England.	00	05	00
Practice of true Devotion, 12ves.	00	02	06
New Manual of Devotions, in 3 Parts.	00	03	00
Nuptial Dialogues and Debates, 2 Vols. 12ves.	00	05	06
Nelſon's Abridgment of the Law, 3 Vols. Folio.	04	10	00

O

	l.	s.	d.
Ozanam's Courſe of the Mathematicks. Done from the French by Dr. Deſaguliers, and others, 5 Vols. 8vo.	01	02	06
Ovidii Metamorphoſes in Uſum Delphini.	00	06	06
Tranſlated into Engliſh Verſe, and publiſh'd by Dr. Sewell, 2 Vols.	00	05	06
Osborn's Works, 2 Vols. 12ves.	00	05	06
Oſtervald's Cauſes of the Corruption of Chriſtians.	00	04	06
Orleans's Hiſtory of the Stuarts, recommended by Echard, 8vo.	00	04	06
Ovid De Triſtibus in Engliſh Verſe	00	01	00
Ogilby's and Morgan's Pocket Book of the Roads, 8vo.	00	01	06
Ovid's Epiſtles, Engliſh, with Cuts, 12ves.	00	03	00
Art of Love, with Cuts, 12ves.	00	03	00
Oldham's Works, 2 Vols. 12ves.	00	05	00

P

	l.	s.	d.
Philips's Engliſh Dictionary, Folio.	01	00	00
Patrick's (Bp.) Devout Chriſtian Inſtructed, 12ves.	00	03	00
Chriſtian Sacrifice, 12ves.	00	03	00
Menſa Myſtica, 8vo.	00	05	00
Sermons, on Contentment, 8vo.	00	05	00
Help to Young Communicants, 24°	00	00	06
Patrick's (Dr.) Pſalms, 12ves.	00	02	00
Potter's (Biſhop) Greek Antiquities, 2 Vols. 8vo.	00	12	00
Pembroke's Arcadia, 3 Vols. by Sir Philip Sidney, 1725.	00	15	06

Puffendorf's

	_l._	_s._	_d._
Puffendorf's Introduction to the Hiftory of Europe, 8vo.	00	06	00
Pomfret's Poems, 12ves.	00	02	00
Plurality of Worlds. Tranflated from the French of Fontenell, By Gardner.	00	02	06
Poftman robb'd of his Mail: Or, A Collection of Letters, written by the beft Wits of the prefent Age, 12ves.	00	03	00
Prior's Poems, 2 Vols. 12ves.	00	05	06
Parnell's Poems, 8vo.	00	03	06
Pope's Homer's Iliad, 6 Vols. 12ves. with Cuts.	00	18	00
Odiffey, in 5 Vol. 12ves.	00	15	00
Mifcellanies, 2 Vols. 12ves.	00	05	06
Prideaux's Connection of the Old and New Teftament, 4 Vols. 8vo.	01	00	00
Life of Mahomet, 8vo.	00	03	06
Palladio's Architecture, 4to.	00	04	00
Pomet's Hiftory of Druggs, 4to.	01	01	00
Perfian Tales, 3 Vols. 12ves.	00	09	00
Patrick's (Bifhop) Paraphrafe on all the Poetical Books of the Old Teftament.	00	18	00
Commentary on the Hiftorical Books of the Bible, 2 Vols. Folio.	02	08	00
Pearfon, on the Creed, Folio.	00	12	00
Pitt's (Rev. Mr.) Poems on feveral Occafions.	00	03	06

Q

Quarles's Emblems, 12ves.	00	04	00
Divine Poems, 12ves.	00	03	00
Queen's Clofet open'd, 12ves.	00	02	00
Quiney's Pharm. Officinalis, 8vo.	00	06	00
Lexicon Medicum, 8vo.	00	05	06
Sanctorius Aphorifms, 8vo.	00	05	06
Quintus Curtius, 2 Vols. Englifh.	00	06	00

R

Row's Callipœdia, 12ves.	00	01	06
Richardfon of Painting, 2 Vols. 8vo.	00	10	00
Robinfon (Dr.) on the Stone and Gravel, 8vo.	00	04	00
On Confumptions, 8vo.	00	04	00
Royal French Grammar.	00	02	06
Robert's (Capt.) Voyages to the Cape de Verd Iflands.	00	05	00
Ray's Wifdom of God in the Creation.	00	04	06
Phyfico-Theological Difcourfes, 8vo.	00	05	06
Ratcliff's Life, 12ves.	00	01	06
Religious Philofopher, 2 Vols. 4to.	00	16	00
Reflections on Ridicule, 2 Vols.	00	05	00
Ronayne's Algebra, 8vo.	00	06	00
Row's Lucan's Pharfalia, 2 Vols. 12ves.	00	06	00
Salluft, Englifh	00	02	06

S

Selden's Works, 6 Vols Publifh'd by Dr. Wilkins	07	16	00
Stevens's Englifh and Spanifh Dictionary.	01	01	00
Stanhope (Dr.) on the Epiftles and Gofpels, 4 Vols, 8vo.	01	02	00
Sherlock (Dr.) of Death, 8vo.	00	03	06
The fame in 12ves.	00	01	06
on Judgment, 8vo.	00	04	00
on a FutureState, 8vo.	00	04	06
on Providence, 8vo.	00	04	06
of Religious Affemblies, 8vo.	00	04	00

Sherlock's

	l.	s.	d.
Sherlock's (Dr.) Sermons, 2 Vols. 8vo.	00	09	00
Secret History of Whitehall, 2 Vols. 12ves.	00	05	06
Select Novels, 2 Vols. with Cuts, 12ves.	00	06	00
Strother's Pharm. Practica, 12ves.	00	03	06
Sydenham's (Dr.) Works English, 8vo.	00	04	06
Scrivener's Guide, 2 Vol. 8vo.	00	11	00
Salmon's Family Dictionary, 8vo.	00	06	00
Smith's Art of Painting in Oil, 12ves.	00	01	00
Symson's New Voyage to the West Indies.	00	03	06
South's Maxims, 8vo.	00	01	06
Sylvius de la Boie's Practical Physick, 8vo.	00	04	00
Salluftius in Usum D lphini, 8vo.	00	04	00
Schrevelii Lexicon, 8vo.	00	06	06
Spectator, 8 Vols.	01	00	00
Seneca's Morals. By Sir R. Leftrange, 8vo.	00	05	00
Stanhope's (Dr.) Christian Pattern, 8vo.	00	04	06
Parsons Christian Directory.	00	04	06
St. Auftin's Meditations.	00	04	06
Epictetus's Morals, 8vo.	00	04	06
Salmon's Druggift Shop open'd, 8vo.	00	07	06
Suetonius, English, 2 Vols.	00	05	00
Spinke's Sick Man visited, 8vo.	00	05	00
Steel's (Sir Richard) Plays.	00	03	00
Southern's Plays, 2 Vol.	00	06	00
Strother's Effay on Health, 8vo.	00	05	06
Salmon's Review of the History of England, 2 Vols.	00	10	00
against Burnet's History, 2 Vos.	00	10	00
Effay on Marriage.	00	04	06
Shaw's Practice of Physick, 2 Vols. 8vo.	00	09	00
Tranflation of Boerhave's Chymiftry.	00	18	00
Sutherland's Ship-Building unveil'd, Folio.	00	15	00
Sydenham's Practice of Physick, English.	00	05	06
Shaftsbury's Characterifticks, 3 Vols.	00	18	00
Stanhope's (Dr.) 12 Sermons on feveral Occasions, 8vo.	00	05	06
Swinden's Enquiry into the Place of Hell.	00	05	06
South's Sermons, 6 Vols. 8vo.	01	10	00
Shaw's Edinburgh Difpenfatory.	00	04	00
Sharp's Sermons, 4 Vols.	00	18	00

T

	l.	s.	d.
Taylor's (Bp.) Life of Chrift, now in the Prefs.			
Rules for Holy Living and Dying.	00	05	00
Contemplations on the State of Man.	00	02	06
Golden Grove, 12ves.	00	01	00
Tyrrel's Bibliotheca Politica, Folio.	00	18	00
Tournfort's Voyage into the Levant, 2 Vols. 4to.	01	10	00
Tatler, 5 Vols. 12ves.	00	12	06
Tacitus, English, 3 Vols. 12ves.	00	09	00
Terentius in Usum Delphini, 8vo.	00	05	06
English'd by Echard, 12ves.	00	02	06
Travels of an English Gentleman from London to Rome on Foot, 12ves.	00	01	06
Turretin of Fundamental Principles in Religion, 8vo.	00	01	00
Turner's Surgery, 2 Vols. 8vo.	00	11	00
Difeafes of the Skin, 8vo.	00	05	06
Syphilis, 8vo.	00	04	06
Temple's Works, 2 Vols. Folio.	01	12	00
Tillotfon's (Bifhop) Works, 3 Vols. Folio.	02	10	00
Tale of a Tub, 12ves. with Cuts.	00	02	06

Vauban

	l.	s.	d.

V

VAuban, of Fortification, 8vo.	00	06	00
Vida's Art of Poetry, in Englifh, 12ves.	00	02	00
Vertot's Revolutions of Rome, 2 Vols. 8vo.	00	10	00
of Sweden, 8vo.	00	04	06
of Portugal, 8vo.	00	03	00
Vanbrugh's (Sir John) Plays, 2 Vols.	00	05	00

W

WHeatley on the Common Prayer, Folio.	00	18	00
Whitby, on the New Teftament, 2 Vols.	02	02	00
Difquifitiones Modeftæ, 8vo.	00	03	00
Ward's London Spy, in 6 Vols. 8vo.	01	07	06
N. B. Moft of the Pieces may be had fingle.			
Nuptial Dialogues 2 Vols. 12ves.	00	06	00
Webfter's Arithmetick in Epitome, 12ves.	00	02	06
Book-keeping, 8vo.	00	01	06
Wycherley's Plays, 2 Vols. 12ves.	00	05	00
Ward's Young Mathematician's Guide.	00	06	00
Woodward's Effay towards a Natural Hiftory of the Earth, 8vo.	00	04	00
Wifeman's Surgery, 2 Vols. 8vo.	00	10	00
Week's Preparation to the Sacrament, 12ves.	00	01	00
Wood's Inftitutes of the Common Law, Folio.	01	04	00
of the Civil and Imperial Law, 8vo.	00	06	00
Wake's (Abp.) Genuine Epiftles.	00	05	06
Commentary on the Church Catechifm.	00	02	00
Warder's Monarchy of Bees, 8vo.	00	01	06
Well's Sacred Geography of the Old and New Teftament, 8vo. 4 Vols.	01	00	00
Courfe of the Mathematicks, 5 Vols. 8vo.	00	18	00
Watts's Aftronomy, 8vo.	00	04	06
Logick, 8vo.	00	04	06
Sermons, 3 Vol. 12ves.	00	09	00
Pfalms, 12ves.	00	01	06
Wingate's Arithmetick, 8vo.	00	04	06

Y

YOUNG Clerk's Tutor, 12ves.	00	01	06
Young, (Dr.) on the Laft Day, 12ves.	00	01	00
Poem on Lady Jane Gray, 8vo.	00	01	00

Libri in Ufum Scholarum.

BAiley's Ovid's Metamorphofis, 8vo.
    Ovid De Triftibus, 12ves.
    Phædrus, 8vo.
    Cato, 12ves.
    Exercifes, Englifh and Latin, 12ves.
    Exercitia Latina: Or, Latin for Garretfon's Exercifes, 12ves,
Busby's Greek Grammar, 8vo.
    Englifh Introduction to the Latin Tongue.
    Syntaxis Erafmiana Conftruction, 8vo.
    Ditto, Conftrued, 8vo.
Beza's Latin Teftament, 12ves and 24o.

Clavis Homerica, 8vo.
Clark's Introduction to the making of Latin
Florus, 8vo.
Nepos, 8vo.
Eutropius, 8vo.
Erasmus, 12ves.
Corderius 12ves.
} All with Literal Translations.
Castalio's Latin Bible, in 4 neat Vols.
Latin Testament, 12ves.
Cornelius Nepos, 12ves.
Celsar, 12ves.
Demosthenes, 12ves
Dyche's Vocabulary, 8vo.
Youth's Guide to the Latin Tongue,12ves.
English Particles Latiniz'd, 8vo.
Phædrus, 12ves.
Electa Majora, 8vo.
Minora, 8vo.
Eutropius, 12ves.
Epigrammatum Delectus, 12ves.
Erasmus, Dublin, 12ves.
Familiar Form, 12ves.
Farnaby's Rhetorick, 8vo. English and Latin.
Garretson's English Exercises, 12ves.
Gradus ad Parnassum, 8vo.
Gregory's Nomenclatura, 8vo.
Hederici Lexicon, 4to.
Homeri Ilias, Greek and Latin, 8vo.
Helvici Colloquia, 12ves.
Hoadley's Phædrus, 12ves.
Horace, 12ves. sine Notis.
King's Heathen Gods, 12ves.
Lock's Æsop Interlineary, English and Latin.
Leed's Greek Grammar, 12ves.
London Vocabulary, by Greenwood, 12ves.
Leusden's Compendium, 8vo.
Martialis Epigrammata, 12ves.
More's English Examples, for the Use of Bury School, 8vo.
Pantheon. By Tooke, 8vo. with Cuts.
Phædrus Delphini, 8vo.
Ra's Nomenclatura. 8vo.
Royal Grammar, 12ves.
Urmston's Help to the Accidence, 8vo.
London Spelling Book, 12ves.
Walker's Art of Teaching, 12ves.
Engl. Examples, 12ves.
Particles, 8vo.
Wettenhall's Gr. Grammar,12ves.
Well's Dionysius, 8vo.
Ware's Practical Grammar, 8vo.
Xenophon de Cyri Institutione, Greek and Latin.

Most of the Classicks in Usum Delphini.

BOOKS lately publish'd.

I. THE Entertaining Novels of Mrs. Jane Barker. Containing, 1. Exilius: Or, The Banish'd Roman. 2. Clelia and Marcellus: Or, The Constant Lovers. 3. The Reward of Virtue: Or, The Adventures of Clarinthia and Lysander. 4. The Lucky Escape: Or, The Fate of Ismenus. 5. Clodius and Scipiana: Or, The Beautiful Captive. 6. Piso: Or, The Leud Courtier. 7. The Happy Recluse: Or, The Charms of Liberty. 8. The Fair Widow: Or, False Friend. 9. The Amours of Bosvill and Galesia. The 2d. Edition. In 2 Vols. Price 5 s.

II. A Patchwork Screen for the Ladies: Or, Love and Virtue recommended, in a Collection of Instructive Novels, related after a Manner entirely New, and interspers'd with Rural Poems, describing the Innocence of a Country Life. Price 2 s. 6 d.

III. A Lining for the Patchwork Screen: Designed for the farther Entertainment of the Ladies. Price 2 s. 6 d. These Two by Mrs. Barker.

IV. The Life of Charlotta du Pont, an English Lady, taken from her own Memoirs: Giving an Account how she was trapann'd by her Step-Mother to Virginia; how the Ship was taken by some Madagascar Pyrates, and retaken by a Spanish Man of War; of her Marriage in the Spanish West-Indies, and Adventures while she resided there, with her Return to England; and the History of several Gentlemen and Ladies whom she met withal in her Travels, some of whom had been Slaves in Barbary, and others cast on Shore on the Barbarous Coasts up the great River Oroonoque; with their Escape thence, and safe Return to France and Spain. A History that contains the greatest Variety of Events ever yet publish'd. By Mrs. Aubin. Price 2 s.

V. The Tragical History of the Chevalier de Vaudray and the Countess de Vergi. In Two Parts. To which is annex'd a short Novel, entitled, The Inhuman Husband. Done from the French by Mr. Morgan. Price 2 s.

VI. The Agreeable Variety: Being a miscellaneous Collection in Prose and Verse, from the Works of the most Celebrated Authors. In Two Parts, viz. Part I. Containing Instructive Discourses on the most useful Subjects, for the happy Conduct of human Life. 2. Characters of the most Illustrious Personages of both Sexes, of our own, and other Nations, particularly the remarkable Manner of Life of the excellent Princess of Parma. Written by herself, and found among her Papers after her Decease. 3. Choice Poems, and Select Passages, extracted from the most Celebrated Poets. Part II. Containing Original Poems; Sixty familiar Letters upon Education, Love, Friendship, &c. none of which ever before Publish'd. The Whole Collected and Publish'd by a Lady. Price 3 s. 6 d. The 2d Edition.

VII. Miscellanea Aurea: Or, The Golden Medley. Consisting of, 1. A Voyage to the Mountains of the Moon, under the Æquator: Or, Parnassus reform'd. 2. The Fortunate Ship-wreck: Or, A Description of New Athens, being an Account of the Laws, Manners, Religion, and Customs of that Country. By Morris Williams, Gent. who resided there above twenty Years. 3. Albetoni: Or, A Vindication of that Cardinal. 4. The Secret History of the Amours of Don Alonzo Duke of Lerma, and Grandee of Spain. 5. The Garden of Adonis: Or, Love to no Purpose; being about twenty Copies of Verses and Love Letters. By a Lady. 6. Mahomet no Impostor; written in Arabick, by Abdulla-Mahunied Omer. 7. An Account of Bad and Good Women, antient and modern. With several other Epistolary Essays in Prose and Verse. By Mr. Milton; the Lady W ‒ ‒ ‒ ‒ ‒, Mr. Philips, and several Others. In Octavo. Price 4 s.

VIII. The

VIII. The four Years Voyage of Captain George Roberts: Being a Series of uncommon Events, which befel him in a Voyage to the Islands of the Canaries, Cape de Verde, and Barbadoes, from whence he was bound to the Coast of Guinea; the Manner of his being taken by three Pirate Ships, Commanded by Low, Ruffel,, and Spriggs, who after having plundered him, and detained him ten Days, put him aboard his own Sloop without Provisions, Water, &c. and with only two Boys, one of eighteen, and the other of eight Years of Age; the Hardships he endured for above twenty Days, till he arriv'd at the Island of St. Nicholas, from whence he was blown off to Sea (before he could get any Suftenance) without his biggeft Boy and Boat, whom he had fent afhore, and after four Days Difficulty and Diftrefs, was Ship-wreck'd on the unfrequented Ifland of St. John; where, after he had remained near two Years, he built a Veffel to bring himfelf off. With a particular and curious Defcription and Draught of the Cape de Verd Iflands, their Roads, anchoring Places, Nature and Production of the Soil; the Kindnefs and Hofpitality of the Natives to Strangers, their Religion, Manners, Cuftoms, and Superftitions, &c. Together with Obfervations on the Minerals, Mineral Waters, Metals, and Salts, and of the Nitre, with which fome of thofe Iflands abound. Written by himfelf now living at Shad-Thames, 1726. Price 5 s.

IX. The Travels of an Englifh Gentleman from London to Rome on Foot: Containing a Comical Defcription of what he met with Remarkable in every City, Town, and Religious Houfe, in his whole Journey: Alfo an Account of their ridiculous Proceffions, and Ceremonies, in their Churches, through their Streets, and in the Woods. Likewife the Debauch'd Lives, and Amorous Intriegues of the Priefts and Nuns: With a pleafant Account of the Opening the Holy Gate of St. Peter's Church. Alfo Reflections upon the Superftition and Foppifh Pageantry of the whole Ceremony of the laft Grand Jubilee at Rome. The 4th Edition. Now Publifh'd for the Diverfion and Information of the Proteftants of England. Price 1 s. 6 d.

X. Saduciffimus Triumphatus: Or, A full and plain Evidence concerning Witches and Apparitions. In Two Parts. The Firft treating of their Poffibility; the Second of their real Exiftence. By Jofeph Glanvill, Chaplain in Ordinary to King Charles II. and F. R. S. The 4th Edition, with Additions. With fome Account of Mr. Glanvill's Life and Writings. Price 6 s. 1726.

XI. The Works of the Honourable Sir Philip Sidney, Knt. In Profe and Verfe. Containing, 1. The Countefs of Pembroke's Arcadia. 2. The Defence of Poefy. 3. Aftrophel and Stella. 4. The Remedy of Love. 5. The Lady of May: A Mafque. 6. The Life of the Author. The 14th Edition. In Three Vols. 8vo. 1725. Price 13 s. 6 d.

XII. The New Defcription and Prefent State of the Kingdom of France. Containing, 1. An Hiftorical Account of its Kings, their Antiquity, Prerogatives, &c. With a Defcription of all the Royal Palaces, and of the Paintings, Statues, and other Curiofities therein contained. 2. Of the Parliament, and all Officers, Civil and Military, belonging to his Majefty, and the Princes of the Blood. 3. Of the Bifhopricks, other Church Dignities, Monafteries, and Clergy, of the Univerfities, Faculties therein ftudied, and of the French Academy. 4. The Peerage of France; the three Orders of Knighthood, the Nobility and Marfhals, and the Coats of Arms of each refpective Family truly Emblazoned. 5. A Defcription of the City of Paris, and all the Publick Buildings, Churches, Libraries, and Collection of Rarities, and whatfoever elfe is remarkable. 6. The Roads from one Town to another, with the exact Diftances from Place to Place, not only in France, but from thence through Spain, Italy, Germany, and the Netherlands. In Two Volumes, 12ves. The 2d Edition, 1726. Price 6 s.

XIII. Mechanical

XIII. Mechanical Essays on the Animal Oeconomy; wherein not only the Conduct of Nature in Animal Secretion, but Sensation and human Generation, are distinctly consider'd, and Anatomically explain'd; as also the particular Manner of the Operation of a Medicine is accounted for, and many other Curious and Uncommon Subjects are treated of; necessary for all that study Nature, and particularly those that make Physick or Surgery their Practice. By James Handley, Surgeon, Author of Colloquia Chirurgica, 8vo. Price 5 s.

XIV. England's Interest: Or, The Gentleman and Farmer's Friend: Shewing 1. How Land may be improv'd from 20s. to 8 l. and so to 100 l. per Acre, per Annum, with great Ease, and for an inconsiderable Charge. 2. The best and quickest Way of raising a Nursery. 3. How to make Cyder, Perry, Cherry, Currant, Gooseberry, Mulberry, and Birch Wines, as Strong and Wholsome as French and Spanish Wines, and the Cyders and Wines so made to be sold at 3 d. per Quart, tho' as good as Wine now sold for 18 d. 4. Directions for Brewing the finest Malt Liquors, better and cheaper than hitherto known. 5. Instructions for Breeding Horses, Husbandry of Bees, and ordering Fish and Fish-Ponds. Lastly, Physick for Families; containing many useful Medicines for several Distempers, particularly the Plague. By Sir J. Moore, 12ves. Price 1 s. 6d.

XV. English Liberties: Or, The Free-born Subject's Inheritance. Containing Magna Charta, Charta de Foresta, the Statute de Tallagio non Concedendo, the Habeas Corpus Act; with several other Statutes, and Comments on each of them: Likewise the Proceedings in Appeals of Murder, of Ship-Money, of Tunnage and Poundage, of Parliaments, of the Three Estates and of the Settlement of the Crown by Parliament. Together with a short History of the Succession, not by any Hereditary Right, also a Declaration of the Liberty of the Subject, the Petition of Right; with a short, but impartial Relation of the Difference between King Charles I. and the Long Parliament; of Tryals by Juries, and of the Qualifications of Jurors, their Punishment for Misbehaviour, and of Challenges to them. Lastly, Of Justices of the Peace, Coroners, Constables, Church-Wardens, Overseers of the Poor, Surveyors of the Highway, &c. With many Law-Cases throughout the Whole. Compiled first by Henry Care, and now continued with large Additions. By W. Nelson, of the Middle-Temple, Esq; The 4th Edition. Price 4s. 6d.

XVI. A Crown of Glory, the Reward of the Righteous: Being Meditations upon the Vicissitude and Uncertainty of all Sublunary Enjoyments, viz. 1. Honour, Riches, and Pleasure. 2. The Nature and Cause of Afflictions. 3. The great Benefit of Afflictions. 4. Of our Resignation to the Will of God. To which is added, A Manual of Devotions for Times of Trouble and Affliction, also Meditations and Prayers for the Holy Communion, both before, at, and after receiving; with some general Rules and Directions for our Daily Practice. Compos'd for the Use of a Noble Family. By the Right Reverend Dr. Thomas Kenn, late Lord Bishop of Bath and Wells. Price 2 s. 6d.

XVII. The Devout Christian's Hourly Companion: Consisting of Holy Prayers, and Divine Meditations. Done into English from that Spiritual Drexelius. The 3d Edition, in 12ves. Price 1 s.

XVIII. The Gentleman Angler: Containing short, plain, and easy Instructions, whereby the most ignorant Beginner may in a little Time, become a perfect Artist in Angling for Salmon, Salmon-Peal, Trout, Pike, Carp, Perch, Barbell, Tench, Bream, Chub, Greyling, Mullets, Flounders, Roach, Dace, Gudgeon, &c. With several Observations on Angling, Angle-Rods, and Artificial Flies, how to choose the best Hair, and Indian Grass; of the proper Times and Seasons for River and Pond Fishing. To which is added, The Angler's new Song, the Laws of Angling, and the Form of a
Licence

Licence and Deputation for Angling. Together with an Appendix : Containing the Method of Rock and Sea Fifhing, an Explanation of Technical Words ufed in the Art of Angling ; choice Receipts for drefling Fifh ; and how to improve Barren Ground, by turning it into Fifh-Ponds. By a Gentleman, who made Angling his Diverfion upwards of twenty eight Years, 1725. Price 1 s. 6 d.

XIX. A Practical Difcourfe of Religious Affemblies, under the following Heads : 1. Of Religion in general. 2. What Religious Worfhip is. 3. Of Publick Worfhip, and the Danger of forfaking Publick Affemblies. 4. The Seafonablenefs of this Difcourfe. 5. Concerning Speculative Atheifts. 6. The Inclination of Human Nature to Religious Worfhip. 7. Atheifts fhould not wholly forfake Religious Affemblies. 8. Nor intermeddle in the Difputes of Religion. 9. Concerning the Practical Atheift. 10. The Danger of Irreligion, both with refpect to this World and the next. 11. Concerning Parochial Communion. 12. Concerning the Neglect of the Publick Prayers of the Church. 13. Concerning the great Neglect of the Sacrament of the Lord's Supper. By William Sherlock, D. D. late Dean of St. Paul's. The 4th Edition, 1726. Price 4 s.

XX. Spiritual Communion Recommended and Enforced from Scripture, from the Primitive Fathers and Councils, from Reafon, and from Experience, in an Examination and Defence of the Doctrine, Worfhip, Rites, and Ceremonies of the Church of England. In Two Parts. By a Lay Hand, 8vo. 1725. Price 2 s. 6 d.

XXI. Arithmetick in the Plaineft and moft Concife Method hitherto extant; with new Improvements for Difpatch of Bufinefs in all the feveral Rules ; as alfo Fractions, Vulgar and Decimal, wrought together after a new Method that renders both eafy to be underftood in their Nature and Ufe. The Whole perufed and approved of by the moft Eminent Accomptants in the feveral Offices of the Revenues, viz. Cuftoms, Excife, &c. as the only Book of its Kind, for Variety of Rules, and Brevity of Work. By Geo. Fifher, Accomptant. The 2d Edition, with large Additions and Improvements, 12ves. 1725. Price 2 s. 6 d.

XXII. A new Method of treating Confumptions; wherein all the Decays incident to Human Bodies are mechanically accounted for, with fome Confiderations, touching the Difference between Confumptions, and thofe Decays that naturally attend Old Age. To which are added, Arguments in Defence of the Poffibility of curing Ulcers in the Lungs, as alfo Reafons demonftrating that the irregular Difcharges of all the Evacuations in Confumptions, arife from the Refiftance of the Heart not decaying in a fimple Proportion to the Refiftance of the other Parts. 8vo. Price 5 s.

XXIII. A compleat Treatife of the Gravel and Stone, with all their Caufes, Symptoms and Cures accounted for. To which are added, Propofitions demonftrating that the Stone may be fafely diffolved without any Detriment to the Body, drawn from Reafon, Experiments, and Anatomical Obfervations. The 2d Edition, with large Additions. 8vo. Price 4 s. Thefe two by Nicholas Robinfon, M. D.

XXIV. An Effay towards a Natural Hiftory of the Earth, and Terreftrial Bodies, efpecially Minerals; as alfo of the Sea, Rivers, and Springs · With an Account of the Univerfal Deluge, and of the Effects it had on the Earth. By John Woodward, M. D. Profeffor of Phyfick in Grefham College. The 3d Edition. Price 4 s.

XXV. The

XXV. The Demonftration of True Religion, in a Chain of Confequences from certain and undeniable Principles;' wherein the Neceffity and Certainty of Natural and Revealed Religion, with the Nature and Reafon of both are proved and explained; and in particular the Authority of the Chriftian Revelation is eftablifhed, not only from the Natures and Reafons of Things, but alfo from the Relation it bears to the Scriptures of the Old Teftament. In 16 Sermons preached at Bow Church in the Years 1724, and 1725, for the Lecture founded by the Honourable Robert Boyle, Efq, In two Volumes, 8vo. Price 9 s.

XXVI. An Effay upon Government: Or, The Natural Notions of Government, demonftrated in a Chain of Confequences from the fundamental Principles of Society. By which all the niceft Cafes of Confcience relating to Government, may be, and many of them are here refolved, with refpect to the Authority of Government in general, the End and Manner of making and executing Laws, the Meafures of Submiffion to Princes, and the Lawfulnefs or Unlawfulnefs of Revolutions, in a Method altogether new. Price 1 s. 6 d. The two laft by Thomas Burnett, D. D. Prebendary of Sarum, and Rector of Wefthington in Wiltfhire.

PLAYS, on Elziver Letter, at One Shilling each.

A Bramule,
All for Love,
Anatomift,
Ambitious Stepmother,
Artful Husband,
Artful Wife,
Beaux's Stratagem,
Beaux's Duel,
Beggar's Bufh,
Biter,
Boarding School,
Bold Strike for a Wife.
Briton,
Bufiris,
Bufy Body,
Caius Marius,
Campaign,
Carelefs Husband,
Cato,
Chances,
Committee,
Confcious Lovers,
Country Wife,
Sir Courtly Nice,
Cruel Gift,
Devil of a Wife,
Diftrefs'd Mother,
Don Sebaftian,
Double Gallant,

Drummer,
Duke of Gloucefter,
Earl of Effex,
Æfop,
Fair Penitent,
Fair Quaker of Deal,
Fall of Saguntum,
Fatal Marriage,
Gamefter,
Hamlet,
Hob,
Humours of Purgatory,
Jane Shore,
Jane Gray,
Inconftant,
Ignoramus,
Ifland Princefs,
King Lear,
London Cuckolds,
Love and a Bottle,
Love for Money,
Love makes a Man,
Love's laft Shift,
Mariamne,
Meafure for Meafure,
Merry Wives of Windfor,
Northern Heirefs,
Northern Lafs,
Oroonoko,

Orphan,
Othello,
Phædra and Hippolitus,
Pilgrim,
Plain Dealer,
Provok'd Wife,
Recruiting Officer,
Rehearfal and Chances,
Relapfe,
Revenge,
Royal Convert,
Rule a Wife,
She Gallant,
Sauney the Scot,
She wou'd and fhe wou'd'nt,
She wou'd if fhe cou'd,
Siege of Damafcus,
Sophonisba,
Spartan Dame,
'Squire of Alfatia,
Tamerlane,
Theodofius,
Tunbridge Wells,
Twin-Rivals,
Venice preferv'd,
Ulyffes,
Sir Walter Raleigh,
Wife's Excufe,
Wonder.

With great Variety of Plays, Poetry, Novels, &c.

ADDITIONS

AND

ALTERATIONS

IN THE

Second Edition

OF THE

CREDIBILITY

OF THE

GOSPEL HISTORY:

OR, THE

FACTS

Occasionally mention'd in the

NEW TESTAMENT,

Confirmed by

PASSAGES of Ancient Authors, who were contemporary with our SAVIOUR or his Apostles, or lived near their time.

With an Appendix concerning the time of *Herod*'s death.

By *NATHANIEL LARDNER.*

LONDON:

ADVERTISEMENT

Concerning the

SECOND EDITION.

 NOW allow, that the words of St. *Luke*, ch. ii. 2. are capable of the fenfe, in which they are underftood by *Herwaert* and *Perizonius.* But as I ftill difpute moft of the examples alledged by thofe learned men in fupport of that fenfe, there is but a fmall alteration made in that article. The Reverend Mr. *Maſſon* has * given me occaſion to conſider afreſh what I had ſaid concerning *Macrobius*'s paſſage. I hope, what is now added will be to his and others ſatisfaction. I have alſo taken this opportunity to add ſome farther obſervations on *Joſephus*'s ſilence about the ſlaughter of the infants at *Bethlehem.* But the moſt important addition is a curious obſervation on *Joſephus* concerning the *Egyptian* impoſtor, which I received from Mr. *Ward.* Theſe and the few other alterations and additions made in this edition can need no apology with thoſe who underſtand the nature of this deſign. As the Additions are printed by themſelves, and may be had ſeparate, I hope the firſt edition is not much prejudiced hereby.

Note ; *The Additions are to be given to thoſe who are poſſeſſed of the firſt Edition.*

* See his Slaughter of the children in *Bethlehem*, as an hiſtorical fact, vindicated, &c. in the dedication to the Biſhop of *Coventry* and *Lichfield.*

BOOK

BOOK I.

Note: The figures included within Crotchets are the Pages of the second edition; the other are the pages of the first edition.

CHAP. II.

PAGE [47] 70. l. 2. — *and to intimate, that they ought not to expect to be restored to the authority they wished for, whilst they were so universally corrupt* (a).

Note added, (a) There is a remarkable passage to this purpose in the speech of *Josephus* to the *Jews* in *Jerusalem*, while *Titus* with the *Roman* army lay before the city. Πόθεν δ' ἠρξάμεθα δελείας; ἆρ᾽ ἐχὶ ἐκ στάσεως τῶν προγόνων, ὅτε ἡ Αρισοβέλε κỳ Υρκανε μανία, κỳ ἡ πρὸς ἀλλήλες ἔρις, Πομπήιον ἐπήγαγε τῇ πόλει, κỳ Ῥωμαίοις ὑπέταξεν ὁ Θεὸς τὲς ἀναξίες ἐλευθερίας. Joseph. de B. l. v. c. 9. §. 4.

Page [151] 243. At the end of Chap. iii. *Add:* It appears from a verse of *Horace* (b), that the *Jewish* zeal in making proselytes was very extraordinary, and much taken notice of.

(b) ———— ———— Ac veluti te Judaei cogemus in hanc concedere turbam.
Lib. i. Sat. iv. ver. ult.

Page [213] 346. At the end of Chap. vii. *Addition.* §. XVII. St. *John* says [*Ch.* xix. 39, 40.] *There came also* Nicodemus, *and brought a mixture of myrrhe*

A 2   *and*

and aloes, about an hundred pound weight. Then took they [Jofeph *of* Arimathea *and* Nicodemus] *the body of Jefus, and wound it in linen clothes, with the fpices, as the manner of the* Jews *is to bury.* This may feem to fome a large quantity of fpices, to be beftowed on a fingle body at its interment. And it has been made an objection by a modern (c) *Jew* againft the hiftory of the *New Teftament.* And yet according to St. *Mark* [Ch. xvi. 1.] and St. *Luke* [Ch. xxiii. 55, 56] *Mary Magdalene,* and fome other women, having obferved the *fepulchre, and where the body was laid, went and bought fweet fpices, that they might anoint him. And on the firft day of the week, early in the morning, they came to the fepulchre, bringing the fpices which they had prepared.*

But the largeneffe of this quantity will not furprize any, who confider the *Jewifh* cuftom ; and that they were wont not only to embalm, or *anoint* the body, but to lay it alfo in a bed of fpices. 'Tis faid of *Afa* [2 Chron. xvi. 14.] *They buried him in the bed which was filled with fweet odors, and divers kinds of fpices prepared by the apothecaries art: and they made a very great burning for him.* The *Jews* of this time feem not to have fallen fhort of their anceftors in this kind of expenfe. For *Jofephus* in the account of *Herod*'s funeral proceffion fays : " The foldiery was followed by five " hundred flaves and freed-men bearing fweet fpices (d)." He mentions the fame number in the *War,* and in the *Antiquities.* 'Tis likely there were fpices here for a *burning,* as well as for a bed to lay *Herod*'s body in.

It is likewife objected by the fame *Jew,* that the quantity of fpices mentioned by St. *John* was a load
for

(c) *Amram,* in *B. Kidder,* affirms, that this was enough for two hundred dead bodies, and that it could not be carried with lefs than the ftrength of a mule, and therefore not by *Nicodemus. Kidder*'s *Demonftrat. of the Meffias,* Part III. Ch. iii. §. 11.

(d) Πενταληιοι δ υπ' αυ ης ᾿ʹ οικετῶν κ᾿ απελευθέρων αρω- μαιοφερι. De B. J. l. i. c. ult. §. 9. Τότοις ειπονlο πενlακοσιοι οικετῶν αρωμιιοφο᾿ ꞌ. Antiq. l. 17. c. 8. §. 3. As Bifhop *Kidder* has not quoted thefe paffages, I hope they will not be unacceptable here.

for a mule, and therefore could not be carried by *Nicodemus*. One would not have expected such an objection from a reasonable creature, who might know it to be a very just, as well as common way of speaking, to ascribe to any person that which is done by his order or direction. St. *John* has made particular mention of *Joseph* and *Nicodemus*, as present at the burial of *Jesus*. They were both of them men of substance, and may be supposed to have order'd the attendance of some of their servants on this occasion.

Chap. viii. Page [253] 413, and the first three lines of p. 414. are altered thus: But I apprehend (*e*), that St. *Paul* tells them, he perceived they were *in all things very devout*. This would give no offense at *Athens*. It was their peculiar character (*f*); the encomium, which they were fond of above any other.

(*e*) The conclusion of the note, page 413. is altered from a paraphrase to a literal version thus. I think therefore that St. *Paul* says: *I perceive, that ye are in all things very devout. For as I passed along, and observed the objects of your worship, I found also an altar with this inscription:* To the unknown God, *Whom therefore ye worship without knowing him, him do I declare unto you.*

(*f*) Note added: Εἰ γάρ τι ἄλλο τῆ Ἀθηναίων πόλεως, ϗ τῦτ᾽ ἐν πρώτοις ὅξιν ἐγκώμιον, τὸ ϖεὶ πάντΘ ϖεῆγμα]Θ, ϗ ἐν παν]ὶ καιρῷ τοῖς θεοῖς ἕπεσθαι, ϗ μηδὲν ἄνευ μαν]ικῆς ϗ χϱησμῶν ἐπιτελεῖν. Dionyf. Hal. de Thucydid. Judic. §. 40. Vid. & omnino Sophoc. Oed. Col. v. 1000. & feq. It was customary for eminent strangers, who spoke in public at *Athens*, to give them in their first discourse some commendation, taken from the wisdom of their lawes and institutions, or some other topic. St. *Paul* had good reason not to be defective in this point upon so nice an occasion. He could very truly say they were a devout people. It was extremely to h s purpose, and they would be much pleased to hear it from him. Ἡ μὲν δὴ διάλεξις ἔπαινοι ἦσαν τῆ ἄςεως, ϗ ἀπολογίαι ϖϱὸς τὰ Ἀθηναί-ες, ὑϖὲρ τῶ μὴ ϖϱότεϱον ϖϱὸς αὐτὰς δεῖχθαι. Philoft. vit. Alexand. Sophift. §. 3. Ἀθηναίοις μὲν γὸ ἐπιδεικνυὶμΘ αὐτος δίκης λόγες, ὅτε ϗ ϖϱῶτον Ἀθήναζε ἀφίκελο, ἐκ ἐς ἐγκώμιον κατέςησο᾽ ἑ ωτὸν τῆ ἄςεως, τοσῦτων ὄντων, ἅ τις ὑπὲρ Ἀθηναίων εἴποι. Id. vit. Polem. §. 4. It was therefore a singularity in *Polemon*, a most proud man, that in his discourse at *Athens*, at his first visit, he said nothing in their praise. There is another like example particularly observed in *Adrian* the sophift. Μεσὸς ᵹ ἕτω παϱϱησίας ἐτὶ τῆ θϱόνον παϱῆλθε, τῆ Ἀθήνησιν ὡς ϗ ϖϱοοίμιον οἱ χϱήσθαι τῆ ϖϱὸς αὐτὰς δια-

A 3

λέξεως,

λέξεως, μὴ τ̇ ἐκείνων σοφίαν, ἀλλὰ τ̇ ἑαυτῶ. Id. vit. Adrian. §. 2. *Grotius* underſtood St. *Paul* to ſpeak here of the *Athenians* in the way of commendation, as I do.

Page [256] 416. *How can it be thought then, that theſe governours ſhould undertake to ſuppreſs the (g) firſt Chriſtians*, &c.

(g) *Note added.* When the *Romans* permitted the *Jewiſh* ſynagogues to uſe their own laws, and proper government; Why, I pray, ſhould there not be the ſame toleration allowed to the Apoſtolical Churches? The *Roman* cenſure had as yet made no difference between the judaizing ſynagogues of the *Jews*, and the *Chriſtian* ſynagogues or churches of the *Jews*, Nor did it permit them to live after their own laws, and forbid theſe. Dr. *Lightfoot Hebr. & Talm. Exerc*, on Matth. iv. 23.

Page [262] 426. in the note, after *chief Roman officers*, add: or as *Philoſtratus* expreſſes it, Judges who had the ſword: δίκας ὃ δεῖσθαι αὐτὰς [δίκας ἐπὶ μύιχης, &c.] ξιφῶ ἔχον]ῶ. Vit. Sophiſt. l, i. n. 25. §. 2.

Chap. x. p. [299] 488. l. 17, after, *ſhould be ſet at liberty*, add: *Lucian* ſays, that " at the requeſt of " *Athenodorus*, of *Tarſus*, the ſtoic philoſopher, and " preceptor of *Auguſtus*, the city of *Tarſus* obtained " freedom from tribute (*h*) ".

(h) Ἀθηνόδωρῶ, ταρσεύς, ϛωϊκὸς, ὃς κỳ διδάσκαλῶ ἐγένετο Καίσαρῶ Σεβαϛῶ θεῦ, ὑφ᾽ ῦ ἡ Ταρσέων πόλις κỳ φόρων ἐκυφίσθη, κ. λ, Vol. 2, edit. Amſt. p. 473. *Lucian. Macrob.*

Page [313] 512. at the end of Ch. x. add: *Heliodorus*, the ſophiſt, being in a certain (*i*) iſland, fell under a charge of murder. " Whereupon, ſays (*k*) " *Philoſtratus*, he was ſent to *Rome*, to anſwer for him " ſelf before the Prefects of the Praetorium."

(i) About A. D. 223. (k) Λαβὼν ἤ ἐν τῇ νήσω φονικὴν αἰτίαν, ἀνεπέμφθη ἐς τ̇ Ῥώμην. ὡς ἀπολογησόμην ῶ τοῖς τῶ ϛρατοπέδων ἡγεμόσι. Vit. Sophiſt. l. 2. num. 32.

BOOK II.

Ch. i. p. [369] 73. in the notes, inſtead of *a learned and ingenious friend*, read, my learned and ingenious friend, Mr. *Ward*.

Page [401] 129. the lines 13—22 are to be thus read. But methinks this is a defect which may be dispensed with, if that be the only difficulty. For my own part, I dare not absolutely reject it : but yet I am not fully satisfied, that this is the sense of the words. *I think myself obliged*, &c.

Page [411] 148, after *commentaries*, and *p.* 149, 150, 151, 152. are altered thus : But though I contest all these instances (as thinking I have given the true meaning of all those places) it must be allowed, that *Perizonius*'s example from *Aristophanes*, and another from *Alexander Aphrodisius* (*l*) alleged by others in this cause, prove that πρῶτον, used adverbially is put without περ following it to denote the priority they contend for. How far the argument will hold by way of analogy from adverbs to adjectives, I cannot say. It ought also to be allowed, that the πρῶτός μοι τῦ Ἰεδα of 2 *Sam.* xix. 43. (but not found in all the copies of the *Seventy*) is an equivalent phrase to that in St. *Luke*, and to be understood in the same sense, which is put upon St. *Luke*'s words. The passage from the *Maccabees, Last of all after the sons the mother died*, contains also a parallel phrase. To these I add two other instances (*m*) of πρῶτΘ itself, which I am unwilling to contest, and shall leave with the reader.

Perizonius's way of accounting for this construction by the ellipsis of a preposition to be understood, when not expressed, is well argued from the two instances he has alleged of περ subjoined to πρῶτΘ. I add another like instance from *Eusebius* (*n*). Though perhaps the

A 4 other

(*l*) Ἡ πληγὴ πρῶτον τ᾽ ἀϛαπῆς τ᾽ βρόντην ἀποτελεῖ, ἢ ἄμα. Ictus prius tonitru perficit quàm fulgur, aut simul. *Alexand. Aphrod.* Problem. l. 1.   (*m*) Πρὸ τῶ ὄντως ὄντων, κỳ τῶ ὅλων ἀρχῶν ὅτι θεὸς ἦς, πρῶτΘ κỳ τε πρώτε θεῦ κỳ βασιλέως. Ante eas res quae vere sunt, & ante principia universalium est unus deus prior etiam primo deo & rege. *Iambl.* de mysteriis, §. 8. c. 2. Καὶ πρῶτΘ ἐϛεφανῦτο τῶ ἄλλων. primus ante alios corona honoratus est. *Dionys.* Hal. Hist. Rom. l. iv. c. 3.   (*n*) Αὐτίκα γῦν μάλα θεασώμεθα, ὅπως

other way of suppofing πρώτη ufed for προτέρα (o)
need not be quite rejected.

I prefume this may be fufficient to fhew, that the
phrafe in St. *Luke* is capable of the fenfe contended for
by thefe learned men. But I cannot yet perfwade my
felf, that it is the real fenfe of the text for the following
reafons.

1. This is a very uncommon ufe of the word πρῶτος.
This, I think, is evident, in that the Critics have been fo
much at a loffe for inftances. *Stevens* knew of none (p), befide that produced above from *Aphrodifius*, where πρῶτον
is ufed adverbially. There are alfo almoft innumerable
other ways of expreffing this priority of time (q). The
reafon of the *Greek* writers fo rarely ufing this word thus
is very obvious. It can hardly be done without caufing
fome ambiguity ; therefore when they ufe it in this
fenfe, we fee they often fubjoin πρὶ. That this ufe of
πρῶτος was defignedly avoided, feems to me evident
from a paffage (r) of *Herodotus* ; where having in the
former part of the fentence twice ufed the fuperlative,
in the latter he takes the comparative ; either to avoid
ambiguity, or as more agreeable to the genius of the
Greek language.

2. It does not appear, that any of the firft *Chriftians*
underftood St. *Luke* in this fenfe. That they did not fo
interpret this text, we are affured from the *Syriac*, *Vulgate*, and other verfions; from *Juftin Martyr*, *Eufebius*,
and from the paffage of *Julian* above quoted ; in which
he certainly reprefents the common opinion of people
in his time, of *Chriftians* and others.

Page

ὅπως μὲν ὁ Πλάτων τὺς πρὸ αὐτῶ πρώτυς ἔσκωπ]εν, ὅπως ἢ τὺς
Πλάτωνος διαδόχυς ἄλλοι. Praepar. Ev. l. 14. c. 2.   (o) Ἔςι
δέ τις δύναμις, ουσίας μὲν δευτερα, ψυχῆς ἢ πρώτη. Eft autem
quaedam vis effentiâ quidem inferior, fed nobilior animo. *Salluft.* de
mundo. c. 8.   (p) Πρῶτον ; προτερον, prius. Alexander Aphrodifius, ἡ πληγὴ, κ. λ. Quem alioqui ufum apud vetuftiores rariffi-
mum effe puto : affertur tamen & ex *Ariftotelis* Rhet. πρῶτον ἤ, pro
prius quàm. Thefaur. Gr. Tom. 3. 567. A.   (q) Πρὸ, πρότερον, πρῶτον [adverb.] προτέρα, πρώτη πρὸ, πρὶν, &c.
    (r) The fame as in the firft edition, p. 152.

Chap. ii. p. [439] 197. after *horrid inhumanity*, add :
In a word, the objection againſt this relation of St. *Matthew* muſt be founded on the ſilence of the *Greek* and *Roman* hiſtorians, or of *Joſephus*. As for the ſilence of the
former, the *Roman* republick or empire about this time
was ſo vaſt, that the affairs of many dependent princes
have been loſt in the crowd. *Tacitus* goes over the hiſtory of the *Jews* from *Pompey*'s conqueſt of *Judea* to the
government of *Felix*, mentioned in the *Acts*, in one ſhort
chapter. Of *Herod* he ſays: ' The kingdome he receiv-
' ed from *Antonie* was enlarged [or confirmed] by *Au-
' guſtus*. And that after his death his kingdome was di-
' vided between three of his ſons (*s*).' Without ſo much
as naming the ſons of *Herod*, who arrived at ſovereign
power, and ſucceeded their father. *Strabo* ſays, ' *Herod*
' obtained the title of king firſt from *Antonie*, and then
' from *Auguſtus*. Some of his ſons he put to death, as
' guilty of deſigns againſt himſelf : others he appointed
' his ſucceſſors, dividing hls kingdome among them.
' But his ſons were not happy, for they fell under ſome
' accuſations. One of them was baniſhed into *Gaul*, and
' the other two by means of a great deal of ſubmiſſion with
' much difficulty kept their ſeveral tetrarchies (*t*).' He
does not ſo much as name thoſe ſons whom *Herod* killed,
nor thoſe that ſucceeded him. 'Tis with a like brevity
that ſome other writers have mention'd *Herod*. *Dio Caſſius*'s hiſtory of affairs about the latter part of *Herod*'s reign
is

(*s*) Regnum ab Antonio Herodi datum, victor Auguſtus auxit [al.
ſanxit]. Poſt mortem Herodis, nihil expectato Caeſare, Simon quidam regium nomen invaſerat. Is a Quinctilio Varo obtinente Syriam
punitus. Et gentem coercitam liberi Herodis tripartito rexere. Tacit.
Hiſt. l. v. c. 9.   (*t*) Ἡρώδης — ὥςε κ᾽ βασιλεὺς ἐχρημάτισε,
δόνῳⒻ τὸ μὲν πρῶτον Αντονίⱪ ⸆ ἐξυσίαν, ὕςερον ᾑ κ᾽ ΚαίσαρⒻ
τῦ Σεβαςῦ. ᾑΰ ᾑ υἱῶν τῶϳ μὲν αὐτὸς ἀνεῖλεν, ὡς ἐπιβυλεύσαντας
αὐτῷ. τῶϳ ᾑ τελευτῇϳ διαδόχυς ἀπέλιπε, μεείδας αὐτοῖς ὑποδύς.
— ΰ μέν τοι ευτύχησαν οἱ παῖδες, ἀλλ᾽ ἐν αἰτίαις ἐγένοντο. κ᾽ ὁ
μὲν ἐν φυγῇ διετέλεσε, παρὰ τοῖς Αλλόβερξι Γαλάτας λαβὼν ὀι-
κυσιν. ᾑ ᾑ θεραπεία πολλῆ μόλις ἔνερυτο καθοδον, τετεαρχίας
ὑποδοθείσης ἐκατέρῳ. Strabo. l. 16. p. 765. ęd. Caſaub.

is wanting. I leave it to any one to judge, whether it be reasonable to expect the particular fact at *Bethlehem* from historians, who plainly content themselves with delivering the succession of princes, without relating their affairs, or so much as recording all their names.

As for *Josephus*; his silence is no more an objection against St. *Matthew*, than the silence of other writers is against him. *Josephus* has said a great deal of *Herod*'s liberality to foreigners, to *Antioch*, *Berytum*, *Tyrus*, *Sidon*, *Damascus*, and many other cities in *Syria*; to the *Athenians*, *Lacedemonians*, *Rhodians*, and other people of *Greece*. Of his benefaction to the *Eleans*, he says, ' It was a com-' mon benefit not to *Greece* only but to all the world (*u*)': and ' that he was so remarkable for his liberality, that ' *Augustus* and *Agrippa* often said; *Herod*'s kingdome ' was too small for him, and that he deserved to be king ' of all *Syria* and *Egypt* (*x*).' I suppose people take these things upon *Josephus*'s authority. I cannot conceive how the single silence of *Josephus* (and of *Justus* of *Tiberias* if you please to add him) should be an objection against St. *Matthew*; when the silence of the *Greeks* and *Syrians*, people that abounded so much in writers (several of which are also still in being) is no objection against *Josephus*: who has recorded many things done by *Herod* for those people, of which they have made no mention, that we know of.

It has been pretended indeed, that *Josephus* was a great enemy to *Herod*, and seems willing to tell all his various acts of cruelty. But this is not certain, for *Herod*'s character in *Josephus* has a mixture of good and bad. He has related a great many things to his advantage, which can be verified by no other writers. *Herod* put to death every member of the *Jewish* great Council in *Hyrcanus*'s time, except *Hillel* and *Shammai*; yet *Jo-*
sephus

(*u*) Antiq. l. 16. c. 5. §. 3, 4. de Bell. l. 1. c. 21. §. 11, 12. Τὸ ϑ Ἠλείοις χαεισθὲν, ὐ μόνον κοινὸν τ̃ Ἑλλάδ῀Θ, ἀλλ' ὅλης τ̃ οἰκεμέ-νης δ̃ ῶεον. ibid. §. 12. (*x*) Καὶ φασὶν αὐτόν τε Καίσαεα κ̃ Ἀγείππαν πολλάκις εἰπεῖν, ὡς ὑποδ'έοι τὰ τ̃ ἀρχῆς Ἡρώδ'η τ̃ ἄσης ἐν αὐτῷ μεγαλοψυχίας· ἄξιον ϑ εἶναι κ̃ Συείας ἁπάσης κ̃ Αἰ-γύπ]ε τ̃ βασίλειαν ἔχειν. Antiq. l. 16. c. 5. §. 1;

ſephus mentions this very ſlightly (y). He even takes part with *Herod* againſt the *Phariſees* in an account of an execution made at *Jeruſalem* in the later part of his reign. Though *Joſephus* were an enemy to *Herod*, he might have inducements to ſhew him favour upon ſome occaſions. *Agrippa* the younger was living, when *Joſephus* wrote; and he had ſome acquaintance with him, and obligations to him (z). It was not for the honour of the *Jewiſh* nation to make a mere monſter of *Herod*, who had reigned over them between thirty and forty years. A particular recital of all *Herod*'s cruelties could not but make the uneaſineſſe of the *Jewiſh* people under the *Roman* government appear very unreaſonable. They might be thought a ſtrange people who rebelled againſt the *Romans*, and yet had bore with a man who had ſpared neither young nor old; who had ſlaughtered all the members of their great council, and the innocent infants of a whole town and all its diſtrict. I have ſometimes thought, that this was really one reaſon, why *Joſephus* made ſo ſlight mention of the cutting off the members of that ſenate. It might alſo be ſome inducement not to relate the ſlaughter of the infants.

But *Joſephus*, as a firm *Jew*, had certainly a particular reaſon for paſſing over this event at *Bethlehem*: He could not mention it without giving the *Chriſtian* cauſe a great advantage. To write, that *Herod* at the latter end of his reign had put to death all the young children at *Bethlehem*, on occaſion of a report ſpread at *Jeruſalem*, that the *King of the Jews* had been newly born there, would have greatly gratified the Chriſtians; ſince it was well known, when he wrote, that about thirty years after the death of *Herod*, *Jeſus*, being then about thirty years of age, had been ſtiled the *King of the Jews*, and had been publickly crucified at *Jeruſalem* with that title; and it was firmly believed by all his followers that he was the great perſon ſpoke of under that character, and was now advanced to dominion and power.

Nay,

(y) Ant. l. xix. c. 9. §. 4. xv. 1.   (z) Vid. Joſ. vit. §. 65.

Nay, I do not fee how any ferious and attentive Heathen, who had heard any thing of *Jefus*, could read a relation of this event in *Jofephus* (a *Jewifh* hiftorian, known to be no favourer of thofe called *Chriftians*) but he muft be difpofed to think, the *Chriftian* belief deferved fome confideration. For if there was a report fpread at *Jerufalem*, the Capital city of *Judea*, that the *King of the Jews* had been newly born ; and if this report was fo far credited, that *Herod*, notwithftanding his numerous iffue, thought it needful to make away with all the young children at *Bethlehem*, and its borders, in order to fecure the fucceffion in his own family : this is at once a ftrong argument, that the *Jewifh* expectation of a great perfon to arife from among them is no new thing, and that there were fome reafons to think that great perfon had been born at that time. Moreover, he muft alfo fuppofe it poffible, that the Child, whofe life was aimed at, efcaped, notwithftanding the care of *Herod*. For it is plain, he did not certainly know the child, of whom the difcourfe was : if he had, he would not have given orders for deftroying all the young children under fuch an age.

The more any Heathen knew of the *Jewifh* expectations, or of the ftory of *Jefus*, either from hearfay from the *Chriftians*, or by having looked into any of the Gofpels, the more would he have remarked fuch a relation in this hiftorian.

For this reafon *Jofephus* could by no means be willing to relate this event, with its moft peculiar circumftances ; though I think he has given a general account of *Herod*'s cruelty at that time, as I have fufficiently fhewn already.

Page [444] 197. After, *A voice was heard in Rama*, add : This event is alfo mentioned in *Irenaeus* (a), who lived in the fame century ; and by *Origen* (b) in the third century, in his anfwer to *Celfus*, where he fays : ‘ *Herod* put to death all the little children in *Bethlehem* ‘ and its borders, with a defign to deftroy the *King of*
the

' *the Jews*, who had been born there.' 'Tis needlefs to make any more quotations of *Chriſtian* (c) writers.

(*a*) Propter hoc & pueros eripiebat, qui erant in domo David, bene fortiti in illo tempore nafci, ut eos praemitteret in fuum regnum; ipfe infans cum eſſet, infantes hominum martyres parans, propter Chri-ſtum, qui in Bethlehem natus eſt Judae, in civitate David, interfeſtos fecundum fcripturas. *Contra Haer.* l. iii. c. 16 §. 4. al. c. 17. In qua [Ægypto] & dominus noſter fervatus eſt, effugiens eam perfecutionem quae erat ab Herode. ibid. c. 21. §. 3. al. c. 28.   (*b*) Ο δ᾽ Ἡρώ-δης ἀνᾶλε πάντα τὰ ἐν Βηθλεεμ κỳ τοῖς ὁρίοις αὐτῆς παιδία, ὡς συναγαιοήσων τ᾽ γ̣υνθέντα Ιᴧδαίων βασιλέα, l. 1. p. 47.   (*c*) Vid. Eufeb. Hiſt. Ec. l. i. c. 28. P. Orof. l. vii. c. 3, &c. &c.

Page [445] 198. After *Ariſtobulus* add : This is what I faid of this paſſage in the firſt edition. I would now add : It ought to be allowed, that *Auguſtus* did paſs this jeſt upon *Herod,* upon fome occaſion or other, and that *Macrobius* has given us exaſtly the words of the jeſt. This paſſage alfo ſhews, that *Herod*'s ſlaughter of the infants in *Judea* was a thing well known in *Macrobi-us*'s time, and was not conteſted by Heathens.

If we could be aſſured, that *Macrobius* tranſcribed this whole paſſage, not only the jeſt it felf, but the oc-caſion of it likewife, from fome more ancient author, it would be a proof, that this event was well known in that author's time alfo. And we ſhould have a great deal of reafon to fuppofe, that author was a Heathen; becaufe it is moſt likely, that *Macrobius,* a bigotted Heathen (*d*) himfelf, did not much deal in Chriſtian writers.

But it is poſſible, that *Macrobius* found only the jeſt in his author, and added the occaſion, having collected it from the common difcourfe of the Chriſtians of his time, who frequently fpoke of this cruel aſtion of *Herod.* There is fome reafon to fufpeſt this, becaufe it is very likely that *Auguſtus*'s reflexion upon *Herod* was occaſion-ed by the death of one of thofe fons whom *Jofephus* has
mentioned ;

(*d*) This is very evident from his works. And the reader may fee a full proof of it in the Rev. Mr. *Maſſon*'s ſlaughter of the children in *Bethlehem,* as an hiſtorical faſt, vindicated. §. 3.

men ione ,

flaughter of the infants at *Bcthlehem*. This fufpicion may be farther ftrengthened by the great agreement of *Macrobius* with St. *Matthew* in the words he ufes concerning the children (*e*). *Macrobius* being ignorant of *Herod*'s ftory, and having heard of the flaughter of the infants; when he met with this jeft in fome author, concluded there had been fome young child of *Herod* put to death together with them.

I am content therefore to leave it a doubtful point, whether *Macrobius* tranfcribed this whole paffage, or the jeft only, from fome more ancient author.

Upon the whole then, there lies no objection againft this relation of St. *Maothew*. There is nothing improbable in the thing it felf, confidering the jealous, cruel temper of *Herod*. The filence of *Jofephus*, or of the ancient *Greek* and *Roman* hiftorians, can be no difficulty with any reafonable perfon. This fact is confirmed by the exprefs teftimony of very early Chriftian writers, and by *Macrobius*, a Heathen author, in the latter end of the fourth century; from whom it appears, that this event was not then contefted, and that it was even better known, than the fate of thofe fons of *Herod*, whom *Jofephus* fays he put to death at man's eftate.

(*e*) *Children within two years of age, which* Herod *King of the* Jews *commanded to be flain.*

Chap. vii. p. [541] 360. l. 10. after *underftood*, add: I place another remarkable inftance from *Cicero* in the margin (*f*).

(*f*) Quid ea, quae NUPER, id eft paucis feculis, medicorum ingeniis reperta funt? De Nat. Deor. l. 2. c. 50.

Chap. viii. p. [551] 376. after, *And that is fufficient*, add: Thefe were my thoughts concerning this difficulty formerly. But I have now an obfervation to offer to the reader, which I think will not only reconcile St. *Luke* with *Jofephus*, but likewife *Jofephus* with himfelf;

num ers.   1 0 ervation a   een communicate to me by the truly learned and accurate Mr. *John Ward*, Rhetorick Profeffor at *Grefham Colledge*.

The hiftory of this impoftor feems to lye thus. He came firft to *Jerufalem*, went from thence into the country, and taking a circuit by the wildernefs returned again to the mount of *Olives*. In the *Antiquities* (which contain the fhorter account of this affair) *Jofephus* mentions only the beginning and end of the ftory, that is, the impoftor's coming at firft to *Jerufalem*, and at laft to the mount of *Olives*; and drops the middle part, of which he had given a fufficient account in the books of the *War*. The chief captain's *four thoufand* therefore were the men carried out of *Jerufalem*, who were afterwards (g) joined by others in the country to the number of *thirty thoufand*, as related by *Jofephus*. 'Tis likely alfo, that before he left the city, he had fo concerted matters with fome friends, whom he left behind him, as to entertain hopes, that upon his return his defign would be favoured by great numbers of *Jews* in *Jerufalem*, and that he fhould have no oppofition from any but the *Romans*. But upon his arrival at the mount of *Olives*, finding the *Romans* drawn out to attack him, and the citizens in general prepared to oppofe him, he did not dare to venture an engagement, but prefently fled with a body of his moft trufty friends, as is ufual in fuch cafes. With thefe in particular the *Roman* foldiers were ordered to engage, neglecting the reft, who were only a confufed multitude, and immediately made off as they could by different wayes. When therefore *Jofephus* fays, *the Egyptian fled accompanied by a few* (h) *only*, he is to be underftood of that body which at firft fled away with the impoftor, and were but *a few* with refpect to the whole *thirty thoufand*. When he

(g) The words ἐξαγαγὼν in St. *Luke*, and ἀθροίζει in *Jofephus*, feem very well adapted to this diftinction.
(h) Τὸν μὲν ᾿Αιγύπτιον φυγᾶν μετ᾿ ὀλίγων.

he fays, *the greateft (i) part, or moft of thofe who were with him were flain or taken prifoners,* which in the *Antiquities* are faid to be *four hundred killed, and two hundred taken,* he means the *greateft part* of thofe *few that fled* with him. Nor need it be thought ftrange, that the number of the flain and the prifoners is no greater; fince, as it feems, *Jofephus* fpeaks only of that body of men who fled with the impoftor. 'Tis poffible, fome of the reft of the multitude might be killed likewife, though *Jofephus* takes no notice of them; but 'tis moft likely not many. For it feems by *Jofephus,* as if only the *Roman* foldiers marched out againft them, while the *Jewifh* people in *Jerufalem* ftood upon their defence, if any onfet had been made upon them.

Thus then, though there were but *four thoufand* of thefe men at firft, they might be joined by others afterwards to the number of *thirty thoufand.* So St. *Luke* is reconciled with *Jofephus.* And the number, faid by *Jofephus* to be *flain or taken prifoners,* might be a *great number,* or the *greateft part,* of that body which fled with the *Egyptian* upon the attack made by *Felix* and his foldiers. Thus *Jofephus* is reconciled with himfelf.

(*i*) Διαφθαρῆναι ἢ ᾗ ζωγρηθῆναι πλείσες σὺν αὐτῷ.

Page [555] 380. Inftead of the laft paragraph read: I hope therefore, that the account, which *Jofephus* has given of this impoftor will be no longer reckon'd an objection againft St. *Luke,* but a confirmation of his hiftory.

F I N I S.

Juft Publifhed,

By the fame AUTHOR.

A Vindication of three of our Bleffed SAVIOUR's Miracles, *viz.* the Raifing of *Jairus*'s daughter, the Widow of *Naim*'s fon, and *Lazarus.* In anfwer to the objections of Mr. *Woolfton*'s *Fifth Difcourfe on the Miracles of our Saviour.*

Lightning Source UK Ltd.
Milton Keynes UK
UKHW021334250219
337978UK00013B/1459/P

9 780282 353933